World rights reserved. This book or any portion thereof may not be copied or reproduced in any form or manner whatever, except as provided by law, without the written permission of the publisher, except by a reviewer who may quote brief passages in a review.

The author assumes full responsibility for the accuracy of all facts and quotations as cited in this book. The opinions expressed in this book are the author's personal views and interpretations, and do not necessarily reflect those of the publisher.

This book is provided with the understanding that the publisher is not engaged in giving spiritual, legal, medical, or other professional advice. If authoritative advice is needed, the reader should seek the counsel of a competent professional.

Facsimile Reproduction
As this book played a formative role in the development of Christian thought, the publisher feels that this book, with its candor and depth, still holds significance for the church today. Therefore, the publisher has chosen to reproduce this historical classic from an original copy. Frequent variations in the quality of the print are unavoidable due to the condition of the original. Thus the print may look darker or lighter or appear to missing detail, more in some places than in others.

Copyright © 2014 TEACH Services, Inc.
ISBN-13:978-1-47960-354-1 (Paperback)
Library of Congress Control Number: 2014932368

Published by

TEACH Services, Inc.
P U B L I S H I N G
www.TEACHServices.com • (800) 367-1844

*"Wherewithal shall a young man cleanse his way?
by taking heed thereto according to Thy word."*

GOD'S GREAT PLAN

BIBLE LESSONS FOR THE EIGHTH GRADE

SARAH E. PECK

Published for the

*Department of Education
of the General Conference
of Seventh-day Adventists*

(Revised 1926, 1940)

PACIFIC PRESS PUBLISHING ASSOCIATION
MOUNTAIN VIEW, CALIFORNIA

OMAHA, NEBRASKA   CRISTOBAL, CANAL ZONE   PORTLAND, OREGON

BIBLE LESSONS SERIES

Third Grade—When the World Was Young
Fourth Grade—From Egypt to Canaan
Fifth Grade—The Last of Old Testament Times
Sixth Grade—The Life of Jesus
Seventh Grade—The Gospel to All the World
Eighth Grade—God's Great Plan

Copyright, 1922, 1940, by
PACIFIC PRESS PUBLISHING ASSOCIATION

TO THE TEACHER

The Purpose or Aim. The one great purpose of these lessons is not only to give our boys and girls a clear mental vision of the plan of salvation before they leave the church school, but to enable them to see their own personal relation to it—to weave it into their daily Christian experience. If the recitations are allowed to dwindle into a formal drill on memory verses, locating texts of Scripture, explaining various questions—merely reciting well-prepared lessons, however important these things are in themselves, the work will be like "the letter" that "killeth." The "ministration of the Spirit" must be present if worth-while results are obtained. Therefore, it is hoped that the teacher will make the preparation of every lesson a subject of special prayer, and open every recitation with a short, sincere petition for the presence of the Holy Spirit, remembering that the Holy Spirit must always be the real Teacher of God's Word.

The teacher should also endeavor to make plain to the pupil the relation of each lesson to the plan of salvation. Teach the pupil to *study*, to dig deep into the beautiful and precious but often hidden meaning of the treasures of God's Word. Dwell on the thought until the mind digests the bread of life. Then give the Holy Spirit opportunity to cause the spiritual food to be assimilated by the soul and thus become a part of the pupil's spiritual life.

"There is but little benefit derived from a hasty reading of the Scriptures. One may read the whole Bible through, and yet fail to see its beauty or comprehend its deep and hidden meaning. One passage studied until its significance is clear to the mind, and *its relation to the plan of salvation* is evident, is of more value than the perusal of many chapters with no definite purpose in view and no positive instruction gained."—*"Steps to Christ," page 95.*

"The book of Revelation, in connection with the book of Daniel, especially demands study. Let every God-fearing teacher consider how most clearly *to comprehend and to present the Gospel* that our Saviour came in person to make known to His servant John,—'The Revelation of Jesus Christ, which God gave unto Him, to show unto His servants things which must shortly come to pass.'"—*"Education," page 191.*

In harmony with this instruction, it should be the constant aim of the teacher to see in every lesson "its relation to the plan of salvation," "to comprehend and to present the Gospel."

In the development of these lessons, an effort has been made to help the pupils to grasp the beautiful and simple unity in God's great library — the Scriptures; to help them to appreciate the golden chain of God's love upon which all Bible truth hangs; to help them to see the relation of the scattered facts of Bible history previously studied, to God's great plan for all His created intelligences both in heaven and on earth.

General Outline. The nature and scope of the lessons have made possible considerable variety in style. Bible studies and memory gems characterize the lessons in chapter one. In this chapter not only is God's plan explained, but an effort is made to answer in a simple and satisfactory way questions that almost always trouble children's minds; such as: Could not God have prevented sin? Why is sin allowed to continue? Why was it necessary for Jesus *to die?* Why would not an angel have been a sufficient sacrifice? How can we be sure that sin will never again mar God's universe? Chapters two and three, missionary patriarchs and the missionary nation as teachers of God's plan, are based on historical facts already familiar to most of the children. Therefore exercises on the "Use of Concordance" are here introduced. Chapter four is a book study of Daniel, presenting briefly the simpler prophecies, and showing their relation to God's great plan. Chapter five, "The Man Christ Jesus Working Out God's Plan," deals again with familiar material. As the pupils see how much it has cost to secure the keys of death and the grave, and make possible our release from Satan's dark prison house, they are prepared for chapter six — *their* part, as Christian missionaries, in God's great plan. In these lessons on how to come to the Father's house and discharge the responsibilities as members of the royal family, we return to the Bible study style of presentation. The remainder of the lessons are a book study of God's great plan as presented in "The Revelation,"—that book which has so fittingly been called "a panorama of the glory of Christ." The outline on page 335 shows how this book most wonderfully reveals the working out of God's plan for His "family in earth"; how, after the struggle is past, Satan and all his agents are destroyed, while the church of God dwell triumphant in the holy city.

The Workbook. An attractive and helpful workbook has been prepared to accompany these lessons, and no student can afford to be without it. The workbook contains nine outline maps to be filled out, and also sixteen diagrams with picture cut-outs to illustrate each. These diagrams include all the prophecies of Daniel and Revelation that are given in the "Bible Lessons." When intelligently and correctly filled out by the student, the workbook will be worth preserving, as it will prove a definite help in his future Bible study.

Memory Work. Instead of a maximum of disconnected memory verses, the student is directed to larger thought units—a study of the general contents of certain characteristic chapters in the Bible. He will thus be able to follow through the books of Daniel and Revelation, giving the subject of each chapter consecutively. The subject of a few other chapters in the Bible also forms a part of "Chapters to Remember." In Revelation, five sections are memorized; the mastery of this material leads to a "Memory Certificate." This certificate is in the workbook. The key texts given at the head of lessons are not memory verses. They are merely to direct the mind to the great central theme of the lesson.

Study Plan. The "How to Study" suggestions and the frequent "Reviews" are for the busy teacher whose time to prepare work of this kind is limited. They are also for the inexperienced teacher who always appreciates help. When the entire work seems too heavy, the teacher should feel at perfect liberty to make selections, or to prepare assignments and reviews better adapted to the needs of his students. The "Dictionary Work" is at the option of the teacher. Footnote references are for the teacher only.

Concordance Drills. Concordance drills are to teach the student how to use a concordance. It is not intended that students be required to memorize the location of the texts found.

Oral Composition. Frequent attention should be given to oral composition—connected, logical expression of Bible truth. As almost nothing else can do, these exercises will help to prepare our boys and girls to tell in their own simple language, God's plan to others.

It is hoped that a study of these lessons will whet the appetite for a fuller, richer study of the wonderful words of God. That they may prove a real help to many teachers in their efforts to lead their pupils to a deeper Christian experience, and that they may be an anchor to the soul of many boys and girls, is the sincere prayer of

THE AUTHOR.

ACKNOWLEDGMENTS

Many writers on Biblical subjects have been consulted in the preparation of this volume, but to none is the author more deeply indebted than to the numerous and able productions of Mrs. E. G. White. Grateful acknowledgment is hereby made for permission to draw freely from her books.

The author desires also to express appreciation to the many teachers, ministers, and parents who by reading the manuscript or offering valuable suggestions have so greatly aided in its production.

The following is a list of the authorities quoted, with the abbreviations used:

P. P.— Patriarchs and Prophets
P. K.— Prophets and Kings
D. A.— Desire of Ages
A. A.— Acts of the Apostles
G. C.— Great Controversy
E. W.— Early Writings
Ed.— Education
Test.— Testimonies for the Church
S. P.— Spirit of Prophecy
S. B.— Source Book
D. R.— Thoughts on Daniel and the Revelation
Seer — Seer of Patmos
B. R.— Bible Readings (new edition)
S. A. M.— Second Advent Movement
Hist. of Sab.— History of the Sabbath (fourth edition)
C. S.— The Cross and Its Shadow
W. H. P.—Wylie's History of Protestantism
H. Y. M.—Hundred Years of Missions

The texts referred to under "Use of Concordance" are all found in the small concordance (1921) published by the American Bible Society. This society also publishes a Bible in excellent type containing this concordance.

CONTENTS

First Period

CHAPTER I—*God's Plan Explained*

1. God's Plan to Create a Family 1
2. Review Questions with Bible Texts 7
3. The Plan Told to the Angels 8
4. Review Questions with Bible Texts 11
5. Lucifer's Rebellion in Heaven Against God's Plan . . . 12
6. Review Questions with Bible Texts 16
7. Satan's Opposition on Earth to God's Plan 17
8. God's Family Separated from Him 21
9. Review Questions with Bible Texts 25
10. The Mysterious Secret 26
11. Review Questions with Bible Texts 29
12. The Secret Explained to the Angels 29
13. The Secret Told to Man 34
14. Review Questions with Bible Texts 40
15. Could Not God Have Prevented Sin? 41
16. Why Is Sin Allowed to Continue? 44
17. Why Was It Necessary for Jesus to Die? 48
18. Review Questions with Bible Texts 51
19. Why Could Not an Angel Have Been the Sacrifice for Sin? . 52
20. Bible Study on the Law of God 55
21. The Authority of God's Law Forever Settled . . . 55
22. Bible Study on the Seal of God 59
23. The Everlasting End of Sin 60
24. Reunion of God's "Whole Family in Heaven and Earth" . 63
25. Review Questions with Bible Texts 66
    Review of Chapter I 67

Second Period

CHAPTER II—*The Patriarchs, Teachers of God's Plan*

1. God's First Missionaries 71
2. Noah, a "Preacher of Righteousness" 76
3. Man's First Effort to Establish a World Empire . . . 82
4. "Our Father Abraham" 85
5. Isaac a Type of the Sacrifice of God's Only Son . . . 91
6. Jacob's Preparation to Be a Missionary 96
   Review of Chapter II 100

CHAPTER III—*The Missionary Nation*

1. Abraham's Seed Becoming "a Great Nation" . . . 103
2. Satan Plots to Destroy the Missionary Nation . . . 107
3. God's Plan Rejected by Egypt 111
4. The Birthday of God's Missionary Nation—1491 B. C. . 115
5. The Missionary Nation and School Organized . . . 119
   Review 124
6. The First Semester of the Missionary School . . . 125

7. The Second Semester of the Missionary School	132
8. "Final Examination Day" in God's Church School	136
9. A Bible Study on the Day of Atonement	141
Review	142
10. Satan's Prison House First Opened	142
11. The Nation Ready for Service	147
12. Christian Education a Part of God's Plan—Under the Judges, About 1500 to 1000 B. C.	152
13. Israel the Light of the World—Under the United Kingdom, About 1000 B. C.	155
14. The Nation's Failure to Carry Out God's Plan—Under the Divided Kingdom, About 1000 to 606 B. C.	160
Review	166

Third Period

CHAPTER IV—*God's Plan Worked Out in Captivity*

Under Nebuchadnezzar

1. God Honored by Daniel Because of Christian Education	Dan. 1	169
2. Daniel Honored by God	Dan. 2:1-36	173
3. God's Plan Revealed to the World's King	Dan. 2:36-49	177
4. God's Power Published to All the World	Dan. 3	183
5. A Victory for God	Dan. 4	187
Review		192

Under Belshazzar

6. Daniel's First Vision of the Great Controversy	Dan. 7:1-8, 19, 22	193
7. The Angel's Explanation of the Four Beasts	Dan. 7:11, 12, 15-17, 23, 24, 26, 27	197
8. The Angel's Explanation of the Little Horn	Dan. 7:20-22, 24, 25	200
9. The 1260 Years of Papal Persecution	Dan. 7:11, 25-28	202
10. A Glimpse into Heaven's Great Court Room	Dan. 7:9, 10, 13	206
11. Examination of Cases	Dan. 7:14, 22	209
Review of Daniel 7		211
12. Daniel's Second Vision of the Great Controversy	Dan. 8:1-8, 16, 20-22	212
13. Satan's Masterpiece of Deception	Dan. 8:9-27	216
Review of Daniel 8		219
14. The Downfall of the First World Empire—538 B. C.	Dan. 5	220

Under Darius

15. The Plot to Destroy Daniel	Dan. 6	226
16. Gabriel Sent to Answer Daniel's Prayer	Dan. 9:1-3, 20-24	231
17. Gabriel's Explanation of the 2300 Days	Dan. 9:25-27	234
Review of Daniel 5, 6, 9		237

Under Cyrus
18. Preparations to Return to Jerusalem Dan. 10, 11 . . . 238
19. The Second Coming of Christ Foretold Dan. 12:1-3 . . . 242
20. Daniel's Work Ended . . . . Dan. 12:4-13 . . 245

Under Darius and Artaxerxes
21. The Nation's Second Opportunity for Service 249
    Review of Daniel 10, 12 254
    General Review 255

Fourth Period

CHAPTER V—*The Man Christ Jesus Working Out God's Plan*
1. Preparing for the Coming Redeemer 257
2. The Reception of Jesus 261
3. The Messiah Anointed for Service—27 A. D., Autumn . . 267
4. Satan's Effort to Destroy the Prince of Peace 273
5. Jesus Rejected by Priests and Rulers 277
6. Jesus Rejected at Nazareth 281
7. Jesus Rejected by the Galileans 284
8. Jesus Rejected by the Samaritans 287
9. Priests and Rulers Rejected by Jesus 290
10. The Birthday of the Christian Church 295
11. Satan Cast Out of the Councils of Heaven 300
12. Jesus Securing the Keys of Satan's Prison House—31 A. D., Spring 305
    Review of Chapter V 310

CHAPTER VI—*Christian Missionaries*
1. The Church of Christ to Be God's Missionaries 313
2. Born of the Spirit into God's Family 318
3. The First Step Homeward 321
4. The Second and Third Steps Homeward 324
5. "Of the Household of God" 327
6. The Adoption Ceremony 329
7. Bible Study on Baptism 333
   Review of Chapter VI 334

Fifth Period

CHAPTER VII—*God's Plan Revealed Through His True Church*
Introductory Outline of God's Great Plan as Given in "The Revelation" 335
1. A Sabbath Day in Exile . . . Rev. 1 337
2. The Message to the Church of Ephesus . . . . . . Rev. 2:1-7 . . . 341
3. The Message to the Church of Smyrna . . . . . . Rev. 2:8-11 . . . 346
4. The Message to the Church of Pergamos . . . . . . Rev. 2:12-17 . . . 349
5. Message to the Church in Thyatira . Rev. 2:18-29 . . . 356
6. The Message to the Church in Sardis Rev. 3:1-6 . . . 362
7. The Message to the Church in Philadelphia . . . . Rev. 3:7-13 . . . 370
8. The Message to the Church of Laodicea . . . . . . Rev. 3:14-22 . . . 377

Review of Revelation 1-3 381
CHAPTER VIII—*Satan's Opposition Through the Apostate Church*
1. At the Throne of God . . . . Rev. 4; 5:1, 9 . . 385
2. The Book with Seven Seals . . . Rev. 5 389
3. Opening the First and Second Seals . Rev. 6:1-4 . . . 392
4. Opening the Third, Fourth, and Fifth
   Seals . . . . Rev. 6:5-11 . . . 394
5. The Sixth Seal Opened . . . . Rev. 6:12-17; 7:1-8 . 397
6. The Seventh Seal Opened . . . Rev. 8:1; 7:9-17 . 402
   Review of the Seven Seals 406

CHAPTER IX—*Satan's Opposition Through the Nations of Earth*
1. Rome Weighed in the Balances—The
   First Four Trumpets . . Rev. 8:2-13 . . . 409
2. The Twin of the Papacy—Fifth
   Trumpet, or First Woe . . Rev. 9:1-12 . . . 414
3. The Sixth Trumpet, or Second Woe . Rev. 9:13 to 11:14 . 417
4. God's Message in "the Little Book" . Rev. 10 422
5. The Mystery of God Finished—
   Seventh Trumpet, or Third Woe . Rev. 10:7; 11:15-19 . 425
   Review of the Seven Trumpets 430

Sixth Period

CHAPTER X—*The Opposition of Three Persecuting Powers*
1. Wrath of the Dragon . . . . Rev. 12 433
2. The Leopard Beast . . . . . Rev. 13:1-10 . . . 437
3. The Last and Crowning Deception . Rev. 13:11-14 . . 441
4. The Mark of the Beast . . . . Rev. 13:15-18; 14:1-5 445
   Review of Revelation 12 and 13 448

CHAPTER XI— *God's Last Appeal to Man*
1. The Hour of God's Judgment . . Rev. 14:6, 7 . . 451
2. "Babylon Is Fallen" . . . . Rev. 14:8 456
3. Satan's Plot Unmasked . . . . Rev. 14:9-20 . . . 460
   Review of Revelation 14 464

CHAPTER XII—*The Climax of Satan's Destructive Reign*
1. Preparation for the Seven Last
   Plagues . . . . Rev. 15 467
2. First Five Plagues Poured Out . . Rev. 16:1-11 . . . 469
3. The Sixth Plague . . . . . Rev. 16:12-16 . . 472
4. The Seventh Plague . . . . . Rev. 16:17-21 . . 477
   Review of the Seven Last Plagues 481

CHAPTER XIII—*The Triumph of God's Plan*
1. The Hallelujah Chorus at the
   Marriage of the Lamb . . . Rev. 19:1-10 . . 483
2. Satan's Time for Undisturbed
   Reflection . . . . . . Rev. 20 486
3. A New Heaven and a New Earth . Rev. 21:1-7 . . . 492
4. The Holy City . . . . . . Rev. 21:11-27; 22:1-5 496
5. God's Plan Finished—"It Is Done" . Rev. 22:4, 10, 17 . 502
   Review of Revelation 19, 20, 21, 22 505

First Period—Chapter I

OUTLINE OF CHAPTER I

Topics —
God's Plan to Create a Family
The Plan Told to the Angels
Lucifer's Rebellion in Heaven Against God's Plan
Satan's Opposition on Earth to God's Plan
God's Family Separated from Him
The Mysterious Secret
The Secret Explained to the Angels
The Secret Told to Man
Could Not God Have Prevented Sin?
Why Is Sin Allowed to Continue?
Why Was It Necessary for Jesus to Die?
Why Could Not an Angel Have Been the Sacrifice for Sin?
The Authority of God's Law Forever Settled
The Everlasting End of Sin
Reunion of God's "Whole Family in Heaven and in Earth"
General Review

The angels of heaven are "ministering spirits, sent forth to minister for them who shall be heirs of salvation."

CHAPTER I

God's Plan Explained

1. GOD'S PLAN TO CREATE A FAMILY

"According to His own purpose [plan], . . . which was given us in Christ Jesus before the world began." 2 Tim. 1:9, last part.

1. Making Plans. Most people like to lay plans. There seems to be something rather fascinating in thinking and contriving what we can do to please or help some one. Especially do we enjoy it if we can keep it a secret for a time, and then give our friends a happy surprise. Some people lay plans that they are unable to carry out. Perhaps it is because they lack money; or more time or labor may be required than they had thought; or perhaps they plan to do something that after all they lack wisdom to accomplish; or it may be that those who are asked to help in carrying out the plan fail to do their part; or some one who is not on the program may become jealous and try to break up the plan, or he may try to get others to think it isn't a good plan, thus making it very unpleasant for himself and everyone else.

2. God's Plan—When? Where? For Whom? The plan that these lessons are about is one that God laid many years ago. It is "the eternal purpose [plan] which He purposed [planned] in Christ Jesus our Lord" "before the world began." It is not yet fully worked out, but "God, that cannot lie," has promised it. So wonderful is this plan, that "the prophets have inquired and searched diligently" to understand it, and even "the angels desire to look into" it. The more we know about this eternal plan, the more wonderful it seems to us.

This great plan originated in the secret councils of God; yet both the inhabitants of heaven and all who live on earth, have a part to act in carrying it out. It is called the plan of salvation.

3. Why God's Plan Cannot Fail. Before ever this world was created, God lived. No finite mind can comprehend eternity; but

---
References Used: P. P., pp. 45-51, 108; S. P., Vol. 1, pp. 66, 67, 81; Eph. 3:11; Titus 1:2; 1 Peter 1:10, 12; Dan. 7:9; Heb. 12:22; Luke 3:38; Gen. 1:26; 2:10; Rev. 22:2.

we know that God is eternal, that He is "from everlasting to everlasting." Daniel calls Him "the Ancient of Days." No one created God, for He is Himself "the fountain of life."

The only-begotten Son of God is also "from everlasting," "from the days of eternity"; and "as the Father hath life in Himself; so hath He given to the Son to have life in Himself." The Holy Spirit also is "eternal," and is everywhere present, executing the plans of

God commanded, and the angels were created.

the Father and the Son. From eternity, the Father, the Son, and the Holy Spirit have been associated in every plan; and for this reason, They are said to be one — one in character, one in purpose, and one in power. Not only is all eternity Theirs, not only are They perfectly united in Their work, but They possess all power, all wisdom, and all the riches of the universe. Therefore it is impossible for any plan laid by Them ever to fail.

4. Why the Heavenly Family Was Created. Heaven has always been the dwelling place of these three persons of the Godhead — the Deity. But They were too unselfish to enjoy heaven alone; so, at some time in eternity — we are not told just when — God commanded, and the angels were created. They were "an innumerable company," and God was the Father of this vast heavenly family.

And on this family the Father lavished a wealth of love. For His pleasure "they are and were created." But His pleasure lay in making His creatures happy.

5. Why the Earthly Family Was Created. God's love is as boundless as His character is infinite. Therefore, as eternity rolled on, the Deity held another council, and planned to create another family, so that Their opportunity to serve and bless might have a still wider field of expression. Thus one more link would be added to this great chain of unselfish love. Together the Father and the Son planned to create a new and glorious world. It would be a place where the angels would delight to visit, and thus their range of happiness be enlarged.

6. The Beautiful Earth Planned by the Deity. The Deity planned to diversify the surface of the earth with mountains, hills, and plains, with here and there "noble rivers and lovely lakes." The hills and mountains would not be broken and ragged, with inaccessible steeps and dangerous, rocky chasms, as they so often are now. Everywhere the framework of the earth would be covered with fertile soil, which would produce a luxuriant growth of verdure. Nowhere would there be unhealthful swamps or hot, barren deserts. The soil would be covered with a rich, soft carpet of green grass, made still more beautiful with graceful shrubs. Never-fading flowers would brighten the landscape with their attractive colors, and fill the air with the richest, most delicate perfume. The hills would be crowned with majestic trees, many of which would be filled with luscious fruit. Gold and silver would adorn the earth, instead of being hid beneath its surface as it is now, and little streams would ripple over bright-colored pebbles of precious stones.

7. The Animals as Planned by the Deity. To make the beautiful earth as attractive as possible, the Deity planned to enliven the streams and lakes with all kinds of fish, and cheer the woods with happy songsters. Beasts of the field also would be created. The noble yet gentle lion, the king of beasts, would be there, with the little lambs sporting peacefully around him. And great, good-natured bears would enjoy the shade of the trees, while graceful antelopes and deer in gleeful play would chase one another over the plains.

Not until we tread the streets of the city of gold shall we get a true idea of the beauty and perfection of what God intended this

The Father and the Son planned to create a new and glorious world.

home to be. But we know that it was to be gorgeous beyond description, filled with all the comforts and riches and beauties and pleasures that an all-powerful, wealthy, loving Father could bestow.

8. The People for the Beautiful Earth. In order that there might be some one to live in, enjoy, and take care of this wonderful place, God said, "Let Us make man in Our image, after Our likeness: and let them have dominion over the fish of the sea, and over the fowl of the air, and over the cattle, and over all the earth." These beings were to be called "the sons of God." At first, but two were to be made, and they should become the father and the mother of a noble race of beings.

"Both in outward resemblance and in character," they were to be like God Himself, with minds capable of comprehending divine things, with affections pure, and their entire nature in harmony with the divine will. In form they were to be "of lofty stature and perfect symmetry," their countenances glowing "with the ruddy tint of health." No trace of sickness or feebleness was to exist — only that which would give unbounded life and joy.

These people were to be free moral agents, with the fullest liberty to do just as they should desire. God would not enforce their obedience to His holy will; but if, when their loyalty should be tried, they of their own free will should render loving, cheerful obedience,

The home of Adam and Eve was a beautiful garden.

He would finally grant them eternal life and everlasting joy with the Creator Himself.

9. The Home for the First Parents. For Adam and Eve, the father and mother of this race, the Deity planned to provide a special home — not a prisonlike castle or palace that would partly exclude the cheery sunshine and the fresh, pure air. No, indeed! Their home was to be a garden, a veritable little paradise spot on this earth, and this home "was to be a pattern for other homes as their children should go forth to occupy the earth." In the center of this garden there was to be an inexhaustible fountain of living water, the source of the river of life. As the river of life left the garden, it "was parted, and became into four heads;" and from these heads, streams were to go forth and water the whole earth. On either side of the river of life would grow the tree of life, bearing "twelve manner of fruits," a new fruit for each month. And in the midst of the garden would be the tree of knowledge.

10. Man's School. For the instruction of these favored beings, and to give them still further pleasure, it was planned that the angels would often visit them. As their Teacher, God Himself also would walk and talk with them, explaining the laws and operations of creation, the secrets of the life of leaf and flower and tree. He would make them familiar with every living creature, "from the mighty leviathan that playeth among the waters, to the insect mote that floats in the sunbeam." "God's glory in the heavens, the innumerable worlds in their orderly revolutions, 'the balancings of the clouds,' the mysteries of light and sound, of day and night,"— these would be some of the lessons that man would study in this Eden school. It was the Creator's plan that every leaf of the forest and every stone of the mountains should speak to them "of infinite wisdom and power." And they would ever be discovering some new attraction that would fill "their hearts with deeper love" and call forth "fresh expressions of gratitude."

11. The Sabbath. It would seem as if nothing was omitted that would make this plan the most wonderful that even God could conceive. But the best part of it yet remains. Every seventh day, the people were to have a Sabbath, a special day set apart for their special joy,— a day when God would rest "from all His work" and spend the time with these favored ones. On this day, they, too, would lay aside all their work, pleasant though it had been, and spend the sacred hours with the Deity. Do you think Adam and Eve would welcome the weekly arrival of this precious day?

> "O day of sweet reflection,
> Thou art a day of love;
> A day to raise affection
> From earth to things above;
> On thee, the high and lowly,
> Who bend before the throne,
> Sing, Holy, holy, holy,
> To the Eternal One."

How to Study: First, read the lesson through without interruption, and try to get a clear picture of just what God planned to do. Then see if you can recall the different parts of the plan by looking at the lesson topics. After that, you should be able to give full descriptions as follows:

Oral Composition
1. Describe the earth that God planned to create.
2. Describe the animals.
3. Describe the people.
4. Describe man's home.
5. Describe man's school.

Dictionary Study: Find in the dictionary the exact meaning of: salvation, Deity. By analysis tell the meaning of: in-finite; in-numer-able; in-exhaust-ible.

Memory Work: Memorize Psalms 36:9. When you have learned this verse so that you can recite it without help, write the reference in the first star of the "cross" on the "Service Flag." This flag (or pennant) is found on one of the pages in "Bible Workbook" for the eighth grade. Continue to enter on the cross the references for other memory verses as you learn them. After the cross is finished, fill out the "crown" in the same way.

2. REVIEW QUESTIONS WITH BIBLE TEXTS

1. How long ago was God's great plan laid? By whom? 2 Tim. 1:9.
2. What was the first part of this plan? Ps. 148:2, 5.
3. What was the second part? Isa. 45:18, first half.
4. Why was the earth created? Rev. 4:11.
5. Who were to be associated in the work of creation? Gen. 1: 1, 2; Heb. 1:2.
6. What is Their relation to one another?
7. How long have They lived? Ps. 90:2; Micah 5:2, margin; Heb. 9:14.
8. What enables the Father to create? * Ps. 36:9, first half.
9. What enables the Son to create? * John 5:26.
10. Where is the dwelling place of the Deity? Acts 7:48, 49; Ps. 80:1.

How to Study: In this and all other Bible studies, as you read the Bible texts, find and write down the expression that answers the question, and then try to remember the exact language of that part of the text. Remember the references for all memory verses. These verses are always starred. Since four of the texts in this lesson are in Psalms, and two in Hebrews, it will save time to put bookmarks at these places in your Bible when you begin to study.

Memory Work: Memorize John 5:26. Review Psalms 36:9. When you have recited John 5:26 correctly without help, write the reference in the second star of the "cross" on your "Service Flag."

3. THE PLAN TOLD TO THE ANGELS

"The morning stars sang together, and all the sons of God shouted for joy."
Job 38:7.

1. Preparing to Tell the Plan. In the great council chamber of heaven, God's plan to create a new world and another family was completed. How the Father, with His Son and the Holy Spirit, must have enjoyed the thought of telling it to the angels! How surprised and glad they would be! How all "the sons of God" would shout for joy! How the arches of heaven would echo and reëcho with their songs of praise!

At last, the great day came. Let us try to imagine the scene. The Father takes His place upon His "great white throne," while His Son sits at His right hand. Their glory is indescribable. About the throne is a dazzling rainbow, and in the firmament above the throne is the appearance of many precious stones reflecting the firelike brightness that radiates from the Father and the Son. That majestic, noble-looking, commanding angel standing in the presence of the Creator is Lucifer, the day-star, "son of the morning." The "ceaseless beams of glory enshrouding the eternal God" rest upon him. A special light beams in his countenance and shines around him, brighter and more beautiful than that around the other angels. Next to Christ, he is the most honored of God, holding the highest position of power and glory among the angels. His forehead is high and broad. He is "full of wisdom, and perfect in beauty" as he walks "up and down in the midst of the stones of fire." The rainbow that surrounds the throne encircles him. He is "the anointed cherub that covereth," the leader of the heavenly choir, and this exalted position he has held since the day that he was created.

Round about is the angelic host, radiant with the light ever flowing from the throne. It is their joy to know and do the will of their Creator. They delight "in reflecting His glory and showing forth His praise." Their love to God is supreme, and their love for one another is confiding and unselfish. They love and honor Lucifer, the prince of angels, and delight in executing his commands.

2. Satan's Jealousy. The plan of God is made known. A chorus of rejoicing and praise bursts forth from "ten thousand times ten thousand, and thousands of thousands," of angel voices. But in the

---
References Used: P. P., pp. 35-37.

It is their joy to know and do the will of their Creator.

heart of Lucifer, a strange spirit is felt. For a long time, he had been jealous of Christ. Little by little, he had indulged the desire to occupy the highest position. His heart was lifted up because of his beauty. Little by little, his feeling of jealousy had increased. "Why was not *I* chosen to represent God in creating this new and beautiful world?" he thought. "Why should not *I* thus be honored? Am I not as wise and as beautiful as Christ? Why should *He* have the supremacy?"

3. How God Tried to Prevent Trouble. God read the secret thoughts of Lucifer's heart. He knew that if this spirit were communicated to the other angels, the result would be ruin to Lucifer and to all who might sympathize with him. The course that Lucifer was taking caused great sorrow to the loving heart of God. What should He do to prevent, if possible, the on-coming disaster? There is one thing that God cannot or will not do. He will not compel anyone to serve Him. But He would place before every angel the exact facts in the case, so that, in the struggle which seemed inevitable, they might not be deceived.

Before the great contest had time to develop, "the King of the universe summoned the heavenly hosts before Him, that in their presence He might set forth the true position of His Son, and show the relation He sustained to all created beings." He carefully explained to them the work of Jesus as Creator; He reminded them that "the Son of God had wrought the Father's will in the creation of all the hosts of heaven; and to Him, as well as to God, their homage and allegiance were due." He told them that in the creation of a new world, His Son should be associated with Him as He had been when *they* were created. He further explained that this creation was not for the purpose of exalting Himself, but as another expression of His beneficence and love.

4. The Response of the Angels. When He had thus set the matter before them, the angels, with hearts full of loyal gratitude, poured out their love and adoration. "Lucifer bowed with them; but in his heart there was a strange, fierce conflict. Truth, justice, and loyalty were struggling against envy and jealousy. The influence of the holy angels seemed for a time to carry him with them. As songs of praise ascended in melodious strains, swelled by thousands of glad voices, the spirit of evil seemed vanquished; unutterable love thrilled his entire being; his soul went out, in harmony with the sinless worshipers, in love to the Father and the Son. But again he was filled with pride in his own glory. His desire for supremacy returned, and envy of Christ was once more indulged."

5. Why Lucifer Could Not Be Creator. Perhaps God would have chosen Lucifer in the work of creation if Lucifer had been capable of such a work; and if such a thing had been possible, Jesus would gladly have given him the honor. But no created being can himself create. God only can create. Jesus can create, because He is equal with God. "As the Father hath life in Himself; so hath He given to the Son to have life in Himself." But although Lucifer held the highest place in heaven, next to Jesus; although he was "full of wisdom, and perfect in beauty"; although he was the "covering cherub,"— yet he could not create, for he himself had been created, and in him was not "the fountain of life." For him to attempt such an impossibility would mean only disaster to himself and others.

More than this, the one who is Creator must unselfishly love those whom he creates. No personal ambition can possibly actuate him. The highest good and happiness of his subjects will be his chief aim, his constant thought, his only pleasure. He will be not only their Lord and Master, but their humble servant. He will so love them that if need be he would even die for them. Was Lucifer willing to be all this? Ah, no! Lucifer was seeking his own selfish purposes. He desired to exalt himself. He had an entirely false conception of a great ruler, for he thought that a ruler was to be served rather than to serve.

6. Lucifer's Decision. As Lucifer thought of his beauty, his wisdom, his exalted position, he felt that he had been treated with great injustice. Was not he the prince of angels? Was he not as much entitled to reverence and honor as the Son of God? Had not God Himself said of him, "Thou sealest up the sum, full of wisdom, and perfect in beauty"? He thought God was unfair and unjust, partial to Jesus because He was His Son. O Lucifer, Lucifer! How could you thus doubt God's wisdom and love! Why did you allow wicked pride and envy and rebellion to enter and rule your heart!

Oral Composition:
1. Describe the scene in heaven when God's plan was told to the angels, taking up the following points:

    The Father and His throne The plan announced
    The Son The rejoicing of the angels
    Lucifer The spirit of Lucifer
    The angel host

2. Describe God's effort to prevent trouble, telling about:

    The meeting held with the angels The response of the angels
    The work and position of Jesus Lucifer's experience
    His relation to the plan

Dictionary Work: Find the exact meaning of: Lucifer, rebellion.

Memory Verse: Job 38: 7.

---

4. REVIEW QUESTIONS WITH BIBLE TEXTS

1. Upon what does God sit? Rev. 20: 11.
2. Describe the brightness around Him. Eze. 1: 26-28.
*3. Describe the covering cherub. Eze. 28: 12 (last part), 14.
*4. What other position did the covering cherub occupy? Eze. 28: 13, last part.

*5. What was his name? Isa. 14: 12, first part.
6. How many angels surround the throne? Rev. 5: 11; Heb. 12: 22.
7. What did the angels do when God's plan was told them? * Job 38: 7.
8. What spirit arose in Lucifer's heart?
*9. Could Lucifer create? Why not? Eze. 28: 13, last part.
10. What else unfitted Lucifer to be a ruler?

How to Study: As previously directed, recite from memory all **starred verses** and give their location. When a **question is starred**, this indicates that the text given is from a **memory chapter**; you should be able to tell in what chapter the answer to the question is found. Answer all other questions, as far as possible, in the language of the Bible, giving only that part of the text which directly answers the question.

Put a bookmark in Ezekiel and Revelation before beginning to study.

Chapters to Remember: Isaiah 14 and Ezekiel 28 tell about the position and sin of Lucifer. It will help you to remember these chapters if you notice that 28 is just two times 14.

Memory Work: Review the three memory verses you have had.

---

5. LUCIFER'S REBELLION IN HEAVEN AGAINST GOD'S PLAN

"I will ascend into heaven, I will exalt my throne above the stars of God: . . . I will be like the Most High." Isa. 14:13, 14.

1. Jesus and Angels Try to Help Lucifer. As Lucifer cherished his evil thoughts, they increased, until at last he could not keep them within his own breast. He began to spread them among the angels. "Now the perfect harmony of heaven was broken. Lucifer's disposition to serve himself instead of his Creator, aroused a feeling of apprehension when observed by those who considered that the glory of God should be supreme. In heavenly council the angels pleaded with Lucifer. The Son of God presented before him the greatness, the goodness, and the justice of the Creator, and the sacred, unchanging nature of His law. God Himself had established

---

References Used: P. P., pp. 35-41; Jude 9; 1 Thess. 4: 16; John 5: 25.

the order of heaven; and in departing from it, Lucifer would dishonor his Maker, and bring ruin upon himself. But the warning, given in infinite love and mercy, only aroused a spirit of resistance. Lucifer allowed his jealousy of Christ to prevail, and became the more determined."

2. Spreading Discontent Among the Angels. When the spirit of rebellion became manifest, Lucifer was no longer permitted to remain as the covering cherub. He was cast out "as profane . . . from the midst of the stones of fire." "Leaving his place in the immediate presence of the Father, Lucifer went forth to diffuse the spirit of discontent among the angels. He worked with mysterious secrecy, and for a time concealed his real purpose under an appearance of reverence for God. He began to insinuate doubts concerning the laws that governed heavenly beings, intimating that though laws might be necessary for the inhabitants of the worlds, angels, being more exalted, needed no such restraint, for their own wisdom was a sufficient guide. *They* were not beings that could bring dishonor to God; all *their* thoughts were holy; it was no more possible for them than for God Himself to err."

Lucifer told them that their freedom as well as his own was about to be taken from them, that "an absolute ruler had been appointed," to whose authority all would be compelled to pay homage. "But," he promised with subtle deception, "if you will remain loyal to me, I will protect you from such unjust tyranny. I will secure for you your freedom." Thus artfully did Lucifer seek to undermine their confidence in the Creator.

3. The Father's Effort to Help Lucifer. "In great mercy, according to His divine character, God bore long with Lucifer. The spirit of discontent and disaffection had never before been known in heaven. It was a new element, strange, mysterious, unaccountable. Lucifer himself had not at first been acquainted with the real nature of his feelings; for a time he had feared to express the workings and imaginings of his mind; yet he did not dismiss them. He did not see whither he was drifting.

"But such efforts as infinite love and wisdom only could devise, were made to convince him of his error. His disaffection was proved to be without cause, and he was made to see what would be the result of persisting in revolt. Lucifer was convinced that he was in the wrong. He saw that 'the Lord is righteous in all His ways, and holy in all His works;' that the divine statutes are just, and that he ought to acknowledge them as such before all heaven.

"Had he done this, he might have saved himself and many angels. He had not at that time fully cast off his allegiance to God. Though he had left his position as covering cherub, yet if he had been willing to return to God, acknowledging the Creator's wisdom, and satisfied to fill the place appointed him in God's great plan, he would have been reinstated in his office."

4. Satan's Final Decision and Declaration of War. "The time had come for a final decision; he must fully yield to the divine sovereignty, or place himself in open rebellion. He nearly reached the decision to return; but pride forbade him. It was too great a sacrifice for one who had been so highly honored to confess that he had been in error, that his imaginings were false, and to yield to the authority which he had been working to prove unjust."

At last, filled with wounded pride, and urged on by disappointed rage, Lucifer made the final plunge into the abyss of ruin. In sullen anger, he determined to defeat God's plan, if he could, destroy the confidence of the angels in their divine Ruler, and undermine their loyalty to His government. Having won to his side as many as possible of the angels, he would gain possession of the newly created earth, and there set up a government of his own. Finally, he would take possession of heaven by force, dethrone God, and he himself be God. Deep down in his jealous heart he resolved: "I will ascend into heaven, I will exalt my throne above the stars [princes] of God: . . . I will be like the Most High." Thus was the declaration of war published. "Thus it was that Lucifer, 'the light bearer,' the sharer of God's glory, the attendant of His throne, by transgression became Satan, 'the adversary' of God and holy beings, and the destroyer of those whom Heaven had committed to his guidance and guardianship."

5. War in Heaven. The war in heaven was not a struggle with gun and cannon, with sword and spear. It was a struggle with "spiritual wickedness in heavenly places." "Michael and His angels fought against the dragon; and the dragon fought and his angels." The word "Michael" means "one who is like God." It is a name given to Christ; for, as we learn from several texts of Scripture, Michael is the great Archangel, and "the voice of the Archangel" is "the voice of the Son of God."

The loyal angels entreated Satan to submit to God's government of love. They told him that there could be no happiness without obedience. They warned him that He who had created could as easily overthrow and punish.

"Rejecting with disdain the arguments and entreaties of the loyal angels," Satan "denounced them as deluded slaves." "Great numbers of the angels signified their purpose to accept him as their leader. Flattered by the favor with which his advances were received, he hoped to win all the angels to his side, to become equal with God Himself, and to be obeyed by the entire host of heaven."

There was war in heaven, and Satan was cast out into the earth.

Loyal angels continued to urge those who sympathized with Satan to repent, and many were disposed to heed this counsel. "But Lucifer had another deception ready. The mighty revolter now declared that the angels who had united with him had gone too far to return; that he was acquainted with the divine law, and knew that God would not forgive. He declared that all who should submit to the authority of Heaven would be stripped of their honor, degraded from their position. For himself, he was determined never again to acknowledge the authority of Christ. The only course remaining for him and his followers, he said, was to assert their liberty, and gain by force the rights which had not been willingly accorded them."

6. The Fate of Satan and His Angels. "So far as Satan himself was concerned, it was true that he had now gone too far to return. But not so with those who had been blinded by his deceptions. . . . Had they heeded the warning, they might have broken away from the snare of Satan."

And so the terrible struggle continued. Where false accusation failed, Satan resorted to flattery and deceit, until at last he drew "the third part of the stars of heaven, and did cast them to the earth." Thus nearly half of the angels of heaven had placed themselves on the side of rebellion. But if all but one had deserted the Father, that one would have been in the ascendancy, for "one with God is a majority."

At last, the conflict reached its climax, and every angel had made his decision. Though Satan and his followers desired to get entire possession of heaven, they "prevailed not; neither was their place found any more in heaven. And the great dragon was cast out, that old serpent, called the devil, and Satan, which deceiveth the whole world: he was cast out into the earth, and his angels were cast out with him."

In speaking to the seventy of this conquest, Jesus said, "I beheld Satan as lightning fall from heaven." So quickly can God dispose of an evildoer when he has passed the limits of His forbearance.

How to Study: As you read the lesson, write a list of events in the order in which they are related, placing several under each lesson topic. From this list, try to tell the story in connected form, using good English. By picturing the scenes to yourself, make the story just as real as you can.

---

6. REVIEW QUESTIONS WITH BIBLE TEXTS

*1. What was the first open act in the casting out of Lucifer? Eze. 28: 16, last part.
*2. What had God said about Lucifer's wisdom and beauty? Eze. 28: 12.
*3. What was Lucifer's final decision, which plunged heaven into open conflict? Isa. 14: 13, 14.
*4. On what two sides were the angels lined up? Rev. 12: 7.
5. Who is Michael?

*6. How many of the angels went over to Satan's side? Rev. 12:4, first part.
7. What was the nature of the war in heaven? *Eph. 6:12.
*8. What was the result of this war? Rev. 12:8, 9.
9. What was Satan's fall from heaven like? Luke 10:18.

How to Study: Follow the plan for previous Bible studies. "Bookmark" chapters or books that are referred to more than once.

Memory Work: Memorize Ephesians 6:12.

Chapter to Remember: Revelation 12 tells about the war in heaven. Notice that two questions refer to Ezekiel 28 and one to Isaiah 14. What special events are told in these chapters? Three questions refer to Revelation 12.

7. SATAN'S OPPOSITION ON EARTH TO GOD'S PLAN

"The serpent said unto the woman, Ye shall not surely die." Gen. 3:4.

1. The Disappointment of Satan and His Angels. When Satan was cast out of heaven, he knew that never again would he be permitted to enter its gates. Never again could he lead the heavenly choir in their songs of grateful praise. Never again could he enjoy the peaceful associations of the angels of light. A terrible darkness filled his soul. His happiness was gone. "The angels which kept not their first estate, but left their own habitation," were gloomy and despairing. As the result of disappointed hopes, strife and discord were among them. Instead of gaining greater good as Satan had promised them, they were experiencing the sad results of disobedience.

2. Satan's Plan to Capture Adam and Eve. Satan's only hope of holding the confidence of his followers was to cause Adam and Eve to desert God, join him in his rebellion, and become his servants. He could then take possession of Eden and make that the seat of his government on earth. How could this be accomplished? Although Satan was allowed to make this earth his abode, he was not left free to wander hither and thither, harassing Adam and Eve with constant temptation. He could have access to them only at the tree of knowledge of good and evil.

References Used: P. P., pp. 53-57; S. P., Vol. 1, pp. 38-40; Jude 6; Isa. 14:29.

3. Adam and Eve Warned Against the Foe. God knew that Satan's purpose was to set up a government of his own upon the earth in opposition to the government of heaven. He knew the danger which Adam and Eve would have to meet, and He took every precaution to protect them. He had made them capable of understanding His requirements, of comprehending the justice of His law

Satan could have access to Adam and Eve only at the tree of knowledge of good and evil.

and the good that would result from obeying it. They also understood that disobedience would forfeit His gifts, and bring upon them misery and ruin.

As soon as Satan was cast out to the earth, two angels were sent to warn Adam and Eve of their foe. They told them about this rebel angel, but assured them that "while they were obedient to God, the evil one could not harm them; for, if need be, every angel in heaven would be sent to their help." They cautioned the holy pair to keep close together as a means of safety. They were to have free access to every part of Eden except the tree of knowledge. Of this tree God said, "Ye shall not eat of it, neither shall ye touch it, lest ye die." This was to be the test of their loyalty to God.

But it was not an arbitrary test. Every command of God is for our good, and this was for their good. God was desirous of protecting them from the wily temptations of Satan, who was lurking in the tree of knowledge, watching for an opportunity to cause their fall. "Should they attempt to investigate its nature, they would be exposed to his wiles." If they obeyed God and kept away from this tree, Satan would at last be compelled to give up his efforts and acknowledge his defeat. With all these explanations and warnings and promises, God trusted Adam and Eve to prove themselves loyal.

4. Eve Deceived and Captured. One day, while engaged in pleasant occupation in the garden, Eve unconsciously wandered away from Adam, and finally found herself at the forbidden tree. A strange sense of fear took hold of her as she realized that Adam was not with her. She was alone and felt as one lost. But as she looked upon the tree, which was "pleasant to the eyes," she shook off the feeling of danger with the thought that she was wise enough and strong enough to protect herself. She remembered that the angels had cautioned her not to approach this spot; but Satan certainly was not here now, so why should she fear? She looked at the tempting fruit, and wondered why God had told them not to eat it.

As she gazed upon the fruit-laden tree, something suddenly arrested her attention. It was a voice, sweet and musical, speaking to her! Was it Adam? Was it an angel? No; there it is! It is a serpent, a beautiful creature, with wings as bright as burnished gold. "Now the serpent was more subtle [knowing] than any beast of the field which the Lord God had made." But God had not given it the power of speech. How did it learn to talk? Though Eve had been warned against Satan, she never dreamed that *this* could be he.

Again the serpent spoke. "Yea," it said, in a tone of surprise calculated to make her doubt the wisdom and love and truthfulness of God, "hath God said, Ye shall not eat of every tree of the garden?" O Eve! Why do you not flee from this enchanted spot?

But no! Surprised to hear the echo of her own thoughts, she lingered to listen further to the strange serpent. To his cunning question she answered, "We may eat of the fruit of the trees of the garden: but of the fruit of the tree which is in the midst of the garden, God hath said, Ye shall not eat of it, neither shall ye touch it, lest ye die."

Covering his feeling of hatred for God's commands under a persuasive voice, Satan, speaking through the serpent, said assuringly: "Ye shall not surely die: for God doth know that in the day ye eat thereof, then your eyes shall be opened, and ye shall be as gods, knowing good and evil."

"By partaking of this tree, he declared, they would attain to a more exalted sphere of existence, and enter a broader field of knowledge. He himself had eaten of the forbidden fruit, and as a result had acquired the power of speech. . . . The tempter intimated that the divine warning was not to be actually fulfilled; it was designed merely to intimidate them. How could it be possible for them to die? Had they not eaten of the tree of life?"

Satan ingeniously concealed the fact that by transgression he had become an outcast from heaven. Cautiously but carefully he insinuated that the reason God had forbidden her to eat the fruit of this tree was because He did not want her to receive its benefits, lest she should be exalted to equality with Himself in power and wisdom. He told her that God was jealously withholding good, and was "seeking to prevent them from reaching a nobler development, and finding greater happiness."

Had Eve refused to listen to the serpent, had she sought her husband, and had they "related to their Maker the words of the serpent, they would have been delivered at once from his artful temptation." But, in spite of the sense of danger, Eve, infatuated and flattered, had listened with more than idle curiosity to the deceptive argument of the serpent, and she believed his words. Now was Satan's opportunity. He plucked the fruit, and, with an air of generosity and personal interest in her welfare, placed it in her half-reluctant hands. "See," he argued, "it does not hurt you to touch it, neither will it hurt you to eat it! Try how delicious it is!" And as he spoke, he again ate of the fruit with evident satisfaction.

"And when the woman saw that the tree was good for food, and that it was pleasant to the eyes, and a tree to be desired to make one wise, she took of the fruit thereof, and did eat."

5. Adam Overcome. Having herself disobeyed, Eve became the agent of Satan in causing Adam's disobedience. She filled her hands with the forbidden fruit, and, with an unnatural excitement, sought for Adam. She told him where she had been and what had occurred, and wanted to conduct him at once to the tree of knowledge. Adam was astonished and alarmed. He replied that he who had persuaded her to eat of the forbidden fruit must be the foe against whom they had been warned.

Eve explained to Adam that the serpent had said she would not die, and she thought this must be true, for since she had eaten the fruit, she "realized a delicious, exhilarating influence, thrilling every faculty with new life, such, she imagined, as inspired the heavenly messengers." And again she urged Adam to taste the fruit.

Adam was greatly troubled. What should he do? He knew that sooner or later Eve must die. Her society had been to him his greatest joy. It seemed to him that he could not live without her. He resolved to share her fate. Since she must die, he would die with her. He seized the fruit and quickly ate. The awful deed was done! What would be the consequences?

How to Study: First, read the lesson through without interruption, trying to get a clear idea of the condition of the fallen angels, Satan's plan to win Adam and Eve to his side, God's protection and faithful warning, Eve at the forbidden tree, her conversation with the serpent, her disobedience, Adam's distress and sin.

In connection with this, read carefully Genesis 2:17; 3:1-6. Then try to tell the whole story, using the five lesson topics, if you need them, to get all the points in their proper order.

Dictionary Work: Subtle. Notice that the root of this word is *tela*, a web, which comes from *texere*, to weave. What does *sub* mean? Does this help to explain Satan's crafty, sly, deceptive methods?

Chapter to Remember: Genesis 3 tells about man's fall.

---

8. GOD'S FAMILY SEPARATED FROM HIM

"Your iniquities have separated between you and your God, and your sins have hid His face from you." Isa. 59:2.

1. Sorrow in Heaven. When the news of man's transgression spread through heaven, every harp was hushed. In disappointment and sorrow, the angels cast their crowns from their heads. All heaven was in agitation. How could man show such base ingrati-

---
References Used: P. P., pp. 60, 62; Ed., pp. 23, 25; S. P., Vol. 1, pp. 42, 54; Ex. 33:18-20; Gen. 2:17; 1 John 3:4; Rom. 6:23.

tude in return for the rich bounties God had provided! A council was held to decide what must be done with the guilty pair. "Holy angels were immediately commissioned to guard the tree of life." Around these angels, flashed beams of light having the appearance of a "flaming sword which turned every way, to keep the way of the tree of life." Never again were Adam and Eve permitted to partake of its life-giving fruit.

2. Separated from God. In their innocency, Adam and Eve had been granted direct communion with their Maker. Free and happy, as children of God, they had talked with Him face to face. But now of their own free will they had chosen to obey Satan instead of God. They became the servants of Satan; for "to whom ye yield yourselves servants to obey, his servants ye are to whom ye obey." They were slaves — sold under sin. No longer could they look upon the face of their kind and loving Father, for He dwells in the light which no sinful man can approach unto. No sinful man has ever seen the Father or ever can see Him. "Your iniquities have separated between you and your God, and your sins have hid His face from you," is the word of God to us. This does not mean that God is angry with us, or that He does not want us to be near Him, as Satan would like to have us believe. No, indeed! God greatly loved Moses; but He said to him, "Thou canst not see My face: for there shall no man see Me, and live." God has not separated Himself from us, but our iniquities have separated us from Him.

When the news of man's transgression spread through heaven, the angels were bowed with grief.

3. Satan, the God of This World. When Adam and Eve chose to follow Satan, not only did they themselves become subject to him, but the dominion over which God had placed them at creation passed to their conqueror. It was thus that Satan became "the god of this world." As its representative, he then claimed a right in the council of "the sons of God" at the gate of heaven, to urge the interests, and defend if possible the supposed rights, of his usurped kingdom.

4. The Father of Lies. What was the character of this ruler? He "abode not in the truth, because there is no truth in him. When he speaketh a lie, he speaketh of his own: for he is a liar, and the father of it." Assuring them that they would receive some desirable good, the enemy had said, "Your eyes shall be opened, and ye shall be as gods, knowing good and evil." Did he speak the truth?

"Their eyes were indeed opened; but how sad the opening! The knowledge of evil, the curse of sin, was all that the transgressors gained." "The knowledge of good had been freely given them; but the knowledge of evil,— of sin and its results, of wearing toil, of anxious care, of disappointment and grief, of pain and death,— this was in love withheld." Instead of becoming like God, they became like Satan. They had given themselves to him, to be his children, and now they became partakers of his nature.

5. The Father of Death. Of Satan we are further told that "he was a murderer from the beginning." And truly he was. Full well he knew the truth of God's word, "In the day that thou eatest thereof thou shalt surely die." Not that the luscious fruit of the tree of knowledge was poisonous; nor did the sin lie merely in yielding to appetite, but in disobedience to God and in rejecting the authority of His law. "Sin is the transgression of the law," and "the wages of sin is death."

"The warning given to our first parents did not imply that they were to die on the very day when they partook of the forbidden fruit. But on that day the irrevocable sentence would be pronounced. Immortality was promised them on condition of obedience; by transgression they would forfeit eternal life. That very day they would be doomed to death." And it was on that fatal day that they were cut off from the tree of life. "In order to possess an endless existence, man must continue to partake of the tree of life. Deprived of this, his vitality would gradually diminish until life should become extinct."

6. Effects of Sin upon Creation. Adam and Eve soon learned that sin had changed not only them, but everything in nature. The ground became infested with thorns and noxious weeds, and the earth gradually became less and less productive. "As they witnessed, in drooping flower and falling leaf, the first signs of decay, Adam and his companion mourned more deeply than men now mourn over their dead. The death of the frail, delicate flowers was indeed a cause of sorrow; but when the goodly trees cast off their leaves, the scene brought vividly to mind the stern fact that death is the portion of every living thing."

When Adam rebelled against *God's* law, the inferior creatures, once obedient to him, were in rebellion against *his* rule. The birds that once responded to his call now flew from him in nervous fear. Many of the animals, once gentle and submissive, became wild and dangerous.

Under the reign of "the prince of the power of the air," the atmosphere manifested extremes of heat and cold hitherto unknown; the wind became fierce, and destructive storms rent the air. And now disturbances of various kinds, as earthquakes, volcanoes, and floods, are rapidly on the increase. The same spirit that works in the air, works also in the children of disobedience, resulting in almost unceasing war and bloodshed. Pain and sorrow, famine and pestilence, sickness and death, have nearly filled the cup of human woe.

7. A Sad Outlook. Sad indeed were the terrible consequences of disobedience. In spite of the pleadings of loyal angels, in spite of the tender wooings of the Holy Spirit, in spite of earnest entreaties from Jesus, in spite of the most solemn reasoning of the Father Himself, Lucifer and his followers had scornfully refused to repent and be saved. "Never! Never will we submit," was their defiant determination, their final decision. And now Adam and Eve have fallen — victims to the deceptive power of man's archenemy.

Earth is wrapped in gloom. Heaven is bowed with grief. "The world that God had made was blighted with the curse of sin, and inhabited by beings doomed to misery and death." Is there no escape? Must the whole family of Adam finally perish? Will Satan after all be the ruler of the universe?

How to Study: After reading the lesson straight through, you should be able to give a clear, full answer to each of these questions:
1. How was the tree of life protected after man sinned? Why?
2. Why does God not allow us to see Him?
3. What double loss came as a result of sin?
4. What four names are given to Satan in this lesson? Explain why he received each. To what council did he claim a right?
5. What effect did sin have upon vegetation? upon the animals? upon the atmosphere?

Memory Work: Memorize Isaiah 59:2.

Dictionary Work: Find by analysis the meaning of: im-mortal'ity; ir-rev'oc-able.

9. REVIEW QUESTIONS WITH BIBLE TEXTS

*1. How was the tree of life guarded after man sinned? Gen. 3:24. Why?
*2. What was the sentence pronounced upon man? Verse 19, last part.
*3. How did sin affect the earth? Verse 18, first part; Gen. 4:12, first part.
4. How did sin affect vegetation of all kinds? animal life?
5. Under whose dominion has the air been since sin? Eph. 2:2. What has been the result?
6. Instead of having freedom, in what condition are those who obey Satan? Rom. 6:16.
7. How did sin change man's relation to God? *Isa. 59:2.
8. Why cannot sinful man approach God? 1 Tim. 6:16, first part; Ex. 33:20.
9. As "god of this world," what does Satan do? 2 Cor. 4:4.
10. What council did he attend? Job 1:6. Where was it held?
11. What is the character of this ruler? John 8:44.
*12. Why is he called a liar? a murderer? Gen. 3:4, 5.

Memory Work: Review all the memory verses; namely, Ps. 36:9; John 5:26; Job 38:7; Eph. 6:12; Isa. 59:2. What truth does each of these verses teach?

10. THE MYSTERIOUS SECRET

"God so loved the world, that He gave His only-begotten Son, that whosoever believeth in Him should not perish, but have everlasting life." John 3:16.

1. Satan's Hopes. "Satan exulted in his success." Having led the parents of the human family to desert God and unite with him, he encouraged his angels to think that his kingship over the whole earth was now assured, and that it would be only a matter of time when they would be able to take possession of heaven. But his hopes were doomed to receive a fatal blow.

2. God's Secret. The most wonderful part of God's great plan has not yet been told. It is called "the mystery, which was kept secret since the world began," or, as another version expresses it, "the mystery which hath been kept in silence through times eternal." It is also called "the mystery of godliness." What is this mystery? Why was it kept secret? When was it revealed?

3. In the Council of Peace. Away back in the "times eternal," before there was a created being, in that great council of the Deity, "the council of peace," regarding the creation of "the whole family in heaven and earth," a most solemn question was considered. God was planning to create the angel family, and heaven was to be their home; after that, the human family were to be created, with this earth as their home. As with the angels, so with man, the Father desired that their lives should measure with His own, that they might live with Him forever.

But before everlasting life could be granted them, angels as well as men were to be placed on probation; that is, their loyalty to the Creator and His law was to be proved. If, when the test came, they remained true, immortality and eternal life would be theirs. But if not — what then?

4. The Provision to Save Sinners. So long as everything pleased them, there could be no test. But suppose something should arise that did not please them; would they still be willing to trust the Father's love and wisdom? Would they delight to do His will, to obey His law? Or would they insist on having their own way? Would they ever refuse to give Him the loyal support and grateful obedience which alone could insure their own happiness and safety?

References Used: P. P., p. 57; 1 Tim. 3:16; Eph. 3:15; 1 John 3:4; Rom. 6:23; Isa. 9:6; Matt. 19:5; 5:6; Zech. 6:12, 13; Eze. 28:15.

If they should rebel or disobey, there could be but one result — they must die! In order to preserve heaven itself and the whole universe from utter ruin, God must destroy sin. "Sin is the transgression of the law," and "the wages of sin is death." Could there be no release from this terrible fate? Only one. "Since the divine law is as sacred as God Himself, only one equal with God could make atonement for its transgression." Who was the only one equal with God? It was His Son. "In Him dwelleth all the fullness of the Godhead bodily." The Son of God was the only one who could pay the wages of this ruinous debt. Would He die for sinners, if ever sin should enter God's universe? Would He?

It was an awful moment. Jesus had always been at the right hand of the Father. He was the Father's "wonderful Counselor." No one else could fully comprehend and enter into all the Father's plans and purposes. No one else could share His responsibilities, for no one else was equal with Him. How could the Father consent? How *could* He?

Yet how could He *not* consent? How could He refuse to give all that He had, to protect and to save those whom He Himself had brought into existence? They were His own children, even though they might become wayward. Then, of all times, they would need their Father's special care. No, He could not let them go. He loved them with an everlasting love.

5. **The Gift of Jesus.** Very carefully was the matter considered. At last, the decision was made. Jesus gave Himself. God gave His Son. With a breaking heart, the Father gave the command, "Awake, O sword, against My Shepherd, and against the Man that is My fellow." Yes, Jesus was God's "fellow," His partner in all His possessions, His comrade, His bosom companion; for Jesus "is in the bosom of the Father." Between the Father and the Son existed a fellowship, the strength and sweetness of which no human being can fully comprehend, though perhaps God tried to illustrate their perfect oneness when He said of man and *his* companion, "They twain shall be one flesh."

"God so loved the world, that He gave His only-begotten Son, that whosoever believeth in Him should not perish, but have everlasting life." It was a terrible struggle. But while God is God, and while God is love, it was the only thing He could do. Now, if sin ever *should* enter the universe, a remedy is provided. No wonder that eternity only can reveal such love! Then, and not till then, shall we fully comprehend the force of the truth, "He that spared not His own Son, but delivered Him up for us all, how shall He not with Him also freely give us all things?"

6. A Double Sacrifice. And this was "the secret" of the Deity "which hath been kept in silence through times eternal." It originated in "the council of peace," so called because it was God's plan of restoring peace in His universe should any created being ever rebel against His government. "And the council of peace shall be between Them both." It was "between Them both" because the sacrifice of both was equal. Both gave Their all, and this decision won for Jesus one of His most distinguished titles, "the Prince of peace." Is it any wonder that God has pronounced a special blessing upon "the peacemakers"? Is it any wonder that in a special sense "they shall be called the children of God"?

7. Why the Mystery Was Kept Secret. Of Lucifer it is said, "Thou wast perfect in thy ways from the day that thou was created, till iniquity was found in thee." We are not told how long it was after the angel family was created, before sin was found in the heart of Lucifer. But we know that it was manifest when this earth was created. Up to that time, the secret had not been revealed, because until the need for it arose, it could not possibly have been understood by loyal beings who knew nothing but happy obedience. Had sin *never* arisen, the secret would forever have been "kept in silence," locked in the heart of Deity.

How to Study: First, read the lesson straight through. Then see if you can discuss each topic without omitting any important item.
What thought in this lesson impresses you the most?

Memory Work: Memorize Romans 8: 32. If you do not already know John 3: 16, memorize that also.

Dictionary Study: By analysis, tell the meaning of: at-one-ment; counsel-or.

Chapter to Remember: Matthew 5 contains the Beatitudes, or blessings. What Beatitude in this lesson? This chapter is a part of Christ's Sermon on the Mount, which is given in Matthew 5, 6, 7.

11. REVIEW QUESTIONS WITH BIBLE TEXTS

1. What is the mystery "which was kept secret since the world began"? Rom. 16: 25.
2. Why was it kept a secret? When would it have been told had sin never come?
3. Why did God give His Son? *John 3: 16.
4. Why was the Son of God a sufficient sacrifice? Col. 2: 9.
5. Why was it hard for the Father to give up His Son? Zech. 13: 7; John 1: 18.
6. What kind of council is that said to be where God gave His Son? Why?
*7. Who did Jesus say shall be called the children of God? Matt. 5: 9.
8. In giving Jesus, how much did God give? *Rom. 8: 32.

Time Limit Drill: See how many of the verses given in the preceding questions you can turn to in three minutes.

Chapter Drill: Turn to the chapter and find the place that tells the following:

1. The Beatitudes
2. The war in heaven
3. The fall of man
4. Satan's declaration of war
5. Lucifer, the covering cherub
6. The Sermon on the Mount
7. Lucifer a created being
8. Lucifer the leader of the angels' choir
9. The first curse upon the earth
10. Lucifer cast out from God's presence

Verse-Finding Drill: Turn to the verses containing these expressions. See how long it takes you to find them all.

1. With Thee is the fountain of life.
2. The Father hath . . . given to the Son to have life in Himself.
3. All the sons of God shouted for joy.
4. We wrestle not against flesh and blood.
5. Your iniquities have separated between you and your God.
6. God so loved the world, that He gave His . . . Son.
7. How shall He not with Him also freely give us all things?

12. THE SECRET EXPLAINED TO THE ANGELS

"He that spared not His own Son, but delivered Him up for us all, how shall He not with Him also freely give us all things?" Rom. 8: 32.

1. Sorrow and Anxiety Among the Angels. The angels did not know about the provision that had been made to save sinners. They

---

References Used: P. P., pp. 63-65; D. A., pp. 23, 49, 117; S. P., Vol. 1, pp. 45-49; Rom. 8: 3; Phil. 2: 7, 8; Heb. 4: 15; 1: 14; Rev. 14: 6; John 17: 5; Isa. 53: 3, 11.

knew that Satan had boasted that he would exalt his throne above the stars of God,— that he would be like the Most High. They knew that he claimed to have been unjustly treated, and that he was determined to secure what he called his rights. They knew that multitudes of the heavenly family had joined him. And now they saw the family of earth choosing to follow him. They did not believe that he was in the right, but they wondered what it all meant. They were in great perplexity. Throughout the heavenly courts there was mourning for the ruin that sin had wrought. Anxiously the angels waited in the council that had been called to consider what must be done with these guilty ones.

2. The Son in Counsel with the Father. Upon the countenance of the lovely Jesus there was "an expression of sympathy and sorrow." As He approached the Father, a bright light enshrouded Them both. They were in close converse. Although in the "times eternal" the Father had consented to give up His Son, now that the occasion had really come, it was to Him a terrible struggle. He knew that Satan hated His Son even more bitterly than when he was cast out of heaven. He knew that when His Son should come to this world, where Satan claimed to be the ruler, and endeavor to win back any of his subjects to obedience and loyalty to God, Satan would use every wickedness and cruelty that he and all the wicked angels could think of to make His work a failure, and to discourage and overthrow even Christ Himself.

Jesus must take upon Himself the weakness of sinful flesh; He must be tempted in all points just as we are, with no more help than we may have. Would He endure the test? Could it be possible that He *might* fail? Yes, this was even true. He offered Himself at the fearful "risk of failure and eternal loss." And the Father knew all this. Do you wonder that He yearned over His Son when He thought of the awful peril? Yet He risked His Son for you, for me! Such is the greatness of the infinite sacrifice made for our salvation.

With anxious suspense the angels waited while Father and Son communed together. Three times Jesus was "shut in by the glorious light about the Father." Three times His life was put in the balance with our salvation. "Jesus might have remained at the Father's side. He might have retained the glory of heaven, and the homage of the angels. But He chose to give back the scepter into the Father's hands, and to step down from the throne of the universe," that you and I may one day be with Him.

3. Jesus Met with Angels. When at last Jesus came forth from the Father's presence and met the angels, His countenance was calm, "free from all perplexity and trouble," shining "with benevolence and loveliness, such as words cannot express." "He then made known to the angelic host that a way of escape had been made for lost man." "God so loved the world, that He gave His only-begotten Son, that whosoever believeth in Him should not perish, but have everlasting life." This was the secret of redeeming love.

Jesus told the angels that to save men, He would lay aside His divine glory, and take upon Himself the form of a servant, and be made in the likeness of men. He told them that He would bear man's iniquities; that in doing this, He would be "despised and rejected of men; a man of sorrows, and acquainted with grief;" that He would "pass long hours of agony so terrible that angels could not look upon it, but would veil their faces from the sight;" and that at last He would become "obedient unto death, even the death of the cross." He concealed nothing from the angels, but opened before them the great plan of God, the plan of salvation, the plan that had been kept secret through times eternal.

4. The Angels' Response. Not only the Father and the Son, but all the angels of heaven, were involved in the infinite sacrifice. At first the angels could not rejoice. How could they give up their beloved Commander to a life of humiliation and suffering? They prostrated themselves before Him. They would yield *their* glory. They offered *their* lives.

5. How Jesus Comforted Them. Jesus comforted and cheered them. He told them that in His weakness they would be sent to strengthen Him, and in His sufferings to comfort and encourage Him. He also told them that on the third day He would come forth from the grave, and that they should act a part in His resurrection. More than this, He told them that they might have a part to act in the work of redeeming fallen man, sharing with Him not only the sacrifice but the joy, for they would be "ministering spirits, sent forth to minister for them who shall be heirs of salvation."

Jesus told the angels that as they should go forth on their mission of love, they would encourage and win back to God many whose struggling hearts were groping after help. They would guard from

The heavenly host touched their harps and filled heaven with the sweet refrain:
"Glory to God in the highest,
And on earth peace, good will toward men."

the power of evil angels and turn the footsteps of many toward their eternal home. Through His suffering and death, and through their ministry, a great multitude from "every nation, and kindred, and tongue, and people," would be rescued from the grave. And when He had finished the work which the Father had given Him to do, the Father would glorify Him with the glory which He had with Him before the world was. Then, as the "King of glory," He would return to heaven, while all the redeemed throng would sing alleluias richer and more lofty than any music they had yet heard. He told them they might give the welcome when the King of glory should come in. Then He would "see of the travail of His soul" and "be satisfied," for God's "whole family in heaven and earth" would once more be united in peace and harmony and love.

6. Joy Among the Angels. As the heavenly host were told that in this way and only in this way fallen man could be freed from the snares of Satan and once more enjoy the associations of heavenly beings, they became reconciled to the plan. "Then joy, inexpressible joy, filled heaven." The heavenly host touched their harps, and in a note higher than they had sung before, they filled heaven with the sweet refrain, "Glory to God in the highest, and on earth peace, good will toward men." "With a deeper gladness now than in the rapture of the new creation, 'the morning stars sang together, and all the sons of God shouted for joy.'"

Oral Composition: After reading the story through, tell it from the following outline:
1. Sorrow and Anxiety Among the Angels
    Cause — what the angels knew; what they did not know
2. Jesus in Counsel with the Father
    Jesus' countenance
    Cause of struggle — Jesus' suffering; Satan's hatred; the great risk
    Three times shut in with the Father
3. Jesus Meets with the Angels
    Change in countenance
    Tells the plan to save man
4. The Angels' Response
    How they feel — their offer
5. How Jesus Comforts Them
    Tells their part —"ministering spirits"
    Result — many saved; family reunited
    Welcoming the King of glory

6. Joy Among the Angels
  Why reconciled — songs of rejoicing

Memory Work: Memorize Hebrews 1:14, and enter the reference in the proper star on the "Service Flag." Review Romans 8:32.

Chapter to Remember: Psalms 24 tells about the welcome for the King of glory.

---

13. THE SECRET TOLD TO MAN

"I will put enmity between thee and the woman, and between thy seed and her Seed; It shall bruise thy head, and thou shalt bruise His heel." Gen. 3:15.

1. Jesus, the Link Binding Man to God. Although sin had separated man from God, the plan of salvation made it possible for the Father to communicate with him through Jesus and the angels. God's love for His family on earth was so great that He was willing to let His only-begotten Son die in order still to keep close to man and help him. Therefore, when the secret of redemption was to be told to Adam and Eve, the Father sent the Saviour to carry the glad tidings.

2. Seeking the Lost Ones. It was Jesus whose voice Adam and Eve heard as He walked in the garden of Eden seeking the lost ones. As He called to them, is it any wonder that these guilty ones were ashamed and afraid to meet their Lord? They knew they had shamefully deserted Him. They knew they deserved to be punished. They tried to hide, but that was impossible. His voice, full of grieved yet tender sympathy, won from them a response. He did not scold them. He did not blame them. Kindly, yet very seriously and with deep sadness, the Saviour questioned them regarding their course of action. "Hast thou eaten of the tree? Hast thou disobeyed Me, Adam?"

Confused and terrified, they at first tried to cast the blame upon others and to excuse and justify themselves. Adam even insinuated that God Himself was somewhat responsible, since He had given him the woman who had led him to transgress. But this was no excuse for Adam; for though Eve was deceived, "Adam was not deceived."

References Used: P. P., pp. 61, 62, 66, 366; S. P., Vol. 1, pp. 43, 44, 50; 1 Tim. 2:14; Rev. 22:4; Isa. 1:18-20; 2 Peter 2:4; Gen. 3:11, 17, 21; 4:16.

3. Words of Hope from the Saviour. "Adam and Eve stood as criminals before the righteous Judge, awaiting the sentence which transgression had incurred; but before they heard of the life of toil and sorrow which must be their portion, or of the decree that they must return to dust, they listened to words that could not fail to give them hope."

Speaking to the serpent, the Lord said, "I will put enmity between thee and the woman [the church], and between thy seed and her Seed [the Saviour]; It [the Seed of the woman] shall bruise thy head [causing Satan's final overthrow and death], and thou shalt bruise His heel." These words revealed the fate of Satan, and they revealed also the promise of the Saviour. The bruising of Christ's heel referred to the pathway of sorrow and suffering that He and His followers would tread in order to rescue fallen man from the pit of sin into which Satan had plunged him.

While these words foretold warfare between man and Satan, they were to Adam and Eve a promise of final victory. The Son of God assured them that though they had sold themselves under sin, though they had chosen to become the servants of Satan and were now in bondage to him, yet if they would unyieldingly fight the good fight of faith, He would again create in them a clean heart and restore in them the image of God — the nature of their Creator.

He told them that although they must now live in Satan's domain, yet if, through the strength which He would give them, they would resolutely turn away from the enemy, refusing to obey him, and give themselves fully to God, He would through His own suffering and death rescue them and at last purchase back the home which they had forfeited. Then with the redeemed once more they should see the Father's face. "Come now," He pleads with sinful man, "let us reason together: . . . though your sins be as scarlet, they shall be as white as snow; though they be red like crimson, they shall be as wool. If ye be willing and obedient, ye shall eat the good of the land: but if ye refuse and rebel, ye shall be devoured with the sword: for the mouth of the Lord hath spoken it."

4. Messages from the Angels. Angels also were sent to visit and encourage the fallen pair, and to tell them more fully of the plan of salvation. The angels told them that He who had created them had been moved with pity as He viewed their hopeless condition, and had volunteered to take upon Himself the punishment due to them, and die for them. They related to them the grief, distress, and anguish that was felt in heaven, as it was announced that they had transgressed the law of God, and how this had led Christ to offer His own precious life as a sacrifice for them.

They told them that through this sacrifice a door of hope was opened to them. Another probation was offered them. They were told that if now, through faith in God, they would resist the devil, he would flee from them. Angels from heaven would be sent to help

Angels were sent to visit and encourage the fallen pair, and to tell them more fully of the plan of salvation.

them in every time of temptation. "God is faithful, who will not suffer you to be tempted above that ye are able; but will with the temptation also make a way to escape, that ye may be able to bear it."

5. Repentance of Adam and Eve. The tender love of God broke the hearts of these erring ones. "The sacrifice demanded by their transgression, revealed to Adam and Eve the sacred character of the law of God; and they saw, as they had never seen before, the guilt of sin, and its dire results. In their remorse and anguish they pleaded that the penalty might not fall upon Him whose love had been the source of all their joy; rather let it descend upon them and their posterity." But they were told that since the law of Jehovah is the foundation of His government in heaven as well as upon the earth, not even the life of an angel could atone for its transgression. Only the Son of God could pay the penalty.

6. The Results of Sin. Very plainly the Saviour then explained the unavoidable consequences of sin. He told them that they would no longer be allowed to remain in the garden of Eden, that they must make their home without. He told them that hereafter, as a result of their sin, instead of the pleasant and invigorating occupation which they had enjoyed in cultivating the garden, they would have to "tear their bread from a reluctant soil." Now that they had chosen to eat of the tree of knowledge, the Lord declared, "In sorrow shalt thou eat of it all the days of thy life;" that is, "they should be acquainted with evil all the days of their life," and finally they would die and return to the dust from which they had been taken.

7. Man's Confession. It was a terrible punishment, but they knew that it was just. They knew that He who "spared not the angels that sinned" could not spare them. Acknowledging their guilt, they confessed that they had forfeited all right to that happy abode, but pledged themselves for the future to yield strict obedience to God.

8. Evidence of Acceptance. At creation Adam and Eve were clothed with a beautiful drapery of light such as the angels wear. But sin caused this covering of light to disappear. As they walked with God in the cool of the day, they now felt a strange chill in the evening air; and before sending them away from their Eden home, the thoughtful Redeemer made them "coats of skins, and clothed them." The animals slain for this purpose represented Jesus, the Lamb of God, slain from the foundation of the world. By this act Adam and Eve knew that Jesus accepted their repentance. Then with sorrow of heart, yet with humble, penitent gratitude, they passed beyond the gates of Paradise into the domain where Satan held sway, out into the homeless earth where rested the curse of sin. But they went not alone, for Jesus their Saviour went with them even to death.

9. Satan's Fears. When Satan heard the words of Christ, he knew that his work would be hindered, that in some way man would have help to resist his power. But he told his angels that his plans had thus far been successful upon the earth, and that when Christ

With sorrow of heart, yet with humble, penitent gratitude, Adam and Eve passed beyond the gates of Paradise into the domain where Satan held sway.

should take upon Himself man's weak, sinful, human nature, he could overpower Him, and thus hold the human family in spite of the Son of God.

10. Our Part in the Conflict. When Adam and Eve left Eden, the long, sad conflict between right and wrong, the "great controversy between Christ and Satan," the great war of the ages, really began. Everyone who lives on this earth is lined up on one side or the other of this great struggle. This earth is God's great battle

"The garden of Eden remained upon the earth long after man had become an outcast from its pleasant paths."

field. It is impossible to get away from this warfare, for there is no neutral ground. "He that is not with Me is against Me; and he that gathereth not with Me scattereth abroad."

11. The Garden of Eden. "The garden of Eden remained upon the earth long after man had become an outcast from its pleasant paths. The fallen race were long permitted to gaze upon the home of innocence, their entrance barred only by the watching angels. At the cherubim-guarded gate of Paradise the divine glory was revealed. Hither came Adam and his sons to worship God. . .'. When the tide of iniquity overspread the world, and the wickedness of men determined their destruction by a flood of waters, the hand that had planted Eden withdrew it from the earth."

How to Study: As you read this lesson, try to imagine how Jesus felt as He talked to Adam and Eve and to the serpent, and how Adam and Eve felt,—criminals, causing the death of their best Friend, causing untold sorrow to their Maker, and anguish among the angels, yet every one of these willing to do *anything* to rescue them.

After reading the lesson through, look back over the lesson topics and try to recall the important thoughts suggested by each.

Be able to explain each expression in Genesis 3:15.

Memory Work: Memorize 1 Corinthians 10:13. If you do not already know Genesis 3:15, memorize that also. Place both these references on the "Service Flag."

14. REVIEW QUESTIONS WITH BIBLE TEXTS

1. In what likeness did Jesus come to this earth? Rom. 8:3.
2. What experience did He have in order to help us meet temptation? Heb. 4:15.
3. What part do the angels act in the plan of salvation? *Heb. 1:14.
4. When Jesus has finished His work, what will God give back to Him? John 17:5.
*5. What will He then be called? Ps. 24:10.
6. Who will be saved as a result of God's plan? Rev. 7:9.
7. What great family will then be reunited? Eph. 3:15.
*8. In what words did Jesus encourage Adam and Eve after their sin? *Gen. 3:15.
9. Though liberty had been promised them, in what condition were they when they were overcome by Satan? 2 Peter 2:19.
10. What encouragement does God give those who are tempted? *1 Cor. 10:13.
11. How can we cause the devil to flee from us? James 4:7.
12. How did Adam and Eve feel after Jesus and the angels had talked with them?
13. How did Satan feel about his sentence?
14. On which side of this conflict are we lined up? Matt. 12:30.

How to Study: This is another review lesson. From the study you have had in the last two lessons, you should be able to answer correctly every question. The purpose of this lesson is to show you where these truths are found in the Bible. Notice that questions 3, 8, and 10 are answered by memory verses that you already know. Answer these questions by quoting the verses in full.

Time Drill: The following are the texts to find in this lesson. See how many you can turn to in five minutes.

Rom. 8:3	Ps. 24:10	1 Tim. 6:12
Phil. 2:6, 7	Rev. 7:9	Isa. 1:18-20
Heb. 4:15	Isa. 53:11	James 4:7
John 17:5	2 Peter 2:19	Matt. 12:30

15. COULD NOT GOD HAVE PREVENTED SIN?

"This is the victory that overcometh the world, even our faith."
1 John 5:4, last part.

1. Sin, a Mystery. Children, and grown people also, sometimes wonder how it was possible for Lucifer, a beautiful angel in heaven, one who had been created perfect, to sin. "It is impossible to explain the origin of sin so as to give a *reason* for its existence. . . . Sin is an intruder, for whose presence no reason can be given. It is mysterious, unaccountable; to excuse it, is to defend it. Could excuse for it be found, or cause be shown for its existence, it would cease to be sin." The Bible calls it "the mystery of iniquity."

2. How the First Sin Grew. While it is impossible to explain how sin could originate, we know that it did not develop in a day. "Little by little, Lucifer came to indulge the desire for self-exaltation. . . . Not content with his position, though honored above the heavenly host, he ventured to covet homage due alone to the Creator." Little by little, his attitude of complaining and doubt drove out of his heart the spirit of contentment and faith. Had Lucifer been satisfied with what God had seen fit to give him, had he believed that God was doing the very best for him, sin would have found no place in his heart. Faith would have driven away discontent and doubt. Perfect faith would have cast out sin. And it will do the same for us; for the Bible says, "This is the victory that overcometh the world, even our faith."

3. How God Might Have Prevented Sin. But could not God have *prevented* sin from the very first? Yes; "God might have created man without the power to transgress His law; He might have withheld the hand of Adam from touching the forbidden fruit; but in that case man would have been, not a free moral agent, but a mere

---
References Used: P. P., pp. 35, 49; G. C., pp. 492, 493; Ed., p. 24; Heb. 11:6.

automaton. . . . His obedience would not have been voluntary, but forced. There could have been no development of character. Such a course . . . would have been unworthy of man as an intelligent being, and would have sustained Satan's charge of God's arbitrary rule."

God could have prevented sin from entering both heaven and earth, for He could have made Lucifer, the other angels, and man just as He made the graceful fish, the happy birds, and the noble beasts of the field — beautiful, useful, submissive to His authority, simply another kind of animal, without the power of faith, adoration, and worship.

4. Angels and Men Different from Animals. But God wanted the angels and man to be His associates, His companions, His friends, His own dear children, "sons of God." He wanted us to be different from the animals. He wanted us to be like Himself. He had a wealth of love and kindness too great to find its full expression on anything but the highest order of creation. So He created angels and men of a higher order than animals, beings with a heart and soul capable of receiving His great overflow of peace and good will.

5. Who Are Our Friends? But how could God tell whether these created beings would be true friends? How do *we* tell who are *our* true friends? We never know who are real friends until something arises that tests their loyalty. Those who are friendly only when everything moves along smoothly, but who desert us in times of test, are friends in name only. A true friend trusts us so fully that he will not believe an unfavorable report. He will refuse to listen to it. Much less will he do us harm by trying to influence others against us.

6. What Eve Lost Through Unbelief. Yet Eve did this. She believed what the serpent said, though she knew it was contrary to God's expressed word. She then influenced Adam to turn away from God also. Had she believed God, she would have been satisfied with what He had seen fit to give her. When Eve allowed discontent and envy to enter her heart; when she became dissatisfied with what she had, and desired that which for her own good God was withholding; when she distrusted God and believed the serpent, "she cast away faith, the key of knowledge," the very key that would have given her that for which she longed. Had she refused to believe the lie that Satan told, God in His own good time would have opened to her all the treasures of wisdom and knowledge. Through false education, Satan is still causing people to cast away their faith. Instead of giving them true knowledge, he robs them of the very key which would unlock to them the great treasure house of wisdom.

7. Faith a Test of Loyal Friendship. Loyalty is not true loyalty if given only when it is to one's personal advantage. Even though to Eve it might have appeared that she was being deprived of some benefit when access to the tree of knowledge was refused her, yet her faith and confidence in her Maker should have convinced her that He would never withhold from her anything that was for her good. Without such faith as this, it is impossible for us to please God, or to be His friend. No love or service can be acceptable to God unless it is given willingly and cheerfully,— just because we want to please Him. This is true loyalty — true friendship.

8. Why God Created Us with Power of Choice. God has given His all to us; He gave it of His own free choice. If we are to be His companions and friends, is it too much for us to give our all to Him, and give it of our own free choice? It is this wonderful interchange of love, this freewill offering between God and the angels and between God and man, that made them and us superior beings — God's companions and friends. And this is why God created Lucifer, the other angels, and man with power to love and obey or to refuse to love and obey. What a pity that any of these beings, created perfect, chose to disobey! What a pity that, whether intentionally or unintentionally, they cast away faith, the key that would have unlocked to them all the treasures of God, and given them victory over every temptation!

How to Study: After reading the lesson through carefully, you should be able to answer the following questions:
1. How did sin grow in Lucifer's heart?
2. What would have kept him from sin?
3. What will give *us* victory in overcoming sin? *1 John 5: 4, last part.
4. How could God have prevented sin?
5. How are we different from the animals?
6. What only will please God? Heb. 11: 6.
7. How did Eve cast away faith? If she had kept her faith, what else would have been given her?

Dictionary Study: Automaton. What other words can you think of, that contain the root *auto?* What does this root mean?

Memory Work: Memorize 1 John 5: 4, last part. When this verse is learned and the reference written in the "Service Flag," the "cross" will be complete.

Chapter to Remember: Hebrews 11 gives many examples of people who had true faith in God. It is sometimes called the faith chapter of the Bible.

16. WHY IS SIN ALLOWED TO CONTINUE?

"The Lord is . . . not willing that any should perish, but that all should come to repentance." 2 Peter 3: 9.

1. Result of Destroying Satan at Once. God knew the sorrow and suffering that disobedience would bring into the world. He knew that the very floodgates of woe would thus be opened. He knew that He would have to give up His beloved Son to be tempted and insulted and mistreated and falsely accused by Satan and his followers, and at last to be mocked and scourged and crucified. He knew, too, that Satan and all his associates would finally be lost in the lake of fire. Why, then, did He not at once blot Satan out of existence, and thus prevent all this sorrow?

It is true that God might have destroyed Satan, but it does not follow that this would have put an end to the trouble. The angels and the inhabitants of other worlds could not have understood such an act on the part of Him whom they had always believed to be so patient, so merciful, so kind and good. And many of them might have concluded that after all God was not really the kind Father that they had thought He was, and perhaps Lucifer was right. They might have reasoned that having destroyed Lucifer, the most exalted one among them, He would sometime destroy them too, and in that case their only final safety would be in having another ruler and a different government. And so the immediate destruction of Satan, instead of settling the trouble, would doubtless have caused other rebellions to spring up in heaven. It would also have caused some to serve God from fear instead of from love.

2. How Satan Misrepresented God's Character. Through falsehood, flattery, and cunning deceit, Satan misrepresented God's character and His law. Because God chose His Son instead of Luci-

---

References Used: P. P., pp. 35-42, 68.

fer as His associate in creation, Satan accused God of being partial and unjust. Because, in order to promote the happiness and insure the safety of the angels, God required them to obey His law, which is "holy, and just, and good," Satan told them that they were deluded slaves of a powerful despot, that they were compelled to obey because God was stronger than they. Because God could not yield to Satan's desire for self-exaltation, Satan argued that God was seeking honor for Himself. In order to keep his followers from repenting and returning to God, Satan said that the Father was unforgiving. Because God finally cast him and his followers out of heaven, Satan declared that He was tyrannical. When God tried to protect Adam and Eve from a knowledge of evil, Satan said that God was trying to hold them in ignorance. When it was known that Jesus was to be a Mediator between God and sinners, Satan said it was because the Father was stern, unapproachable, and unloving. In every conceivable way did this archrebel misrepresent God's character.

3. The Guilt of Judging. It is well for us to notice that the very traits of character that Satan said God possessed, were the traits that were in his own life. How careful we should be in our judgment of others, lest we fall into the same error! When tempted to think or speak unkindly of others, let us remember the words of Paul: "Therefore thou art inexcusable, O man, whosoever thou art that judgest: for wherein thou judgest another, thou condemnest thyself; for thou that judgest doest the same things."

4. Satan's False Promises. Satan worked so artfully that many were deceived and led astray. He claimed that he was not in rebellion, that he was only seeking their good, and if they would desert God and follow him, he would secure for them their freedom; he would set up a government that would allow them perfect liberty to do as they pleased.

5. Why Satan Was Not Destroyed at Once. Because Satan had misrepresented God's government, it was necessary to demonstrate before the inhabitants of heaven, and of all the worlds, that God's government is just, that His law is a "perfect law of liberty," and that obedience to it is necessary to the very existence of the universe. "The true character of the usurper, and his real object, must be understood by all. He must have time to manifest himself by his wicked works. The discord which his own course had caused in heaven, Satan charged upon the government of God. . . . He claimed that it was his own object to improve upon the statutes of Jehovah. Therefore God permitted him to demonstrate the nature of his claims, to show the working out of his proposed changes in the divine law. His own works must condemn him. . . .

"For the good of the entire universe through ceaseless ages, he must more fully develop his principles, that his charges against the divine government might be seen in their true light by all created beings, and that the justice and mercy of God and the immutability of His law might be forever placed beyond all question." This was why Satan and his followers, instead of being destroyed at once, were cast out of heaven and were allowed to come down to Eden, to this beautiful sinless earth.

6. When and How Fully Sin Will Be Destroyed. But when Satan's plan is fully worked out, so that angels as well as men understand the folly and wickedness of it all, when it is fully demonstrated to them that God's law is a "law of liberty," that it is "holy, and just, and good," and that our only safety is in obeying God, then sin and sinners will be destroyed with Satan in the lake of fire "prepared for the devil and his angels." They will be destroyed, root and branch. "The earth also and the works that are therein shall be burned up." The earth will be brought back to just where it was in the beginning. It will again be "without form, and void," cleansed from every trace of sin.

7. Re-Creation and the Re-Creator. Then God will re-create the earth more beautiful than at first, and people it with holy beings. Who will these beings be? Those who accept God's plan. Those who while living on this earth turn resolutely away from the temptations of Satan, and bravely, nobly, faithfully live for God. You and I may be among these holy ones if we let Him take all sin and disobedience out of our heart, and create in us a new, clean heart. This is the work of redemption; and Jesus, who created all things in the beginning, is the re-creator, the Redeemer.

8. How Long Will God's Mercy Last? But has not the evil of Satan's reign now been fully shown? Why, then, does God allow sin to continue? Only God knows when His work will all be finished. He has not revealed to us the exact time when probation's door will be forever closed. We know that "His mercy endureth forever." Gently and persistently He knocks at the door of our hearts. He is "not willing that any should perish, but that all should come to repentance." Therefore, so long as His family are not all rescued from Satan, so long as there is one soul earnestly seeking for divine help, His mercy will still linger.

9. The Angel of Mercy Soon to Leave the Earth. But, as we look about us, how few we see who are really seeking after God with all their hearts! How few there are even of those who profess to be the children of God, who are willing to obey God at any cost! How few there are who feed as regularly upon the bread of life as they partake of their necessary physical food! How many there are who are "lovers of their own selves," how many who are "proud, . . . disobedient to parents, unthankful"! How many there are who are "lovers of pleasures more than lovers of God"! How many, many there are who carelessly, thoughtlessly "neglect so great salvation"!

Is it any wonder that the angel of mercy, rejected and neglected, is folding her wings, ready to depart from the earth? You and I are living in the time when the great Judge is separating the just from the unjust. Soon this work will be finished, and the decree will go forth: "He that is unjust, let him be unjust still: and he which is filthy, let him be filthy still: and he that is righteous, let him be righteous still: and he that is holy, let him be holy still." When that decree goes forth, in which class will you be found? In which class shall I be found?

The Lord is "not willing that any should perish, but that all should come to repentance."

How to Study: When you have gone through the lesson, you should be able to answer these questions:
1. How did Satan misrepresent God's character?
2. Why was he not destroyed at once? What would have been the result if he had been?
3. Why is God still merciful to sinners? *2 Peter 3: 9.
4. When will this sinful earth be burned up? 2 Peter 3: 10.
5. How fully will sin be destroyed? Mal. 4: 1.
6. Why is the angel of mercy now folding her wings, ready to leave this earth?

Time Drill: The following texts are used in this lesson; see how many of them you can turn to in three minutes.

Matt. 25: 41	Rev. 22: 11
Rom. 7: 12	Ps. 106: 1
James 1: 25	2 Tim. 3: 2, 4
Rom. 2: 1	Mal. 4: 1
2 Peter 3: 9, 10	Heb. 2: 3

Memory Work: Memorize 2 Peter 3: 9, and enter the reference in one of the stars on the rim of the "crown" on the "Service Flag." The next thirteen memory verses will complete the rim of the crown. As you learn them, enter them in their proper places.

Dictionary Study: By analysis tell the meaning of: immutable, im-mut-able. *Mercy* and *merchant* come from the same root, which suggests the thought of paying a full price. God's mercy pays the full "wages of sin" and forgives the debt.

17. WHY WAS IT NECESSARY FOR JESUS TO DIE?

"I the Lord have called Thee in righteousness, . . . to bring out the prisoners from the prison." Isa. 42: 6, 7.

1. An Illustration. Why did Jesus have to *suffer* and *die?* Why could He not have saved us without making such a terrible sacrifice?

Let us suppose that two great nations are at war with each other. One general is fighting for his own selfish ambition, simply that he may be a great and powerful monarch. The other general is fighting to secure to his subjects their liberty and their homes. The time comes at last for the great decisive battle. The good general carefully instructs his officers just where to station their troops. He tells them about the pitfalls of certain dangerous localities, and warns them against these places. But they do not fully realize the importance of exactly obeying the instructions of their general, and in an unguarded moment they station themselves at one of the very

---

References Used: D. A., p. 785; Isa. 14: 16, 17, margin or A. R. V.; Zech. 6: 12, 13; also those given in lesson 18.

points that has been designated as a danger point. Therefore, when they meet the enemy, they are easily deceived by his false and tricky maneuvers, and every man in the army is captured. In exceeding cruelty every prisoner is locked in a dark and lonely cell to perish, with no hope of ever being released. The general alone escapes.

The good general who had planned to secure such happiness to his subjects is broken-hearted. He at once sets about to free his people. He takes the matter up with his government, whose king is his own father. He is the only one who can open the prison doors of the enemy, and he begs his father's consent to undertake the perilous task. Full well he knows that his enemy will put him to death if he undertakes to meddle with the prisoners. But his great heart of sympathy cannot be satisfied, himself to enjoy the blessings of life and liberty while his men languish in prison. They are *his* men, and he would rather die than leave them to perish.

The father king shares equally in his sympathy for the prisoners, for they are his subjects. But how can he allow his son, his only son, the one who is his constant companion in all the work of the kingdom, his vicegerent — how can he allow his son to sacrifice his life? How can he give him up? But no one else can open the prison doors; and, with his son, he too feels that something must be done. Since he can, he must save his subjects, or he is unworthy to be their king. At last he consents.

The general enters the prison; — the deed is done, and release is secured to the prisoners. But the good general himself is taken and tried and hanged.

2. Satan's Prison House. Like this good general, the Son of our heavenly King entered Satan's prison house, the grave, to release us, His subjects, who through sin had become prisoners of death, "hid in prison houses." It was the only way to unlock the door of the prison. For Satan himself would never have opened "the house of his prisoners"; he would "let not loose his prisoners to their home." If the captives are ever released, Jesus, the life-giver, the liberty lover, must enter the grave where the captives are. He must get the key to the prison house.

3. The "Council of Peace." At the close of the great world war, the representatives of all the nations met in a great peace council to discuss and arrange terms of peace. So, away back in times eternal, in that wonderful "council of peace" between the Father and the Son, before the world had been created, then it was that Jesus offered to enter Satan's prison house, the grave, so as forever to settle the question with the angels and with men,— to show beyond a doubt that God's law is a perfect law of liberty, that unselfish, self-sacrificing love is God's only motive in all His dealings with man. Thus He was "the Lamb slain from the foundation of the world."

4. Can Satan Hold Jesus in His Prison? But, unlike the good general, Jesus was able to say: "I lay down My life, that I might take it again. No man taketh it from Me, but I lay it down of Myself. I have power to lay it down, and I have power to take it again." Satan could not hold the Son of God in the grave prison. The Father had promised, "I . . . will hold Thine hand, and will keep Thee." And He kept His word. The voice of the mighty angel was heard at Christ's tomb, saying, "Thy Father calls Thee."

Had there been one stain of sin in the life of Jesus, He could not have come forth from the grave. That one sin would have held Him in Satan's prison, for "the wages of sin is death." But because Jesus was free from sin, "it was not possible that He should be holden of" death. Only one who had never sinned, one who had the perfect righteousness of God's law, could release man from himself paying the wages of sin, the transgression of that law. If Christ had not died, then man must have died, and died eternally,— his sin would have held him in the grave. He would have been Satan's prisoner forever.

5. How the Prisoners Are Released. Jesus is the resurrection and the life. He has promised, "Because I live, ye shall live also." When He came forth from the grave, He brought with Him the master key of death and the grave, so that now He is able to unlock the door of every grave and release every prisoner. How will He do this? "Marvel not at this: for the hour is coming, in the which all that are in the graves shall *hear His voice*, and shall come forth." Although sin must be destroyed, not one sinner need be lost. Everyone may have eternal life; but only through the merits of Christ, for He alone holds "the keys of the grave and of death."

"Thanks be to God, which giveth us the victory through our Lord Jesus Christ."

How to Study: After studying topics 2, 3, 4, and 5, write at least five questions that can be answered by what is given under these topics. Perhaps your teacher will let you use these questions to test your classmates. How is Christ's mission expressed in the key text of this lesson?

Chapters to Remember: Isaiah 42 tells about Satan's prison house. 1 Corinthians 15 is the resurrection chapter. Read Isaiah 42: 6, 7, 22, and 1 Corinthians 15: 51-57.

Dictionary Work: vice-gerent.

Chapter Drill: Turn to the chapters that tell about —

1. Satan's prison house
2. The Sermon on the Mount
3. "The King of glory"
4. The fall of Lucifer
5. War in heaven
6. Wisdom and beauty of Lucifer
7. The fall of man
8. Victory over death
9. The Beatitudes
10. The faith chapter

18. REVIEW QUESTIONS WITH BIBLE TEXTS

Before beginning to study this lesson, put a bookmark in your Bible at Isaiah 42, Revelation 1, and John 5. All except two of the references given are in these three books. These two are Acts 2 and 1 Corinthians 15. Can you find these five places in two minutes? Try it.

Remember in what chapter the texts that answer the starred questions are found.

*1. Where has Satan hidden those whom he has robbed and spoiled? Isa. 42: 22.
2. What does he refuse to do? Isa. 14: 17, last part. Read also the margin. Read the connection, verses 12-17.
3. In what council was the plan arranged for Jesus to give His life and thus release the prisoners of Satan?
4. When was Jesus placed in Satan's prison house?
5. When was it decided that Jesus should be slain for man? Rev. 13: 8, last part.
*6. What promise did God give Him, that He might bring out the prisoners from the prison? Isa. 42: 6, 7.
7. Why was Jesus able to unlock Satan's prison house? Acts 2: 24; John 10: 17, 18.
8. Could anyone else have done this? Why not? *John 5: 26.
9. When He came forth from the grave, what did He bring with Him? Rev. 1: 18.
10. How will Jesus use these marvelous keys? John 5: 28, 29.

11. Because Jesus came forth from the grave, what does He say that He is? John 11: 25, first part.

*12. For what should we be thankful? 1 Cor. 15: 57. Read also verses 55 and 56.

---

19. WHY COULD NOT AN ANGEL HAVE BEEN THE SACRIFICE FOR SIN?

"Love is the fulfilling of the law." Rom. 13:10.

1. Another Question. There is still another question that we should understand: Why must the Father suffer the loss of His Son in order to pay the penalty of His broken law? Why must heaven itself be thus risked? Could not an angel have paid the price?

2. The Character of God's Law. In answering this question, we must first consider the character of God's law and understand what is meant by the broken law. The perfect God is the one who made the law. God is unchangeable; for if a perfect being should change he would that moment be imperfect, and if he were imperfect he could not be God. God's law is the expression of His own life and character, the very foundation of the government of the universe both in heaven and in earth. Like God, the law is everlasting. "All His commandments are sure. They stand fast forever and ever." God's law is "holy, and just, and good." It is a "law of liberty." It is "spiritual." Like Him who made it, "the law of the Lord is perfect." If it should ever be changed it would become an imperfect law, unholy, unjust, and bad; a law of bondage, a carnal law. When we say that God's law has been broken, we do not mean that the law itself has been injured or changed. We simply mean that it has not been obeyed in some one's unholy, imperfect, carnal heart.

3. One Needed "More Excellent" than an Angel. Yet God's law is to be repaired,— repaired in our hearts, where it has been broken. Could an angel do this? Suppose I have a gold vase. One day an enemy ruthlessly breaks the beautiful treasure. If I mend it with any other material than that of which it was originally made, will it still be all of gold? Of course not. At best it will be but a patched, unsightly article, wholly unfit to occupy the place it once held. But

---

References Used: Ps. 19:7; 36:9; 111:7, 8; Rom. 3:20; 7:12, 14; James 1:25; 1 John 4:8; Matt. 19:17; Heb. 1:4; John 10:17, 18.

with genuine gold the expert jeweler, he who made the vase in the first place, can so fuse the parts together that no trace of the break can ever be detected. It will be just as beautiful, just as valuable, as before.

When the lawyer asked, "Master, which is the great commandment in the law?" Jesus answered: "Thou shalt love the Lord thy God with all thy heart. . . . This is the first and great commandment. And the second is like unto it, Thou shalt love thy neighbor as thyself. On these two commandments hang all the law and the prophets." Every commandment of God's law is included in the two great commandments, love to God and love to man. "Love is the fulfilling of the law," and "God is love." Not one jot or tittle can ever pass from this perfect law of love.

Since God's law is perfect, and since "there is none good but one, that is, God," only one who is Himself God, only He who is the fullness of love, can step into the breach that sin has made in this law of love, and fully restore it, so that not one jot or tittle shall be lost. No angel could do this. The only-begotten Son of God, who "hath by inheritance obtained a *more excellent* name,"— He who is of a higher order than the angels — only He can perfectly repair God's broken law, for only in Him "dwelleth all the fullness of the Godhead bodily."

4. One Needed in Whom Is "the Fountain of Life." Only He in whom is "the fountain of life" could break the bands of death, and unlock the door of the grave and come forth. Only the Son of God could do this, for only to His Son has the Father given the fountain of life. All the angels are created beings. They received their life from God. They have no power to give life, for in none of them is the fountain of life. For this reason no angel, not even Lucifer, the chief of the angels, could have said: "I lay down my life. . . . I have power to lay it down, and I have power to take it again."

Had Lucifer instead of Christ been accepted as "the Lamb," not only would he have remained in the grave himself, but all others who entered the grave would have remained there. There could have been no resurrection. God's whole family would have been eternally lost, for only one who is Himself God could by death pay the wages of disobedience and come forth from the grave. Only God could repair the breach in that law which is an expression of His own life, and redeem us who have broken the law.

5. Destruction of Sin Will Repair God's Law. Satan had denied the authority of God's law, and it was his purpose to destroy it completely; for the law unfailingly pointed out his sin. "By the law is the knowledge of sin." Since his fall, he has been constantly endeavoring to cause men to think that obedience to the commandments of God is no longer required. If his deceitful arguments were true, disobedience and sin could never be banished from this earth,— God's law would forever remain broken in our hearts.

Some people teach the error that *Christ* came to destroy God's law; yet He Himself said He came not to destroy, but to fulfill. He came to "magnify the law, and make it honorable." Had it been possible to dispose of sin by destroying or changing the law, Christ need not have died. But only by His death was the great Captain of our salvation able to pay the wages of sin,— the penalty of God's broken law. In no other way could God's law have been repaired.

6. God's Law Must Be Repaired in Our Hearts. Instead of destroying God's law, it is Christ's purpose to write it indelibly in our hearts, so that with Him we also shall say, "I delight to do Thy will, O my God: yea, Thy law is within my heart." To those who have His law written in their hearts, He says, "I will . . . be their God, and they shall be My people." And when this conflict with sin is over, those who have from the heart obeyed God's law will hear the glad words, "Blessed are they that do His commandments, that they may have right to the tree of life, and may enter in through the gates into the city."

How to Study: After studying this lesson, you should be able to answer these questions:

1. Why could only one like God in character repair God's law?
2. Who was this One? Col. 2: 9.
3. What has the Father given His Son that enables Him to pay the wages of His broken law and be victorious over death? *John 5: 26.
4. Why could not an angel repair God's law? Ps. 148: 2, 5.
5. If Lucifer had been accepted as "the Lamb," what would have been the result to himself? to the human family?
6. Instead of repairing God's law, what did Satan want to do? Why?
7. If sin could have been disposed of by destroying God's law, what would have been unnecessary?

20. BIBLE STUDY ON THE LAW OF GOD

1. What did Christ say were the two great commandments of the law? Matt. 22: 36-40.
2. How can God's law be said to be an expression of His character? 1 John 4: 8.
3. How only can we know what is sin? Rom. 7: 7.
*4. Instead of coming to destroy the law, what did Christ come to do? Matt. 5: 17, 18.
5. How only can the law be fulfilled? Rom. 13: 10.
6. How do we show that we love God? John 14: 15.
7. What did Christ say He would do for the law? Isa. 42: 21.
8. Instead of destroying God's law, where will Christ write it? Jer. 31: 33.
9. What will those do in whose hearts God's law is written? Ps. 40: 8.
10. What reward is promised to those who keep God's commandments? *Rev. 22: 14.

How to Study: Learn this lesson so well that you can give a Bible reading on the law of God. What did Christ say about God's law in His Sermon on the Mount? See how many texts you can find in the Bible that combine *love* with *God's law*.

Memory Work: Memorize Revelation 22: 14.

21. THE AUTHORITY OF GOD'S LAW FOREVER SETTLED

"Forever, O Lord, Thy word is settled in heaven." Ps. 119: 89.

1. A Seal Expresses Authority. No law or document of any kind is of value without the proper signature or seal. It is this that gives it authority. In a state, a law becomes effective after the governor has officially signed his name. In the United States, the president's signature is necessary. A seal is an impression pressed into the paper or parchment on which an official document is written. It may or may not contain the official signature, but it has the force of a signature, and is often used in addition to the signature, to give dignity to the document. It represents the authority of the state, nation, firm, corporation, or other body possessing the seal. It is impossible to erase or change the impression made by a seal. To attempt it would be to destroy the document itself.

A seal on a document has the force of a signature, and expresses authority.

2. The Crime of Breaking a Seal. When Daniel was thrown into the den of lions, a stone was brought, and laid upon the mouth of the den; and the king sealed it with his own signet. When the body of Jesus was laid in the sepulcher, a great stone was rolled to the door, and the tomb was sealed. In either case, the stone could not be removed without breaking the seal. No one would dare to do this, for it would be an offense against the highest authority in the land. An attempt to imitate a signature or to use a seal for private purposes would be a state-prison offense, subject to the most severe punishment that could be inflicted.

3. The Seal of God's Law. The government of the United States is expressed in the supreme law of the land, its constitution. The government of heaven is expressed in the law of its supreme Ruler — the law of God. The Sabbath commandment contains the seal which shows the authority of God's government. Here, in the very heart of God's perfect law, is found His signature,—"the seventh day is the Sabbath of *the Lord thy God,*" that God who "made heaven and earth, the sea, and all that in them is, and rested the seventh day: wherefore the Lord blessed the Sabbath day, and hallowed it." This tells who God is, what His kingdom is, and why He commands His creatures to reverence the Sabbath day.

4. Lucifer and God's Seal. If to tamper with the seal of an earthly ruler is so great a crime, what must be the enormity of the sin of one who would dare to tamper with the seal of God's law! Yet Lucifer dared to do this. He rebelled against the authority of the God of the universe — his own Creator. He wanted to be the Creator. He wanted *his* name in the seal. It is because this could

Not only in His life but in His death Jesus confirmed the dignity and authority of God's law.

not be given him that he now attacks the Sabbath commandment with special hatred. This is why, in the last days, when he knows that his time is short, he is wroth with God's people, and makes war with those who keep the commandments of God.

5. How Jesus Restored the Broken Seal. How did Jesus confirm in the minds and hearts of all created intelligences the dignity and authority of God's law? How did He repair the broken seal? He did it by His own death. He threw His own life into the breach that sin had made in His Father's law. Jesus was laid to rest in Satan's prison house, the grave, just at the edge of the Sabbath; and there He lay during its sacred hours, behind the seal of the Roman government. Then very early in the morning of the day following the

Sabbath, He took His life and came forth from the tomb amid great manifestations of angelic glory on earth and rejoicing in heaven.

6. The Double Blessing on the Sabbath. When the angels saw Jesus die on the cruel cross, when they saw His bleeding body laid to rest in Satan's prison house, they needed no further evidence that Satan was a murderer. Then as never before they realized the justice of God's government, the infinite love of God. Then it was that the authority of God's law of love, the sacred character of its seal, was forever and unquestionably settled among the angels in heaven. Some day it will be as unquestionably settled in the hearts of men on earth. At creation God blessed and sanctified the Sabbath day; through redemption Jesus has doubly blessed and sanctified the Sabbath day and forever glorified it. Thus the Sabbath is a memorial not only of creation but of re-creation, or redemption.

7. What It Means to Keep the Sabbath. God has promised to write His law in our hearts. By keeping the Sabbath holy — the entire day "from even [when the sun did set] unto even," we show that we recognize the authority of His law. We show also that we accept the death of Christ to repair in our hearts the broken law of God and free us from the bondage of Satan.

8. How to Keep the Sabbath. The Sabbath is a day for our sweetest pleasures, a day for the whole family to spend together with Him who made the Sabbath, a day to study the precious promises of God's word and to learn more of the creative and re-creative power of God both in His book of revelation and in His great book of creation — the book of nature. To seek our own pleasure, to talk about commonplace, everyday matters, to read that which will keep our thoughts on ordinary things — this is not true Sabbath keeping. While the Sabbath is not a day for common visiting, it is proper to visit and encourage the sick or those who are shut in, and help them to see new attractions in Jesus. On the Sabbath, with clean clothes and clean bodies and clean hearts, we should attend the "holy convocation" where God's people assemble for worship. In every way our deportment at these gatherings should be just what it would be if instead of the minister, Jesus "went into the synagogue on the Sabbath day, and stood up for to read," as was His custom when He lived here. It should be just what we would want it to be should an angel accompany us, as was the case with Adam and Eve in Eden. If by our careless conduct we drive away the angel of light, an angel of darkness stands ready to take possession of our hearts. When we have done this, we have broken the seal of God's law in our hearts; we have denied the authority of His law in our lives.

If we carefully observe God's law, if we delight to do His will, if we honor His holy day, we shall bear the honored title "repairer of the breach."

How to Study: On each topic in the lesson, write a question on what you think is its most important thought. Bring these to class and see if your classmates can answer them. Avoid questions that can be answered by "yes" or "no."

Memory Work: Memorize Psalms 119: 89.

Chapter to Remember: Psalms 119 is the longest chapter in the Bible; God's law is referred to in nearly every verse.

---

22. BIBLE STUDY ON THE SEAL OF GOD

*1. What part of God's law contains the seal of His name? Ex. 20: 8-11.

2. What day did Christ, by His death, pay "the wages of sin," the penalty of God's broken law?

3. Of what two events is the Sabbath a memorial?

*4. After the death of Christ for sin, how was the authority of God's law regarded in heaven? *Ps. 119: 89.

*5. How does Satan now feel toward those who honor God's Sabbath? Why? Rev. 12: 17.

6. What two things do we show to the world by keeping the Sabbath day holy?

7. What portion of time does the Sabbath cover? Lev. 23: 32; Mark 1: 32.
*8. What should we refrain from doing on the Sabbath? Isa. 58: 13, 14.
9. What kind of deeds are lawful on the Sabbath? Matt. 12: 12, last part.
10. What two great books should we study on the Sabbath? For what purpose?
11. What shows that attendance at church is a part of true Sabbath keeping? Lev. 23: 3; Luke 4: 16.
12. What should be our conduct at these "holy convocations"?
13. How may we obtain the title "repairer of the breach"? Isa. 58: 12 (last part), 13.

How to Study: Be able to give a Bible reading on the seal of God, using only those questions that refer to Bible texts.

Chapters to Remember: Exodus 20 contains the Ten Commandments. Isaiah 58 tells about repairing the breach in God's law.

23. THE EVERLASTING END OF SIN

"Affliction shall not rise up the second time." Nahum 1: 9.

1. An Important Question. Since God has created man and angels with power to do as they desire — to obey or to refuse to obey — how can we be *sure* that sin and affliction will never again mar the universe, even after Satan and his angels have been destroyed in the lake of fire, and this earth has been purified and repeopled with the redeemed? Surely this is a serious and important question, but one quite easy to answer.

2. The Lesson of Life's Experience. Let me ask you another question: Will a child who has once been seriously burned put his hand again on a hot stove? And why not? Oh, he has learned the

References Used: Rev. 22: 3; John 10: 28, 29; Heb. 2: 14.

consequences. So will it be with the redeemed from this earth as well as with all the inhabitants of God's entire universe. For nearly six thousand years they have suffered from the cruel and deceitful workings of Satan. They have seen the ruin that sin has wrought not only in the vegetable and the animal world, but in the lives of otherwise noble men and women and even in innocent, unsuspecting children. They have also experienced the love of God in the wonderful plan of salvation. Do you think they will ever again choose the ruin that comes from serving the wicked one?

3. The Lesson of Eternity. The love that God's plan unfolds will be the science and the song of the entire family of God throughout the ceaseless ages of eternity. The longer the redeemed hosts study this science and sing this song, the more they will realize the value of all that Jesus has purchased for them, the more they will appreciate God's love for them; and as the ages roll on they will be removed farther and farther from any inclination or thought of sin. How could anyone desire to exchange the riches and joy of heaven for the poverty and sorrow of earth? How could anyone ever choose to live again in a world of sickness and pain and death? How could anyone prefer the bondage and destruction of sin to liberty and eternal life? Could we choose to crucify again the Son of God, our everlasting Benefactor? No, indeed! After our bitter experience with sin, after once becoming acquainted with Jesus face to face, we could never again choose to wound Him and harm ourselves by sinful disobedience.

4. The Assurance of God's Word. On this point we have the still stronger assurance of God's word. Of the tempter who is constantly scheming to lead us into sin, we are told: "I will bring forth a fire from the midst of thee, it shall devour thee, and I will bring thee to ashes upon the earth in the sight of all them that behold thee. All they that know thee among the people shall be astonished at thee: thou shalt be a terror, and never shalt thou be any more." *"Never shalt thou be any more."* God's word is sure. "Affliction *shall not* rise up the second time." "There shall be *no more* curse."

5. The Eternal Reminder of Sin. But, as if to make assurance doubly sure, Jesus throughout eternity will carry on the palms of His hands the marks of the cruel nails that made Him our sin bearer and our Redeemer — a constant reminder of the results of our disobedience. But instead of appearing as ugly scars, they are resplendent with a glory more dazzling than flashes of light from the most brilliant diamonds. In describing this, the prophet says:

> "His glory covered the heavens,
> And the earth was full of His praise.
> And His brightness was as the light;
> He had rays coming forth from His hand;
> And *there* was the hiding of His power."

Jesus has graven us upon the palms of His hands, and we have His own assuring words: "Neither shall any pluck them out of My hand. My Father, which gave them Me, is greater than all; and no man is able to pluck them out of My Father's hand." Thus the crucifixion, the very means by which Satan thought to defeat God's plan and hold us in his iron grip, becomes the power by which God keeps and protects us, and gloriously establishes and perpetuates His plan.

6. Paul's Assurance. The good apostle Paul appreciated this when he confidently declared, "I am persuaded, that neither death, nor life, nor angels, nor principalities, nor powers, nor things present, nor things to come, nor height, nor depth, nor any other creature, shall be able to separate us from the love of God, which is in Christ Jesus our Lord."

How to Study: After studying the lesson through, you should be able to answer the following questions. Where Bible texts are given, find the answers in the Bible.

1. What lesson will the experience with sin in this life teach us?
2. How shall we feel about sin the longer we live in the new earth?
*3. What will become of Satan, the tempter, when this life is past? Eze. 28: 18, 19. Read also verses 12-17.
4. What reminder of the cost of our salvation shall we always have? Isa. 49: 16.
5. What will the prints of the nails in Jesus' hands be like? What is hidden in them? Hab. 3: 4. Read the margin. Read also A. R. V.
6. What direct statement does God's word give about a second outbreak of sin? Nahum 1: 9.
7. What assurance does Paul give? *Rom. 8: 38, 39.

Memory Work: Memorize Romans 8: 38, 39.

24. REUNION OF GOD'S "WHOLE FAMILY IN HEAVEN AND EARTH"

"God sent forth His Son . . . to redeem [purchase] them that were under the law, that we might receive the adoption of sons." Gal. 4: 4, 5.

1. God's Family at Creation. When God created Adam and Eve they were subjects of His kingdom, under His all-wise, kind rule. He had created them perfect, and He wanted them to be perfectly happy, so He placed them under His perfect law. Anyone without law is lawless, and it is impossible for a lawless person to be happy or to make others happy. But Adam and Eve were more than subjects of God's kingdom. They were the children of His family in earth.

2. God Robbed by Satan. When Satan blinded their minds and led them to desert their own Father, he claimed them as *his* servants. He also claimed that, since King Adam had of his own free choice accepted his rule, the dominion over which the Creator had placed Adam was now *his* dominion, and that henceforth *he* was "the god of this world." What would you think of a man who would thus come into your home and take possession? Even though he were allowed to hold that which he had taken by unfair play, would it really be his by right? No, indeed! At best it could be only a usurped possession. God is still the rightful owner of every man and woman and every boy and girl living. We may refuse to recognize His ownership, but this does not change the facts. God has made us, He daily gives us the life we have, and we are His.

3. The Family Purchased Back. It is true that man sold himself to Satan — sold himself for naught, and less than naught. He sold himself for a knowledge of evil. He sold himself to become the bond servant of the most severe taskmaster. But Satan had no right to take such unfair advantage of innocent, unsuspecting creatures. It would have been perfectly just had God required him to return the captives he had unlawfully taken. But had He done this, Satan would doubtless have accused God of wresting from him those who of their own free choice had come over to his side to be his servants. Therefore God would not dispute the question with

---

References Used: Col. 1: 11-13; 2: 9; John 1: 18; 14: 26; Heb. 1: 3; 2 Cor. 6: 18; 1 John 1: 9; Phil. 4 · 7; 1 Cor. 10: 13; James 1: 5; Ps. 91: 10, 11.

His unfair enemy. What will He do? Oh, He will *purchase* them back!

4. The Price Paid. Man sold himself to Satan for naught, but what was the price paid to win him back? He was redeemed "without money," but with that which is more precious than money, even the life of Him in whom "dwelleth all the fullness of the Godhead bodily;" it was the life of "the only-begotten Son, which is in the bosom of the Father;" it was the life of Him who created all things and who "upholdeth all things." In this transaction God risked everything He had in heaven and in earth. Could He have done more to demonstrate to the universe His absolute fairness to Satan? Could He have done more to prove His love and loyalty to us as our Father? Could He have done more to show forth the beauty of holiness in His own character?

The price paid for our salvation was so great that our only hope of ever securing any benefit from it is to accept it as a free gift. So, when God invites sinners to accept the gift that restores them to their Father and to a place in His family, He says:

"Ho, everyone that thirsteth, come ye to the waters,
And ye that hath no money; come ye, buy, and eat;
Yea, come, buy wine and milk *without money and without price*. . . .
Let the wicked forsake his way, and the unrighteous man his thoughts:
And let him return unto the Lord, and He will have mercy upon him;
And to our God, for He will abundantly pardon."

This gift is "without price" because it is priceless. Its value is too great to be measured in gold or silver; it is therefore offered to us "without money." By this priceless gift of our Father, we are doubly His — first, by right of creation; second, by right of redemption, or purchase. How ungrateful, how against our own interests it would be for us not to accept such a gift and return to our Father's family!

5. The Family Adopted. That the transaction may be trebly sure, it is God's plan to make up His family by adopting every human being who will accept His priceless gift. When a child is adopted into a family, he legally becomes just as much a member of the family as are the natural children. He takes the family name and often he receives a new first name. After the papers are drawn up and sealed, he is received into the family as a son, and has all the rights and privileges of a child born in the family. As a son he shares in the father's estate, a joint heir with the natural children.

In consideration for all this he also shares in the duties and responsibilities of the family life and becomes subject to the authority of the father.

It is the same with God's adopted family. When we give ourselves to be led by the Holy Spirit, we receive "the adoption of sons," and we bear the name of Christ. We are then no longer servants of Satan, but God becomes a Father to us, and we become His sons

God's family in their own Father's house.

and daughters; "and if children, then heirs; heirs of God, and joint heirs with Christ."

6. Value of Adoption in This Life. What does it mean to us to be adopted into God's family?

It means *forgiveness of sins.* "If we confess our sins, He is faithful and just to forgive us our sins, and to cleanse us from all unrighteousness."

It means *peace with God.* "The peace of God, which passeth all understanding, shall keep your hearts and minds through Christ Jesus."

It means *help in temptation.* "God . . . will not suffer you to be tempted above that ye are able; but will with the temptation also make a way to escape, that ye may be able to bear it."

It means *strength to be patient.* "Strengthened with all might, according to His glorious power, unto all patience and long-suffering with joyfulness."

It means *a liberal education.* "If any of you lack wisdom, let him ask of God, that giveth to all men liberally, and upbraideth not; and it shall be given him."

It means *a good memory.* "The Comforter, which is the Holy Ghost, . . . shall . . . bring all things to your remembrance, whatsoever I have said unto you."

It means *protection during the plagues.* "There shall no evil befall thee, neither shall any plague come nigh thy dwelling."

7. **Future Value of Adoption.** For the future, adoption into God's family means translation to heaven and becoming "partakers of the inheritance of the saints in light." In fact, it means that as joint heirs with Christ, all the treasures of heaven, all that we can ask or think, awaits our demand and reception. What more can we ask? Yet it means even more — *more* than we can ask or think — "exceeding abundantly above all that we ask or think." And finally, when the family of God according to His original plan is fully made up and the plan of salvation for fallen beings finished, God's entire family, His family in heaven and His adopted family on earth, will be at home, reunited in their own Father's house.

How to Study: As you read each section, write down first the section topic, then two or three sub-topics. This will help you to notice and remember the main thoughts of the lesson. Use this outline for your class recitation.

Memory Work: Memorize Isaiah 55: 1, 7.

Dictionary Study: redeem. By analysis give the meaning of: law-less; price-less.

---

25. REVIEW QUESTIONS WITH BIBLE TEXTS

1. Since man's fall, what is Satan called? 2 Cor. 4: 4.
2. For how much did man sell himself? Isa. 52: 3.
3. How much did it cost to redeem, or purchase him back? *Isa. 55: 1, 7; *Rom. 8: 32.
4. Why did God redeem us? Gal. 4: 5, last part.
5. When God adopts us, whose heirs do we become? Rom. 8: 17.
6. What does adoption bring to us in this life?
7. How much is God able to do for us? Eph. 3: 20.
8. How much does God's whole family include? Eph. 3: 15.

How to Study: Before beginning to study, notice that two texts are in Isaiah, two in Romans 8, and two in Ephesians 3. "Bookmark" these places. Recite the starred verses from memory.

Review of Memory Verses for the Period: Ps. 36:9; John 5:26; Job 38:7; Eph. 6:12; Isa. 59:2; Rom. 8:32; John 3:16; Heb. 1:14; 1 Cor. 10:13; Gen. 3:15; 1 John 5:4; 2 Peter 3:9; Rev. 22:14; Ps. 119:89; Rom. 8:38, 39; Isa. 55:1, 7. Be able to recite all these verses without any help.

Verse-Finding Drill: Without using a concordance, turn to or tell where the memory verses are found that begin —

With Thee is the fountain of life
As the Father hath life in Himself
When the morning stars sang together
We wrestle not against flesh and blood
Your iniquities have separated
He that spared not His own Son
God so loved the world
Are they not all ministering spirits
There hath no temptation taken you

I will put enmity between thee and
This is the victory
The Lord is not slack
Blessed are they that do His commandments
Forever, O Lord, Thy word is settled
For I am persuaded, that neither death
Ho, every one that thirsteth

Chapter Drill: Turn to the chapter that tells about —

1. Repairing the breach in God's law
2. Victory over death and the grave
3. God's law in nearly every verse
4. Lucifer's declaration of war
5. The covering cherub
6. The longest chapter in the Bible
7. Satan's prison house
8. The first promise of a Saviour
9. The Beatitudes
10. The law of God
11. The faith chapter
12. War in heaven
13. The fall of man
14. The fall of Lucifer
15. The King of glory
16. The Sermon on the Mount

REVIEW OF CHAPTER I

Test Questions: See how many of these questions you can answer in the language of the Bible without looking up the text. Be able to recite all starred verses. Be able to tell the subject of chapters following all starred questions. The paragraph numbers refer to previous lessons.

1, 2. When was God's great plan laid? Eph. 3:11.
   What two families did He plan to create? Eph. 3:15.
   Why did He want to create beings like Himself? Rev. 4:11.
   How can God create and give life? *Ps. 36:9; *John 5:26.
3, 4. How many angels surround the throne? Rev. 5:11.
   *What two positions did Lucifer occupy? Eze. 28:13, 14.
   What did the angels do when God's plan was told them? *Job 38:7.
5, 6. *Describe the war in heaven. *Eph. 6:12; Rev. 12:7-9.
   *What decision of Lucifer opened the war? Isa. 14:13, 14.
   7. Why did Satan go to the tree of knowledge?
   *How did the serpent compare in ability with the other animals? Gen. 3:1.
8, 9. How did sin affect the earth? vegetation? animals?

How did Adam and Eve meet death the day they sinned?
What separated man from God? *Isa. 59:2. Why?
Why did man feel that his punishment was just? 2 Peter 2:4; 1 John 3:4 with Rom. 6:23, first part.

10, 11. Why did God keep secret His plan to save?
Why did God give us His Son? *John 3:16.
Why was it a struggle for the Father?
In giving Jesus how much did He give? *Rom. 8:32.

12-14. When Jesus stepped down from the throne as God, what did He take upon Himself? Phil. 2:7, 8; Rom. 8:3.
What was the first promise of a Saviour? *Gen. 3:15.
What part do the angels have to act? *Heb. 1:14.
What is our relation to this conflict? Matt. 12:30.
What help do we have under temptation? *1 Cor. 10:13.
Who will be saved as a result of God's plan? Rev. 7:9.
How will Jesus then feel? Isa. 53:11.

15. How could God have prevented sin?
How are God's children different from the animals?
What is the victory that overcomes the world? *1 John 5:4.

16. Why was Satan not destroyed at once?
Why does God allow sinners to live? *2 Peter 3:9.
How fully will sin at last be destroyed? Mal. 4:1.

17, 18. From the following texts, explain why Jesus must die to save us: Isa. 42:22; 14:17; John 5:26; 10:17, 18; Rev. 1:18; John 14:19.

19, 20. Why could not the life of an angel have saved us? Ps. 148:2, 5; Heb. 1:4.
Give two texts showing that Jesus did not come to destroy His Father's law.
If God's law could have been destroyed, what would have been unnecessary?
What reward is promised to those who keep God's law? *Rev. 22:14.

21, 22. Of what two events is the Sabbath a memorial? Explain.
Explain how the Sabbath is the seal of God's law.
How is God's law regarded in heaven? *Ps. 119:89.
*How does Satan feel toward those who honor God's law? Rev. 12:17.
Who are the "repairers of the breach"? Isa. 58:12, 13.
Give two verses that show when the Sabbath begins and ends.

23. What assurance have we that sin will never again mar God's universe? Nahum 1:9.
What does Paul say about our not being separated from God? *Rom. 8:38, 39.
How will the cost of our salvation forever be remembered? Isa. 49:16; Hab. 3:4.

24, 25. How much did it cost to redeem man? *Isa. 55:1, 7.
When God adopts us, whose heirs do we become? Rom. 8:17.
When redemption is finished, what family will be reunited? Eph. 3:15.

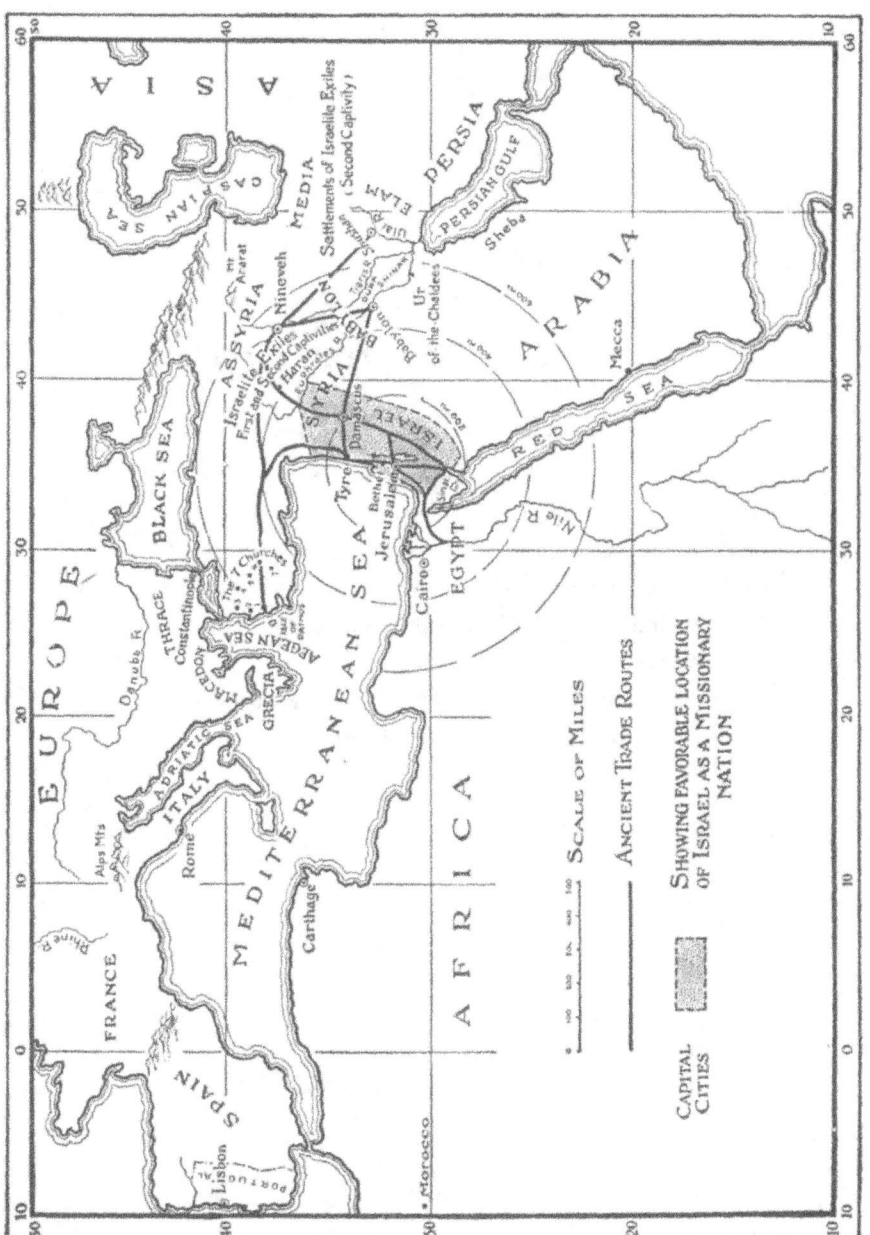

Map of Bible Lands

Second Period—Chapters II and III

OUTLINE OF CHAPTER II

Topics —	B. C.
God's First Missionaries — Adam and Enoch	4004
Noah, a "Preacher of Righteousness"	2348
Satan's First Effort to Establish a World Government	
"Our Father Abraham"	1921
Isaac a Type of the Sacrifice of God's Only Son	
Jacob's Preparation to Be a Missionary	
Review	

CHAPTER II

The Patriarchs, Teachers of God's Plan

1. GOD'S FIRST MISSIONARIES

B. C. 4000 to B. C. 3000

"Behold, the Lord cometh with ten thousands of His saints."
Enoch's Message, Jude 14.

1. God's Preknowledge of His Family. When, in the council of peace, the Deity planned to create "the whole family in heaven and earth," every item of this wonderful undertaking was carefully comprehended. In all His work, God considers not only the great things, but the small things as well. "The hand that hung the worlds in space is the hand that fashions the flowers of the field." He who has numbered "the very hairs of your head," He who knows our thoughts even before we utter them, knew in the beginning every detail regarding His prospective family. David says, *"Thine eyes did see my substance, yet being unperfect ["mine unformed substance," A. R. V.] ; and in Thy book all my members were written, what days they should be fashioned, when as yet there was none of them." Marvelous as it is, our Creator Father knew each one of His family by appearance and by name, when as yet there was none of us — yes, before we were "fashioned," or created. He knew just how many angels there were to be in His heavenly family, and He knows just how many people there will be in His earthly family.

2. God's Original Plan Will Be Worked Out. Although Satan wrecked the family on earth, he cannot wreck God's plan. That is still the same. The very number that God planned for in the council of peace before creation, will yet be counted when He makes up His jewels. Everyone who has ever lived on this earth or who ever will live here has had or will have an opportunity to be a member

---

References Used: P. P., pp. 68, 82-89, 92; Ed., p. 114; S. P., Vol. 1, p. 53; Matt. 10: 30; Gen. 1: 28; John 1: 29; Jude 14, 15.

(71)

THE WORKING OUT OF GOD'S PLAN

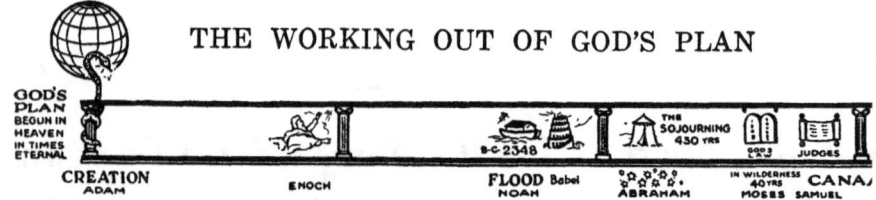

DIAGRAM NO. 1. This diagram covers the scope of the entire book — from the entrance of sin to the end of the millennium, when the holy city comes down and the earth is made new. We are now living in the closing hours of the preparation for the second coming of Christ. Soon this generation will close and the end will come, for God "will finish the work, and cut it short in righteousness." The prophecies of Daniel, including the 1260 years of papal persecution and the prophecy of the 2300 days, are shown in their relation to God's plan.

of that family. When the full number is made up, probation will close, God's work will be finished, and those who have refused a place in the Father's family — those who have refused to connect with "the fountain of life"— will be cut off from among the living.

3. Man as God's Agent. In His original plan, God designed to use man as His agent in making up this family. When He created our first parents, He said, "Be fruitful, and multiply, and replenish the earth." Then, as soon as the earth should be replenished, as soon as the full number of His family should be born, God's original plan would be accomplished. It is still His plan that righteous human beings shall replenish the earth. So, even though we have sinned, God still trusts us to have a part in His great plan by carrying to others a knowledge of the *second* birth. Now, by the spiritual birth instead of the natural birth, we may bring others into God's family on earth, gathering them out from the wreckage of sin.

4. Adam, God's First Missionary. When Adam learned that he might be associated with Jesus and the angels in gathering together the family of God, his heart filled with gratitude. He knew that he did not deserve such favor, but he resolved that so long as God spared his life, he would not only be obedient to all God's requirements, but he would also endeavor to teach others the great plan of salvation. Thus Adam, the father of the human family, the first to disobey, was the first to repent. His name was the first to be entered in God's family record book above. He was God's first missionary.

Through his long life, extending over nearly one thousand years, Adam brought to the cherubim-guarded gates of Paradise his children and his children's children to nine generations. Here he told

DURING THE REIGN OF SIN

them the story of creation, of the garden of Eden, of the tree of life and the tree of knowledge, and then of his sin and expulsion from Eden. He also told them of God's plan to save. As he offered the innocent lamb as a sacrifice, Adam explained to them about the suffering that Jesus was willing to endure — that He was "the Lamb of God, which taketh away the sin of the world."

5. The First Sacrifice. "To Adam, the offering of the first sacrifice was a most painful ceremony. His hand must be raised to take life, which only God could give. It was the first time he had ever witnessed death, and he knew that had he been obedient to God, there would have been no death of man or beast. As he slew the innocent victim, he trembled at the thought that his sin must shed the blood of the spotless Lamb of God. This scene gave him a deeper and more vivid sense of the greatness of his transgression." But in Christ he saw a star of hope which lighted up the dark future.

6. Trials and Results of Adam's Labors. During his long life, Adam lived among men, faithfully warning them against the subtle temptations of Satan, and instructing them regarding the sacredness of God's law. The godly life and faithful labors of Adam did much to spread a correct knowledge of God. "Yet there were but few who gave heed to his words. Often he was met with bitter reproaches for the sin that had brought such woe upon his posterity. . . . He witnessed the wide-spreading corruption that was finally to cause the destruction of the world by a flood; and though the sentence of death pronounced upon him by his Maker had at first appeared terrible, yet after beholding for nearly a thousand years the results of sin, he felt that it was merciful in God to bring to an end a life of suffering and sorrow."

7. Enoch's Preparation to Be a Missionary. Enoch, the seventh from Adam, was another missionary for God. From the lips of Adam he had learned the dark story of the fall, and the cheering promise of the Saviour. Enoch walked and talked with God. "To him prayer was as the breath of the soul; he lived in the very atmosphere of heaven." Through holy angels, God revealed to Enoch

The offering of the lamb gave Adam "a deeper and more vivid sense of the greatness of his transgression."

many events of the future. He told him of the flood to come, and He opened more fully the plan of redemption. He also "carried him down through the generations that should live after the flood, and showed him the great events connected with the second coming of Christ and the end of the world."

8. The Preaching of Enoch. Enoch preached these great truths to those who lived on the earth at that time, and there were some who believed his message. To Cain and his descendants he carried the good news of Christ's coming and the warning of God's judgment. "Behold," he declared, "the Lord cometh with ten thousands of His saints, to execute judgment upon all, and to convince all that are ungodly among them of all their ungodly deeds."

9. Translation of Enoch. "For three hundred years, Enoch had been seeking purity of soul, that he might be in harmony with Heaven. For three centuries he had walked with God. Day by day he had longed for a closer union; nearer and nearer had grown the communion, until God took him to Himself. He had stood at the threshold of the eternal world, only a step between him and the land of the blest; and now the portals opened, the walk with God, so long pursued on earth, continued, and he passed through the gates of the holy city,— the first from among men to enter there."

The translation of Enoch was for the encouragement of all who live on the earth. "Satan was urging upon men the belief that there was no reward for the righteous or punishment for the wicked, and that it was impossible for men to obey the divine statutes." Enoch's life taught men that even while living among the wicked, it is possible to resist temptation, *"for before his translation he had this testimony, that he pleased God." His translation is also an assurance to those who shall live in the end of time that "as Enoch was translated to heaven before the destruction of the world by water, so the living righteous will be translated from the earth before its destruction by fire."

How to Study: Prepare to tell this lesson as oral composition under the three following heads:
1. How God will work out His original plan. Topics 1-3.
2. The missionary Adam. Topics 4-6.
3. Enoch as a missionary. Topics 7-9.

Under each head write such "catch words" as you may need in order not to omit any important thought.

Dictionary Study: replenish. (The root of this word means *plenty*.) Form the *habit* of never allowing yourself to pass over words whose meaning you do not quite understand. Get "the dictionary habit."

Use of Concordance: Find and read from the Bible the two texts starred under topics 1 and 9. Key words: member, translation. Which of these texts is found in "the faith chapter"? In what book of the Bible will you find the text telling what David says?

Memory Work: Memorize Enoch's message in Jude 14, 15.

For Your Workbook: Begin to make diagram No. 1. In the proper place indicate (1) when Jesus came to earth (by a large star); (2) the eras B. C. and A. D.; (3) the present year; (4) God's plan begun in "times eternal"; (5) God's plan finished in the new earth; (6) creation, Adam, and Enoch.

The blank on which to fill out this diagram is a page in "Bible Workbook" for the eighth grade. The necessary pictures are also given in the workbook.

2. NOAH, A "PREACHER OF RIGHTEOUSNESS"

B. C. 3000 to B. C. 2000

"By faith Noah . . . prepared an ark to the saving of his house." Heb. 11:7.

1. Noah's Relation to Other Patriarchs. A thousand years had passed since Adam sold himself for naught. In spite of the earnest efforts of God's faithful missionaries, but few had fully turned away from Satan and joined God's family. Many scoffed at God's plan and refused to obey His law.

About a thousand years after the beginning of this world's history (B. C. 3000), a man was born whose name was Noah. "Noah" means *comfort;* and surely Noah was to be a comfort to the righteous, and he must have been a great comfort to God. Noah was one of the greatest missionaries this world has ever known. He was the great-grandson of the man who "walked with God." Noah's life covered almost the entire period of the second thousand years, for he lived 950 years — twenty years longer than Adam had lived.

2. Increase of Unbelief and Evil. Even while Adam lived, sin, like deadly leprosy, had made terrible inroads among the inhabitants of earth. Men "did not like to retain God in their knowledge." But they "could not deny the existence of Eden while it stood just in sight, its entrance barred by watching angels. The order of creation, the object of the garden, the history of its two trees so closely connected with man's destiny, were undisputed facts. And the existence and supreme authority of God, the obligation of His law, were truths which men were slow to question while Adam was among them." But now that Adam was gone, evil rapidly increased until at last "God saw that the wickedness of man was great in the earth, and that every imagination of the thoughts of his heart was

---

References Used: P. P., pp. 82, 84, 95-98, 105-108, 112, 630; Isa. 52:3; Rom. 1:28; Gen. 6:5, 6, 11; 7:16; 9:11; Ps. 104:8, R. V.

only evil continually. . . . The earth also was corrupt before God, and the earth was filled with violence."

3. God's Repentance. This awful condition filled the heart of the Creator with intense sorrow; the Bible says, "It grieved Him at His heart," so that "it repented the Lord that He had made man on the earth."

God's repentance is not like man's repentance. When man repents, he changes his mind, and takes a different course of action from the one he was following, because he sees that his former course was not right or best. But God's actions and plans are always perfect, and therefore they cannot change. So when God repents, He changes circumstances in order that His original purpose may be accomplished and that right may triumph.

In the days of Noah, iniquity had become so terrible and widespread that the whole world was fast approaching destruction. Yet amid the wickedness there were a few righteous souls. What could be done to save these honest ones from the threatened ruin, and put an end to the wretchedness of the wicked? Our Father always *"knoweth how to deliver the godly out of temptations." He had a plan by which all who would obey His instructions might be separated from the wicked, and be saved. Those who persisted in their wicked course would reap the fruit of their own disobedience and rebellion. What was God's plan? And how did He carry it out?

This is a fragment of a baked clay tablet on which is inscribed a Babylonian account of the flood. The original is in the British Museum, London.

4. Noah Chosen to Be God's Missionary. What a "comfort" at such a time as this to find some one who could be trusted, some one who would be true and loyal even amid sneers and persecutions!

Noah, though at this time nearly five hundred years old, was just such a man. To him God sent an angel to tell him His purpose to destroy the earth by a flood, and to direct him to build an ark into which all might go who desired to be saved. Noah is called a *"preacher of righteousness." For one hundred twenty years, he faithfully told the people of the coming destruction and of God's plan to save them. Not only did Noah devote his time to warning the world, but the angels in heaven were busy in the work of persuading, encouraging, and helping those whom Satan was so deceitfully drawing away to destruction.

Many at first appeared to receive the warning; but when they saw the unbelief all around them, "they finally joined their former associates in rejecting the solemn message. Some were deeply convicted, and would have heeded the words of warning; but there were so many to jest and ridicule, that they partook of the same spirit." Many even of those who professed to serve God, rejected the preaching of Noah, regarding him as a fanatic.

Still God held in check the elements of destruction, until every one had either accepted or rejected God's plan for him. Had the antediluvians believed the message of God, and repented, the Lord would have spared them as He afterward spared Nineveh. But by persistently disobeying Him, they at last closed their period of probation. Enoch had told his children what God had shown him in regard to the flood. Methuselah, Noah's grandfather, and others worked with Noah in an effort to give a knowledge of the true God, and warn the world of the coming destruction. These assisted Noah in building the ark. Noah's father, Lamech, died about five years before the flood; and Methuselah, whose name means, "When he is dead, it shall be sent," died the very year of the flood, 1656 years after creation. Others also were laid to rest before the storm broke.

5. In the Ark. Finally the ark was finished. Only Noah and his family, eight persons in all, were prepared to enter. "And the Lord shut him in." "A flash of dazzling light was seen, and a cloud of glory, more vivid than the lightning, descended from heaven, and hovered before the entrance of the ark. The massive door, which it was impossible for those within to close, was slowly swung to its place by unseen hands. Noah was shut in, and the rejecters of God's mercy were shut out. The seal of heaven was on that door; God had shut it, and God alone could open it."

Preserved by angels that excel in strength, the ark safely rode the tempestuous billows of a shoreless ocean, sheltering its inmates from harm. At last, one year and seventeen days after the door of the ark was closed, "an angel descended from heaven, opened the massive door, and bade the patriarch and his household go forth upon the earth."

6. The Rainbow of God's Covenant. "Lest the gathering clouds and falling rain should fill men with constant terror, from fear of

"I do set My bow in the cloud, and it shall be for a token of a covenant between Me and the earth."

another flood, the Lord encouraged the family of Noah by a promise: 'I will establish My covenant with you; . . . neither shall there any more be a flood to destroy the earth. . . . I do set My bow in the cloud, and it shall be for a token of a covenant between Me and the earth.' . . . It was God's purpose that as the children of after generations should ask the meaning of the glorious arch which spans the heavens, their parents should repeat the story of the flood, and tell them that the Most High had bended the bow, and placed it in the clouds." They were to explain that as the rainbow around the throne of God and above the head of the Saviour is a token of God's mercy toward us when we repent of our sins, so the rainbow in the cloud was an assurance that the waters should never again overflow the earth.

7. God's Record in the Earth. "The entire surface of the earth was changed at the flood. A third dreadful curse rested upon it in consequence of sin. . . . In many places, hills and mountains had

These are photographs of part of a fossil elephant's tusk and the remains of a palm leaf found buried in Alaska, within the arctic circle. Here also are found many remains of other tropical and semitropical plants and animals. This shows that before the flood the climate in this frozen region was warm and pleasant. These plant remains now form large coal beds.

disappeared, leaving no trace where they once stood; and plains had given place to mountain ranges." "The mountains rose, the valleys sank down unto the place which Thou hast founded for them." The earth at this time became a vast burial ground. "Men, animals, and trees, many times larger than now exist, were buried, and thus preserved as an evidence to later generations that the antediluvians perished by a flood." Thus God left in the very earth itself a record to cause men to believe His word.

8. How and Why Satan Works Against This Record. Satan cannot remove this record, but through false education, he is making every effort to destroy its influence. Because geologists have found these relics in the earth, some of them teach that long before the time of creation, the earth was peopled by a race of beings larger than any now living. They also teach that the earth was evolved during vast indefinite periods of time, when strange forms of life existed and finally passed away. This theory is called evolution. It is one of Satan's devices to lead people not to believe in that God who "in six days . . . made heaven and earth, the sea, and all that in them is, and rested the seventh day: wherefore the Lord blessed the Sabbath day, and hallowed it." To those who understand his deceptive schemes and his hatred for God's law, it is plain that his efforts are thus directed against the Sabbath commandment, the seal of God's law and the sign of His authority.

9. God's Weapons in the Earth. The immense forests that were buried at the time of the flood "have since been changed to coal, forming the extensive coal beds that now exist, and also yielding large quantities of oil. The coal and oil frequently ignite and burn beneath the surface of the earth. Thus rocks are heated, limestone is burned, and iron ore melted. The action of the water upon the lime adds fury to the intense heat." Earthquakes and volcanoes are a result of these disturbances. As the depths of the earth contained the weapons that were used in destroying the world at the time of the flood, so now the earth is stored with fire, the weapon that will be used in its final destruction,— it is *"kept in store, reserved unto fire against the day of judgment."

How to Study: After studying the lesson, you should be able to answer these questions:
1. What relation to Noah was Enoch?
2. What helped to check unbelief and evil while Adam still lived? What condition developed after his death?
3. What is the difference between the repentance of man and God?
4. What efforts were made to save man from evil? With what results?
5. Who helped Noah build the ark? Describe the scene when the ark was closed; when it was opened. What year B. C. is 1656 after creation?
6. What relation has the rainbow on earth to the one in heaven?
7. What record has God left of the flood? Why? How does Satan try to destroy its influence? Why?
8. With what is the earth now stored? For what purpose?

Dictionary Study: antediluvian (ante-diluvian), geologist (geo-logist). Can you think of another word that has the root *geo?* What word meaning *flood* has the same root as "diluvian"?

Use of Concordance: Find the texts that are starred under topics 3, 4, 9. Key words: godly, preacher, fire.

Chapters to Remember: Genesis 6, 7, and 8 tell the story of the flood. 2 Peter 3 tells about the destruction of the earth by fire. From what memory chapter is the quotation under topic 8? the one at the head of the lesson?

For Your Workbook: Locate "the flood" on diagram No. 1.

For Class Discussion: What were the first two curses upon the earth? Gen. 3: 17, 18; 4: 10-12.

3. MAN'S FIRST EFFORT TO ESTABLISH A WORLD EMPIRE

B. C. 3000 to B. C. 2000

"There is none other name under heaven given among men, whereby we must be saved." Acts 4:12.

1. In the Plain of Shinar. Noah lived for 350 years after the flood; and Shem, his son through whose descendants the Saviour was to come, lived for 500 years after the flood. During this time, people again multiplied upon the earth. For a time, they lived among the mountains where the ark had rested. As their numbers increased, there were those among them who did not want to obey and worship the Creator as Noah and Shem did. At last, more than one hundred years after the flood, they separated themselves from those who remained in the hills. They journeyed to the plain of Shinar, on the banks of the Euphrates River. The location was beautiful, the soil fertile, and here they decided to build a city and a tower and make their home.

2. Satan Plans a Monarchy. Satan saw this as his opportunity to establish a monarchy that would finally control the whole earth, a government in which God would have no recognition. He sought to bring contempt upon the sacrificial offerings that pointed forward to the death of Christ; "and as the minds of the people were darkened by idolatry, he led them to counterfeit these offerings, and

---
References Used: P. P., pp. 118-123; Gen. 11: 1-9; Rev. 17: 5.

sacrifice their own children upon the altars of their gods." Others who had come to the plains he led to deny the existence of God. Still others, though believing that there is a God, yet knowing that He had destroyed the earth by a flood, thought of Him only as one who was ready to punish, instead of one who was seeking to save the lost.

3. The Tower Builders Defy God. These people determined that they would protect themselves from any future calamity like the flood. By their actions, they declared: "We do not need God. We can save ourselves." So they built that great tower of Babel. They planned to build it higher than the waters of the flood had reached, and they reasoned that then they would be beyond danger.

4. Prayer Defeats Satan's Plans. Among these people who dwelt in the plain of Shinar, there were some who feared the Lord, but who had been deceived and drawn into the schemes of the ungodly. When the true nature of the work of building the tower was discovered, these sons of God tried to turn the others from their evil course, but without avail. Then they cried to God for help. "And the Lord came down to see the city and the tower, which the children of men builded."

For the sake of the faithful ones, and that the wicked might have time to repent, God delayed His judgments. But most of the people were determined to carry forward their heaven-daring undertaking. "When the tower had been partially completed, a portion of it was occupied as a dwelling place for the builders; other apartments, splendidly furnished and adorned, were devoted to their idols. The people rejoiced in their success, and praised the gods of silver and gold. . . . Suddenly the work that had been advancing so prosperously was checked. Angels were sent to bring to naught the purpose of the builders. . . . Lightnings from heaven . . . broke off the upper portion of the tower, and cast it to the ground."

5. The Language Confounded. Up to this time, all men had spoken the same language; but now the language was confounded. As a result, the different groups of workmen could not understand one another, and, amid confusion and fear, building operations ceased. Then those who could understand one another united in companies, some going one way, and some another. Thus "the Lord scattered them abroad from thence upon the face of all the earth."

6. God's Purpose. But all this was done in love. It was God's purpose in the beginning that men should scatter abroad and people the earth, so that in all parts of the earth might be those who could tell future generations of His plan to save. Satan thought to defeat this plan by centering the people in one place where he could more successfully influence them against God. Had these people under his direction gone on unchecked, a mighty power would have been exerted to banish peace, happiness, and safety from the earth.

Those who could understand one another united in companies, some going one way and some another.

It is the same principle that Satan tried to carry out in heaven; and for the good of all concerned, God in mercy brought their efforts to an end.

Through calamity, God worked for their good, hoping that when separated from one another, they would reflect on the course they were taking, and see how foolish it was. He sent angels to impress their hearts with the need of the Saviour and to encourage them to forsake their evil ways. And so even in our waywardness and folly and sin, God still loves us and longs to help us. Even trouble and disaster are permitted that we may see our need of Jesus.

7. "Mystery, Babylon the Great." The tower of Babel was near the spot where afterward the great city of Babylon was built — that city which was Satan's counterfeit of the New Jerusalem. The motive in building it was the beginning of a great system of wickedness having for its foundation the idea that man can save himself, and denying the truth that "there is none other name under heaven given among men, whereby we must be saved," but the name of Jesus only. In the Bible this "mystery of iniquity" is called "Babylon," "Babylon the Great," or "that great city Babylon." Remember this, for you will study more about it in future lessons.

8. Recent Discoveries. Ruins believed to be those of the tower of Babel, still exist. During the last hundred years, bricks have been discovered on which are written characters that are thought to identify the ancient tower. God has doubtless brought these things to light in these closing days of earth's history so that the world may have convincing evidence that His word is true. He will do everything that can be done to help men everywhere to turn away from the deceptions of Satan and find refuge in the Saviour.

How to Study: Write one leading question on each topic of the lesson, numbering the questions to correspond with the topic. Perhaps your teacher will let you use your questions to test your classmates.

Map Work: Locate the plain of Shinar; Euphrates River; Babylon. See map on page 69.

Dictionary Study: Bab-el,— Babylon. The word Bab-el means "the gate of god." The word Babylon means "confusion" (Gen. 11:9, margin).

Chapter to Remember: Genesis 11 tells about the tower of Babel.

For Your Notebook: Locate the tower of Babel on diagram No. 1.

For Class Discussion: What relation do the events of this lesson have to the great controversy between Christ and Satan? to the verse at the beginning of the lesson?

4. "OUR FATHER ABRAHAM"

About 2000 B. C.

"By faith Abraham, when he was called to go out into a place which he should after receive for an inheritance, obeyed; and he went out, not knowing whither he went." Heb. 11:8.

1. The Patriarchs as Missionaries. Ever since the fall of Adam, the story of God's great plan had been told from family to family by the fathers, or patriarchs. Adam was the first patriarch. It was God's plan that the first-born son of each patriarch should be the succeeding patriarch. This meant that he would have the honor and the responsibility during his lifetime, or generation, of telling to others the story of God's great plan. In a special sense, he was to be God's missionary. By right of birth, Cain was the second patriarch. But he forfeited his birthright; he proved himself unfit

References Used: P. P., p. 125; Joshua 24:2; Gen. 12:1-3, 7; 13:14, 15; 15:13, 15; 17:4, 8; Heb. 11:8, 10, 13, 15, 16; Acts 7:5; Rom. 4:13; Gal. 3:29; John 8:39, 56.

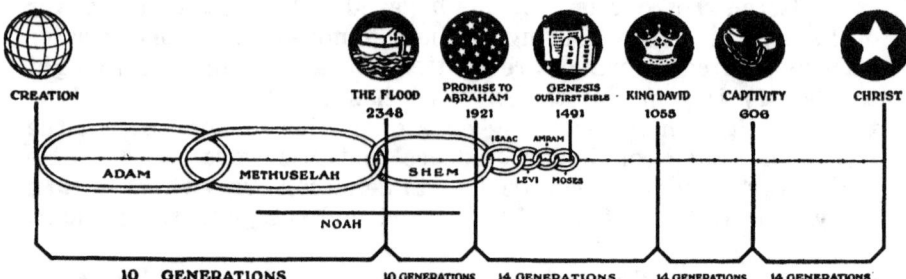

DIAGRAM No. 2. This diagram covers Old Testament times, showing the groups of generations pointing to the birth of Christ. It shows also how easily the stories of creation, the garden of Eden, the fall, the flood, and other stories of patriarchal days were handed down to Moses, who wrote them in the book of Genesis, our first Bible. The lives of Adam and Methuselah span the time from creation to the flood, while seven links complete the chain from creation to Canaan. Adam lived with Noah's grandfather for 243 years; Methuselah lived with Noah's son Shem 98 years; and Shem, who lived nearly a century before the flood, talked with Abraham and Isaac.

to teach the plan of salvation, because by bringing of the fruit of the ground instead of a lamb for an offering, he showed his lack of faith in the sacrificial system that pointed forward to the Saviour. As Abel had been killed, Seth, the next eldest son, received the birthright and became the patriarch, the missionary for his generation. Enos, the eldest son of Seth, became the third patriarch, and so on down the line, each patriarch representing a generation, or family of people. In this way, the patriarch was God's divinely appointed representative on earth. As you will see by examining the diagram on page 506, several patriarchs lived at the same time. How many lived during the life of Noah? How many antediluvian patriarchs were there? How many postdiluvian patriarchs? Which one was both antediluvian and postdiluvian?

2. A Loyal Man Needed. Four hundred years had passed since the people were dispersed from Babel. God looked down upon His children as a good shepherd might look upon his flock, torn and scattered and lost. Almost the whole earth was given over to idolatry, but here and there He saw honest hearts longing for a better life. He would send some one to them to tell them of His plan to save. But whom could He trust with His message of love?

One time during the great war, General Pershing wanted to send a special message to President Wilson. He looked for some one whom he could trust — some one whom he knew to be thoroughly loyal to the cause of liberty for which we were fighting, some one who was faithful, some one who would not even in the slightest degree betray his trust to one of the enemy, some one who would obey his instructions to the last letter. God at this time was looking for just such a man. Did He find him?

3. Abram Called. Over in Ur of the Chaldees, God saw a man who, although surrounded by superstition and heathenism, refused to yield to these evil influences. Even though Terah, his own father, "served other gods," yet Abram steadfastly adhered to the worship of the one true God. "Idolatry invited him on every side, but in vain." This was the man God wanted — a man who would be loyal to Him right in his own home, even when influences were against him. "Now the Lord had said unto Abram, Get thee out of thy country, and from thy kindred, and from thy father's house, unto a land that I will show thee: and I will make of thee a great nation, . . . and in thee shall all families of the earth be blessed."

4. Abraham, the Father of a Missionary Nation. As years passed by, the number of inhabitants increased in the earth, and gradually they moved farther and farther from the cradle of the race — the small territory where the patriarchs had lived. God saw that soon it would be impossible for a few patriarchs to reach all these distant places and converse with all the people; so He decided to organize a missionary nation, and He chose Abraham to be the father of this nation. "I will make of thee a great nation," were the words of the promise. "Thou shalt be a father of many nations." As a sign that He would surely fulfill this covenant, God changed Abram's name to Abraham, which means "father of a great multitude."

5. Abraham, the First Foreign Missionary. No man has ever been more highly honored than the patriarch Abraham. He was the first who was called to leave his home and native land and carry the gospel to distant lands — he was God's first foreign missionary. Did he refuse? No! "By faith Abraham . . . obeyed; and he went out, not knowing whither he went." But God knew, and that was enough for Abraham. From place to place he traveled, erecting altars to God, and winning souls in every land.

6. The Land of Canaan Promised to Abraham. When Abraham first entered the land of Canaan, the Lord appeared to him, and said, "Unto thy seed will I give this land." A few years later, the Lord again appeared to the patriarch, and repeated this promise. "Lift up now thine eyes, and look from the place where thou art northward, and southward, and eastward, and westward: for all the land which thou seest, to thee will I give it, and to thy seed forever." When Abraham had been nearly twenty-five years in Canaan, the Lord appeared to him again, and once more repeated the promise, "I will give unto thee, and to thy seed after thee, the land wherein thou art a stranger, all the land of Canaan, for an everlasting pos-

Abraham entering the land of Canaan.

session." Yet, during his whole life, all that Abraham owned of the land of Canaan was the rock-hewn tomb in the cave of Machpelah in which he and Sarah his wife were buried; and even this he purchased at an exorbitant price.

7. The Fulfillment of the Promise. Abraham was a man of great wealth. He might have lived in Ur in luxury and ease. Even after leaving his home, if he had been mindful — mind-full — of that country from which he came out he might have had opportunity to return. But no! Abraham was not the man to turn back after having put his hand to the plow. He was willing to become a stranger and a pilgrim on the earth and give all his wealth to win his fellow men into the family of God. But what did God mean by promising Abraham a country and then never giving him even the smallest possession, "no, not so much as to set his foot on"? Had God's word failed?

When God made the promise to Abraham, saying, "All the land which thou seest, to thee will I give it, and to thy seed forever," He said also, "Know of a surety that thy seed shall be a stranger in a land that is not theirs . . . four hundred years. . . . And thou shalt go to thy fathers in peace; thou shalt be buried in a good old age." The future is just as plain to God as the present. In fact,

Abraham "looked for a city which hath foundations, whose builder and maker is God."

there is neither past nor future with Him; all time is present with God; He is the great "I AM." To Abraham, God lifted the curtain; and because Abraham believed God, he too saw into the distant future. Thus Abraham understood that he himself should not possess the land, but that a few centuries later the promise would be fulfilled to his seed.

It was also God's thought that Abraham and his seed, or descendants, should be "heir of the world," not in its present sinful state, but when it should finally be made new. The earthly Canaan was a type of the heavenly Canaan, the new earth. Abraham understood this, "for he looked for a city which hath foundations, whose builder and maker is God." He desired "a better country, that is, an heavenly." "And if *ye* be Christ's, then are ye Abraham's seed, and heirs according to the promise." We may be partakers of the promise to Abraham if we accept Christ into our lives and if we are obedient to God as Abraham was — if we "do the works of Abraham."

8. The Looked-for Redeemer. The work with which God was to honor this chosen nation is expressed in the words, "In thee shall all families of the earth be blessed." By this, God meant that in Abraham's line of descendants in the nation that He was about to organize, the Redeemer of the world should come — the One who would bless all families of the earth. Abraham understood this; for Jesus Himself said, "Your father Abraham rejoiced to see My day: and he saw it, and was glad." From that time until Jesus was born in Bethlehem, many a parent in Israel looked for the fulfillment of this promise and fondly hoped that *his* son might be the honored one. Would not your interest be aroused if you knew that one in your family might one day be president of the United States, or the king of England, or some other great ruler? How much more if he were to be the King of heaven!

How to Study: Study to recite from the given topics. In preparing to do this, read one section at a time, then write several "catch words" or sub-topics under the main head, that will help you to see and remember the important points. For instance:

1. The Patriarchs as Missionaries
    The first patriarch
    The birthright — privileges and duties
    Cain, Abel, and Seth; other patriarchs
    Patriarchs living at the same time

Map Work: Locate Abram's home; the land of promise. See map, page 69.

Dictionary Study: post-diluvian, kindred (kin), mind-ful, patri-arch. What other word have we learned containing the syllable *arch*? Before looking for these words in the dictionary, try to tell their meaning by analysis.

Chapter to Remember: Genesis 12 tells about the call of Abraham.

For Your Workbook: On diagram No. 1 locate the call of Abraham. Gen. 12:1, date in margin.

Begin diagram No. 2 — "The Patriarchal Chain." Fill it in as far as Abraham. The blank diagram to be filled in is a page in "Bible Workbook" for the eighth grade. Pictures for this diagram are also in the workbook.

There were 60 generations from Adam to Christ. Which two are counted twice in the diagram? See Matthew 1 and diagram page 86.

For the Ambitious Student: Abraham paid 400 shekels of silver for the cave of Machpelah. (Gen. 23:16.) The value of a shekel is given as 64 cents, or in English money, 2s. 8d. How many days' labor would this amount to at

15 cents a day, the regular wage of a day laborer in the time of Christ? (Matt. 20:2, margin.) At $5.00 a day, an average wage for day labor to-day, how much would a burial place cost one to-day, if one had to pay at the rate Abraham paid?

5. ISAAC A TYPE OF THE SACRIFICE OF GOD'S ONLY SON

"Take now thy son, thine only son Isaac, whom thou lovest, . . . and offer him . . . for a burnt offering." Gen. 22:2.

1. Abraham's Knowledge of Patriarchal Stories. When Abraham was sent forth to tell the world of the Redeemer, and of God's great plan, he did not have the Bible from which to explain the will of God to the people; for at that time, the Bible had not been written. The stories of creation, the garden of Eden, the fall, God's plan to save, the flood, the confusion of languages, and other events of the great controversy between Christ and Satan, had been handed down from father to son, and had thus been written in the hearts of the patriarchs since the days of Adam. Abraham knew these stories well, for he had heard them recounted over and over again by most of the patriarchs since the time of Noah. He had heard the story of the flood from Shem, Noah's son, who had helped to build the ark and was one who had been sheltered within it. And Shem had never tired of listening to the stories of creation told by his great-grandfather Methuselah, who for over two hundred years had himself heard these same stories from the lips of Adam.

2. Lessons from the Offering of Isaac. But Abraham had more than these patriarchal stories, thrilling with interest though they were, to tell the people. He himself had many wonderful personal experiences to relate. But no experience given to this aged patriarch contained more lessons, or threw more light on God's plan, than the call to offer his son as a burnt offering,— the very son through whom God had promised, "All nations of the earth shall be blessed." Why did God command Abraham to slay his son? The answer to this question reveals another view of Satan's deceptive scheming and of God's supreme righteousness. Before the birth of Isaac, Abraham had shown a lack of faith in God's promises, and he had disobeyed one of God's commandments. Because of this, Satan,

---
References Used: P. P., pp. 148, 154, 155; Gen. 21:12; 22:10, 12; Rev. 12:10.

*"the accuser of our brethren," had accused him before the angels and before God as being unworthy of the blessings that God had promised him.

3. Perfect Obedience Alone Acceptable. God knew that Abraham's lack of faith and consequent disobedience were not the result of willful rebellion, and he "desired to prove the loyalty of His servant before all heaven." He also desired to make it plain "that nothing less than perfect obedience can be accepted." That Satan might have no grounds for further complaint, God's second test of Abraham's faith and obedience was far more severe than the one over which he had previously failed. "Take now thy son, thine only son Isaac, whom thou lovest, . . . and offer him . . . for a burnt offering." With almost breathless anxiety the angels watched. Would Abraham obey? Or would he again fail?

4. Satan's Effort to Defeat Abraham. Satan put forth his best efforts to cause Abraham to disobey God. He suggested, "Abraham, you must be deceived; for has not God commanded, 'Thou shalt not kill'? And would God require that which He has once forbidden? Besides, is not Isaac the child of promise? Is it not through his descendants that the Saviour is to be born? Surely, Abraham, you must be mistaken. Do not under any consideration obey the dictates of your deluded imagination." Thus Satan endeavored to cause Abraham to fall, as centuries before he had caused the fall of Adam. Satan knew it would make his work hard if a whole nation were to be consecrated to the work of explaining the gospel and telling men of his deceptive workings. He must if possible, destroy this plan at its very beginning.

5. Abraham Obtains Victory Through Faith and Prayer. Poor, wretched Abraham! It was a time of terrible agony with the father of an only son. What *should* he do? What only *could* he do? He could pray. And pray he did. In his perplexity and anguish, "he bowed upon the earth, and prayed as he had never prayed before. . . . He went to the place where he had several times met with the heavenly messengers, hoping to meet them again, and receive some further direction; but none came to his relief. Darkness seemed to shut him in; but the command of God was sounding in his ears, 'Take now thy son, thine only son Isaac, whom thou lovest.' "

Abraham believed God. He would no longer hesitate and delay. Cost what it might, he would be obedient to the divine command. His only hope was in God's promise, "In Isaac shall thy seed be called." Though he could not understand, he knew that God would not needlessly cause sorrow. He knew that God must have a good reason for the strange command. Moreover, he knew that it was impossible for God to lie. He had promised, and He would perform. If it was God's will that Isaac should die, he knew *"that God was

Abraham told Isaac that if it was God's will that he should die, "God was able to raise him up, even from the dead."

able to raise him up, even from the dead." "In Isaac shall thy seed be called," he repeated over and over to himself. And thus his faltering steps were strengthened for the task before him.

    6. Satan's Defeat, Angels' Joy. It is a familiar story,— that silent journey with Isaac to Mount Moriah, the altar built, and the precious sacrifice tenderly laid in its place. "By faith Abraham . . . offered up Isaac." As he stretched forth his hand and took the knife to slay his son, suddenly a cry from God arrested the blow: "Lay not thine hand upon the lad : . . . for now I know that thou fearest God, seeing thou hast not withheld thy son, thine only son from Me." Satan heard the cry of God, and he knew that Abraham was victorious and that his scheme had again been defeated. "All heaven beheld with wonder and admiration Abraham's unfaltering obedience. All heaven applauded his fidelity. Satan's accusations were shown to be false." *"Abraham believed God, . . . and he was called the friend of God."

    7. Abraham Better Understands God's Sacrifice. Another reason why this great trial was imposed upon him was "to impress Abraham's mind with the reality of the gospel." As the father of a great nation through whom God's great plan was to be made known to the world, and as the father of the faithful, Abraham must have a clear idea of the meaning of the sacrifice that God had made for the salvation of man. The sacrifice of Isaac, Abraham's only son, the son of promise, was a type of the sacrifice of Christ, God's only Son, the promised Redeemer. When Abraham took the knife to slay his son, how very real did Heaven's sacrifice seem to him! Now he could understand to some degree how the heavenly Father felt when in His distress He exclaimed, "Awake, O sword, against . . . the Man that is My fellow." "The agony which he endured during the dark days of that fearful trial, was permitted that he might understand from his own experience something of the greatness of the sacrifice made by the infinite God for man's redemption. No other test could have caused Abraham such torture of soul as did the offering of his son. God gave *His* Son to a death of agony and shame. The angels who witnessed the humiliation and soul-anguish of the Son of God were not permitted to interpose, as in the case of Isaac. There was no voice to cry, 'It is enough.' To save the fallen race, the King of glory yielded up His life."

    8. Angels Better Understand God's Plan. "The sacrifice required of Abraham was not alone for his own good, nor solely for the benefit of succeeding generations; but it was also for the instruction of the sinless intelligences of heaven and of other worlds. The field of the controversy between Christ and Satan,— the field on which the plan of redemption is wrought out,— is the lesson book of the universe. . . .

    "It had been difficult even for the angels to grasp the mystery of redemption,— to comprehend that the Commander of heaven, the

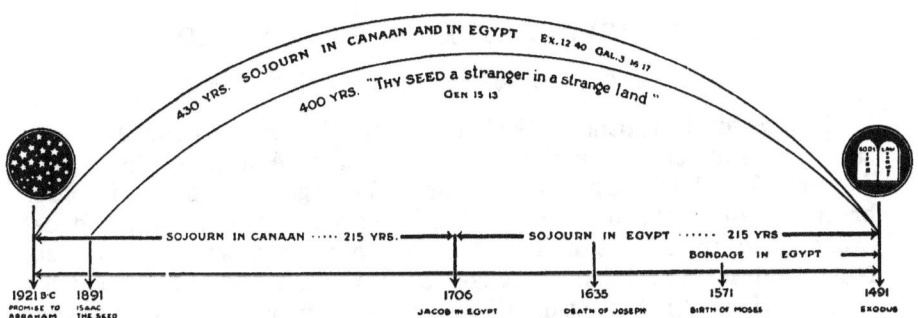

DIAGRAM NO. 3. This diagram makes plain the 400-year and 430-year periods of time.

Son of God, must die for guilty man. When the command was given to Abraham to offer up his son, the interest of all heavenly beings was enlisted. With intense earnestness they watched each step in the fulfillment of this command." And when the test was over, "light was shed upon the mystery of redemption, and even the angels understood more clearly the wonderful provision that God had made for man's salvation."

How to Study: Prepare to tell the story of the offering of Isaac, making plain the following special points:
1. Why God told Abraham to offer his son (Give six reasons)
2. How Satan tried to cause Abraham to disobey God
3. Abraham's struggle in prayer
4. His victory through faith in God's promise
5. Satan's defeat and the angels' joy
6. How this experience threw light on God's plan

Use of Concordance: Find the two texts that are starred under topics 5 and 6. Key words: raise, friend. Which of these is in the "faith chapter"?

Chapter to Remember: Genesis 22 tells about the offering of Isaac.

For Your Workbook: On diagram No. 3 indicate the time when God called Abraham (for date, see Gen. 12:1, margin); also the time when Isaac became "the seed." According to the custom of those days, the child was not counted the seed, or heir, until he was five years of age. Abraham was 75 years old when the promise was made (Gen. 12:4); he was 100 years old when Isaac was born (Gen. 21:5); how many years, then, from the time of "the promise" until Isaac was "the seed"? This was the beeginning of the 400-year period of sojourn spoken of in Gen. 15:13. The 430-year period of sojourn spoken of in Gal. 3:16, 17 began with the promise to Abraham, just thirty years before. The blank diagram to be filled out is a page in "Bible Workbook" for the eighth grade.

6. JACOB'S PREPARATION TO BE A MISSIONARY

"I will not let Thee go, except Thou bless me." Gen. 32:26.

1. Jacob's Deception. God was preparing Isaac's son Jacob to carry forward the work that He had given to Abraham, his grandfather. The birthright of the family belonged to Esau, his older brother. But Esau did not want this sacred responsibility, and because he despised his birthright, God had promised it to Jacob. Nevertheless, this did not excuse Jacob from his sin of securing it by deception. In this act he, like Abraham, tried to do the work that belonged to God and that God had promised to do for him. As a result of his lack of faith in God, Jacob was compelled to flee from home in order to escape the wrath of his brother.

2. His Sin Confessed and Forgiven. Jacob's flight took him through miles of wilderness, where he was exposed to many dangers. The second night out found him far from home, an unprotected, lonely wanderer. But it was not the fear of the dangers around him that distressed him; he feared that because of his sin, "he had lost forever the blessing that God had purposed to give him; and Satan was at hand to press temptations upon him." In brokenness of heart Jacob at last took his troubles to the Lord in prayer, and humbly confessed his sin. Then "he took of the stones of that place, and put them for his pillows, and lay down in that place to sleep."

Had God forsaken him? God dwells "with him . . . that is of a contrite and humble spirit," and He was with Jacob. As he slept, God appeared to him in a dream. "And behold a ladder set up on the earth, and the top of it reached to heaven: and behold the angels of God ascending and descending on it. And, behold, the Lord stood above it, and said, I am the Lord God of Abraham thy father, and the God of Isaac: the land whereon thou liest, to thee will I give it, and to thy seed; . . . and in thee and in thy seed shall all the families of the earth be blessed. And, behold, I am with thee, and will keep thee in all places whither thou goest, and will bring thee again into this land. . . . And Jacob awaked out of his sleep, and he said, Surely the Lord is in this place; and I knew it not. . . . This is none other but the house of God [Bethel], and this is the gate of heaven."

References Used: P. P., pp. 183, 184, 196-199; Hosea 12:4; Gen. 28:11-22; 32:6-8, 28; Isa. 57:15.

3. The Plan of Redemption Revealed to Jacob. "In this vision the plan of redemption was presented to Jacob. . . . The ladder represents Jesus. . . . Had He not . . . bridged the gulf that sin had made, the ministering angels could have held no communion with fallen man." As the ladder connected earth with heaven, so Christ connects man with God. This vision gave Jacob a new understanding of the work of the Saviour. Though at this time

In this vision the plan of redemption was presented to Jacob. As the ladder connected earth with heaven, so Christ connects man with God.

seventy-seven years of age, he experienced a new conversion; and when God in the dream renewed to him the same promise which He had made to Abraham and Isaac, Jacob in gratitude dedicated his life and all that he had to God.

4. Satan's Plan to Destroy Jacob. After twenty years' absence from his father's home, the angel of the Lord directed Jacob to return. As the hills of his native land appeared before him, the thought of Esau troubled him. Did he still want to kill him? In order to assure Esau of his own kind feelings, he sent servants before him with a message of peace. "The messengers returned to Jacob, saying, We came to thy brother Esau, and also he cometh to

8 — B. L., Eighth Grade

meet thee, and four hundred men with him. Then Jacob was greatly afraid and distressed."

Satan knew that Jacob's descendants were to be the chosen nation to carry the plan of salvation to the world; and he determined to destroy him if possible, and thus defeat God's plan. Before the angels of God, this "accuser of our brethren" had claimed that since Jacob had sinned, he belonged to his dominion and he had a right to destroy him. To accomplish this he had revived the old hatred in Esau's heart, and he now moved upon Esau to march against Jacob with an army.

5. Jacob's Night of Wrestling with God. Poor Jacob! He had already bitterly repented of his sin, and the dream at Bethel assured him that God had forgiven him. What more could he do? Jacob had failed in his first test of faith. Now he was to have another test. Would he prove to the angels that he could fully trust God? Would he be able to silence the accusations of Satan? After arranging for the safety of his family and his flocks, he withdrew from the company to spend the night alone with God, in whom was his only hope. "It was in a lonely, mountainous region, the haunt of wild beasts, and the lurking place of robbers and murderers. Solitary and unprotected, Jacob bowed in deep distress upon the earth. It was midnight. . . . With earnest cries and tears he made his prayer before God.

"Suddenly a strong hand was laid upon him. He thought that an enemy was seeking his life. . . . In the darkness the two struggled for the mastery. Not a word was spoken, but Jacob . . . did not relax his efforts for a moment. While he was thus battling for his life, the sense of his guilt pressed upon his soul; his sins rose up before him, to shut him out from God." By forcing upon him a sense of his guilt, Satan was trying to discourage him, and break his hold upon God. But Jacob "remembered God's promises, and his whole heart went out in entreaty for His mercy.

"The struggle continued until near the break of day, when the Stranger placed His finger upon Jacob's thigh, and he was crippled instantly." Jacob now knew that the One with whom he had wrestled was Christ, "the Angel of the covenant." Though suffering with pain, and no longer able to struggle, yet he clung to the Angel. "He wept, and made supplication." "He must have the assurance that his sin was pardoned. . . . The Angel tried to re-

The night of Jacob's wrestling with God is an illustration of the "time of trouble."

lease Himself; He urged, 'Let Me go, for the day breaketh;' but Jacob answered, 'I will not let Thee go, except Thou bless me.' "

6. Satan's Scheme Defeated. Jacob had borne the test. His unyielding faith in God had been proved. Jacob "had power over the Angel, and prevailed." "As an evidence that he had been forgiven, his name was changed." "Thy name," said the Angel, "shall be called no more Jacob [supplanter], but Israel [prevailer]: for as a prince hast thou power with God and with men, and hast prevailed."

"While Jacob was wrestling with the Angel, another heavenly messenger was sent to Esau. In a dream, Esau beheld his brother for twenty years an exile from his father's house; he witnessed his grief at finding his mother dead; he saw him encompassed by the hosts of God. This dream was related by Esau to his soldiers, with the charge not to harm Jacob, for the God of his father was with him." And so once more Satan's schemes are defeated and God's work for the human family moves on triumphantly. Jacob settled with his family in the land of Canaan, where he continued to live for more than thirty years, a beacon of light to the inhabitants of the land.

7. The Time of Jacob's Trouble. The night of Jacob's wrestling with God is an illustration of the experience through which the Israel of God will pass just before their final deliverance from the power of Satan. It is called "the time of Jacob's trouble." Remember this, for we shall study more about it in a future lesson.

How to Study: After reading this lesson through, copy the various lesson topics. Make an outline by placing under each topic two or three sub-topics that will remind you of the important thoughts given. From this outline tell the whole story. Explain how the ladder represented God's plan, why Satan wanted to destroy Jacob, why the Angel wrestled with Jacob, and how God defeated Satan. What qualifications of a true missionary did Jacob develop?

Map Study: Locate the place where Jacob dreamed about the ladder, the place of his exile, the place where his name was changed to Israel (Gen. 32: 22). What does "Bethel" mean?

Use of Concordance: Find the verse containing the expression, "angels of God ascending and descending upon the Son of man." Key word: ascend.

Chapters to Remember: Genesis 28 tells about Jacob's dream. Genesis 32 tells the story of Jacob's wrestling with the Angel. Find these stories in the Bible. Ask your father to read one of them for family worship.

REVIEW OF CHAPTER II

Chapter Drill: Turn to the chapter or chapters that tell about:

1. The flood
2. The Ten Commandments
3. Tower of Babel
4. Call of Abraham
5. Destruction of earth by fire
6. The faith chapter
7. Offering of Isaac
8. Jacob's dream
9. Wrestling with the Angel

Concordance Time Drill: See how many of these texts you can locate from the concordance in five minutes. The key words are starred.

1. In Thy book all my *members were written.
2. Before his *translation . . . he pleased God.

3. The Lord knoweth how to deliver the *godly.
4. Noah, . . . a *preacher of righteousness.
5. Reserved unto *fire against the day of judgment.
6. God was able to *raise him up.
7. Abraham . . . was called the *friend of God.
8. Angels of God *ascending . . . upon the Son of man.

Test Questions and Exercises: Read the questions through, checking any that you are not sure you can answer correctly. Then look up answers to the questions checked. How many do you find it necessary to check? The numbers in the margin refer to previous lessons; starred references are memory verses. When answering starred questions, tell the chapter in which the answer is found.

1. How much did God know about His family before they were created? Ps. 139: 16, margin.
   How did God at first intend to have His "family in earth" made up?
   How will His plan to secure a family be carried out under sin?
   Describe the first sacrifice and its meaning.
   What great truth did Enoch preach? *Jude 14, 15.

2. In which thousand-year period did the flood occur?
   Explain Genesis 6:6. What lesson does the rainbow teach?
   What were the first three curses upon the earth, and what was the effect of each?
   What record of the flood has God left in the earth? Why?
   How are Satan's efforts to misinterpret this record directed against the Sabbath?

3. *What was Satan's plan in the tower of Babel?
   Why did God confound the language of those working on the tower?
   What recent evidence has been found of the existence of this tower?

4. Who was the first foreign missionary? Why did God thus honor Abram?
   *What was God's purpose in calling Abram?
   Explain the promise that he should be "heir of the world."
   What shows that Abram understood the promise?
   Explain: "In thee shall all families of the earth be blessed."

5. Why did God ask Abraham to offer Isaac?
   Relate the experience that won for Abraham the title "friend of God."
   *How did the offering of Isaac throw light on God's Sacrifice?
   What was the difference between the two?

6. *How did the ladder in Jacob's dream represent God's plan?
   Why did Satan influence Esau to kill Jacob?
   How did God defeat Satan's plan?
   *Of what is Jacob's night of wrestling a type?

OUTLINE OF CHAPTER III

Topics —   **B. C.**

Topic	B. C.
Abraham's Seed Becoming "a Great Nation"	
Satan's Plot to Destroy the Missionary Nation	
God's Plan Rejected by Egypt	
The Birthday of God's Missionary Nation	1491
The Missionary Nation and School Organized	
Review	
The First Semester of the Missionary School	
The Second Semester of the Missionary School	
Final Examination Day in God's Church School	
A Bible Study on the Day of Atonement	
Review	
Satan's Prison House First Opened	
The Nation Ready for Service	1451
Christian Education a Part of God's Plan Under the Judges — Schools of the Prophets	
Israel the Light of the World Under the United Kingdom	1095-975
The Nation's Failure to Carry Out God's Plan Under the Divided Kingdom	975-606
Review	

CHAPTER III

The Missionary Nation

1. ABRAHAM'S SEED BECOMING "A GREAT NATION"

"Fear not to go down into Egypt; for I will there make of thee a great nation."
Gen. 46:3.

1. How Satan Discouraged Jacob. Satan taxes every power of his mind, and employs every device possible to his crafty nature, to distress and discourage those who desire to serve God. He will use any means, no matter how dishonorable, in his effort to defeat God's plan. It is God's pleasure to bring relief to those who put their trust in Him — to straighten out the tangled threads of our unhappy experiences and bring victory out of apparent defeat. When the cloud of trouble looks the darkest, then God's deliverances are often the nearest.

So it was with Jacob. On returning to Canaan, he received the sad news of his mother's death; a few years later he was called to part with his devoted wife Rachel. Three years more, and Joseph, the comfort and idol of his old age, was as he supposed torn in pieces and devoured by wild beasts. Then followed the death of his father Isaac, and afterward a terrible famine which threatened to bring final destruction to himself and family.

When he sent his sons to Egypt to secure food, "the lord of the country" accused them of being spies. After keeping them all in prison for three days, he released them, but as a test of their honesty, he commanded that Simeon be bound before them and committed to prison until their next return for food. He further required that as evidence that they were true men and not spies, they bring their youngest brother Benjamin when they came again.

"Jacob was anxiously awaiting the return of his sons, and on their arrival the whole encampment gathered eagerly around them

---

References Used: P. P., pp. 226, 227, 232, 233, 236, 237, 240; Rev. 5:5; Gen. 42:20, 33, 36-38; 45:5-9; 46:3, 4, 27, 29, 30, 34; 48:21; 50:24, 25.

as they related to their father all that had occurred. Alarm and apprehension filled every heart. The conduct of the Egyptian governor seemed to imply some evil design. . . . In his distress the aged father exclaimed, 'Me have ye bereaved of my children. Joseph is not, and Simeon is not, and ye will take Benjamin away. *All these things are against me.* . . . My son shall not go down with you. . . . If mischief befall him by the way in the which ye go, then shall ye bring down my gray hairs with sorrow to the grave.' "

2. **"All These Things" for Jacob's Good.** Poor Jacob! If his faith had lifted the veil that separated the future from him, he would have seen the guiding hand of a merciful Father overruling all these events for his good. In the selling of Joseph and in the famine that followed, Satan thought to destroy those whom God was preparing to use in bringing the light of the gospel to the world. Did he succeed? No, indeed! God, by the touch of His hand, used these very circumstances to deliver His chosen ones.

As was revealed on their next journey for food, "the governor" of the land proved to be their own brother Joseph, whom twenty-two years before they had so cruelly separated from their father and sold as a slave to merchantmen going down into Egypt. But Joseph was not angry with them. He recognized the providence of God in it all, and said: "Be not grieved, nor angry with yourselves, that ye sold me hither: for God did send me before you to preserve life. For these two years hath the famine been in the land: and yet there are five years, in the which there shall neither be earing nor harvest. And God sent me before you to preserve you a posterity in the earth, and to save your lives by a great deliverance. So now it was not you that sent me hither, but God: and He hath made me a father to Pharaoh, and lord of all his house, and a ruler throughout all the land of Egypt. Haste ye, and go up to my father, and say unto him, Thus saith thy son Joseph, God hath made me lord of all Egypt: come down unto me, tarry not."

3. **God's Promise Renewed to Jacob.** And Israel went. As he was on the way, a message from God came to him in a vision of the night. "Fear not to go down into Egypt; for I will there make of thee a great nation: I will go down with thee into Egypt; and I will also surely bring thee up again." This assurance meant much to Jacob. Two hundred fifteen years before, the promise had been

"All the souls of the house of Jacob, which came into Egypt, were threescore and ten." These were the ancestors of the missionary nation.

given to Abraham that his seed should be in number as the stars. Yet at this time "all the souls of the house of Jacob, which came into Egypt, were [only] threescore and ten."

4. Why God Sent Jacob into Egypt. The land of Canaan at this time offered no field for the development of such a nation as had been foretold. It was in possession of powerful heathen tribes whose cup of iniquity would not be full for four more generations. The children of Israel could not therefore drive out these heathen peoples, and if they went to live among them they would be in constant danger of being drawn into their idolatrous practices. "Egypt, however, offered the conditions necessary to the fulfillment of the divine purpose. A section of country [the land of Goshen], well-watered and fertile, was open to them there, affording every advantage for their speedy increase." And the fact that "every shepherd was 'an abomination unto the Egyptians' would enable them to remain a distinct and separate people, and would thus serve to shut them out from participation in the idolatry of Egypt."

5. Jacob's Last Years. When after his years of anxiety and sorrow Israel met Joseph, his long-lost son, he said, "Now let me die, since I have seen thy face, because thou art yet alive." But Jacob did not die. "Seventeen years were yet to be granted him in the peaceful retirement of Goshen. These years were in happy contrast to those that had preceded them. He saw in his sons evidence of true repentance; he saw his family surrounded by all the conditions needful for the development of a great nation; and his faith grasped the sure promise of their future establishment in Canaan. He himself was surrounded with every token of love and favor that the prime minister of Egypt could bestow; and happy in the society of his long-lost son, he passed down gently and peacefully to the grave. . . . Jacob's last years brought an evening of tranquillity and repose after a troubled and weary day. Clouds had gathered dark above his path, yet his sun set clear, and the radiance of heaven illumined his parting hours."

6. "The Lion of the Tribe of Judah." In the prophetic blessings which Israel at the last pronounced upon his sons, the birthright was transferred to Judah. The thoughts of his children were directed to the coming Saviour in these words: "Judah is a lion's whelp. . . . The scepter shall not depart from Judah . . . until Shiloh [the Peacemaker, Christ] come; and unto Him shall the gathering of the people be." The lion, king of the forest, is a fitting symbol of this tribe, from which came David, and the Son of David, Shiloh, the true "Lion of the tribe of Judah."

7. Last Words of Israel and Joseph. Israel's last words to Joseph pointed forward to the fulfillment of the promise: "God shall be with you, and bring you again unto the land of your fathers." And when Joseph was about to die, he likewise encouraged his brethren, saying, "I die; and God will surely visit you, and bring you out of this land unto the land which He sware to Abraham, to Isaac, and to Jacob." "And Joseph took an oath of the children of Israel, saying, God will surely visit you, and ye shall carry up my bones from hence." Through the years that followed, "that coffin, a reminder of the dying words of Joseph, testified to Israel that they were only sojourners in Egypt, and bade them keep their hopes fixed upon the land of promise, for the time of deliverance would surely come."

How to Study: This lesson is arranged under seven topics. On each of the special topics assigned you, write from one to three questions to use in testing your classmates. Try to begin one question with the word "Why."

Memory Work: Learn the names of the twelve children of Israel in order, beginning with the eldest. Ex. 1:2-4. Memorize Romans 8:28 and enter the reference on your "Service Flag." How was this promise fulfilled in the events related in this lesson?

Chapters to Remember: Find the chapters in Genesis that this lesson covers.

For Your Workbook: On diagram No. 3 indicate the time when Israel moved to Egypt; also the time of Joseph's death. For dates, see Genesis 46:1-4 and 50:26, margins. How many years from "the promise" to the end of Israel's sojourn in Canaan? What part of the whole 430-year period of sojourn is it? Indicate this on your diagram.

For Class Discussion: What relation do you think this lesson has to the working out of God's plan? Why did not God develop His nation in Canaan? Gen. 15:16. Why did He choose Egypt? Why is Christ called Shiloh? Gen. 49:9, 10.

---

2. SATAN'S PLOT TO DESTROY THE MISSIONARY NATION

"Every son that is born ye shall cast into the river." Ex. 1:22.

1. The Prosperity of Israel. For seventy years, the seventy souls of the house of Jacob were the favored of all the land of Egypt. While Joseph still lived, Satan had little hope or chance to disturb the working out of God's plan. The king knew that it was through the God of Joseph that Egypt had been supplied with food while other nations were suffering from famine, and he gratefully acknowledged the benefits he and his people had received. During this period of royal favor, the children of Israel "increased abundantly, and multiplied, and waxed exceeding mighty; and the land was filled with them."

2. Plans Again Laid to Destroy Israel. But after the death of Joseph "there arose up a new king over Egypt, which knew not Joseph." He was a wicked king, and Satan was quick to take advantage of what seemed to him an opportunity to destroy the rapidly developing nation which God was preparing to do His work. Through this king the whole nation of Israel was made slaves. The

---

References Used: P. P., pp. 242, 245; Gen. 41:29, 46; 45:6; 46:8-27; 50:26; Ex. 1:5.

people were placed under the most cruel and overbearing taskmasters. "And the Egyptians . . . made their lives bitter with hard bondage, in mortar, and in brick, and in all manner of service in the field."

"But the more they afflicted them, the more they multiplied and grew." Failing in this effort, Satan influenced the king to issue the decree, "Every son that is born ye shall cast into the river." "He

Angels were sent to watch over the little ark among the flags by the river's brink.

knew that a deliverer was to be raised up among the Israelites; and by leading the king to destroy their children he hoped to defeat the divine purpose."

3. The Coming of a Deliverer. It was just at this time that Moses was born. His parents "saw him that he was a goodly child." They also knew that the period of their sojourn in Egypt was nearing a close, and that God would soon raise up a deliverer for His people. Who could say that *their* child might not be the one? *God* knew that he *was* the one, and He answered the mother's earnest prayers to save him. Angels were sent to watch over the little ark "among the flags" by the river's brink in which lay the tiny but precious bundle. Angels directed Pharaoh's daughter thither and moved upon her heart to rescue him and adopt him as her own.

God also used the little sister Miriam to act a part in carrying out His plan. Miriam had been anxiously watching to see what would become of her baby brother, and when she saw the princess trying to quiet the weeping child, she ventured to approach her and ask, "Shall I go and call to thee a nurse of the Hebrew women, that she may nurse the child for thee?" And Pharaoh's daughter said to her, "Go." No more delightful errand had ever been given the happy sister, and she bounded away to her own mother. They soon returned, and the princess said to the mother, "Take this child away, and nurse it for me, and I will give thee thy wages." Thus again "Satan had been defeated in his purpose. The very decree condemning the Hebrew children to death had been overruled by God for the training and education of the future leader of His people."

4. Moses' Early Training. The mother Jochebed now felt sure that her child had been preserved for some great work, and she carefully trained him with this in view. Especially did she teach him to bow down and pray to the living God, to honor and obey His law, and to shun the sin of idolatry. At the age of twelve Moses was taken from his mother to live in the palace of the king. Here, though surrounded with the glitter and pomp of royalty, and in constant touch with heathen practices, yet he did not forget the lessons his mother had taught him.

As the Lord prepared Moses to become the great deliverer of ancient Israel from Egypt, so it is His plan that every boy and girl of the Israel of to-day shall receive an education that will prepare them to do a great work for Him in the final deliverance of His people from this world of sin. Every boy and girl in God's Israel to-day is in a special sense a part of God's great plan.

5. Moses Extending a Knowledge of God. "The elders of Israel were taught by angels that the time for their deliverance was near, and that Moses was the man whom God would employ to accomplish this work. Angels instructed Moses also that Jehovah had chosen him to break the bondage of His people." But Pharaoh was planning to make his adopted grandson his successor to the throne of Egypt, and the youth had been educated for this high station. Before he could be king he must be taught the national religion. "This duty was committed to the priests. But while he was an ardent and untiring student, he could not be induced to participate in the worship of the gods. He was threatened with the loss of the crown, and warned that he would be disowned by the princess should he persist in his adherence to the Hebrew faith. But he was unshaken in his determination to render homage to none save the one God, the Maker of heaven and earth. He reasoned with priests and worshipers, showing the folly of their superstitious veneration of senseless objects. None could refute his arguments, . . . yet for the time his firmness was tolerated."

6. Moses' Choice and What It Meant. But the time soon came when Moses must decide between the throne of the greatest nation of the world with all its riches and worldly honor, and a part in the work of God with its affliction and reproach. It was not hard for him to make a right decision, for he knew that a palace in the city of gold would be worth far more than a palace in Egypt, and the crown of life that God will one day place on the head of the overcomer was to him worth far more than the perishable crown of Egypt.

In the museum in Cairo, Egypt, to-day there lies, among the great and honored of past ages, a dried-up, lifeless, ugly-looking mummy,— all that remains of the once famous Pharaoh. Thousands of people view this mummy with wonder and awe. Had Moses accepted the throne of Egypt, he too would doubtless be lying there in state with other great kings of his time. But he chose "rather to suffer affliction with the people of God, than to enjoy the pleasures of sin for a season; esteeming the reproach of Christ greater riches than the treasures in Egypt." And now where is he? Although he was called to sleep for a short time in the grave, Christ Himself, with the angels who had buried him, came down from heaven, called him forth from the grave, and escorted him in triumph to the throne of God. Moses lost the crown and riches of Egypt; he gained the crown

The mummy of King Rameses II, the Pharaoh of the Oppression, over three thousand years old

and riches of heaven. He lost his place in the Egyptian museum; he won a place in heaven above. Did he make a wise choice?

How to Study: After reading the lesson through, make an outline for oral composition, and tell the story from this outline.

Map Work: Locate the place where Pharaoh's remains now lie.

Memory Work: Memorize Hebrews 11:24-26, and enter the reference on your "Service Flag."

Chapters to Remember: Exodus 1 tells about the oppression of Israel. Exodus 2 tells about Israel's deliverer. What reference to the "faith chapter" is there in this lesson?

For Your Workbook: On diagram No. 3 indicate the time of Moses' birth. For date, see Ex. 2:2, margin.

For Class Discussion: Why were the elders of Israel instructed by the angels about their deliverance instead of learning it from the Bible?

3. GOD'S PLAN REJECTED BY EGYPT

"Against all the gods of Egypt I will execute judgment;" "that thou mayest know that there is none like unto the Lord our God." Ex. 12:12; 8:10.

1. Satan's Effort to Overthrow Moses. When Moses was forty years of age, some of his enemies, urged on by Satan, reported to the king that he designed to lead the Israelites "against the Egyptians, to overthrow the government, and to seat himself upon the throne; and that there could be no security for the kingdom while he lived. It was at once determined by the monarch that he should die." Because of this, Moses fled to Arabia, where he found a home with Jethro, a priest and worshiper of God.

By this act Satan again thought to defeat God's plan, but as usual God used this very circumstance to promote His work. By long contact with the dissipation and splendor of the royal court and the evils of a false religion, Moses had lost to some extent the simplicity and humility of the true religion. But forty years of shepherd life amid the beauties of nature swept away his pride and

References Used: P. P., pp. 247, 251, 259; Ex. 2:23, 24; 3:7, 8, 10; 8:10, 19; 9:15, 16; 10:21; 12:12.

self-sufficiency and made him patient, reverent, and humble, so that
*"the man Moses was very meek, above all the men which were
upon the face of the earth." It was here, under the inspiration of
the Holy Spirit, that Moses wrote the book of Genesis — the stories
that had been handed down by the patriarchs from the days of Adam.

2. Why God Allowed Israel to Be Oppressed. During all this
time the oppression of the children of Israel continued. Yet there
was no deliverer. Had God forsaken them? Would His promise
after all fail? God's promises never fail. They never have failed.
They never will fail. They never can fail. He allowed the oppression in order to prepare His people for deliverance. For four
generations they had dwelt in Egypt, and during this time they
had built homes and accumulated wealth. It would be no easy matter for them to leave their homes and migrate into a land unknown
to them. They were in danger of losing sight of the promise made
to Abraham, Isaac, and Jacob.

To save His people from the disaster of being satisfied to remain in Egypt, God allowed them to feel the iron heel of Egyptian
oppression for many long, weary years. Heavier and heavier
became their burdens, more and more undesirable their surroundings. At last, "the children of Israel sighed by reason of the bondage, and they cried, and their cry came up unto God by reason of
the bondage. And God heard their groaning, and God remembered
His covenant with Abraham, with Isaac, and with Jacob." The
time for Israel's deliverance had come.

3. God's Purpose in Delivering Israel. It was not merely to deliver His people from unjust servitude that God heard their cry.
Under the exactions of their taskmasters it was almost impossible
for them to keep holy the Sabbath day. As a result they were losing the knowledge of God's law and some of their children were even
bowing down to false gods. It was that they might be delivered
from these sinful practices as well as from the cruel bondage, that
the people cried to God. And it was not only for their sakes that
God was about to deliver Israel, but that they might be placed where
they could give to the whole world a knowledge of the true God.

4. Moses Called to Be Israel's Deliverer. One day when Moses
was out with his flocks near Mount Horeb, which is Mount Sinai, he
saw a bush in flames, branches, foliage, and trunk, all seeming to be

burning, yet not consumed. "He drew near to view the wonderful sight, when a voice from out of the flame called him by name." It was the Son of God, the great "I AM," speaking to him. He said: "I have surely seen the affliction of My people which are in Egypt, and have heard their cry by reason of their taskmasters; for I know their sorrows; and I am come down to deliver them out of the hand of the Egyptians. . . . Come now therefore, and I will send thee unto Pharaoh, that thou mayest bring forth My people the children of Israel out of Egypt."

5. God's Efforts to Save the Egyptians. But God was also interested in the Egyptians. He is *"not willing that *any* should perish, but that *all* should come to repentance." Before the time of Moses, He had repeatedly sent His messenger of salvation to the people of Egypt. Both Abraham and Jacob had brought to them a knowledge of the true God. Joseph also had lived among them for nearly a century, witnessing to the saving power of Jehovah. Moses in the royal court had not only stood firm for God by refusing to worship their senseless idols, but he had pointed priests and rulers to the God of heaven. Even as slaves there were those among Israel who "declared to the Egyptians that the object of their worship was the Maker of heaven and earth, the only true and living God. They rehearsed the evidences of His existence and power, from creation down to the days of Jacob." For two hundred fifteen years, one half of the whole period of the sojourning of the children of Israel, had been spent in Egypt. The Egyptians thus had opportunity to become acquainted with the way of salvation.

Moses "drew near to view the wonderful sight, when a voice from out of the flame called him by name."

9 — B. L., Eighth Grade

6. **Why the Plagues Came upon Egypt.** What more could God do for them? By showing them His signs and wonders and finally by sending plagues upon Pharaoh and upon all his servants, He would give them one more opportunity to turn from their worthless idols. "Against all the gods of Egypt I will execute judgment," said the Lord. Several times Moses told Pharaoh God's purpose in the plagues: "that thou mayest know that there is none like the Lord our God." At last, even the magicians were forced to acknowledge, *"This is the finger of God." But Pharaoh persistently hardened his heart until God finally pronounced his doom,—"Thou shalt be cut off from the earth." Pharaoh's probation had closed. Still his life was allowed to continue for a time "for to show in thee My power; and that My name may be declared throughout all the earth." The plagues were nation wide, "over the land of Egypt," giving every one an opportunity to know the utter helplessness of their false gods.

7. **The Plagues a Type.** Further to show them the power of the true God, the land of Goshen where the children of Israel dwelt was protected from the last seven of the ten plagues. Thus the plagues of Egypt were a type of the seven last plagues that will be poured out in the end of time, and from which God's people will be protected.

How to Study: In studying this lesson, try to get a clear idea of why God allowed Moses to go to Arabia, why He allowed oppression to come upon Israel, why He planned to deliver Israel, and why He sent the plagues upon Egypt.

Notice that God hardened Pharaoh's heart after Pharaoh seven times hardened his own heart. In the Bible the number seven indicates completeness.

Use of Concordance: Find the three starred texts quoted under topics 1, 5, and 6. Key words: meek, perish, finger.

Chapters to Remember: Exodus 3 tells about the burning bush. Exodus 7-11 tells about the ten plagues.

For Class Discussion: What was the promise made to Abraham, Isaac, and Jacob? Why is God called the "I AM"?

For the Ambitious Student: Find the seven times that God told Pharaoh the plagues were sent that he might know the true God. One is in Exodus 7, two in Exodus 8, three in Exodus 9, and one in Exodus 10.

4. THE BIRTHDAY OF GOD'S MISSIONARY NATION
First month, 14th day, 1491 B. C.

"Thus saith the Lord, Israel is My son, even My first-born. . . . Let My son go, that he may serve Me." Ex. 4:22, 23.

1. How God's Mercy Is Shown. God is in no way responsible for the existence of sin. But He has pledged Himself and all heaven to remove it from the earth. He will do all that can be done to save people from its ruin. He will be long-suffering and patient with their follies. But when any person or any nation persistently and defiantly refuses to accept the salvation He has provided, He may then destroy them to prevent them from endangering the safety and salvation of others. They have given themselves fully over to Satan, they have separated themselves from the source of peace and joy, and although God's mercy "endureth forever," it is no longer a mercy to spare such unprofitable and dangerous lives. The most merciful thing that can then be done is to put an end to their miserable existence, and thus give others a better opportunity to win out in the struggle with evil. Egypt, at that time the greatest nation in the world, had reached just this place, and now the mercy of God was withdrawn from it. From this time the very name Egypt became a symbol for sin and rebellion against God.

2. Pharaoh's Rebellion. The time had come for the deliverance of Israel, "even My first-born," as the Lord called them. Still Pharaoh rebelliously and stubbornly refused to yield. The first request of Moses was met with the haughty, defiant response: "Who is the Lord, that I should obey His voice to let Israel go? I know not the Lord, neither will I let Israel go." During the first nine plagues, Pharaoh and his people had had special opportunity to learn the power of the God of Moses. Through loss of their harvests, their flocks, and their herds, God had spoken in no uncertain tones. Still Pharaoh refused to listen. By his rebellion he invited the last and most fearful judgment of all. As God's agent, Moses came before him with the terrible announcement: "Thus saith the Lord, About midnight will I go out into the midst of Egypt: and all the first-born in the land of Egypt shall die." God had left this judgment until the last, that if possible it might be averted.

References Used: P. P., pp. 273, 279, 281; Test. Vol. 6, p. 195; Gen. 15:13; Ex. 5:2; 11:4, 5; 12:6-39; John 6:51, 63; 1 Cor. 5:7, 8.

3. How God Protected Israel. To protect the Israelites from the coming judgment, the Lord through Moses told each family to slay a lamb, and with a bunch of hyssop "take of the blood, and strike it on the two side posts and on the upper doorpost of the houses. . . . And they shall eat the flesh in that night, roast with fire, and unleavened bread; and with bitter herbs. . . . And when I see the blood, I will pass over you, and the plague shall not be upon you to destroy you." At evening the parents were to gather the children into their own houses, and the father was to sprinkle the blood as directed. "Any one of the children of the Hebrews who was found in an Egyptian habitation was destroyed."

4. The Believing Egyptians Protected. Were any of the Egyptians spared? Yes; "many of the Egyptians had been led to acknowledge the God of the Hebrews as the only true God, and these now begged to be permitted to find shelter in the homes of Israel when the destroying angel should pass through the land. They were gladly welcomed, and they pledged themselves henceforth to serve the God of Jacob, and to go forth from Egypt with His people."

5. Pharaoh Urges Israel to Leave Egypt. It was at midnight, the hour when Jacob wrestled with the Angel, that God had promised to deliver His people. When that hour struck, "there was a great cry in Egypt; for there was not a house where there was not one dead." But in the houses of the Israelites all were safe. Pharaoh no longer stubbornly refused to let Moses and the children of Israel go. "He called for Moses and Aaron by night, and said, Rise up, and get you forth from among my people, both ye and the children of Israel; and go, serve the Lord, as ye have said. . . . And the Egyptians were urgent upon the people, that they might send them out of the land in haste." And they went out "about six hundred thousand on foot that were men, beside children." That was the birthday of the missionary nation — God's first-born. It was the end of the time revealed to Abraham centuries before,—"Thy seed shall be a stranger in a land that is not theirs, and shall serve them; and they shall afflict them four hundred years."

On an Egyptian monument recently discovered, mention is made of the fact that the Pharaoh of the exodus lost a son; and scholars connect this with the death of the first-born. Thus God is giving the world in these last days evidence upon evidence of the truth of His word.

6. The Meaning of the Passover. The Passover was to be observed by the children of Israel forever; that is, up to the time when it was fulfilled in the sacrifice of Christ, "our Passover." It was not only to keep in remembrance the miraculous deliverance from Egypt, but it expressed faith in the Redeemer as their Deliverer from the bondage of sin. When, in later years, their children should say to them, "What mean ye by this service?" the parents were to explain, "It is the sacrifice of the Lord's Passover, who passed over

The sacrificial lamb represented the Lamb of God —"our Passover, sacrificed for us."

the houses of the children of Israel in Egypt, when He smote the Egyptians, and delivered our houses."

7. The Passover a Type. The sacrificial lamb represented the Lamb of God —"our Passover . . . sacrificed for us." The lamb was slain "between the two evenings," or, as we would say, at three o'clock in the afternoon — the very hour when Jesus gave His last cry of agony as He hung on the cross. The hyssop was the symbol of purification. "Purge me with hyssop, and I shall be clean: wash me, and I shall be whiter than snow." The blood sprinkled on the doorpost was the sign of the Saviour's protection, and kept the destroying angel from entering the home; so the blood of Jesus on the door of our hearts will prevent the destructive power of sin from entering in. The flesh of the lamb was to be eaten; so we are to "eat the flesh of the Son of man" by studying and obeying His word. The bitter herbs symbolized the bitterness of the bondage in Egypt; so when we feed upon Christ,— when we try to obey His words,— it should be with bitter sorrow for our sins. The unleavened bread represented the life free from the leaven of sin; so Paul says to us, "Let us keep the feast, not with old leaven, neither with the leaven of malice and wickedness; but with the unleavened bread of sincerity and truth." The first-born of the king was the inheritor of the throne, and the slaying of the first-born in all Egypt pointed to the final destruction of the kingdom of sin. The entire journey of Israel from Egypt to Canaan, the promised land, is a type of our journey from a world of sin to the heavenly Canaan. "Now all these things happened unto them for ensamples [types]: and they are written for our admonition, upon whom the ends of the world are come." Shall we not listen to the warning which God is thus sending us?

How to Study: As you study this lesson, notice the following comparisons. They show *the meaning* of these things that concern us "upon whom the ends of the world are come."

"These Things Happened unto Them for Types."	"They Are Written for Our Admonition."
1. Bondage of Egypt	1. Bondage of sin
2. Israel was Pharaoh's slave, but secured unjustly	2. Those who serve sin are the servants of Satan
3. Pharaoh's refusal to let Israel go to serve God	3. Satan's unwillingness to let us serve God
4. The Passover	4. Christ our Passover, 1 Cor. 5: 7
5. The sacrificial lamb	5. The Lamb of God
6. The lamb slain "between the two evenings"	6. Christ slain "the ninth hour," Matt. 27: 46
7. Gather the children out of the habitations of the Egyptians	7. Come out from the world, and be separate
8. Put the blood on the door with hyssop	8. "Purge me with hyssop," Ps. 51: 7
9. Journey to earthly Canaan	9. Journey to heavenly Canaan
10. Pillar of cloud and fire	10. Christ our Protector and Guide

Chapter to Remember: Exodus 12 tells the story of the first Passover. Ask your father to read Exodus 12: 1-36 for family worship.

Memory Work: Memorize 1 Corinthians 10: 11, and enter the reference on your "Service Flag."

For Class Discussion: Why did God call Israel His "first-born"? To what do the two symbolic midnight events mentioned under topic 5 point forward?

For Your Workbook: On diagram No. 3 locate the exodus. For date, see Exodus 12, margin. Indicate the number of years Abraham's seed sojourned in Egypt. With what event does this begin? Indicate also the approximate number of years they were in bondage. How old was Moses at the time of the exodus?

5. THE MISSIONARY NATION AND SCHOOL ORGANIZED

"Ye shall be unto Me a kingdom of priests, and an holy nation." Ex. 19:6.

1. The Journey from Egypt. It was in the glorious springtime that God chose to release Israel from the bondage of heathen Egypt — and go with them on that long journey over the fields and through the mountain passes. It was a time such as is described by Solomon in the words:

> "Lo, the winter is past;
> The rain is over and gone;
> The flowers appear on the earth;
> The time of the singing of birds is come,
> And the voice of the turtledove is heard in our land;
> The fig tree ripeneth her green figs,
> And the vines are in blossom;
> They give forth their fragrance."

2. Israel's Invisible Leader. It has been estimated that the hosts of Israel covered at least twelve square miles. In all their journey from Egypt to the promised land, "the Lord went before them by day in a pillar of a cloud, to lead them the way; and by night in a pillar of fire, to give them light." Though they could not see Him, yet Jesus was in the cloud, directing and protecting them. In this way God was teaching His people not to depend on helpless visible idols, but on Him, their mighty invisible Leader. This cloud spread out over them like an immense umbrella, protecting them from the heat of the sun by day, and giving light to that vast multitude as they encamped for the night.

Though Jesus accompanied the people, do not think for a moment that Satan had surrendered and was gone. The great contro-

---

References Used: P. P., pp. 296, 301, 302, 304, 309, 310, 366; Ed., pp. 39, 167; "Historical Sketches," p. 231; S. of Sol. 2:11-13, A. R. V.; Ex. 13:21; 16:35; 19:10-12, 18, 19; 24:17; Ps. 78:24, 25; Heb. 4:12; 12:21; Deut. 33:2.

versy between Christ and Satan begun in heaven still continued, and the dark shadow of the enemy hovered near, watching for the first opportunity to bring in doubt and temptation. As a result, more than once on this long journey they yielded to his suggestions to doubt God's leading; their faith failed them and their thoughts went back to the homes they had left, and, be it said to their everlasting shame, they murmured and complained. But we are also told that they "cheered their way by the music of sacred song," keeping step to the rhythm as they marched along.

At Mount Sinai the missionary nation and school were organized.

3. Sabbath Sacredness Shown by a Threefold Miracle. God was preparing this people to be His special agents to carry to the world a knowledge of His holy law and of the Redeemer whose life had been offered to restore the broken law in the hearts of sinners. But the Israelites during their period of slavery had not always lived in obedience to God's law. Many of them had disregarded the Sabbath day. To restore in their minds and hearts the sacred character of His law and of His holy day, God for forty years "rained down manna upon them to eat" and gave them "the corn of heaven. Man did eat angels' food."

"Every week during their long sojourn in the wilderness, the Israelites witnessed a threefold miracle, designed to impress their minds with the sacredness of the Sabbath: a double quantity of manna fell on the sixth day, none on the seventh, and the portion needed for the Sabbath was preserved sweet and pure, when if any were kept over at any other time it became unfit for use."

4. At Sinai. After journeying for nearly seven weeks, they reached the place where, a short time before, God had talked with Moses out of the burning bush. Before them Mount Sinai lifted its massive front in solemn majesty. "The cloudy pillar rested upon its summit, and the people spread their tents upon the plain beneath. Here was to be their home for nearly a year."

5. The Nation and School Organized. As soon as the camp was in readiness, God called Moses to Him into the mount. The time had come for Israel to be organized as a church, a school, and a nation under the government of God. "Ye shall be unto Me a kingdom of priests [or teachers], and an holy nation," were His words to Moses. Such a government is called a theocracy, because God Himself was to be the King, and the leaders were to receive their instructions direct from Him. This occasion was the fulfillment of God's promise to Abraham, "I will make of thee a great nation."

The school into which God organized the nation was the first church school of which we have any record. More than a million students attended this school — men, women, and children — and they were all in the same class, studying the same lessons. The purpose of the school was to prepare the students to go forth as missionaries to the world. Their course of study was God's great plan,— the good news of the coming Redeemer, the gospel. Their textbook was the law of God, the sanctuary and its services. And the Son of God Himself was the principal Teacher.

6. God's Law Spoken from Sinai. That the people might fully understand that God's law is the very foundation of His government not only in heaven but on earth, God purposed to repeat it to them with the divine voice. Since Adam's sin, all the communion between God and man has been through Christ, the Redeemer. It was God in Christ who gave our first parents the promise of a Saviour; it was He who appeared to the patriarchs; it was He who went before Israel in the cloud; and it was He who, "standing side by side upon the mount" with the Father, spoke the Ten Commandments. The Lord said to Moses, "Go unto the people, and sanctify them to-day and to-morrow, and let them wash their clothes, and be ready against the third day: for the third day the Lord will come down in the sight of all the people upon Mount Sinai." Bounds were also put about the mount, with strict instructions that not a hand should touch it, for "whosoever toucheth the mount shall be surely put to death."

"On the morning of the third day [fifty days from that memorable night of the Passover], as the eyes of all the people were turned toward the mount, its summit was covered with a thick cloud, which grew more black and dense, sweeping downward until the entire mountain was wrapped in darkness and awful mystery. Then a sound as of a trumpet was heard, summoning the people to meet with God; and Moses led them forth to the base of the mountain. From the thick darkness flashed vivid lightnings, while peals of thunder echoed and reëchoed among the surrounding heights. 'And Mount Sinai was altogether on a smoke, because the Lord descended upon it in fire; and the smoke thereof ascended as the smoke of a furnace, and the whole mount quaked greatly.' 'The glory of the Lord was like devouring fire on the top of the mount' in the sight of the assembled multitude. And 'the voice of the trumpet sounded long, and waxed louder and louder.' So terrible were the tokens of Jehovah's presence that the hosts of Israel shook with fear, and fell upon their faces before the Lord. Even Moses exclaimed, 'I exceedingly fear and quake.'

"And He gave unto Moses two tables of stone written with the finger of God."

"And now the thunders ceased; the trumpet was no longer heard; the earth was still. There was a period of solemn silence, and then the voice of God was heard. Speaking out of the thick darkness that enshrouded Him, as He stood upon the mount, surrounded by a retinue of angels, the Lord made known His law."

"He came with ten thousands of saints: from His right hand went a fiery law for them."

7. Effect on the People. As, one by one, the ten brief commands of God's law were slowly and clearly spoken in thunder tones by the Son of God, the Holy Spirit accompanied the words with a power that went to the hearts of the people. As never before they realized that the law of Jehovah is a discerner of the very "thoughts and intents of the heart," and that nothing short of perfect obedience can ever be acceptable. Deeply impressed with their own unworthiness, and overwhelmed with terror, "they shrank away from the mountain in fear and awe."

The national laws given by God to Israel were written in a book by the hand of His servant Moses.

8. The Laws Written. Laws regulating sacrifices for sin had been in operation since the first sacrifice was offered by man, while the ten-commandment law had been in force from "times eternal." For the first time all these laws were now written,— God's eternal law on the tables of stone with His own finger, the other national laws in a book by the hand of His servant Moses. The nation itself was called Israel, and the people Israelites.

How to Study: Study to recite from the paragraph topics.

Dictionary Work: By analysis find the exact meaning of: theocracy; Decalogue.

Use of Concordance: Find the poem quoted in paragraph 1. Since Solomon wrote it, in what book will you look for it?

Chapter to Remember: Exodus 20 contains God's law.

For Your Workbook: On diagram No. 1 indicate the 430 years' sojourn. With what event does this begin? With what event does it end?

On diagram No. 2 finish the "chain" to include Moses. How many links are needed from the time Adam told the first patriarchal story until these stories were written in "the Book"?

For Class Discussion: When and where was the promise made to Abraham? Gen. 12: 2, 3. When and where was it fulfilled? Ex. 19: 6. What is this period of time called? Ex. 12: 40. How long was it?

Why were the people of God's nation not called Jacobites, since they were the direct descendants of Jacob?

What feast, celebrated fifty days after the Passover, commemorated the giving of God's law from Sinai?

For the Ambitious Student: If the estimate given under topic 2 is approximately correct, how much space would there be for one man's family, with his flocks and herds, not counting the "mixed multitude"? Ex. 12: 37, 38.

REVIEW

Chapter Drill: How many of these chapters can you turn to in three minutes?

1. Life of Jacob
2. The oppression of Israel
3. Birth of Moses
4. The faith chapter
5. The burning bush
6. The ten plagues
7. The first Passover
8. The Ten Commandments

Test Questions and Exercises: Read the questions of each paragraph, checking only those that you cannot answer. Then look up answers to the questions checked. Be able to take any one of these sets of exercises and recite on every point. The numbers refer to previous lessons.

1. Why did God choose Egypt instead of Canaan as the place to develop His missionary nation? Recite *Romans 8: 28, and tell how in Jacob's life this promise was fulfilled. To what tribe was the promise of the coming Saviour given?

2. After Joseph's death, how did Satan try again to destroy God's nation? How did God defeat his plan? What is there in this circumstance which shows that God will use children in carrying out His plan? What is His plan for boys and girls to-day? How is He preparing them for this work? Recite *Hebrews 11: 24-26, and tell what was the result of Moses' choice.

3. When Moses was forty years of age, how did Satan again try to defeat God's plan? What was the result? Why did God allow oppression to come to Israel? Why did He deliver them? How did God through the plagues try to save not only Israel but Pharaoh and the Egyptians? Why was Pharaoh finally "cut off from the earth"? Of what are the plagues of Egypt a type?

4. How did God protect His people from the last plague? How did He protect the believing Egyptians? Of what was the Passover a type? Why did all these things happen and why are they written? *1 Cor. 10: 11.

5. By what threefold miracle did God try to teach Israel the sacredness of the Sabbath? Describe the first church school.

6. THE FIRST SEMESTER OF THE MISSIONARY SCHOOL

God's Plan Taught in the Sanctuary

Lesson 1 — Topics 1-6; Lesson 2 — Topics 7-10

"I dwell in the high and holy place, with him also that is of a contrite and humble spirit." Isa. 57:15.

1. God's First Lessons. Before the students of this school were prepared to teach others the importance and sacredness of God's eternal law, they must themselves realize its holy character. God's first lesson to accomplish this was in the giving of the manna. The second lesson was in the speaking of His law from Sinai amid scenes of power and glory. But He did not stop here. A third time He emphasized its importance in a message that He sent by Moses when Moses was in the mount forty days and forty nights receiving instructions to build the sanctuary. The message was: *"Verily* My Sabbaths ye shall keep: . . . it is a *sign* between Me and the children of Israel *forever:* for in six days the Lord made heaven and earth, and on the seventh day He rested."

God knew how determined Satan was that men should forget Him, for if he could succeed in blotting from their minds all thought of their Creator, he could easily lead them to follow and worship *him.* This is why the Sabbath, God's memorial of His creative power, has been the special object of Satan's hatred. It is because men have forgotten their Creator that many now worship false gods or claim not to believe in God at all. Had they always observed the Sabbath, from week to week commemorating the fact that "in six days the Lord made heaven and earth, the sea, and all that in them is, and rested the seventh day,"— had this God been the object of their worship, there never could have been an idolater, an atheist, or an infidel. The keeping of the Sabbath, God declares is a *sign* of our loyalty to the only true God, a sign that we believe in Him who created all things in six days and rested on the seventh day.

2. The Sanctuary to Teach God's Plan. The first half year — the first semester of school — was given to building the sanctuary and making its furniture. As the students worked, God taught them many lessons about the sanctuary in heaven, and His plan to prepare

---

References Used: P. P., pp. 348, 349; "Seer," pp. 363, 367, 368; Ex. 25:8; 31:13, 17; Isa. 53:2; 66:2; Dan. 7:10; 2 Cor. 6:16; 1 Cor. 3:17; 6:20; 1 Peter 3:3, 4; 1 Sam. 16:7.

them to live with Him. "Let them make Me a sanctuary; that I may dwell among them," He said. The earthly sanctuary is called the *"shadow of heavenly things." Together with its services, it was *"a figure for the time then present," an object lesson to teach the people about the work of Christ, our great High Priest in the heavenly sanctuary. It was to be a miniature heaven on earth, where God would dwell with His people and teach them day by day

The sanctuary was an object lesson to teach the people about the work of Christ in the heavenly sanctuary.

about His great plan to save man. For this reason everything was to be made with the greatest care, of the most expensive and beautiful material, and exactly as directed.

3. The Meaning of "Sanctuary." A sanctuary is a place set apart for a sacred purpose. Sometimes a person reserves a room in his home for his own personal, private use, a place where he may get away from the distracting activities and cares of life and be alone. He calls this room his *sanctum*. The word "sanctuary" contains the same thought as "sanctum," which literally means "holy." If the person wishes to emphasize the fact that his sanctum is strictly private, he speaks of it as his *sanctum sanctorum*, which literally means "holy of holies." The sanctuary that Moses was told to build was to contain two apartments, the first called the holy, the second the holy of holies, or the most holy.

4. The Heavenly Sanctuary a Pattern. In heaven there is a sanctuary, *"the true tabernacle, which the Lord pitched, and not man." While Moses was in the mount, God gave him a view of this sanctuary, with the express caution, when instructing him to build the earthly sanctuary: *"See . . . that thou make all things according to the pattern showed to thee in the mount." God gave Moses the exact size and structure of every board and bar, every ring and hook, every curtain and every article of furniture, with all the details concerning each.

When the apostle John was in vision, he was permitted to look into heaven, where he saw both apartments of the heavenly sanctuary. He saw the "seven lamps of fire burning before the throne;" he saw our great High Priest; he saw the Angel stand at the golden altar with a golden censer offering incense; and he also saw "the ark of His testament." We at once recognize these as pertaining to the sanctuary.

5. The Beauty Within. The tabernacle was a type of Christ. Without, it was substantial yet very plain,— a huge, box-looking affair, or as some think, resembling a long houselike tent, completely covered with an immense curtain of badgers' skins to protect it from the weather. But though it was unattractive without, no language can describe the glory of the scene presented within the sanctuary. The ceilings and gold-plated walls were draped with brilliantly colored curtains of blue and purple and scarlet, with figures of shining angels, richly embroidered in gold. At the entrance and between the two apartments hung curtains of the same rich material. The rainbow tints of the curtains beautifully represented the rainbow of glory which surrounds the throne of God. The embroidered figures represented the angels around the heavenly throne, the "thousand thousands" who minister to Jesus our heavenly High Priest, and the "ten thousand times ten thousand" who stand before Him ever ready to do the bidding of their Commander.

6. The First Apartment. In the first apartment of the holy place, the golden walls reflected the light from the golden candlestick, the lights of which were always kept burning. The candlestick, which was made of one piece of pure gold, weighed nearly two hundred pounds. It was almost five feet high and three and one

The ark inclosing the tables of God's law and covered with the mercy seat, together with the glory above, represented God on His throne in heaven, with His law as its foundation.

half feet wide. It represented the church of God, and the lights represented the Spirit of God, which the church is to lift up before the world. The table with its ornamental crown and the altar of incense glittered with gold.

7. The Second Apartment. In the second apartment, or holy of holies, in solitary grandeur was the ark containing the tables of the Ten Commandments. This chest, the most elaborate and expensive article of furniture in the sanctuary, was overlaid within and without with gold, and had a crown of gold about the top. The mercy seat, which formed its cover, was of solid gold, with a golden cherub standing on each end. Above the mercy seat, filling the room with a glorious light, was the manifestation of the divine presence. This glory also shone out over the curtain into the first apartment.

The ark inclosing the tables of God's law and covered with the mercy seat, together with the glory above, represented God on His throne in heaven, with His law as the foundation of His throne. The mercy seat represented the mercy of God in giving Jesus to die for us that we might have forgiveness for our sins,— forgiveness for disobeying His law. The cherubim represented the covering cherubim in the midst of the stones of fire in heaven. "The position of the cherubim, with their faces . . . looking reverently downward toward the ark, represented the reverence with which the heavenly host regard the law of God, and their interest in the plan of redemption."

8. The Sacred Character of God's Law. The constitution of the United States, the fundamental law of our government, was written by the fathers of our nation. This original copy was for years kept in state in the nation's capitol at Washington. A few years ago it was noticed that the ink was fading, and there was danger that time would destroy this valued document; so by act of Congress it was placed in a special dark vault in the Army and Navy Building, where it lies to-day, and only the highest dignitaries are ever permitted to see it. Of all official documents, this one is probably the most revered by the citizens of the United States.

With His own finger, God Himself wrote the fundamental law of *His* government on imperishable stone, to teach the people that *His* law will last *forever*. And it was to teach them to reverence His law, that He told Moses to make that beautiful box for it, and place it in the most holy apartment of the sanctuary, over which hovered the divine presence,—the most sacred spot on earth.

9. Our Body Sanctuary. If we are the true children of Christ, we are "the temple [or sanctuary] of the living God," and of such God has said, "I will dwell in them." We are told to glorify God in our body, and we are warned that "if any man defile the temple of God, him shall God destroy." If we glorify God in our body sanctuary, like Him of whom the glorious sanctuary was a type, we shall be beautiful within. Our adorning will "not be that outward adorning of plaiting the hair, and of wearing of gold, or of putting on of apparel," but it will be "the hidden man of the heart, . . . even the ornament of a meek and quiet spirit, which is in the sight of God of great price." Let us remember that "the king's daughter is all glorious *within*," that "the Lord seeth not as man seeth; for man looketh on the outward appearance, but the Lord looketh on the heart." Our hearts will then become the *sanctum sanctorum* of the Spirit of God. God, who dwells "in the high and holy place," dwells "with him also that is of a contrite and humble spirit" and that trembles at His word. Not only will our hearts be a *sanctum sanctorum*, set apart solely for His use, but God will in turn be *our* "sanctum sanctorum," our refuge to whom we may flee in times of temptation and be sheltered from the enemy.

10. The Value of the Sanctuary. As it is impossible to reckon the value of the redemption that has been purchased for us by the blood of Christ, so it would be impossible for us to estimate accurately the immense value of the gold and silver and the other materials used in the sanctuary. Something of its value is, however, revealed to us. The gold weighed 29 talents and 730 shekels; the silver weighed 100 talents and 1,775 shekels. Besides the immense

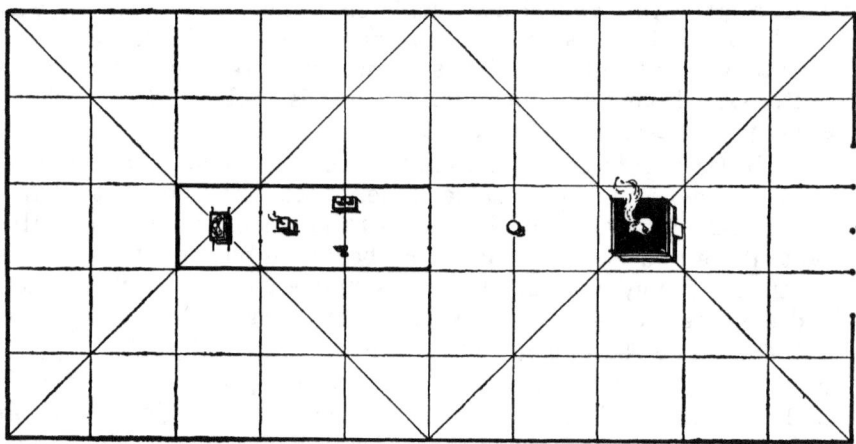

DIAGRAM No. 4. The sanctuary and the court

amount of gold and silver, there was other expensive material, to say nothing of the value of the skillful labor employed during the six months that it was under construction. All this was to give the people and us some small idea of the salvation that has been purchased for us at an infinite cost, and that is given to us "without money and without price."

Lesson 1 — Topics 1-6

How to Study: In studying these lessons, get a clear idea of the beauty and value of the sanctuary and its furniture — try to *see* it. Be an ambitious student, and solve some of the "Problems for the Ambitious Student."

Use of Concordance: Find the four starred verses under topics 2 and 4. Look for them in Hebrews. Which chapters?

Memory Work: Memorize Psalms 45:13, and write the reference on your "Service Flag."

Chapters to Remember: Exodus 24-32 tells about Moses' forty-day stay in the mount, when God wrote the law on tables of stone, and gave him full directions for making the sanctuary. Hebrews 8 and 9 compare the earthly and heavenly sanctuaries.

For Your Workbook: Diagram No. 4. Draw a plan of the sanctuary, showing the exact location of the different articles of furniture. Draw the construction lines very faintly. The blank for this diagram is a page in "Bible Workbook" for the eighth grade.

Copy the first column below, and in a column opposite write that which corresponds in "the true tabernacle," using the references given.

The Earthly Sanctuary	*The Heavenly Sanctuary*
1. The earthly tabernacle	1. Heb. 8: 2, last part
2. The table of shewbread	2. John 6: 48
3. The candlestick of pure gold	3. Zech. 4: 2
4. The seven lights	4. Rev. 4: 5, last part
5. Curtains of blue, purple, and scarlet	5. Rev. 4: 3, last part
6. The embroidered angels	6. Rev. 5: 11
7. The golden altar	7. Rev. 8: 3

Lesson 2 — Topics 7-10

8. The ark	8. Rev. 11: 19, first part
9. God's righteous law	9. Ps. 97: 2, margin; James 2: 12
10. The mercy seat above which was the presence of God	10. Prov. 20: 28, last part
11. The covering cherubim	11. Eze. 28: 14, first part
12. God's presence above the mercy seat	12. Rev. 7: 10, last part

For Class Discussion: Who was one of the covering cherubs in heaven? Who now occupies that position? Why would keeping God's Sabbath have prevented the existence of an idolater, an atheist, or an infidel?

Problems for the Ambitious Student: (A shekel of silver is said to be valued at 64 cents; a shekel of gold at $9.60. A talent of silver is valued at $1,920.00; a talent of gold at about $27,275.00.)

1. What was the total value of the sockets into which the tenons of the boards fitted? Ex. 38: 27.
2. What was the value of the rest of the silver used? Ex. 38: 25.
3. What was the value of the gold used? Ex. 38: 24.
4. What was the total value of the silver and gold used?
5. What would be its purchasing value to-day, with a day's labor then worth 15 cents and now $5.00?
6. What would the candlestick and its vessels be worth in to-day's money value? Ex. 37: 20, 24.
7. A talent weighed about 96 pounds avoirdupois; how many tons did the 29 talents of gold plus the 100 talents of silver weigh?

7. THE SECOND SEMESTER OF THE MISSIONARY SCHOOL

God's Plan Taught in the Daily Services of the Sanctuary

Lesson 1 — Topics 1-4; Lesson 2 — Topics 5-7

"Present your bodies a living sacrifice, . . . which is your reasonable service."
Rom. 12:1.

1. The Work of the Second Half Year. While during the first half of the year the lessons were on the building of the sanctuary, the last half of the year they were on its daily services. Like the building itself, the services also were a "shadow [a type, or illustration] of heavenly things." They explained the work of Jesus, the heavenly High Priest, the Redeemer of the world. By observing the work of the priests in the earthly sanctuary and taking part in the service, the people learned of the work that Christ is doing in the heavenly sanctuary. The sanctuary with its service was a "prophecy of the gospel," wonderfully revealing God's great plan. Because of this, there is no subject in the Bible more important for us to understand.

2. The Daily Service. The daily service consisted of the morning and evening burnt offering at the brazen altar in the court, and the offering of sweet incense on the golden altar in the first apartment, or holy place, and the trimming of the lights of the golden candlestick. The shewbread on the table was also a part of the daily sacrifice. All these were continual services throughout the year. Besides these there were special sin offerings for individual sins.

3. The Special Sin Offering. Every morning and evening a lamb was offered for the entire congregation, but at special times the individual sinner offered a lamb for a special sin offering. Then he brought the lamb to the door of the sanctuary, placed his hands on the head of the offering, and confessed his sins. Thus in a figure, or type, his sins were laid on the lamb, just as our sins when confessed are laid on Christ, the Lamb of God. Then with his own hand he killed the innocent victim. The priest then took the blood in a basin into the holy place, where hidden from the view of the people, he sprinkled it seven times with his finger before the veil behind which

---

References Used: P. P., pp. 348, 352-355; Lev. 4:13-21, 27-35; 6:9-13, 26; 9:24; 24:2, 6, 8; 1 Peter 2:24; Ps. 69:9; Ex. 25:30; 27:20, 21; 29:38-42; 30:7, 8; Num. 4:7; 28:9, 10.

was the ark containing the law which had been transgressed. This illustrated how our sins when confessed and forgiven are covered in God's great record book in the heavenly sanctuary. The horns of the golden altar were also touched with the blood. In some cases, instead of taking the blood into the holy place, the priest ate the flesh of the sacrifice. But he ate it in the holy place, away from the view of the people. Thus he bore the sins "in his own body," and thus they were transferred to the sanctuary. The blood of the animal could not remove sin, but in this way the sinner expressed his faith in the sacrifice of Christ, by whose blood all our sins may be blotted out.

The sin offering represented how their sins when confessed were laid on Christ, the Lamb of God.

4. The Daily Burnt Offering. In the burnt offering the lamb was first slain, and then the entire sacrifice was laid upon the brazen altar and burned. Every morning and evening the nation thus gave themselves anew to God. They thus showed not only that they surrendered all sin, but they pledged their lives to be laid on the altar of Christ and wholly consumed in His service. It was said of Christ, "The zeal of Thine house hath eaten Me up." And so our zeal for God's house — His work — should fully consume our time, our talent, and our possessions. All our plans and desires should daily be consecrated in this way to be carried out or given up as God may direct. The Spirit of God appeals to our honor and loyalty in the words, "I *beseech* you . . . by the mercies of God, that ye present *your* bodies [your hands, your feet, your eyes, your lips, your ears — your whole bodies] a *living* sacrifice." Is this too much for us to do? God says it is but our "reasonable service." Nothing less than this complete consecration can ever properly express a sincere faith in the work which the Lamb of God "ever liveth" to do for us.

The lamb offered was to be "of the first year" and "without blemish," showing that the offering we make of ourselves should be as early in life and as nearly perfect as possible. God has given

His best for us, and nothing less than our best for Him is a fitting expression of our appreciation. And so the lamb represented not only Christ as He offered Himself for us, but it represented the people as they gave themselves to Him. True worship includes both faith in God and work for God. On the Sabbath the burnt offering consisted of *two* lambs morning and evening.

The fragrant incense which rose with the prayers represented the righteousness of Christ that covered those who prayed in sincerity.

5. The Daily Incense Offering. While the lamb was offered on the brazen altar, the priest offered the sweet incense on the golden altar. As he did this he looked toward the ark in which lay the tables of God's law which had been transgressed. At the same time, the people outside united in silent prayer for forgiveness of sin. The fragrant incense which rose with their prayers represented the righteousness of Christ which covered those who prayed in sincerity, and gave assurance that their prayers were answered. It also represented the prayers which Christ offers in heaven for us.

Thus before the veil of the holy place at the brazen altar there was continual sacrifice to represent atonement for sin, while before the veil of the most holy place at the golden altar there was continual incense to represent the intercession of Christ for forgiveness of sin.

The hours of morning and evening sacrifice were sacredly set apart for worship, and correspond to our morning and evening periods of prayer. The fire on the brazen altar was kindled by God Himself, and it never went out. Day and night it was kept burning, the priests in turn officiating. Only by this continual offering could the service properly represent the continual sacrifice of Christ. Likewise the fire upon the golden altar, which also was kindled by God, was sacredly cherished. "Day and night the holy incense diffused its fragrance throughout the sacred apartments, and without, far around the tabernacle." This illustrated how Jesus "ever liveth to make intercession" for us.

6. The Shewbread and Its Meaning. The shewbread on the table in the holy place was also a perpetual offering. There were twelve cakes, one for each tribe, arranged in two rows. The table was never without this bread. Thus the bread fitly represented our constant dependence upon God for food, both physical and spiritual. On every Sabbath day the bread was removed and replaced by fresh loaves. Thus, while we should have spiritual food every day, at every Sabbath service we should receive a fresh supply of the bread of life.

7. The Light and Its Meaning. The lights shining from the golden candlestick were never allowed to go out, but shed their beams by day and by night. They represented the light of the Holy Spirit, which at some time in life shines into the heart of every individual. It was the duty of the priest to trim the lamps morning and evening and keep them brightly burning. So we are to keep our lights trimmed and burning, that others by our lives may see the way to Christ. To let our light grow dim might cause some one to stumble and fall and lose his way to heaven.

How to Study: Copy the following "types," and, in a column opposite write the corresponding "antitype" as given in the texts. Notice that three texts are in John, and two in Hebrews.

Lesson 1 — Topics 1-4

THE SIN OFFERING

Type	Antitype
1. The lamb for the sin offering	1. John 1:29
2. Sacrifice "without blemish"	2. 1 Peter 1:19; Eph. 5:27
3. Sin confessed and placed on the sacrifice	3. Heb. 9:28, first part
4. The sinner killed the innocent lamb	4. Isa. 53:5, first part
5. The blood sprinkled seven times	5. Heb. 7:25, first part
6. Morning and evening sacrifice	6. Ps. 55:17

THE BURNT OFFERING

1. Sacrifice entirely consumed by fire — 1. *Rom. 12:1
2. Fires kept burning day and night — 2. Gal. 6:9

Lesson 2 — Topics 5-7

THE INCENSE OFFERING

1. Incense rose continually — 1. 1 Thess. 5:17; Heb. 7:25, last part

THE SHEWBREAD

1. The shewbread — 1. John 6:35, first part, 51, 63

THE CANDLESTICK

1. Lights never went out — 1. John 1:9; Matt. 5:14, 16
2. Candlestick — 2. Zech. 4:2

Memory Work: Memorize Romans 12:1.

---

8. "FINAL EXAMINATION DAY" IN GOD'S CHURCH SCHOOL

A Lesson on the Finishing of God's Plan

"Some men's sins are open beforehand, going before to judgment; and some men they follow after." 1 Tim. 5:24.

1. The Yearly Service. While the daily service was performed every day at the altar of burnt offering in the court outside the tabernacle, and in the first apartment, or holy place, the yearly serv-

---

References Used: P. P., pp. 355, 358; G. C., pp. 480-484; Heb. 9:6, 7, 9; Eccl. 12:14; Matt. 12:36, 37; Mal. 3:16; James 2:12; Ps. 85·10; Lev. 16:5-24; 23·29; also those used in the following Bible study; E. W., p. 52.

ice came once a year, and closed the continual round of sacrifices. At this time, in addition to services in the court and in the first apartment, a special service was performed in the second apartment, or most holy place. The priests performed the work connected with the daily service, but the high priest did the work of the yearly service. No other human eye ever looked into the second apartment of the sanctuary, and only once a year was the high priest permitted to enter there.

2. The Record Books in Heaven. In the great record book of God, every evil deed and every idle word, with every secret thing, is faithfully recorded. This book has sometimes been called the "book of sins" or the "book of death." There is another book, called the "book of remembrance," which contains a record of our good deeds and of pardon for sins confessed. It is written "for them that feared the Lord, and that thought upon His name." God keeps this book "before Him."

3. The Sanctuary Polluted. As in the earthly sanctuary for those who confessed their sins, the blood of the lamb was sprinkled before the veil, behind which was the presence of God, so in the heavenly sanctuary Christ pleads His blood in the presence of the Father whenever we truly repent of sin. Then the record of our forgiveness is written in the "book of remembrance" which is "before God." But, though confessed and forgiven, our sins are not at that time blotted out. Just as the sins of the people transferred in the blood to the holy place polluted the earthly sanctuary, so the record of our sins, though they are forgiven, defiles the heavenly sanctuary. On the last day of the year, there was a special service, when the earthly sanctuary was cleansed "from the uncleanness of the children of Israel." So in the day of judgment at the end of the world our sins written in the books of heaven, if repented of and forgiven, will be blotted out, never again to be remembered against us.

4. The Day for Cleansing the Sanctuary. The day for the cleansing of the sanctuary was called the day of atonement — the day of at-one-ment with God. The tenth day of the seventh month, the yearly harvest time, was the day appointed for this solemn service. It was observed as a day of fasting and prayer. All business and all regular home duties were laid aside, and every true child of God spent the day earnestly examining his own heart and putting away his sins. It may very fittingly be called "final examination day" for this school. In the antitype, the results of this day decide whether we are prepared for promotion from the school of earth to the higher grade, the school above.

5. Cleansing the Sanctuary. On the day of atonement the high priest brought two goats to the door of the tabernacle. Upon these goats lots were cast to decide which was to be sacrificed for the Lord

The service in the most holy place on the last day of the year represented the last work of our High Priest in heaven for sinners. When *Christ* throws down *His* censer there is no more forgiveness of sin.

and which was to be the scapegoat. The goat upon which the first lot fell was slain as a sin offering for the people. His blood was carried into the most holy place and sprinkled by the high priest with his finger upon the mercy seat above the tables of the law, and before the mercy seat seven times. The law of God within the ark is the great rule of righteousness and truth. By it every sinner will be judged. Justice demands that he who transgresses the law shall die. But above the law is the mercy seat, and above all is the presence of a just yet merciful Father. Through His mercy all who repent of their sins are forgiven and are at peace with God. Thus in this service of the sanctuary, "mercy and truth are met together; righteousness and peace have kissed each other."

After sprinkling the blood in the most holy place, the high priest went into the holy place and touched the horns of the golden altar with the blood and sprinkled of the blood upon it with his finger seven times. This service in a figure hallowed, or cleansed, both apartments of the sanctuary "from the uncleanness of the children of Israel." After the sanctuary had been cleansed, the high priest, in a figure, took the sins of all the people upon himself and left the sanctuary. He had "made an end of reconciling." If at that time anyone had not confessed his sins he was "cut off from among his people."

6. The Typical Scapegoat. At the door of the tabernacle the high priest laid "both his hands upon the head of the live goat" (the scapegoat), and confessed over him "all the iniquities of the children of Israel, . . . putting them upon the head of the goat." Then the goat, bearing these sins, was sent away into the wilderness, never to return. Thus in a figure the sins were regarded as forever separated from the people.

7. Satan the Real Scapegoat. In the real ministration of Christ, when as our High Priest He has finished the work of pleading His own blood before the Father to atone for our transgression of the law, the heavenly sanctuary will be cleansed, and the sins of all who have truly repented will be blotted out from the books of heaven. Then Jesus will come forth from the heavenly sanctuary and proclaim, "He that is unjust, let him be unjust still: and he which is filthy, let him be filthy still: and he that is righteous, let him be righteous still: and he that is holy, let him be holy still." Then He will place our sins upon Satan, the scapegoat, the originator of all sin, and Satan will bear the final penalty, first upon this desolate wilderness earth during the thousand years when the redeemed are in heaven, and at last in the lake of fire.

But Satan will bear the sins of those only who before the day of judgment have confessed every known sin and received the assurance of pardon, those whose "sins are open beforehand, going before to judgment." "Repent ye therefore, and be converted, that your sins may be blotted out, when the times of refreshing shall come from the presence of the Lord." To those who are thus ready, Jesus promises, "I will not blot out his name out of the book of life, but I will confess his name before My Father, and before His angels." If we neglect to confess our sins, Jesus cannot confess our names. Our sins will then "follow after" and condemn us in that

In the ministration of Christ, our heavenly High Priest will at last place our sins upon Satan, the real scapegoat, who will bear the final penalty.

great and terrible day. And as a result, instead of our sins' being blotted out of God's book, our names will be blotted out of the book of life, and we shall be forever cut off from God's people.

8. Purifying the Court. After the scapegoat had been sent away into the wilderness, the high priest returned to the holy place, removed his priestly garments, and put on other garments. Then he came into the court again, where he offered burnt offerings. At last nothing was left but ashes. Thus the court itself was purified. So when our heavenly High Priest has finished His work for sinners, He will remove His priestly garments and put on the garments of the "King of kings." Then, when Satan's thousand-year period of confinement amid the ruins of this desolate earthly wilderness is ended, Jesus will purify this earth by fire until neither root nor branch is left of sin,—it "shall be ashes . . . in the day that I shall do this, saith the Lord of hosts."

9. Each Year a Type of the Entire Priestly Work of Christ. Thus each yearly round of the sanctuary service represented the entire work of Christ as our High Priest. While the daily services taught the people about the death of Christ and His work for their salvation, "once each year their minds were carried forward to the closing events of the great controversy between Christ and Satan, the final purification of the universe from sin and sinners." In this way Jesus, the Teacher in God's great church school, taught the people the gospel, the plan of salvation which they were to teach to the world.

How to Study: Get a clear idea of each part of the services on the day of atonement, and be able to tell its meaning.

Memory Work: Memorize 1 Timothy 5: 24.

Chapter to Remember: Leviticus 16 describes the day of atonement service. Ask your father to read this chapter for family worship. Follow the reading carefully.

For Class Discussion: When did Jesus enter the most holy place of the heavenly sanctuary and begin the work of the antitypical day of atonement? What is this work called?

---

9. A BIBLE STUDY ON THE DAY OF ATONEMENT

Copy the following "types," and in a column opposite write the corresponding "antitype" from the given texts:

Type	Antitype
The Day of Atonement	*The Judgment*
1. The High Priest	1. Heb. 9: 11, first part
2. God's glory shining upon the mercy seat	2. Ps. 31: 16
3. The blood sprinkled seven times	3. Heb. 7: 25, first part
4. The sanctuary cleansed	4. Acts 3: 19
5. "An end of reconciling"	5. Rev. 22: 11; 3: 5
6. The scapegoat in the wilderness	6. Rev. 20: 2, 9, last part
7. The high priest changed his garments	7. Rev. 19: 16
8. The sacrifice burned — the court cleansed	8. 2 Peter 3: 10; Mal. 4: 1

REVIEW

Chapter Drill: See how long it takes you to find all these chapters:

1. Moses called to deliver Israel
2. Death of the first-born
3. Leaving Egypt
4. God's law
5. The faith chapter
6. Moses' forty-day stay in the mount
7. Day of atonement
8. The ten plagues

Test Questions and Exercises: The numbers refer to previous lessons.

6. Describe the first apartment of the sanctuary; the second apartment. What lesson may we draw from the beauty of the tabernacle within? *Ps. 45: 13. Why are our bodies called God's temple? What does the immense value of the sanctuary teach us about God's plan? Be able to tell what each part of the earthly sanctuary corresponds to in the heavenly sanctuary.

7. Name the daily services. Describe the special sin offering and tell what it meant. Of what was the daily burnt offering a pledge? What did God require which showed that we should offer ourselves in His service early in life? How did the Sabbath service differ from the daily? What did the incense represent? Why were the fire on the altar and the light of the candlestick kept burning always? Recite *Romans 12:1, and tell what relation it has to the offerings.

8. What record books are kept in heaven? What is the purpose of each? Why did the earthly sanctuary need cleansing? On what day was this service? What was it called? Why? Describe the service. Whom did the scapegoat represent? Whose sins will Satan bear? What did the purifying of the court represent? What did the entire yearly round of services represent? Which class of people mentioned in *1 Timothy 5:24 will be saved?

---

10. SATAN'S PRISON HOUSE FIRST OPENED

"Michael the Archangel, when contending with the devil . . . about the body of Moses, . . . said, The Lord rebuke thee." Jude 9.

1. Our First Bible. Israel had now dwelt under the shadow of Mount Sinai for a year. Up to this time the only part of the Bible that had been written was the book of Genesis, unless, as some think, the book of Job had already been written. The book of Leviticus and probably Exodus were written by Moses during the sojourn at Sinai, while Numbers and Deuteronomy must have been written on the later journeys. These five books are often called the Penta-

References Used: P. P., pp. 251, 410, 472, 477-479; Num. 1: 45, 46; 9: 1-5; 14: 2, 28-33; 20: 8-11; Gen. 49: 9; 15: 16; Rev. 5: 5; Deut. 32: 49, 50; 33: 26, 27; 34: 5, 6; Isa. 48: 21; 1 Cor. 10: 4.

teuch, which means "consisting of five books." They are also called "the law," "the law of Moses," "the book of the law," and "the book of Moses." In this writing Moses was directed by the Holy Spirit, and these books may be called our first Bible.

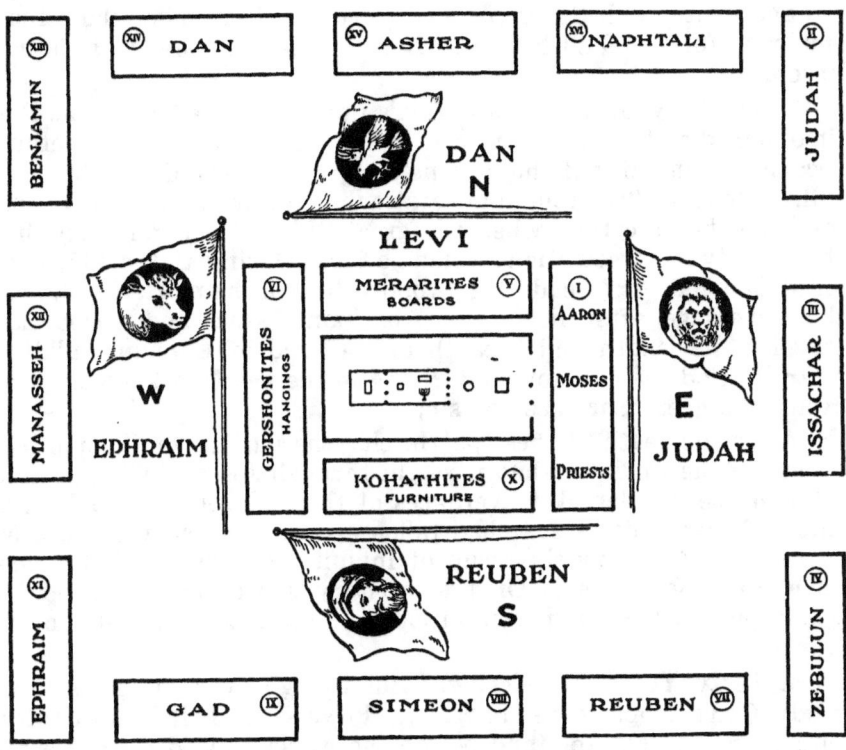

DIAGRAM No. 5. The camp of Israel, showing the line of march.

2. Leaving for Canaan. And now the pillar of cloud was about to lift, indicating an onward journey. Just before Israel left Sinai, the Passover was celebrated, and again in the beautiful springtime they set out on their journey to Canaan. This time they took with them the tabernacle, and "the Book" containing complete instructions for their missionary undertaking. Perfect order characterized the forward march of this church school,—a worthy example for every other church school. This vast multitude of more than half a million besides women and children was arranged under four standards. The color of Judah's standard was green and his emblem a *lion;* the emblem of Reuben was a *man;* the emblem of Ephraim's standard was an *ox* or *calf* and its color gold; Dan's standard was red and white, with the emblem of an *eagle.* Remember these four emblems, for we shall have occasion to refer to them in a future lesson.

3. The Way Open. It was God's purpose to lead Israel at this time immediately into the promised land. He could not do so before, because the iniquity of the nations occupying the land was "not yet full." But now "the fourth generation" had come since Jacob went into Egypt — the time when the great "I AM" had foreseen that the iniquity of these nations would be full. During all the 430 years since God had first made the promise to Abraham, He had given them message after message. Abraham, Isaac, and Jacob had traveled the length and breadth of the land of Canaan, building altars to God the Creator, and giving to the people a knowledge of Jesus, the great Sacrifice for sin.

After the death of these patriarchs, the nations of Canaan had known of the work God had wrought through Joseph in Egypt, and later of the wonderful deliverances of the children of Israel. Because of these things, fear had fallen upon them; but they refused to repent. And now their cup of iniquity was full, and God was about to remove them. On the territory which they occupied He would place His own chosen nation, to be a beacon of light to the world.

4. Forty Years' Wandering. But though everything else was ready, God's people were not ready. Because of their lack of faith, Israel proved unfit to stand before the world as God's representative. When the spies who had been sent ahead to examine Canaan, returned and told of the giants who lived there, the people exclaimed, "Would God we had died in this wilderness!" And God took them at their word. "As truly as I live," He said, "as ye have spoken in Mine ears, so will I do to you." Because the children of Israel despised the land that God wanted to give them, they were left to wander in the wilderness for forty years, until all that were twenty years old and upward who had murmured against God had fallen in death. Out of all that multitude only faithful Caleb and Joshua lived to see the land of Canaan. Thus the sin of murmuring and unbelief "dashed from their lips the cup of blessing," and Satan rejoiced that God's work had been marred and delayed by His own chosen people.

5. The Sin of Moses. Even Moses was not permitted to enter the promised land. And why not? While the people were at Sinai a living stream of water flowed from the smitten rock in Horeb and supplied their need. This represented Christ, the water of life. The rock also represented Christ. He is the "Rock of Ages, cleft

The smitten rock, from which flowed refreshing streams, represented Jesus smitten for us, that we might drink of the water of life.

for me." When Israel left Sinai, the rock at that place ceased to give out its sparkling stream; but wherever they camped, "He caused the waters to flow out of the rock for them." *"They drank of that spiritual Rock that followed them: and that Rock was Christ."

As they neared the end of their forty years' wandering, God tested their faith in Him by withholding the supply of water. As their fathers had done before them, so they also murmured and rebelled. Then Moses prayed to God. And God said, "Take the rod, and gather thou the assembly together, . . . and speak ye unto the rock before their eyes; and it shall give forth his water." But Moses, impatient of their complaining, instead of speaking to the rock, smote it twice with the rod. As he did this, he exclaimed, "Hear now, ye rebels; must *we* fetch you water out of this rock?" He thus not only disobeyed God and took to himself the glory due to God alone, but he spoiled the figure through which God was teaching the people of Jesus, who was smitten but once. Besides, by his lack of patience, the people were led to question whether in the past he had been directed by God. Had Moses gone on unpunished, they would have rejected all the reproofs that God had sent them through him.

6. Moses' Last Days, His Death and Burial. Moses confessed his sin not only to God but to the people, and he tried to strengthen their faith. His farewell sermons are recorded in the book of Deuteronomy. In these sermons he reviewed the laws which God had given them, and encouraged the people to obey them faithfully. Among his last were these beautiful words: "As thy days, so shall thy strength be," and *"The eternal God is thy refuge, and underneath are the everlasting arms." Then, following God's command, he climbed to the top of Mount Nebo. Here in prophetic vision God gave him a view of the land of promise, "not as it then appeared, but as it would become, with God's blessing upon it, in the possession of Israel. He seemed to be looking upon a second Eden." Then on down the stream of time he saw Israel's apostasy, Jesus the Babe of Bethlehem, His life on earth, and His crucifixion. He saw the disciples as they went forth to carry the gospel to the world. And at last he saw the earth as it will be when all sin is removed. Then "the vision faded, and . . . like a tired warrior, he lay down to rest." And the Lord "buried him: . . . but no man knoweth of his sepulcher."

7. Christ Opens Satan's Prison House. Moses was a type of Christ; and as Christ was raised from the dead, so Moses did not remain long in the tomb. "Christ Himself, with the angels who had buried Moses, came down from heaven to call forth the sleeping saint. Satan had exulted at his success in causing Moses to sin against God, and thus come under the dominion of death. . . . The power of the grave had never been broken, and all who were in the tomb he claimed as his captives, never to be released from his dark prison house. For the first time, Christ was about to give life to the dead. As the Prince of life and the shining ones approached the grave, Satan was alarmed for his supremacy. With his evil angels he stood to dispute an invasion of the territory that he claimed as his own. . . . He declared that . . . Moses . . . had taken to himself the glory due to Jehovah,— the very sin which had caused Satan's banishment from heaven,— and by transgression had come under the dominion of Satan. The arch-traitor . . . repeated his complaints of God's injustice toward him." "Yet Michael the Archangel, when contending with the devil he disputed about the body of Moses," would not stoop to discuss the matter with Satan, but said, "The Lord rebuke thee."

The Saviour then "began His work of breaking the power of the fallen foe, and bringing the dead to life. Here was an evidence that Satan could not controvert, of the supremacy of the Son of God. The resurrection was forever made certain. Satan was despoiled of his prey; the righteous dead would live again."

How to Study: Study to recite from the lesson topics. Write out at least five good questions on topics 5, 6, and 7. What were the four standards under which Israel was arranged? Why were Caleb and Joshua allowed to enter Canaan? On diagram No. 1 point out the 430 years' sojourn.

Dictionary Study: What is the literal meaning of: Scriptures, Exodus, Leviticus, Deuteronomy, Pentateuch? Can you think of other words with the root *penta?* *script?* the prefix *ex?* Why was the book of Numbers so called? The Scriptures were not called the Bible until nearly 200 A. D. Can you think why?

Use of Concordance: Find the two starred texts under topics 5 and 6. Key words: drank, eternal.

For Your Workbook: Fill in diagram No. 5, showing the arrangement of the camp of Israel, the standards, and the order of march. Print all names neatly. Color the standards. The blank for this diagram is a page in "Bible Workbook" for the eighth grade.

---

11. THE NATION READY FOR SERVICE
About B. C. 1500

"Be strong and of a good courage; . . . for the Lord thy God is with thee whithersoever thou goest." Joshua 1:9.

1. The Secret of Success. After the death of Moses, God appointed Joshua to be the visible leader of His people. In His commission He three times repeated, "Be strong and of a good courage." And the secret of success He proclaimed in these words: "This book of the law shall not depart out of thy mouth; but thou shalt meditate therein day and night, that thou mayest observe to do according to all that is written therein: for then thou shalt make

---
References Used: Joshua 1:8, 9; 3:16, 17; 14:15; Judges 2:22.

thy way prosperous, and then thou shalt have good success." If Israel had always studied and obeyed God's law, she would have been the most prosperous and successful nation in the world.

2. Crossing the Jordan. The multitude was still encamped east of the Jordan River. Again it was the spring of the year, the time of high water in Jordan, and the banks of the river were full to overflowing. There were no bridges across the river, and the people had no boats. How, then, were they to reach the other side, where lay the land of promise, their future home? Surely this would

God used the crossing of the Jordan, to show His power not only to Israel but to the heathen nations.

seem to be a most unfavorable time for such an undertaking. But "man's extremity is God's opportunity," and God used this occasion to show His power not only to Israel but to the heathen nations. Forty years before, He had made a path for their fathers through the Red Sea; so now He made a path through the Jordan River. At the command of God "the waters which came down from above stood and rose up upon an heap very far from the city Adam: . . . and those that came down toward the sea of the plain, even the salt sea, failed, and were cut off: . . . and the priests that bare the ark of the covenant of the Lord stood firm on dry ground, . . . until all the people were passed clean over Jordan." The city of Adam was thirty miles from the mouth of the Jordan — so far did the

Lord restrain the waters of this swollen stream, that His name might be made known in the earth.

3. Israel Established in Canaan. The miraculous crossing of the Jordan, together with other miracles wrought in behalf of Israel, caused terror to fall upon the inhabitants of the land, and they became an easy prey. Nevertheless, it was not until seven years of struggle that "the land had rest from war." And even then not all the nations were driven out. Some were allowed to remain, that, as God said, "through them I may prove Israel, whether they will keep the way of the Lord to walk therein." Israel now took her

The Plain of Esdraelon or Megiddo

place as an independent nation among other nations of the world. She was ready for service, ready to enter upon her God-given task of carrying to "all families of the earth" a knowledge of the blessing that God had committed to her in the promised Redeemer.

4. The Plain of Esdraelon. When Israel transgressed God's commands and separated themselves from His protection, God permitted the unconquered Canaanite tribes to war against Israel. A little north of the center of Canaan is a plain at that time called the plain of Esdraelon. It is also called the valley of Jezreel. This was the scene of many an ancient battle. In the southern part of this plain was Megiddo, or Ar-megiddo, where the Israelites won a great victory over the Canaanites,— typical, as some think, of the last great conflict among the nations of this war-stricken earth,— the battle of Armageddon.

5. Israel's Favorable Location. Let us look at the map on page 69 and notice the location of Canaan among the other nations or "families" of the world. This shows the inhabited world at the time Israel became a nation. From it you will see that God chose for His people a central location. He placed them at the very heart of the world, at the head of the Great Sea, where the traffic of all the nations was continually passing — the world's natural highway not only for social relations but for war and for commerce.

As the heart is the center of life for the body, sending its life-giving stream to all its parts, so Israel was to be the great spiritual life-giving center of the world. Through every avenue leading away from this chosen nation, spiritual heart throbs were to send streams of salvation to the perishing. And God in heaven above would be the never-failing source of Israel's supply. If she was faithful to her trust, every plan and every ambition of Israel would be prompted and controlled by the one great purpose of giving to others the good news of salvation through the Redeemer to come.

6. Natural Barriers and Their Value. While seemingly exposed to danger from unfriendly nations, the land of Canaan was protected on all sides by natural barriers. On the north the mountains of Lebanon separated it from Syria, on the east and the south were deserts separating it from Babylon and Egypt, and on the west was the Great Sea. By these natural barriers God not only protected His people from warlike invasions, but He separated them from the heathen nations around them, lest by intimate association they be drawn into idolatrous practices, and thus become unfitted for their sacred calling.

7. Association with the World. As a further safeguard against the dangers of familiar association with the world, the Lord strictly commanded Israel not to marry among these outside nations. He knew full well that if in the home either the father or the mother was an idolater, the children of that home would perhaps never gain a clear understanding of the true God of heaven and of His plan to save them. The sins of the parents would thus be visited upon their children, and many of these would be lost. It was to save both the parents and the children from such a calamity that God so frequently emphasized the danger of this sin. And it is for the same

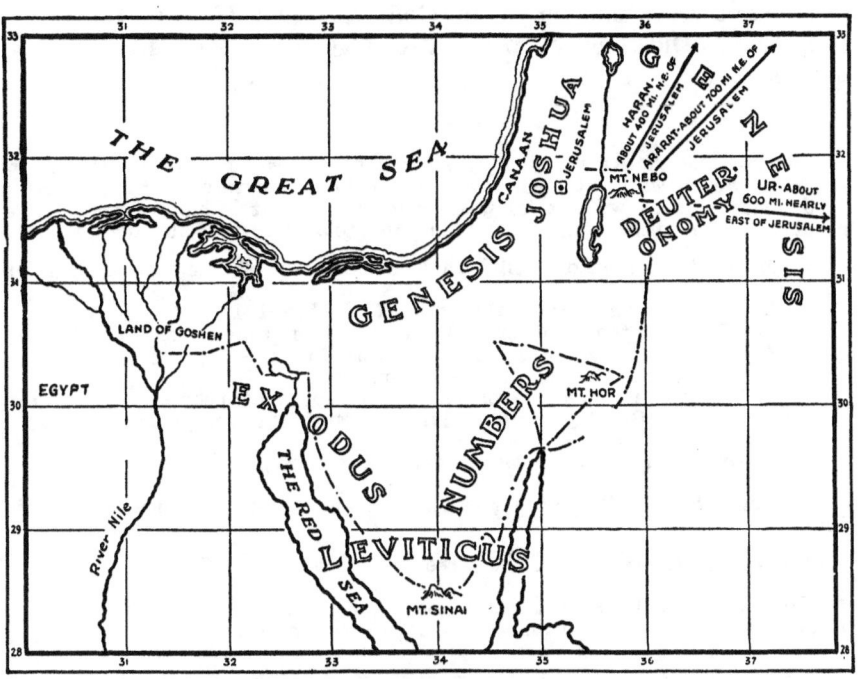

Map showing where the events of the first six Bible books occurred:

Genesis tells the *beginnings* of God's work in this world.
Exodus tells the *going out* from Egypt.
Leviticus records the *laws* given at Sinai.
Numbers records the *numbering* of the tribes.
Deuteronomy gives Moses' *second* statement of the laws.
Joshua (which means savior) tells of the possession of Canaan.

reason that our heavenly Father to-day says to His people, *"Be ye not unequally yoked together with unbelievers: for what fellowship hath righteousness with unrighteousness? and what communion hath light with darkness? and what concord hath Christ with Belial? or what part hath he that believeth with an infidel? and what agreement hath the temple of God with idols?" Did the people obey God? Did they faithfully discharge their responsibility? We shall see.

How to Study: As you read your lesson (instead of afterward), find on the map the places mentioned. Form the habit of never allowing yourself to read about a place without knowing exactly where it is on the map. After reading the lesson through, you should be able to answer the following questions:

1. What did the Lord tell Joshua is the secret of true success? Joshua 1:8.
2. When did Israel cross the Jordan? Joshua 4:19.
3. What was the condition of the river at this time? Joshua 3:15.
4. How wide a path was made across Jordan?
5. For what is the plain of Esdraelon noted?
6. Why was Canaan a favorable location for God's people?
7. How did God try to guard Israel from danger and evil?

Map Work: On the map locate Adam; Esdraelon.

Memory Work: Memorize Joshua 1:8, and enter reference on "Service Flag."

Use of Concordance: Find the verse quoted under topic 7.

For Your Workbook: On outline map No. 1—"The World in Bible Times," locate the nation Israel, outlining the space with crayola.

12. CHRISTIAN EDUCATION A PART OF GOD'S PLAN
Under the Judges — About 1500 to 1000 B. C.

"When the children of Israel cried unto the Lord, the Lord raised them up a deliverer." Judges 3:15.

1. The Experience of Israel. The experience of Israel during the time from Joshua to the anointing of King Saul was a very

---

References Used: Ed., pp. 46-50; Judges 2:7, 10, 12, 14; 3:6; 10:13-16; Ps. 78:37-39; Acts 13:20; 1 Sam. 3:9; Luke 2:49.

checkered one. "The people served the Lord all the days of Joshua, and all the days of the elders that outlived Joshua, who had seen all the great works of the Lord, that He did for Israel." Then "there arose another generation after them, which knew not the Lord, nor yet the works which He had done for Israel. . . . And they forsook the Lord God of their fathers, . . . and followed . . . the gods of the people that were round about them." As a result, "they could not any longer stand before their enemies." In spite of the instruction they had received, Israel "took their daughters to be their wives, and gave their daughters to their sons, and served their gods." As disobedience is sure to bring its unhappy reward, so because of this frequently repeated sin, Israel again and again was brought under the oppression of the surrounding nations.

2. The Work of the Judges. In their distress the people called upon God for deliverance. And God "being full of compassion, forgave their iniquity, and destroyed them not: yea, many a time turned He His anger away. . . . For He remembered that they were but flesh." To free them from the net in which they had become entangled, He raised up judges. It was the duty of these judges to arouse the people to a sense of their sins; and when they had truly repented, so that they could once more be trusted with the sacred work that had been given them to do, God brought deliverance from the enemy. The judges, of whom there were fifteen in all, were the spiritual teachers and leaders of Israel "until Samuel the prophet." During these years Israel so fully forgot the purpose of her existence as a nation and so completely wandered away from God that at six different times she was brought under the oppression of surrounding nations.

3. The Results of Disobedience. Each time that God delivered the Israelites from their oppressor, the heathen learned something of the mighty Deliverer. But Israel lost the blessing and the strength that come from loyal service. Satan wickedly rejoiced in their loss, and in the unhappiness and weakness that he was thus able to bring upon them, and in their consequent unfitness for future service. No wonder that on one occasion God said to them: "Ye have forsaken Me, and served other gods: wherefore I will deliver you no more. Go and cry unto the gods which ye have chosen; let them deliver you in the time of your tribulation." No wonder, either, that a God whose very name is mercy and compassion should, when Israel repented, have His soul "grieved for the misery of Israel," and send them a deliverer. What an opportunity for the angels to behold the long-suffering disposition of the Father!

4. The Children's Part in God's Plan. Samuel was the last of the judges. He was dedicated to the Lord even before his birth. When he was twelve years of age the Lord called to him, and Samuel responded, "Speak, Lord; for Thy servant heareth." And this was Samuel's attitude all the days of his long life of devoted service. As God used the child Samuel, so He will use other children no older than he to do a great work for Him. Moses was but twelve years of age when he was called to stand for God in the court of Pharaoh; and it was when only twelve years of age that Jesus said to His mother, "Wist ye not that I must be about My Father's business?"

5. Schools Established by Samuel. As Samuel grew to manhood, he saw the Hebrew youth drifting into the world and learning the ways of the heathen. Then God directed him to establish church schools where the youth could be taught from the scrolls of the prophets, and where they could be trained as teachers and missionaries to carry to the world the gospel of God's great plan. These schools were called the schools of the prophets, because God chose prophets to be the teachers. The students were called sons of the prophets. The first of these schools was located up in the mountains four or five miles north of Jerusalem, at a place called Ramah. The prophet Samuel, whose home was in this place, was the founder of these schools and one of the first teachers.

"The chief subjects of study in these schools were the law of God, with the instruction given to Moses, sacred history, sacred music, and poetry." The students were also taught the wonderful works of God as seen in nature about them, and in this way they learned lessons of God's power, His goodness and wisdom. Through a study of the sanctuary they learned of the Lamb of God, the great Sacrifice for sin. They were also taught how to pray and to exercise faith, and how to understand and obey the teachings of the Holy Spirit.

6. Church Schools in the Last Days. In these last days God has instructed His people to establish church schools similar to the schools of the prophets, where the children of His people may be taught His plan, and be prepared to do their part in finishing His work in the earth. We are told that "when heavenly intelligences see that men are no longer permitted to present the truth, the Spirit of God will come upon the children, and they will do a work in the proclamation of the truth which the older workers cannot do, because their way will be hedged up." When that time comes, God will use you, boys and girls, if like Samuel and Moses, you are led by His Spirit, and if you are prepared to give from the Bible an intelligent reason for your hope in God. Now is your time to prepare.

How to Study: After studying the lesson through, write six questions that can be answered by what is given under topics 4, 5, and 6. What sin so often caused Israel's captivity? Why?

Memory Work: Memorize 2 Corinthians 6: 14, 15. When this reference is entered on your "Service Flag," the rim of the crown should be complete.

Chapters to Remember: The life of Samuel is told in 1 Samuel. Chapter 3 tells about the Lord's calling him. The schools of the prophets are referred to in 1 Samuel 19: 20; also in 2 Kings 6: 1-7. Read about the schools of the prophets in your Bible.

Concordance Time Drill: See how many of these verses you can find in three minutes. The key word is starred.
1. Be ye not unequally *yoked together with unbelievers.
2. Be *strong and of a good courage.
3. The priests . . . stood *firm on dry ground.
4. The land had *rest from war.
5. He . . . *forgave their iniquity.
6. *Wist ye not that I must be about My Father's business?

For Your Workbook: On diagram No. 1 locate the time when Israel was ruled by judges. This period of time ended at the death of Samuel, the last of the judges. For date, see 1 Samuel 25:1, margin.

13. ISRAEL THE LIGHT OF THE WORLD
Under the United Kingdom — About B. C. 1000

"The Lord God shall give unto Him the throne of His father David: and He shall reign over the house of Jacob forever." Luke 1: 32, 33.

1. From Judges to Kings. When Israel was organized into a nation, God was their King. First through Moses and Aaron, then

---
References Used: P. K., pp. 35-46; Ed., pp. 153, 154; 1 Sam. 8: 5, 19, 20; Acts 13: 22; 2 Sam. 7: 13; Luke 1: 32, 33; 1 Kings 3: 5-12; 4: 34; 10: 6-9, 24; 11: 3, 4, 7, 8; 2 Chron. 6: 32, 33; 7: 12; Isa. 56: 7.

through Joshua, and later through judges of His own selection, He led and instructed His people. As Israel from time to time fell under the power of the nations around them, marrying among them, adopting their ways, and worshiping their gods, they gradually lost a sense of the terrible sin of apostasy, until to a large extent they seemed to have forgotten the purpose of God in making them a nation. They saw the wealth and ambition, the pomp and display, of the kings of these nations, and they desired to be like them.

2. Israel Demands a King. "Make us a king to judge us like all the nations," Israel demanded of Samuel. It was a sad day for Israel when their greatest ambition was to be like the people around them. Samuel remonstrated with them. He told them the dangers of such a departure from the Lord's plan. "Nevertheless the people refused to obey the voice of Samuel; and they said, Nay; but we will have a king over us; that we also may be like all the nations." This was equivalent to denying that God was their King. Although by this course the people had rejected God, yet He did not reject them. He yielded to their demand and gave them a king. God's ways are always the best ways. Still, God never compels us to accept His ways. He often permits us to have our own way, so that through the bitter experience that follows, we may see our folly and repent and learn to trust Him.

3. The First Three Kings. From the time that Israel demanded a king, during a little more than a century, three kings ruled over Israel — Saul, David, and Solomon — each reigning forty years. Israel was still the people of God, and God was still the real Head of the nation. Each of these kings was selected by Him; and so long as they looked to Him for wisdom and direction, He worked for them. At first Saul was humble and God used him; but when he refused to be guided by the Lord and was determined to rule as an independent monarch, he was rejected from being king. Then David was anointed king. The constant purpose of King David's life was to serve and obey God. Though he did not always do right, yet his repentance was humble and sincere. For this reason and because of his high and noble principles, God calls him "a man after Mine own heart."

The throne of David was a type of the throne of Christ, the King of the new earth. This was what God meant when He said, "I will stablish the throne of His kingdom forever." Just before

Jesus was born, the angel who talked with Mary referred to this promise, saying, "The Lord God shall give unto Him the throne of His father David: and He shall reign over the house of Jacob forever." Solomon followed David, and it was during his reign that the kingdom of Israel reached the height of its prosperity.

4. Solomon's Humility. Solomon came to the throne with a humble and teachable spirit — the spirit that every true child of God must have in order to fill his place in God's plan. When the Lord appeared to him in a dream, and said, "Ask what I shall give thee," King Solomon answered:

"O Lord my God, . . . I am but a little child: I know not how to go out or come in. . . . Give therefore Thy servant an understanding heart to judge Thy people, that I may discern between good and bad: for who is able to judge this Thy so great a people? And the speech pleased the Lord, that Solomon had asked this thing. And God said unto him, Because thou hast asked this thing, and hast not asked for thyself long life; neither hast asked riches for thyself, nor hast asked the life of thine enemies; but hast asked for thyself understanding to discern judgment; behold, I have done according to thy words: lo, I have given thee a wise and an understanding heart; so that there was none like thee before thee, neither after thee shall any arise like unto thee." What a revelation this must have been to the universe! What a denial of the falsehood Satan told Eve, that it was God's intention to deprive His children of wisdom!

5. The Temple of Solomon. One of the greatest events in the reign of King Solomon was the building of the magnificent temple of God called Solomon's temple. It was erected on Mount Moriah, the very place where, centuries before, Abraham had offered Isaac. It was a palatial building, garnished with precious stones, surrounded by spacious courts, and lined with carved cedar and burnished gold. In the dedicatory prayer, which Solomon offered, he prayed not only for Israel but for the stranger. "Moreover concerning the stranger, which is not of Thy people Israel, but is come from a far country for Thy great name's sake; . . . if they come and pray in this house; then hear Thou from the heavens, . . . that all people of the earth may know Thy name, and fear Thee." In a night vision God appeared to Solomon and said, "I have heard thy prayer." Had Israel remained true to God, this glorious building would have stood forever, not only as a sign of God's favor to His chosen people, but as "an house of prayer for all people."

6. The Fame of Solomon. Because of Solomon's humility and devotion to God, his fame extended far and near, reaching even to Sheba, a country far to the south in Arabia, on the shores of the Red Sea. When the queen of Sheba heard of Solomon's unparalleled wisdom, she determined to visit the king and judge for herself. The queen asked Solomon many hard questions; but to all these, he

"All the earth sought to Solomon, to hear his wisdom, which God had put in his heart."

was able to give her satisfactory answers. And when she saw his wisdom, his power and riches, she said to the king: "It was a true report that I heard in mine own land of thy acts and of thy wisdom. Howbeit I believed not the words, until I came, and mine eyes had seen it: and, behold, the half was not told me: thy wisdom and prosperity exceedeth the fame which I heard. . . . Blessed be the Lord thy God, which delighted in thee, to set thee on the throne of Israel: because the Lord loved Israel forever, therefore made He thee king, to do judgment and justice."

7. Israel the Light of the World. The queen of Sheba recognized God as the source of Solomon's greatness, and as she returned to her own land she took with her a knowledge of His wisdom and power and justice. Nor was Sheba the only country into which was carried a knowledge of the God of Israel, for "there came of all people to hear the wisdom of Solomon, from all kings of the earth, which had heard of his wisdom." Through King Solomon the name of God was greatly honored, and for a time Israel seemed destined to become what God designed them to be, the light of the world. How easy it is for God to send a knowledge of Himself throughout the world when our greatest desire is, not riches nor honor, but "an understanding heart" that we may do His work!

8. Solomon's Last Days. What a record of loyalty to God Solomon might have left, had he remained true! But "his heart was not perfect . . . as was the heart of David his father." Contrary to the Lord's direct instructions, Solomon took wives of the nations about him, and they "turned away his heart," so that at last he built "high places" or temples "for all his strange wives, which burnt incense and sacrificed unto their gods." What a pity that a reign begun so gloriously should be thus marred! But we are told that "in later years, turning wearied and thirsting from earth's broken cisterns, Solomon returned to drink at the fountain of life."

How to Study: After studying the whole lesson, answer the following:

Why did Israel demand a king? What made David a man after God's own heart? Of what was the throne of David a type? How did Solomon's wisdom extend a knowledge of God? In Solomon's prayer at the dedication of the temple, how did he express his desire that those who knew not God might learn of Him?

Memory Work: Review Joshua 1: 8 and 2 Corinthians 6: 14, 15.

Chapters to Remember: 1 Kings 10 tells of the visit of the queen of Sheba.

For Class Discussion: What book in the Bible records the deeds of Saul? What books record the deeds of David? In what books are the deeds of Solomon found? What poetical book in the Bible was written by David? What three were written by Solomon? What does the name Solomon mean? 1 Chron. 22: 9, margin. Why was this name given him?

14. THE NATION'S FAILURE TO CARRY OUT GOD'S PLAN

Under the Divided Kingdom — About 1000 to 606 B. C.

"The Lord rejected . . . Israel, . . . and delivered them into the hand of spoilers, . . . because they obeyed not the voice of the Lord their God."
2 Kings 17:20; 18:12.

1. Satan's Next Plan to Defeat Israel. The prosperity of Israel must have been a great annoyance to Satan. His efforts to overpower the nation by sending against them the warlike tribes that surrounded them had not succeeded very well. It was evident to these tribes that a power mightier than human was working for Israel. They could not help seeing that "King Solomon exceeded all the kings of the earth for riches and for wisdom." Therefore, instead of overthrowing Israel, "all the earth sought to Solomon, to hear his wisdom, which God had put in his heart. And they brought every man his present, vessels of silver, and vessels of gold, and garments, and armor, and spices, horses, and mules, a rate year by year."

Having been unable to defeat Israel by foes without, Satan next stirred up trouble within. In this he was more successful, for

> "Of all the foes we have to meet,
> None so apt to turn our feet,
> None betray us into sin,
> Like the foes we have within."

The desire in the heart of Israel to be like the nations around them led them to follow Solomon's sinful example. And they took to themselves wives from among the surrounding nations,— the subtle sin that God had so emphatically warned them against. This worldly association resulted, not in turning the heathen away from their sinful practices, but in Israel's adopting their practices, worshiping their gods, and disregarding God's law.

2. The Kingdom Divided. Because Israel deserted God, weakness and division entered the kingdom, and open revolt soon followed. The ten tribes located at the north set up a government of their own and chose their own king. This was called the kingdom

---

References Used: P. K., pp. 96, 407, 408, 453; 1 Kings 10:23-25; 12:28; 16:19; 2 Kings 17:15-18; 24:13, 14; 2 Chron. 34:3, 7, 27-31; Lam. 3:27; Jer. 36:2, 3, 23; Dan. 1:1, 2; Jer. 17:24-27.

of Israel, and the city of Samaria became its capital. The other two tribes — Judah and Benjamin — also had a separate government and king. They were called the kingdom of Judah. Jerusalem was their capital. This period in the history of Israel is known as the Divided Kingdom. "With the rending of the kingdom . . . the glory of Israel began to depart, never again to be regained in its fullness."

3. The Kingdom of Israel. The history of the kingdom of Israel was one long record of sin and apostasy. It began with Jeroboam, the first king, who, desiring to keep the people from attending the feasts at Jerusalem, made two calves of gold, and said to the people, "It is too much for you to go up to Jerusalem: behold thy gods, O Israel, which brought thee up out of the land of Egypt." One of these images he placed in the southern part of his kingdom, at Bethel; the other he put in Dan, at the extreme north. Of the nineteen kings who reigned in Israel, only one, Jehu, made any determined effort to abolish idolatry. The others all walked "in the way of Jeroboam, and in his sin which he did, to make Israel to sin."

4. The Religion of the Court. The worship of Baal — or Baalim, which is the plural of Baal — became the religion of the court and the people. Some of the sacrifices offered to these gods were human beings. The priests danced around the altar and shouted frantically and cut themselves with knives to attract the attention and secure the favor of the god. The worship of Baal was also connected with sun worship, the most ancient and general as well as the most vile and degrading form of heathen religion. The purpose of Satan in Baal worship was to turn the mind away from the Creator to the worship of things created. Christ called this god Beelzebub, the prince of the devils.

5. God's Care for Israel. But through all their apostasy God's mercy and forbearance did not fail. In order if possible to save His people from the path of ruin on which they had started, He chose prophets, through whom He sent messages of warning and instruction. Elijah and Elisha were among the earliest of these prophets. Isaiah was one of the last of the prophets sent to Israel, and Isaiah was martyred by the people whom he tried to help.

6. Israel Taken Captive. A few among Israel listened to the messages of the prophets and turned to the Lord, but as a kingdom Israel continued to follow "the heathen that were round about them. . . . And they left all the commandments of the Lord their God, and made them molten images, . . . and served Baal. And they caused their sons and their daughters to pass through the fire, and used divination and enchantments, and sold themselves to do evil in the sight of the Lord. . . . Therefore the Lord . . . removed them out of His sight: there was none left but the tribe of Judah only." After a terrible siege lasting three years, all Israel was taken captive by the king of Assyria, and carried away out of their own land to Assyria. Some of the captives were left near Haran, the place where, over a thousand years before, Abraham had buried his father, and where had been the old home of Rebekah and Rachel. Others were carried farther east and placed in cities of the Medes. Nineveh, against which Jonah prophesied, was the capital of this same Assyria.

7. The Kingdom of Judah. Twenty kings occupied the throne of David and reigned over the kingdom of Judah. Eight of these "did that which was right in the eyes of the Lord." Under their rule the kingdom prospered, and a knowledge of the living God was extended to the surrounding nations. Because of the righteous lives of these good kings, the kingdom of Judah continued for more than a century after Israel had been taken captive.

8. The Good King Josiah. Josiah, the last of the good kings, was but eight years old when he began to reign. "While he was yet young"— when he was sixteen years old —"he began to seek after the God of David his father;" and when he was twenty years of age, he "cut down all the idols throughout all the land." Then he began the work of repairing the temple of Solomon, which had suffered from years of neglect. One day, while the carpenters were at work, one of the priests discovered a book which proved to be the Book of God that Moses had written. The Book was carried to Josiah, and for the first time in his life the king listened to the reading of the Scriptures — the laws that God had given to His people.

9. Josiah's Reform. When the king saw how Judah had failed to obey God, he rent his clothes in sorrow, and wept before God. But he did more than weep. He "gathered together . . . the priests, and the Levites, and all the people, great and small: and he read in *their* ears all the words of the Book . . . that was found in the house of the Lord." Standing in his place before the people, he promised the Lord that with all his heart he would obey the words that were written in the Book. Then all that were present took the same stand.

10. The Prophet Jeremiah. During the reign of Josiah, God sent many messages through the prophet Jeremiah. Like Samuel, Jeremiah was dedicated from his birth. The divine call came when he was still but a youth. In childhood he had been faithful in little things, and in him God "saw one who would be true to his trust, and who would stand for the right against great opposition." It was Jeremiah who wrote, "It is good for a man that he bear the yoke

One day, while the carpenters were at work, one of the priests discovered a book, which proved to be the Book of God that Moses had written.

in his youth." For forty years Jeremiah faithfully delivered the messages of warning and instruction which God gave him. He told the people that because they had disobeyed God's law and desecrated the Sabbath, Judah was to be taken captive by the king of Babylon. Nevertheless, because Josiah obeyed God, the captivity did not come while he lived.

11. Messages of Hope. Through Jeremiah the Lord sent not only warnings, but messages of hope and comfort. Though the people were to be taken captive, the Lord promised that if while in these strange lands they would be true to Him, He would bring them back to Jerusalem and cause them to dwell safely. These promises brought hope and courage to homes where the word of God was reverenced. Parents who believed the messages of Jeremiah, faithfully taught their children; and many of the children were deeply stirred and gave their hearts to God. Daniel was among the Hebrew children who were thus instructed, and he with other Hebrew lads determined that no matter what came they would obey God.

12. The Roll Written by Jeremiah. After the good king Josiah died, because Jeremiah continued to give the messages of God, he was at last put into prison. Then the Lord said to him, "Take thee a roll of a book, and write therein all the words that I have spoken unto thee against Israel, and against Judah. . . . It may be that

The king seized the roll, and in a fit of anger "cut it with the penknife, and cast it into the fire."

the house of Judah will hear; . . . that they may return every man from his evil way; that I may forgive their iniquity." But when the written message was read before Jehoiakim, the king who was then ruling, he seized the roll, and in a fit of anger "cut it with the penknife, and cast it into the fire that was on the hearth, until all the roll was consumed." By this act he cast away his last opportunity for salvation. From this time, the Lord no longer held in check the king of Babylon.

13. Judah Taken Captive. In response to the command of God, Jeremiah rewrote the roll; but scarcely had it been written when the prophecy it contained began to be fulfilled. "In the third year of the reign of Jehoiakim king of Judah came Nebuchadnezzar king of Babylon unto Jerusalem, and besieged it. And the Lord gave Jehoiakim king of Judah into his hand, with part of the vessels of the house of God; . . . and he brought the vessels into the treasure house of his god." "With mourning and sadness" devoted Jews "secreted the ark in a cave, where it was to be hidden from the

Had Israel remained true to God, this glorious building would have stood forever, not only as a sign of God's favor to His chosen people, but as "an house of prayer for all people."

people of Israel and Judah because of their sins, and was to be no more restored to them." It was at this time that Daniel, then a lad of about eighteen years, Hananiah, Mishael, and Azariah were taken captive.

A little later Nebuchadnezzar carried away the rest of the "treasures of the house of the Lord, and the treasures of the king's house, and cut in pieces all the vessels of gold which Solomon king of Israel had made in the temple of the Lord. . . . And he carried away . . . all the princes, and all the mighty men of valor, even ten thousand captives, and all the craftsmen and smiths: none remained, save the poorest sort of the people of the land." Finally the walls were broken down, Jerusalem was burned, and the beautiful temple destroyed. And all this was the result of rejecting the word of God, which alone could have saved the people and their home.

Thus was fulfilled the prophecy of Jeremiah: "It shall come to pass, if ye diligently hearken unto Me, saith the Lord, to bring in no burden through the gates of this city on the Sabbath day, but hallow the Sabbath day, to do no work therein; then . . . this city shall remain forever. . . . But if ye will not hearken unto Me to hallow the Sabbath day, . . . then will I kindle a fire in the gates thereof, and it shall devour the palaces of Jerusalem, and it shall not be quenched."

Was God right when He told Israel that their demand for a king would be their ruin?

Map Work: Locate the kingdom of Israel, the kingdom of Judah, and the capital of each. Locate the two cities where Jeroboam placed the golden calves. Locate the two countries to which Israel was taken captive. Locate the capital of Assyria; of Babylon.

For Your Workbook: On diagram No. 1 locate the time of the divided monarchy. At the close of whose reign did this period begin? With what event did it close?

For Class Discussion: What two books in the Bible did Jeremiah write? What one did Isaiah write? Ezekiel? Jonah? In what books are the experiences of Elijah and Elisha recorded? What three books record the history of the divided monarchy? During the four hundred years covered by this lesson, a number of the minor prophets gave warnings and messages to God's people. We may read these messages in the books of the Bible that bear their names. Which books were written by the minor prophets? Who were the four major prophets? What five books were written by them?

REVIEW

Test Questions and Exercises: The numbers refer to previous lessons.

10. **From Sinai to Canaan.** What Bible scrolls were written before Israel entered Canaan? What else did the nation have to help them in their missionary work? On diagram No. 5 point out the order of march. On diagram No. 1 point out the 430 years' sojourn. What event marks the beginning of this period? the end? What condition among the Canaanites hindered God from settling His nation in Canaan earlier? What condition in Israel hindered Him still longer? How much longer? Why was Moses not permitted to enter the promised land?

11. In Canaan. By what miracle did God first reveal Himself to the nations of Canaan? What was the effect? Why were some of the wicked nations left in Canaan? Show from the map how Israel's location was favorable to giving the gospel to the world. In what ways was it favorable to Israel's own safety? What instruction did God give from the first regarding association with the heathen? *2 Cor. 6: 14, 15. What did the Lord tell Joshua is the secret of success? *Joshua 1: 8.

12. Under the Judges. What sin brought Israel into bondage to the nations around? What was the effect of this sin on Israel? What was the effect of their deliverance on the nations? What three children were called at the age of twelve to be missionaries? Describe the schools that Samuel established. What were these schools for? What schools in our day should be like them?

13. The United Kingdom. Why was it wrong for Israel to want a king? What three kings ruled during the united kingdom? What did God say about King David? about his throne? Of what was David's throne a type? How fully was a knowledge of God carried to the world during the reign of Solomon? What sin marred Solomon's reign?

14. The Divided Kingdom. Describe Israel's captivity, giving cause, by whom taken captive, and to what places. How many kings reigned over Judah? How many of these were good kings? Who was the last of the good kings? Tell about his experience with the Bible. What work did Jeremiah do? What was the result of his work in the homes of some of the people? What act of Jehoiakim finally brought the captivity of Judah? What four lads were taken captive at this time? By whom? Where? In what year? What prophecy was fulfilled by this captivity?

Chapter Drill: See how quickly you can find the chapters that tell about —

1. The flood
2. The Ten Commandments
3. Tower of Babel
4. Call of Abraham
5. Faith chapter
6. Offering of Isaac
7. Jacob's dream
8. Wrestling with the Angel
9. Moses' birth
10. The burning bush
11. The ten plagues
12. The first Passover
13. The sanctuary
14. The day of atonement
15. Samuel called
16. Schools of the prophets

Book Drill: In what Bible book or books are the following found?

1. Life of Samuel
2. Life of Saul
3. Life of David
4. Life of Solomon
5. Poetry of David
6. Writings of Solomon
7. Writings of Jeremiah
8. Moses' farewell sermons
9. The laws given to Israel
10. Journey from Egypt to Canaan
11. Writings of minor prophets
12. Writings of major prophets
13. The divided kingdom
14. Lives of the patriarchs

Memory Verses for Period Two: Jude 14; Rom. 8: 28; Heb. 11: 24-26; 1 Cor. 10: 11; Ps. 45: 13; Rom. 12: 1; 1 Tim. 5: 24; Joshua 1: 8; 2 Cor. 6: 14, 15.

Third Period—Chapter IV

OUTLINE OF CHAPTER IV

606 to 536 B. C.

Topics —

Under Nebuchadnezzar   Daniel

    God Honored by Daniel Because of Christian Education ... 1
    Daniel Honored by God .... } 2
    God's Plan Revealed to the World's King .... }
    God's Power Published to All the World 3
    A Victory for God 4
    Review

Under Belshazzar

    Daniel's First Vision of the Great Controversy ....
    The Angel's Explanation of the Four Beasts ....
    The Angel's Explanation of the Little Horn .... } 7
    The 1260 Years of Papal Persecution ....
    A Glimpse into Heaven's Great Court Room ....
    Examination of Cases ....
    Review
    Daniel's Second Vision of the Great Controversy .... } 8
    Satan's Masterpiece of Deception .... }
    Review
    The Downfall of Satan's World Government 5

Under Darius

    The Plot to Destroy Daniel 6
    Gabriel Sent to Answer Daniel's Prayer .... } 9
    Gabriel's Explanation of the 2300 Days .... }
    Review

Under Cyrus

    Preparations to Return to Jerusalem 10
    The Second Coming of Christ Foretold .... } 12
    Daniel's Work Ended .... }

Under Darius and Artaxerxes

    The Nation's Second Opportunity for Service
    Review

CHAPTER IV

God's Plan Worked Out in Captivity

1. GOD HONORED BY DANIEL BECAUSE OF CHRISTIAN EDUCATION

Daniel in the King's School — Daniel 1

"The fear of the Lord is the beginning of wisdom: a good understanding have all they that do His commandments." Ps. 111:10.

1. Has God's Plan Failed? Never had Satan's success seemed more certain. Babylon, the place chosen by him years before as the capital of his kingdom, now ruled the world, having conquered not only Judah but Syria, Assyria, and Egypt. Satan greatly rejoiced because God's missionary nation was, as he thought, finally at an end. It is true that Israel's home was destroyed, the beautiful temple was in ruins, and the people were scattered throughout different parts of the world. The prophets also were widely separated,— Ezekiel was among the captives by the river Chebar, Daniel had been taken to Babylon, and Jeremiah was left in Judah.

But did God's work stop? By no means. As the seed rudely scattered by the wind at last takes root and produces plants in many new places, so God would use His loyal, scattered children to hold up the light of salvation in all parts of the world, and make known His great plan. The book of Daniel is a wonderful story of how God caused a knowledge of Himself to be carried to all the nations of the world even while His people were captives in a strange land.

2. Daniel's Early Home Training (1:3, 4). Nebuchadnezzar recognized Daniel and his companions as "children of the king's seed, and of the princes." Their clear complexion and bright eyes testified to the fact that they had lived lives of purity and strict temperance. In the simplicity of their Judean home, they had been

---
References Used: Ed., p. 262; Jer. 40:1-6; Eze. 1:1, 3.

taught by their parents to observe the habits of health. Therefore they were "children in whom was no blemish, but well-favored." At their mother's knee these youth had been taught that the fear of the Lord is the beginning of wisdom. From the book of Moses and the parchment scrolls of the later prophets, they had studied the history of Israel, and they understood God's plan for the world. It was this that fitted them later in life to be statesmen of the highest order. From the great book of nature they had become familiar

IN CAPTIVITY. "How shall we sing the Lord's song in a strange land?"

with natural science and with the God of science. Therefore the king found them "skillful in all wisdom, and cunning in knowledge, and understanding science." It was these qualities, together with a determination of purpose to be true to God and to their home instruction, that gave them "ability to stand in the king's palace."

3. The Test of Loyalty (1: 5, 8-13). Nebuchadnezzar treated these captives not only kindly but with liberality. Recognizing their superior qualities, he decided to place them in the royal school and train them to act a part in the affairs of the government. "And the king appointed them a daily provision of the king's meat, and of the wine which he drank: so nourishing them three years, that at the end thereof they might stand before the king."

This was a time of test to these lads. Seated probably at the same table with Babylonian youth who had no scruples against eating meat offered to idols or drinking wine, would these lads resist the temptation and stand true to their early home training? What if the other boys should laugh at their odd ideas and their peculiar religion! But Daniel remembered the prayers of his mother and how she had taught him that he was to be a light for God when placed under the influences of heathen Babylon. He did not hesitate. He "purposed in his heart that he would not defile himself with the portion of the king's meat, nor with the wine which he drank." And his companions stood with him in this resolve.

Then Daniel "requested of the prince of the eunuchs that he might not defile himself. . . . And the prince of the eunuchs said unto Daniel, I fear my lord the king, who hath appointed your meat and your drink: for why should he see your faces worse liking than the children which are of your sort? then shall ye make me endanger my head to the king." Daniel did not stubbornly refuse to obey; but he earnestly urged: "Prove thy servants, I beseech thee, ten days; and let them give us pulse to eat, and water to drink. Then let our countenances be looked upon before thee, and the countenance of the children that eat of the portion of the king's meat: and as thou seest, deal with thy servants."

4. The Victory and Its Results (1: 14-20). Melzar could not resist the earnest pleadings of this honest youth whom already he had learned to love, and whose conscientious principles he could not help respecting. God honored the noble stand the lads took, "and at the end of ten days their countenances appeared fairer and fatter in flesh than all the children which did eat the portion of the king's meat." The victory was won. They had honored God, and now God honored them. Three times a day, with their faces toward Jerusalem, these youth prayed for wisdom and power. And "God gave them knowledge and skill in all learning and wisdom: and Daniel had understanding in all visions and dreams."

At the end of the three years during which time these youth were to acquire "the learning and the tongue of the Chaldeans," and among other youth, become fitted for royal service, the whole school were brought before Nebuchadnezzar for their final examination. "And among them all was found none like Daniel, Hananiah, Mishael, and Azariah. . . . And in all matters of wisdom and understanding, that the king inquired of them, he found them ten times better than all the magicians and astrologers that were in all his realm." "Therefore stood they before the king."

5. God's Purpose for the Children of To-Day. The life of Daniel and his fellows is an illustration of what God will do for other youth who with their whole heart are steadfast and true to Him. "God's purpose for the children growing up beside our hearths is wider, deeper, higher, than our restricted vision has comprehended. . . . Many a lad of to-day, growing up as did Daniel in his Judean home, studying God's word and His works, and learning the lessons of faithful service, will yet stand in legislative assemblies, in halls of justice, or in royal courts, as a witness for the King of kings."

"Among them all was found none like Daniel, Hananiah, Mishael, and Azariah: therefore stood they before the king."

How to Study: The numbers following the lesson topics refer to verses in Daniel. Read these references in connection with your study. After studying the whole lesson, tell this story from the following outline:

1. Cause of Satan's Joy
    His kingdom rules the world
    God's nation in captivity — Israel's home; temple; people; prophets
2. Daniel's Home Training
    Life of purity and temperance — health habits; results
    Lessons in Bible, history, nature; results of each
    Daniel's determination
3. Test of Loyalty
    At the king's table; the decision
    Ten days' trial; immediate result; later result
4. God's Purpose for the Children of To-day

Map Work: Show from the map that Babylon at this time ruled the world.

Dictionary Work: pulse. What article of food did pulse take the place of?

Memory Work: Memorize Psalms 111: 10, first two parts. Enter this reference in the first star of the middle part of the "crown" on the "Service Flag." Six more memory verses learned will complete this part of the crown.

Chapter to Remember: Daniel 1 tells about Daniel in the royal school at Babylon. Ask your father to read this chapter for family worship.

For Class Discussion: What is a statesman? How did Daniel's study of the Bible and history fit him to be a statesman?

2. DANIEL HONORED BY GOD

God's Wisdom Revealed to "the Wise Men"— Dan. 2: 1-36

"Hath not God made foolish the wisdom of this world? . . . Because the foolishness of God is wiser than men; and the weakness of God is stronger than men." 1 Cor. 1: 20, 25.

1. **The Wise Men of Babylon (2: 2).** During the reign of Nebuchadnezzar, Babylon was the educational center of the world. But this education was filled with heathen ideas. Those who pretended to be able to solve mysteries, reveal secrets, or foretell future events were called "the wise men." Among them were magicians, astrologers, and sorcerers. Magicians were superstitious fortune tellers who pretended to have wonderful things revealed to them by magic. Astrologers studied the stars, from which they pretended to learn future events. Sorcerers pretended to find out mysterious secrets by communicating with the dead. When the king desired to understand the future or to have some mystery explained, he appealed to these so-called wise men. When Daniel and his fellows were graduated from the king's school, they too were classed among the wise men.

2. **The Wise Men Called (2: 1-3).** In the very year that these Hebrew youth finished school and were numbered with the wise men of Babylon, God opened the way for them to teach the heathen about Him. He gave Nebuchadnezzar a remarkable dream, which He used to show the king and his people that the future is known only to the living God, the great I AM. When the king awoke, the dream greatly troubled his mind, yet he could not remember it. Again and again he tried in vain to recall the particulars of the strange dream. So greatly was he troubled that night after night

---

Reference Used: P. K., pp. 491-498.

he could not sleep. At last, in his distress, he called together all classes of the wise men, though Daniel and his fellows for some reason were not called. No doubt God had a hand in Daniel's absence. He would first give the heathen wise men the chance to show the folly of their wisdom, and then through Daniel He would direct their minds to God, the source of all true wisdom. This story illustrates the truth that "the foolishness of God is wiser than men."

3. The Wise Men Condemned to Death (2: 4-13). When the wise men appeared before the king, with cunning flattery they said, "O king, live forever: tell thy servants the dream, and we will show the interpretation." The king was angry. He had expected them to reveal the secret, and they had failed. "The thing is gone from me," he said impatiently. "If ye will not make known unto me the dream, with the interpretation thereof, ye shall be cut in pieces, and your houses shall be made a dunghill. But if ye show the dream, and the interpretation thereof, ye shall receive of me gifts and rewards and great honor."

A second time they asked the king to tell them the dream, with the promise that they would then tell the interpretation. More angry and dissatisfied than before, the king replied: "If ye will not make known unto me the dream, there is but one decree for you: for ye have prepared lying and corrupt words to speak before me, till the time be changed: therefore tell me the dream, and I shall know that ye can show me the interpretation thereof."

In their utter helplessness the wise men responded: "There is not a man upon the earth that can show the king's matter: therefore there is no king, lord, nor ruler, that asked such things. . . . There is none other that can show it before the king, except the gods, whose dwelling is not with flesh." This made the king furious, and the decree went forth that the wise men should be slain.

4. Daniel's Danger and Request (2: 13-16). Then Arioch, the king's captain, sought Daniel and his fellows to be slain. "Daniel answered with counsel and wisdom, . . . Why is the decree so hasty from the king? Then Arioch made the thing known to Daniel." Taking his life in his hands, Daniel ventured into the presence of Nebuchadnezzar, and with calm confidence told the king that if he would give him time he would tell him the dream and its interpretation. God was with Daniel; and the king, influenced by His presence, consented.

5. The Dream Revealed to Daniel (2: 17-24). Daniel at once went to his house, where his companions were, and together they prayed that God would reveal the strange secret. "Then was the secret revealed unto Daniel in a night vision." As the dream and its meaning stood out before Daniel, there came from his lips an

"There is a God in heaven that revealeth secrets, and maketh known to the king Nebuchadnezzar what shall be in the latter days."

outburst of praise and thanksgiving. Going at once to Arioch, he said, "Destroy not the wise men of Babylon: bring me in before the king, and I will show unto the king the interpretation."

6. Daniel Before the King (2: 25-30). No time was lost. In haste Daniel was brought before the king. "Art thou able to make known unto me the dream which I have seen, and the interpretation thereof?" the king asked anxiously. In humility, yet with confidence, Daniel responded: "The secret which the king hath demanded cannot the wise men, the astrologers, the magicians, the soothsayers, show unto the king; but there is a God in heaven that revealeth secrets, and maketh known to the king Nebuchadnezzar what shall be in the latter days. . . . But as for me, this secret is not revealed to me for any wisdom that I have more than any living, but . . . that thou mightest know the thoughts of thy heart."

7. The Dream Related (2:31-36). With intense interest the king listened, as Daniel in straightforward manner continued: "Thou, O king, sawest, and behold a great image. This great image, whose brightness was excellent, stood before thee; and the form thereof was terrible. This image's head was of fine gold, his breast and his arms of silver, his ... thighs of brass, his legs of iron, his feet part of iron and part of clay. Thou sawest till that a stone was cut out without hands, which smote the image upon his feet that were of iron and clay, and brake them to pieces. Then was the iron, the clay, the brass, the silver, and the gold, broken to pieces together, and became like the chaff of the summer threshing floors; and the wind carried them away, that no place was found for them: and the stone that smote the image became a great mountain, and filled the whole earth."

"This is the dream."

" 'This is the dream,' confidently declared Daniel; and the king, listening with closest attention to every particular, knew it was the very dream over which he had been so troubled."

How to Study: Form the habit of referring to the Bible texts given with the lesson topics. Study the lesson through; then copy the seven topics, and from these try to tell the whole story in your own words. Test yourself first on each topic, watching not to omit any important point. Be able to tell accurately every point in the dream.

Dictionary Study: Astrologer (astro-loger). The roots of this word are found in: astronomy, physiology, biology, geology.

Chapter to Remember: Daniel 2 — Nebuchadnezzar's dream of the great image, and Daniel's interpretation.

For Class Discussion: Are there any people in the world to-day like the wise men of Babylon? Who? What shows that Nebuchadnezzar would not tolerate pretense, but that he appreciated honesty? How did Daniel exalt God in this experience? What was the difference between the wisdom of Daniel and that of the other wise men? How does this incident prove that Satan lied to Eve at the tree of knowledge?

3. GOD'S PLAN REVEALED TO THE WORLD'S KING

The Dream Interpreted — Dan. 2: 36-49

"Surely the Lord God will do nothing, but He revealeth His secret unto His servants the prophets." Amos 3: 7.

1. The Purpose of Nebuchadnezzar's Dream. The dream was given to Nebuchadnezzar not only for the purpose of teaching him that God alone can reveal the future, but to impress on his mind the truth that, though he was the king of the world, there is a still greater King than he, One who is above all earthly kings, who "removeth kings, and setteth up kings," and whose kingdom alone shall never end. This dream showed just how long Babylon was to rule the world, and just what kingdoms were to follow to the very end of time. Eight short verses tell the whole story. This is one of the most sublime chapters of history. Is it any wonder that such a dream should so deeply impress the mind of the king?

2. The Head of Gold (2: 37, 38). When Daniel had finished relating the dream, he proceeded at once to tell its wonderful meaning. "Thou, O king, art a king of kings," he said; "for the God of heaven hath given thee a kingdom, power, and strength, and glory. And wheresoever the children of men dwell, the beasts of the field and the fowls of the heaven hath He given into thine hand, and hath made thee ruler over them all. Thou art this head of gold." Can you imagine the feelings of Nebuchadnezzar when he heard this announcement? Yet there was no room for self-exaltation, for Daniel plainly stated that "the God of heaven" had given him the kingdom,

---

Reference Used: D. R. on lesson text.

the power, the strength, and the glory — the God of heaven had made him ruler over all.

Babylon was "the golden kingdom of a golden age." Inspiration itself gives its capital, the city of Babylon, this glowing title: "the glory of kingdoms, the beauty of the Chaldees' excellency." The city was laid out in a perfect square, fifteen miles on each side, inclosed within immense walls. There were fifty streets, twenty-five running each way from wall to wall and crossing at right angles. At the end of each street was an immense gate of solid brass. The grounds were "laid out in luxuriant parks and gardens, interspersed with magnificent dwellings." "Its hanging gardens, rising terrace above terrace, till they equaled in height the walls themselves," were one of the seven wonders of the world. The city contained two royal palaces, one three and a half miles and the other eight miles in circumference. Through the city ran the sparkling waters of the river Euphrates. Along the river banks were walls and gates like those that surrounded the city. The kingdom of Babylon was founded by Nimrod, the great-grandson of Noah, shortly after the flood, near the place where the tower of Babel was begun. From the beginning, it was Satan's plan to have a world empire; and he early designed to make Babylon its capital. This city he patterned after the New Jerusalem, God's capital of the new earth. And now, just as he thought he had succeeded, the Lord through the captive Daniel foretells the fate of this head of gold.

"The interpretation thereof"

3. An Inferior Kingdom (2: 39). "After thee," Daniel continued, "shall arise another kingdom inferior to thee, and another third kingdom of brass, which shall bear rule over all the earth."

Two years after the death of Nebuchadnezzar, a war broke out between the Babylonians and the Medes which finally resulted in the overthrow of the Babylonian kingdom by Darius the Mede, and the

The hanging gardens of Babylon were artificial terraces on which were planted groves of trees, and beautiful shrubs.

setting up of the next world empire, represented in the image by the breast and arms of silver. This kingdom was called Medo-Persia. It began its world reign in the year B. C. 538, only two years before the close of the seventy years' captivity of the Jews. In what respect was Medo-Persia inferior to Babylon? Not in power, for it conquered Babylon; not in extent, for its territory extended far beyond the boundaries of Babylon. It was inferior in wealth and

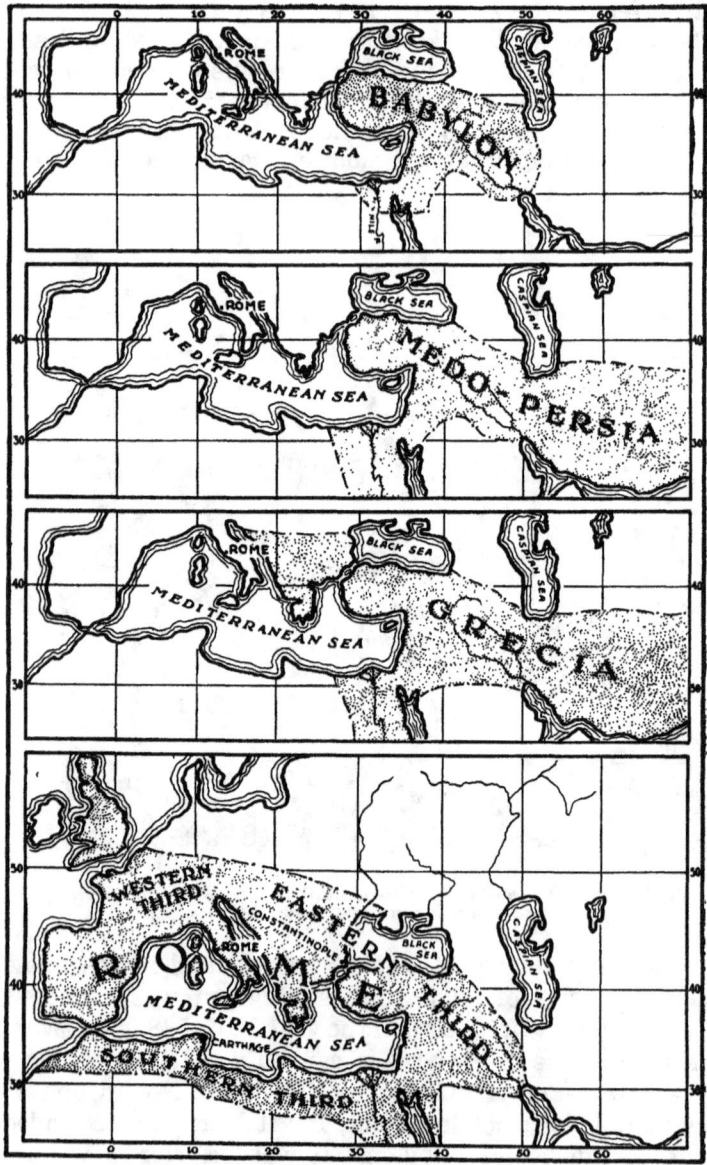

Map showing the four world kingdoms of Daniel's prophecies.

grandeur; it was represented by silver, while Babylon was represented by gold.

4. The Third Kingdom of Brass (2: 39). For about two hundred years, the Medo-Persian kingdom ruled the world. Then Alexander the Great, the king of Greece, overthrew the kingdom, and Grecia, the "third kingdom of brass," began its career as a world kingdom. The decisive battle was fought in the year B. C. 331.

5. The Fourth Kingdom (2: 40). Daniel continues his interpretation, saying: "And the fourth kingdom shall be strong as iron: forasmuch as iron breaketh in pieces and subdueth all things: and as iron that breaketh all these, shall it break in pieces and bruise." The mighty kingdom of Rome succeeded Greece. A great historian, Gibbon, thus describes the conquests of Rome: "The arms of the republic, sometimes vanquished in battle, always victorious in war, advanced with rapid steps to the Euphrates, the Danube, the Rhine, and the ocean; and the images of gold, or silver, or brass, that might serve to represent the nations or their kings, were successively broken by the iron monarchy of Rome." The year B. C. 168 dates the beginning of the Roman Empire as a world power. It included all southern Europe, reaching west into England, south into Africa, and east into Asia. It ruled the world for nearly 500 years after Jesus was born, until 476 A. D.

6. The Iron Kingdom Divided (2: 41-43). But though strong as iron, this kingdom, like all that had preceded, was to crumble and fall. Daniel further explained, saying: "And whereas thou sawest the feet and toes, part of potters' clay, and part of iron, the kingdom shall be divided; but there shall be in it of the strength of the iron, forasmuch as thou sawest the iron mixed with miry clay. And as the toes of the feet were part of iron, and part of clay, so the kingdom shall be partly strong, and partly broken. And whereas thou sawest iron mixed with miry clay, they shall mingle themselves with the seed of men: but they shall not cleave one to another, even as iron is not mixed with clay."

These verses describe the fall of the empire of Rome. The feet and toes of clay and iron represent the divisions of this empire. Among these divisions we may still recognize England, whose people were then called Anglo-Saxons; France, whose people were then called the Franks; Germany, Spain, Italy, Switzerland, and other nations of to-day. Time after time ambitious rulers have endeavored to reunite the parts into another great world power, but the result has always been the ruin of the one who tried it. The last effort in this direction was begun by the German emperor William in 1914. And the world knows the result — the iron would not mix with clay. Emperor William is an outcast, and Germany to-day is a weaker power than before the war. It is not because God has foretold these facts and fixed them so, that the world cannot be united into another world power; but God sees the selfish ambitions in the hearts of men, and He knows that so long as this wickedness exists nations will continue to vie with each other for power, and no one nation can ever be supreme.

7. God's Everlasting Kingdom (2: 44, 45). But the time is soon coming when all who refuse to yield up their selfish hearts for God to cleanse will be destroyed, and only those will remain whose hearts have become fully surrendered to the kingship of King Jesus. Then, with these people as His subjects, "shall the God of heaven set up a kingdom, which shall never be destroyed: and the kingdom shall not be left to other people, but it shall break in pieces and consume all these kingdoms, and it shall stand forever. Forasmuch as thou sawest that the stone was cut out of the mountain without hands, and that it brake in pieces the iron, the brass, the clay, the silver, and the gold; the great God hath made known to the king what shall come to pass hereafter: and the dream is certain, and the interpretation thereof sure."

8. Effect on the King (2: 46, 47). As Daniel finished telling the meaning of the dream, the king, convinced of its truth, and overcome with the thought of its terrible reality, fell upon his face and worshiped Daniel. As soon as he could speak, he exclaimed, "Of a truth it is, that your God is a God of gods, and a Lord of kings, and a revealer of secrets."

9. Daniel and His Fellows Rewarded (2: 48, 49). "Then the king made Daniel a great man, and gave him many great gifts, and made him ruler over the whole province of Babylon, and chief of the governors over all the wise men of Babylon. Then Daniel requested of the king, and he set Shadrach, Meshach, and Abed-nego, over the affairs of the province of Babylon: but Daniel [as the king's representative] sat in the gate of the king." Thus the great

God quietly but certainly brings victory out of what to us looks like hopeless defeat. Already the captivity of God's people, which gave Satan such wicked satisfaction, is being used to promote the work of God. Surely God's plan will finally succeed.

How to Study: As you study the lesson, keep your Bible open to Daniel 2:36-49 for easy reference to verses given with the lesson topics. On map page 180 locate the nations mentioned in each paragraph, before going on to the next paragraph. Notice how each succeeding kingdom grew in extent of territory.

Memory Work: Memorize the names of the four world kingdoms and the year when each came to its end.

For Your Workbook: On outline map No. 3 indicate the four world kingdoms, each in a different color. It would be appropriate to represent Babylon with gilt paper, Medo-Persia with silver paper, Grecia with yellow paper or crayola, and Rome with black paper or crayola.

On diagram No. 1 indicate the time when these four kingdoms ruled the world. Cut out, and mount on diagram No. 6, the great image, then print neatly in the proper places the names of the kingdoms represented, also the dates of the rise and fall of each. The picture for this diagram is in "Bible Workbook" for the eighth grade. So is outline map No. 3.

---

4. GOD'S POWER PUBLISHED TO ALL THE WORLD

In the Fiery Furnace — Daniel 3

"Surely the wrath of man shall praise Thee:
The remainder of wrath shalt Thou restrain."
Ps. 76:10.

1. Nebuchadnezzar's Ambition. Since Daniel told Nebuchadnezzar his dream and gave its interpretation, he and his companions have faithfully performed their duties as officers in the government. They have improved many opportunities to make known the God of heaven. Nebuchadnezzar has often recalled the dream, and especially the words, "Thou art this head of gold." Because prosperity has attended his reign, he is filled with pride and with an ambition that *his* kingdom shall stand forever. He has forgotten God, who plainly told him that his kingdom should not stand forever, but that it would be followed by others.

References Used: P. K., pp. 503-513.

2. Satan's Scheme. Satan was not at all pleased when the king acknowledged the God of heaven as supreme and gave Daniel and his companions places of responsibility in the kingdom. Finally, through the influence of the wise men, he caused the king to represent Babylon by an image *all* of which was gold, and to require all officers in the government to show their loyalty to the king by worshiping it. In this way, Satan still hoped to destroy those who were faithful to God; he still hoped that his dominion would be made secure.

3. Dedicating the Golden Image (3: 1-6). The image which the king made was sixty cubits, or about one hundred feet, high. It was set up in the plain of Dura, and could be seen for miles around. When it was completed, the king called all the rulers of the provinces, and the great men of his kingdom, to come to the dedication. At last the great day came, and all the leading men gathered on the plain of Dura. As they stood before the dazzling statue, gazing at it in wonder and admiration, a herald cried aloud, "To you it is commanded, O people, nations, and languages, that at what time ye hear the sound of the cornet, flute, harp, sackbut, psaltery, dulcimer, and all kinds of music, ye fall down and worship the golden image that Nebuchadnezzar the king hath set up: and whoso falleth not down and worshipeth shall the same hour be cast into the midst of a burning fiery furnace." Soon the music was heard and the rulers bowed in worship before the idol.

4. Three Hebrews Refuse to Worship the Image (3: 8-18). Certain of the wise men who were jealous of the honors that had been bestowed upon Shadrach, Meshach, and Abed-nego, were watching to see what these Jews would do. When they observed that they did not bow before the image, they reported them at once to the king as those who disregarded his commands. In his rage and fury, the king commanded that they be brought before him. "Is it true," he asked; "do not ye serve my gods, nor worship the golden image which I have set up?" Nebuchadnezzar could hardly believe that these who had been so faithful in all their duties in the government would now prove disloyal. He must see it with his own eyes, before he would believe the report. Pointing to the burning furnace, he repeated his command and reminded them of the terrible penalty for disobedience, adding defiantly, "And who is that God that shall deliver you out of my hands?"

"O Nebuchadnezzar," they answered calmly but without hesitating, "we are not careful to answer thee in this matter. If it be so, our God whom we serve is able to deliver us from the burning fiery furnace, and He will deliver us out of thine hand, O king. But if not, be it known unto thee, O king, that we will not serve thy gods, nor worship the golden image which thou hast set up."

5. Cast into the Furnace (3: 19-27). Filled with fury, the king ordered that the furnace be heated seven times hotter than usual. He then "commanded the most mighty men that were in his army

"Lo, I see four men loose, walking in the midst of the fire, and they have no hurt; and the form of the fourth is like the Son of God."

to bind Shadrach, Meshach, and Abed-nego, and to cast them into the burning fiery furnace." The worship of the great image is for a time forgotten. All eyes are turned in the direction of the roaring furnace. The three Hebrews are bound hand and foot. Strong soldiers then pick them up and cast them into the flames. But look! What has happened? The soldiers lie before the furnace — dead! — slain by the exceeding heat of the furnace. The three Hebrews fall down bound into the midst of the burning fiery furnace.

From his royal seat the king looked on. Suddenly his face grew pale. He started from his throne and for a moment looked intently into the flames. Then, turning in alarm to his lords standing near, he exclaimed: "Did not we cast three men bound into the midst of the fire? . . . Lo, I see four men loose, walking in the midst of the fire, and they have no hurt; and the form of the fourth is like the Son of God." Forgetting his own dignity, he rushed as near as possible to the mouth of the furnace, and called out, "Ye servants of the most high God, come forth, and come hither." Before the astonished multitude, these men came forth unharmed. Not a hair of their head was singed, nor was even the smell of fire upon them. Nothing but the cords with which they were bound had burned. Jesus, the God whom they worshiped, had protected them.

"Blessed be the God of Shadrach, Meshach, and Abed-nego, who hath sent His angel, and delivered His servants that trusted in Him."

6. Nebuchadnezzar's Confession (3: 28, 29). The golden image was forgotten in the presence of a God who could do such wonders. Turning to the multitude, Nebuchadnezzar acknowledged his wrong, saying, "Blessed be the God of Shadrach, Meshach, and Abed-nego, who hath sent His angel, and delivered His servants that trusted in Him, and have changed the king's word, and yielded their bodies, that they might not serve nor worship any god, except their own God." Then, remembering how the wise men had influenced him by speaking against these Hebrews and their God, he added, "Therefore I make a decree, that every people, nation, and language, which speak anything amiss against the God of Shadrach, Meshach, and Abed-nego, shall be cut in pieces, and their houses shall be made a dunghill: because there is no other god that can deliver after this sort."

Thus again Satan was caught in the very trap he had laid to ensnare others, and God's loyal children were promoted in the province of Babylon.

How to Study: Study to tell the whole story from the lesson topics. Give the conversational parts as nearly as possible in the words used by the various speakers. These speakers are the herald, Nebuchadnezzar, and the three Hebrews.

Map Work: Locate the plain of Dura. See map on page 69.

Memory Work: Memorize Psalm 76:10. How is this verse fulfilled in this lesson?

Chapter to Remember: Daniel 3 tells about the golden image set up by Nebuchadnezzar, and the deliverance of the three Hebrews from the fiery furnace.

---

5. A VICTORY FOR GOD

Conversion of Nebuchadnezzar — Daniel 4

"He that is slow to anger is better than the mighty; and he that ruleth his spirit than he that taketh a city." Prov. 16:32.

1. God's Interest in Nebuchadnezzar. Inspiration has called Nebuchadnezzar "the hammer of the whole earth." And truly he was, for every nation had felt his telling blows. And now the world was conquered. The whole earth lay prostrate at his feet. Its wealth and honor were at his command. All about him were peace and prosperity. Never a king felt more safe and secure than did he. But just ahead God saw eternal ruin threatening the king. Nebuchadnezzar was nearing the end of his earthly career, and God desired that he who had conquered the world should also conquer himself. He desired that this king of the world should learn that most difficult yet simple lesson: "He that is slow to anger is better than the mighty; and he that ruleth his spirit than he that taketh

---

References Used: P. K., p. 521; Jer. 50:23; Acts 24:25.

a city." He desired that Nebuchadnezzar should at last reign in His everlasting kingdom of gold.

Though hasty and impetuous, though proud of what he had accomplished, yet the king had an honest heart. At different times he had publicly confessed his wrongs, acknowledged his own weakness, and proclaimed the greatness of the God of heaven. And now he was about to approach another crisis in his life. To prepare him for this time of danger, and to enable him to be a victor over his

"Leave the stump of his roots in the earth, even with a band of iron and brass."

wicked temper and pride of heart, God in the quiet hours of the night revealed to the king his own future experience through another mysterious dream.

2. The Dream (4: 4-17). In his dream, the king beheld an immense tree which could be seen from all parts of the earth. "The height thereof reached unto heaven, . . . the leaves thereof were fair, and the fruit thereof much: . . . the beasts of the field had shadow under it, and the fowls of the heaven dwelt in the boughs thereof, and all flesh was fed of it." As he looked at this wonderful tree, suddenly he saw "a Watcher and an Holy One" come down from heaven, who with a mighty voice cried: "Hew down the tree, and cut off his branches, shake off his leaves, and scatter his fruit: let the beasts get away from under it, and the fowls from his branches." But it was not to be entirely destroyed, for the Holy Watcher said: "Leave the stump of his roots in the earth, even with a band of iron and brass, in the tender grass of the field; and let it be wet with the dew of heaven, and let his portion be with the beasts in the grass of the earth: let his heart be changed from man's, and let a beast's heart be given unto him; and let seven times pass over him." But why should such a useful and beautiful tree be destroyed? Said the Watcher, "that the living may know that the Most High ruleth in the kingdom of men, and giveth it to whomsoever He will."

3. The Wise Men Again Fail (4: 9, 18, 19). The dream, which seemed to threaten calamity, greatly troubled Nebuchadnezzar. He called upon the wise men to explain it; but though he told them the dream, they did not understand its meaning. At last he remembered Daniel, who years before had interpreted his dream of the image. When Daniel heard the dream, he was plunged into deep distress, for he knew that it meant trouble for Nebuchadnezzar, whom he loved. For one whole hour he was unable to speak the terrible meaning. If only its meaning might apply to the king's enemies! But no; Daniel must speak the truth, no matter what the consequences. The king, seeing his distress, said reassuringly: "Belteshazzar, let not the dream, or the interpretation thereof, trouble thee." "Tell me the visions of my dream that I have seen, and the interpretation thereof."

4. The Dream Explained by Daniel (4: 20-26). Then said Daniel, "The tree . . . is thou, O king: . . . for thy greatness . . . reacheth unto heaven, and thy dominion to the end of the earth." The cry of the Holy Watcher, he explained, "is the decree of the Most High: . . . they shall drive thee from men, and thy dwelling shall be with the beasts of the field, and they shall make thee to eat grass as oxen, and they shall wet thee with the dew of heaven, and seven times [seven years] shall pass over thee, till thou know that the Most High ruleth in the kingdom of men, and giveth it to whomsoever He will." The leaving of the stump he explained to mean, "Thy kingdom shall be sure unto thee, after that thou shalt have known that the heavens do rule."

5. Daniel's Personal Appeal (4: 27). When Daniel had finished telling the meaning of the dream, he turned to the king, and in earnest, tender tones he pleaded, "O king, let my counsel be acceptable unto thee, and break off thy sins by righteousness, and thine iniquities by showing mercy to the poor; if it may be a lengthening of thy tranquillity."

Nebuchadnezzar was greatly moved. Deep down in his heart he felt that Daniel had spoken the solemn truth. Satan, too, was present. He feared for his dominion. He suggested temptations. Why should the great king act hastily? Better wait a few days. Nebuchadnezzar listened to the tempter. He waited. Like Felix, in his heart he whispered to the Holy Spirit, "Go Thy way for this time; when I have a convenient season, I will call for Thee." The days grew into weeks, and the weeks into months, but the "convenient season" only drifted farther and farther away. Month after

"Is not this great Babylon, that *I* have built by the might of *my* power, and for the honor of *my* majesty?"

month passed by. Month after month Nebuchadnezzar neglected "so great salvation." Month after month God withheld the threatened judgment. As the judgment was delayed, the king more and more indulged his pride, until at last he questioned whether Daniel had given the correct interpretation. A year passed. Still his proud spirit was unconquered.

6. The King Deprived of Reason (4: 28-33). As the king walked in the palace at the end of the year, thinking of his great power and viewing his glorious kingdom, he proudly exclaimed, "Is not this great Babylon, that *I* have built for the house of the kingdom by the might of *my* power, and for the honor of *my* majesty?" Scarcely had the words escaped his lips when a voice from heaven spoke: "O King Nebuchadnezzar, . . . the kingdom is departed from thee. And they shall drive thee from men, and thy dwelling shall be with the beasts of the field: they shall make thee to eat grass as oxen, and seven times shall pass over thee, until thou know that the Most High ruleth in the kingdom of men, and giveth it to whomsoever He will." "The same hour was the thing fulfilled." For seven long years, the king, deprived of reason, wandered about with the beasts of the field.

7. **The King Proclaims God's Power (4: 1-3, 34).** At the end of that time Nebuchadnezzar's reason returned. Then with gratitude and praise he honored the God of heaven. Once more he was established in his kingdom, and excellent majesty was added to him. Then the king issued a decree in which he related the dream, its meaning, and his own experience in its fulfillment. This public proclamation was addressed "unto all people, nations, and languages, that dwell in all the earth," and begins with these words: "Peace be multiplied unto you. I thought it good to show the signs and wonders that the high God hath wrought toward me. How great are His signs! and how mighty are His wonders! *His* kingdom is an everlasting kingdom, and *His* dominion is from generation to generation."

8. **A Victory for Christ (4: 37).** This experience has a deep and beautiful meaning. We have learned how, from the days of Nimrod, Satan had planned to have a world empire with its metropolis at Babel — Babylon — and how success had apparently crowned his efforts. At this city, the very heart of Satan's domain, Christ and Satan now met. Here another spiritual battle in the great controversy was fought. Another victory was won. The battlefield was the heart of the king who occupied the throne of Satan's usurped dominion. Through war and bloodshed and years of terrible conflict, Satan had established on the throne this monarch, proud, ambitious, self-sufficient of heart, refusing to recognize God as the supreme King. Through the quiet influence of the Holy Spirit upon the heart of this same monarch, during the hours when he was inactive in slumber, began a spiritual battle which won a great victory for God. As a result "God's purpose that the greatest kingdom in the world should show forth His praise, was now fulfilled." This victory Nebuchadnezzar himself announced in the last words of his great decree:

"Now I Nebuchadnezzar praise and extol and honor the King of heaven, all whose works are truth, and His ways judgment: and those that walk in pride He is able to abase."

Two years after this decree went forth, after a prosperous reign of forty-three years, Nebuchadnezzar died. It is probable that the Holy Watcher kept him true to the God of Daniel until the last. May we not hope that he who was represented by the head of gold will at last realize his desire to live in a golden kingdom that shall never pass away, by being permitted to walk the golden streets of the New Jerusalem, the metropolis of that kingdom which the God of heaven shall soon set up and which shall stand forever?

How to Study: After studying the lesson carefully, tell it from the following outline:

NEBUCHADNEZZAR'S DREAM OF A TREE
1. Why given.
2. Details of the dream — height and extent of tree; decree of the Watcher; the stump left; like the beasts; "seven times."
3. Interpretation — wise men try; Daniel called.
4. Daniel's appeal to the king.
5. Nebuchadnezzar's neglect.
6. The dream fulfilled.
7. The king restored and converted — his decree — victory for God.

Chapter to Remember: Daniel 4 tells about Nebuchadnezzar's dream of a tree, and his remarkable decree declaring his acceptance of the true God.

REVIEW

Chapter Drill: What is the subject of Daniel 1? 2? 3? 4?

Verse-Finding Drill: Other boys and girls have in five minutes turned to the verses containing these words. How long does it take you to find them all?

1. Daniel purposed in his heart that he would not defile himself.
2. Prove thy servants . . . ten days.
3. Daniel had understanding in all visions and dreams.
4. Tell thy servants the dream, and we will show the interpretation.
5. Then was the secret revealed unto Daniel in a night vision.
6. There is a God in heaven that revealeth secrets.
7. This secret is not revealed to me for any wisdom that I have.
8. Thou art this head of gold.
9. Your God is a God of gods, . . . and a revealer of secrets.
10. Our God . . . is able to deliver us from the burning fiery furnace.

11. There is no other god that can deliver after this sort.
12. I saw, and behold a tree in the midst of the earth.
13. The Most High ruleth in the kingdom of men.
14. Is not this great Babylon, that I have built?
15. Now I Nebuchadnezzar praise and . . . honor the King of heaven.

Test Questions and Exercises: First go through the questions checking those that you are not sure you can answer. Spend your time on the questions you check. Bring to class any to which you fail to find an answer. Numbers refer to preceding lessons.

1. Why did Satan rejoice at the captivity of Judah and Israel? Describe Daniel's home training. What had fitted him to be a statesman? to have a true understanding of science? to have ability to stand in the king's palace? Describe his experience in the king's school.

2. Who were the wise men of Babylon? What circumstance shows that Nebuchadnezzar despised sham? that he appreciated the genuine? How did Daniel give honor to God as he appeared before the king to tell the dream? Relate the dream. What name does God have that shows that He knows the future as well as the present?

3. Explain the meaning of each part of the image. Name the four world kingdoms; show on the map the territory they occupied, and tell when each came to an end. What will be the next world kingdom? How did God use this dream to put Daniel in a position where he could make the true God known to the world?

4. Why did Nebuchadnezzar set up an image all of gold? What did Satan try to accomplish through this experience? How? How did God defeat the enemy? How was a knowledge of the true God thus sent to all the world? Recite *Psalms 76:10, and tell how it was illustrated in this experience.

5. What did God call Nebuchadnezzar? Why? What were the king's greatest faults? What were his good qualities? How did God try to save him from his sins? Relate the dream. What lesson did God thus desire to teach the king? Why did the king fail to learn the lesson? How and when was the dream fulfilled?

---

6. DANIEL'S FIRST VISION OF THE GREAT CONTROVERSY

The Four Beasts — Dan. 7: 1-8, 19, 22

"The Most High ruleth in the kingdom of men, and giveth it to whomsoever He will." Dan. 4: 32.

1. Daniel's Vision (7: 1, 22). Among the kings who reigned over Babylon after the death of Nebuchadnezzar was Belshazzar, Nebuchadnezzar's grandson. In the first year of his reign, Daniel, now about eighty-five years of age, saw in a dream, or vision, important events that were to take place on the earth from his day to the very end of the great controversy — until "the time came that the saints possessed the kingdom."

2. The Sea and the First Beast (7: 2-4). In the vision, Daniel first saw the great sea, not calm and peaceful, but stirred into angry waves by the wind, which blew from every direction. "The four winds of the heaven strove upon the great sea." As he watched the tempest, he saw a great lion come up out of the sea. But this lion was different from other lions, for it had the wings of an eagle.

"The first was like a lion; a second, like to a bear."

After a while the wings "were plucked" and the lion was made to "stand upon the feet as a man, and a man's heart was given to it." This beast ruled over the earth for a little while, but soon its dominion was taken away and its power was gone.

3. The Second Beast (7: 5). After that, another beast came up out of the raging sea. This beast was "like to a bear, and it raised up itself on one side, and it had three ribs in the mouth of it between the teeth of it. And they said thus unto it, Arise, devour much flesh." Like the first beast, the bear ruled the earth "for a season and time." Then its dominion was taken away and its power was gone.

4. **The Third Beast (7: 6).** Again Daniel looked upon the stormy sea. As he gazed, he saw still another beast coming up out of the water. The body of this beast looked like that of a leopard, but upon its back it had "four wings of a fowl; the beast had also four heads; and dominion was given to it." Like the beasts that preceded it, the leopard beast ruled "for a season and time." Then its dominion was taken away and its power was gone.

5. **The Fourth Beast (7: 7, 19, 20).** Once more Daniel's eyes rested on the sea, lashed into fury by the mighty wind. This time,

"Another, like a leopard; a fourth beast, dreadful and terrible."

he saw coming out of the angry waters "a fourth beast, dreadful and terrible, and strong exceedingly; and it had great iron teeth; . . . and it had ten horns;" and the nails on its feet were of brass. As this beast roamed up and down through the earth, it "devoured and brake in pieces" everything it could find; and then, as if that were not enough, it stamped upon and crushed the pieces with its feet. It seemed determined that not one thing should escape its terrible destruction.

6. **The Little Horn (7: 8, 20, 21).** As Daniel looked at the ten horns on the head of the fourth beast, he saw a strange sight. Another horn — a little horn "more stout than his fellows" — was

pompously pushing its way up among the ten. As it arose, three of the ten horns were plucked up by the roots to make room for it. When it was fully up, Daniel saw that this little horn had "eyes like the eyes of a man, and a mouth speaking great things." Its eyes were filled with subtle cruelty, and the words that it spoke were wicked words of blasphemy. "And the same horn made war with the saints, and prevailed against them."

7. The Meaning of Winds and Seas. These beasts had come up out of the sea, which was lashed into fury by a fierce wind. Winds in prophecy are a symbol of strife and war between nations. When Jeremiah prophesied of the last great battle, he called the strife a great whirlwind. He says, "Behold, evil shall go forth from nation to nation, and a great whirlwind shall be raised up from the coasts of the earth. And the slain of the Lord shall be at that day from one end of the earth even unto the other end of the earth." Seas or waters are declared by John the revelator to be a symbol of peoples and nations. "The waters which thou sawest," he said, "are peoples, and multitudes, and nations, and tongues."

How to Study: As you read the lesson try to imagine just how these beasts looked to Daniel. Picture in your mind the storm also. Study to give an accurate description of each beast and the little horn. The meaning of *winds* and *seas* is given in Jeremiah 25: 32, 33 and Revelation 17: 15. Read these texts and remember where they are found. Do not forget the meaning of these two symbols. They frequently occur in prophecy.

Verse-Finding Drill: Turn to the verses containing these expressions. Practice until you can find them all in three minutes.
1. The four winds of the heaven strove upon the great sea.
2. Four great beasts came up from the sea.
3. The first was like a lion.
4. And behold . . . a second, like to a bear.
5. I beheld . . . another, like a leopard.
6. The fourth beast . . . whose teeth were of iron, and his nails of brass.
7. And, behold, in this horn were eyes like the eyes of a man.
8. The time came that the saints possessed the kingdom.
9. A great whirlwind shall be raised up from the coasts of the earth.
10. The waters . . . are peoples, and multitudes, and nations, and tongues.

7. THE ANGEL'S EXPLANATION OF THE FOUR BEASTS

Dan. 7: 11, 12, 15-17, 23, 24, 26, 27

"These great beasts, which are four, are four kings, which shall arise out of the earth." Dan. 7:17.

1. Daniel's Desire to Understand (7: 15-17, 23). That which had been shown to Daniel in vision greatly perplexed him. Turning to one of the angels that stood by, he "asked him the truth of all this." So the angel made known the interpretation of the dream. "These great beasts," he said, "which are four, are four kings, which shall arise out of the earth." These four kings — or kingdoms, as the fourth beast is definitely called — are the same four kingdoms that were revealed in the dream of the image, given to Nebuchadnezzar. What are these four kingdoms?

2. The First Beast Explained. From the interpretation of the great image which God had revealed to Daniel, he already understood that four great kingdoms were to rule upon the earth. But in this vision of the four beasts, God showed him more about the character of these kingdoms. Babylon was represented by a lion, the king of beasts. At first the lion had eagle's wings. This represented the swiftness with which Nebuchadnezzar conquered the nations of the world. But later the wings were plucked, and the lion, once bold and fearless, had the weak, timid heart of a man given to it. This very fittingly represented Babylon after the death of Nebuchadnezzar, when under the rule of kings like the weak and wicked Belshazzar. To what part of the image does the lion correspond? In what year did its power cease?

3. The Second Beast Explained. Medo-Persia was represented by a bear. As the breast and arms of silver were inferior to the head of gold in the image, so the bear is inferior to the lion. This kingdom was made up of two nations, the Medes and the Persians. The bear raised itself up on one side, representing the Persian part of the kingdom, which, though it came up last, yet had the greater power. The three ribs in the bear's mouth are thought to have represented the three provinces of Babylon, Lydia, and Egypt, which were especially oppressed by Medo-Persia. The expression, "Arise, devour much flesh," may mean that this nation was to go on to still greater conquests. To what part of the image does the bear correspond? In what year did its power begin? In what year did it end? How long did it have dominion over the earth?

4. The Third Beast Explained. The leopard with four wings and four heads represented Grecia. The leopard is a swift-footed beast, but the four wings which this leopard had would represent very marked speed. And this was true of Alexander the Great, the king under which Grecia so rapidly overthrew the kingdom of Medo-Persia. In less than eight years, Alexander marched his army hither and thither across the country, from Greece eastward nearly to the Ganges River, and returned to Babylon, a distance of about six thousand miles, capturing every country that lay along his course. In this brief time he became master of the civilized world. But only two years later he died, and his kingdom was then divided among his four generals. These divisions were represented by the four heads of the leopard. To what part of the great image does the leopard correspond? In what year did its power begin? In what year did it end? How long did it have dominion over the earth?

Just as Daniel in his vision saw these beasts one after the other lose their power and finally disappear from the earth, so easily the Most High giveth to whomsoever He will the kingdoms of men whom these beasts represented.

5. Daniel's Anxiety to Understand the Fourth Beast (7: 19, 20). From the fact that the fourth beast was represented as destroying God's people and speaking terrible words of blasphemy, Daniel could see that there was trouble ahead. He was perplexed and anxious, "grieved in spirit," and desired especially to understand about this fourth beast. Scarcely had the angel begun to explain the first three beasts when Daniel interrupted him, saying, "I would know the truth of the fourth beast, which was diverse from all the others, exceeding dreadful, whose teeth were of iron, and his nails of brass; which devoured, brake in pieces, and stamped the residue with his feet."

6. The Fourth Beast Explained (7: 23). Then the angel explained, saying, "The fourth beast shall be the fourth kingdom upon the earth, which shall be diverse from all kingdoms, and shall devour the whole earth, and shall tread it down, and break it in pieces." This fourth beast, with teeth of iron and claws of brass, was the

Roman Empire, the same one that was represented in the image by the legs of iron. For more than six hundred years this pagan empire ruled the whole civilized world.

The first three beasts were wild and ravenous, but the fourth beast was "diverse from all the others, *exceeding* dreadful." Rome did not hesitate to put to death either common people or royalty, even though they were innocent, if only the reigning emperor might prosper. Anyone upon whom rested the least suspicion that he was unfriendly to the government was in danger of death no matter who was the victim, whether father, mother, wife, children, ruler, or the humblest subject. "Thou art not Cæsar's friend" was almost equivalent to a death warrant.

It was under the iron rule of the Roman Empire that King Herod put to death all the innocent babes of Bethlehem in an effort to save his own power. It was under this same iron rule that James and Paul were beheaded, Peter and others martyred. It was under Rome that Jesus was crucified. Under Nero, a Roman emperor, this beast perhaps most cruelly used its "great iron teeth." His hatred was centered largely against the followers of Jesus. Thousands of these innocent people, falsely condemned as rebels against the empire, were thrown to wild beasts or burned alive in the amphitheaters. Vast multitudes assembled to enjoy the sight, and greeted their dying agonies with laughter and applause. On one occasion Nero celebrated a triumphal procession by lighting the highway to Rome with rows of human torches on each side of the road. This terrible sacrifice of life continued with greater or less fury for more than three centuries after the birth of Christ.

The historian Gibbon, describing the power of this kingdom, says: "The empire of the Romans filled the world. And when that empire fell into the hands of a single person, the world became a safe and dreary prison for his enemies. To resist was fatal; and it was impossible to fly." If ever a kingdom had iron teeth with which it devoured the whole earth, if ever a kingdom had claws of brass with which it trod down the earth and broke it in pieces, surely pagan Rome did.

How to Study: Turn to this prophecy in the Bible — the reference given at the head of the lesson. Compare the four beasts of Daniel 7 with the four parts of the great image of Daniel 2. What kingdom did each beast represent, and when did each come to an end? Be able to explain the different features of each beast as follows: 1. eagle's wings, wings plucked, man's heart; 2. raised up on one side, three ribs; "Arise, devour much flesh;" 3. four wings of a fowl, four heads; 4. teeth of iron, nails of brass, "devoured and brake in pieces, and stamped the residue."

For Class Discussion: Who was Cæsar? What did his name represent? What is the allusion under topic 6? John 19:12. Read also Luke 20:24, 25.

For Your Workbook: Cut out and place on diagram No. 6 the beasts of Daniel 7 in their proper places. Fill out the first four parts of the prophecy of Daniel 7. The outline for this diagram and the pictures needed are in "Bible Workbook" for the eighth grade.

8. THE ANGEL'S EXPLANATION OF THE LITTLE HORN
Dan. 7: 20-22, 24, 25

"He shall speak great words against the Most High, and shall wear out the saints of the Most High." Dan. 7: 25, first part.

1. Daniel's Anxiety (7: 20-22). Daniel not only desired to know what the fourth beast represented, but he especially wanted to understand the meaning of its strange horns. "I would know the truth of . . . the ten horns that were in his head," he said anxiously to the angel, "and of the other which came up, and before whom three fell; even of that horn that had eyes, and a mouth that spake very great things, whose look was more stout than his fellows. I beheld, and the same horn made war with the saints, and prevailed against them; until . . . the time came that the saints possessed the kingdom." It was because this horn made such cruel and prolonged war against God's people that Daniel felt troubled.

2. The Horns Explained (7: 25). The ten horns of this beast correspond to the feet and toes of the image, and represent the ten kings, or kingdoms, into which the Roman Empire was finally divided.

After 476 A. D., pagan Rome having been broken up into ten kingdoms, there arose another power different from any that had gone before. This power arose in the church at Rome and was called papal Rome, or the papacy. The man who stood at the head of this power was not called a king; he was called a pope. This pope controlled the people not only in civil matters but in religious matters also. If any dared to oppose him in any way, they were most

Reference Used: D. R. on Dan. 7: 25; S. B., pp. 376, 377.

cruelly punished. The papacy, or papal Rome, tried to get all ten of the kingdoms to recognize its authority, and at last all but three consented. Because these three continued to rebel, they were completely destroyed by the papacy. This was accomplished in the year 538 A. D. In the prophecy this work of the papacy is represented by the little horn which, as it arose, plucked up three of the first horns by the roots.

Describing this horn, the angel said, "He shall speak great words against the Most High, and shall wear out the saints of the Most High, and think to change times and laws: and they shall be given into his hand until a time and times and the dividing of time."

3. The "Great Words" of the Papacy (7: 25). The pope has been called the "Vicegerent of the Son of God," "our Lord God, the Pope," "another God upon earth," "King of kings and Lord of lords," "the Lion of the tribe of Judah, the promised Saviour," and other names that belong only to God. The pope professes to be able to forgive sin, which none but God can do. He claims also to be infallible, that is, incapable of falling or sinning,— a quality that belongs to God alone. Thus the little horn has spoken great and blasphemous words against the Most High. Paul calls him * "that man of sin, . . . who opposeth and exalteth himself above all that is called God, or that is worshiped; so that he as God sitteth in the temple of God, showing himself that *he* is God." He is the mystery of iniquity, of whom we have read in past lessons.

4. Wearing Out the Saints (7: 25). Of this same little horn the angel said, "He shall . . . wear out the saints of the Most High." How has the papacy done this? Historians tell us that 1,000,000 Waldenses perished in France, and 900,000 other Christians were slain in less than thirty years, by the persecuting hand of the papacy. During the same length of time, the Inquisition tortured to death 150,000. Within the space of thirty-eight years, 50,000 more were hanged, beheaded, burned or buried alive, for the crime of heresy — having an opinion different from what the pope commanded. In fact, the total loss of life by papal persecution will never be known. During the first three centuries after Christ, when pagan Rome ruled the world, it is estimated that 3,000,000 Christians perished; yet it is said that the early Christians prayed that this power might continue, for they knew that papal Rome, or the papacy, which was to follow, would be far more cruel.

How to Study: In this lesson there are five important points that you should be able to explain:
1. What the ten horns represent.
2. How and when the little horn arose.
3. What the angel said this horn would do (Daniel 7:25).
4. What the "great words" are that it has spoken.
5. How it has worn out the saints of the Most High.

Dictionary Work: vice-gerent; in-fall-ible; Inquisition. What common word do we use that is similar to "Inquisition"?

Use of Concordance: Find the reference starred under topic 3. Key word: exalt. Of whose proud, boastful statement do these words remind you?

Memory Work: Memorize Daniel 7:25, first half, and enter the reference on the "Service Flag."

---

9. THE 1260 YEARS OF PAPAL PERSECUTION
Dan. 7: 11, 25-28

"He shall think to change the times and the law; and they shall be given into his hand until a time and times and half a time." Dan. 7:25, last part, R. V.

1. The Change in God's Law (7:25). The angel told Daniel that the little horn would not only speak great words against the Most High and wear out the saints of the Most High, but that it would *think* to change "the times and the law" of the Most High. It is impossible for anyone or any power ever really to change God's law or the times that He has established; yet the little horn would *think* to do it, and lead others to think that it had been done. And this very thing the papacy has done, thus fulfilling the prophecy in this respect also. How has it done this? It has thought to change the law of God by omitting the second commandment, which forbids the worship of images. This changes the numbering so that the fourth becomes the third. Then, in order to have ten commandments in all, it has divided the tenth into two. It has also changed the fourth commandment, the only part of God's law that speaks of "times," by substituting Sunday for the Sabbath of the Lord.

The following questions and answers published in a Catholic catechism dated 1909, tell us this:

"Ques.—What is the third [fourth] commandment?
"Ans.— Remember thou keep holy the Sabbath day.

References Used: "The Christian Sabbath," pp. 74, 75; Mark 1:32.

THE LAW OF GOD

AS GIVEN BY JEHOVAH (Abbreviated)	AS CHANGED BY MAN
I Thou shalt have no other gods before Me.	**I** I am the Lord thy God: thou shalt not have strange gods before Me.
II Thou shalt not make unto thee any graven image, . . . thou shalt not bow down thyself to them, nor serve them.	
III Thou shalt not take the name of the Lord thy God in vain; for the Lord will not hold him guiltless that taketh His name in vain.	**II** Thou shalt not take the name of the Lord thy God in vain.
IV Remember the Sabbath day, to keep it holy. Six days shalt thou labor, and do all thy work: but the seventh day is the Sabbath of the Lord thy God: . . . for in six days the Lord made heaven and earth, the sea, and all that in them is, and rested the seventh day: wherefore the Lord blessed the Sabbath day, and hallowed it.	**III** Remember that thou keep holy the Sabbath day.
V Honor thy father and thy mother: that thy days may be long upon the land which the Lord thy God giveth thee.	**IV** Honor thy father and thy mother.
VI Thou shalt not kill.	**V** Thou shalt not kill.
VII Thou shalt not commit adultery.	**VI** Thou shalt not commit adultery.
VIII Thou shalt not steal.	**VII** Thou shalt not steal.
IX Thou shalt not bear false witness against thy neighbor.	**VIII** Thou shalt not bear false witness against thy neighbor.
X Thou shalt not covet thy neighbor's house, thou shalt not covet thy neighbor's wife, nor his manservant, nor his maidservant, nor his ox, nor his ass, nor anything that is thy neighbor's.	**IX** Thou shalt not covet thy neighbor's wife. **X** Thou shalt not covet thy neighbor's goods.
(Ex. 20: 3-17.)	(Butler's Catechism, page 28.)

"Ques.—What day was the Sabbath?
"Ans.— The seventh day, our Saturday.
"Ques.— Do you keep the Sabbath?
"Ans.— No; we keep the Lord's day.
"Ques.—Which is that?
"Ans.— The first day; Sunday.
"Ques.—Who changed it?
"Ans.— The Catholic Church."

From this we see how Satan through the papacy has torn from God's law the Sabbath of Jehovah, the only memorial of Himself that the great God has ever given to man, that which is the seal of His authority, and put in its place the first day of the week, thus indicating that *his* authority is above God's authority. Nothing has ever been done by fallen man that has given Satan such supreme satisfaction as this. Surely that wicked power is worthy to share with the great enemy the titles "man of sin," "mystery of iniquity."

Although the papal church has been used by Satan to do this blasphemous work, we must not think that all who belong to it are opposed to God. Among these people are many who at heart are noble Christian men and women, manifesting a conscientious devotion to their religion that is worthy of our admiration. When these honest ones understand what God requires, they will be as loyal to Him as they have previously been to the commands of the church. Let us remember that God looks not so much on one's profession as upon the heart and the life. He accounted righteous, not the Pharisee who proudly thanked God that he was not as other men, but the poor repentant publican. If we have learned more than others of Bible truth, it is not because we by nature are better than they, or because God loves us more than He loves them, but that we may be His humble servants, showing by a consistent Christian life the power and the value of the truth.

2. Duration of Papal Rule (7:25). "They shall be given into his hand until a time and times and half a time," said the angel. "A time" is one year; "times" represents two years; "half a time" is one half a year — in all, three and one half years. According to Jewish reckoning, a year contained twelve months of thirty days each, or three hundred sixty days. When the Lord foretold to Israel that they were to remain in the wilderness, He said, *"After the number of the days in which ye searched the land, even forty days, each day for a year, shall ye bear your iniquities, even forty years." From this we learn that a day in prophecy represents a year. How many years, therefore, was the papacy to bear rule? Since the authority of the papacy was fully established in the year A. D. 538, the year when the last of the three horns, or kingdoms, was overthrown by the little horn, and since it is to continue 1260 years, in what year would it be broken? Adding 1260 years to 538 brings us to the year 1798. In that year the French army entered Rome, declared the country a republic, and took the pope prisoner. Although the papacy still exists and will to the end of time, yet since 1798 it has not had the cruel persecuting power that it once had. It was during the 1260 years that the Reformation began. Martin Luther and other reformers helped the people to see the wickedness of departing from the word of God, and led them to turn away from the false teachings of the papacy. The time during which the papacy ruled is called in history "the Dark Ages."

3. The End of the Beast (7: 11). In the vision, Daniel saw that at last the fourth beast, because of the blasphemous words that the little horn spoke, "was slain, and his body destroyed, and given to the burning flame." This, then, will be the end of the blasphemous power that dares to tamper with God's holy law and thus exalt himself "above all that is called God."

4. The Kingdom of the Most High (7: 27, 28). After telling Daniel of the destruction of the fourth beast and the little horn, the angel gave him a brighter picture — a picture of God's everlasting kingdom. "The greatness of the kingdom under the whole heaven," he said, "shall be given to the people of the saints of the Most High, whose kingdom is an everlasting kingdom." Still Daniel was greatly troubled. The thought of what this wicked power was to do weighed upon his mind, and the angel left him with a sad countenance and an anxious heart.

How to Study: Be able to explain the following:
1. The three changes that the papacy has thought to make in God's law.
2. That "a time and times and half a time" is 1260 years.
3. A day in prophecy represents a year. Give reference.
4. The duration of the papacy — 538 to 1798.
5. The final fate of the beast and the little horn.
6. When God's everlasting kingdom will be set up.

Memory Work: Finish memorizing Daniel 7:25. Numbers 14:34 is the starred verse under topic 2. Remember where it is located and what it explains.

For Your Workbook: On diagram No. 1 locate the 1260-year period of time. On diagram No. 6 mount the beast with a little horn. Add the points of this lesson to the "Prophecy of Daniel 7."

10. A GLIMPSE INTO HEAVEN'S GREAT COURT ROOM
Dan. 7: 9, 10, 13

"My little children, . . . we have an Advocate with the Father, Jesus Christ the righteous." 1 John 2:1.

1. A Scene in Heaven (7: 9, 10, 13). In the dream which, years before, God had given to Nebuchadnezzar, He revealed the future of earthly governments; but to Daniel He not only revealed events that were to take place on earth, but, drawing aside the curtain, He gave him a view of events connected with the great conflict which are now taking place in heaven. After Daniel had watched the beasts as one by one they came out of the troubled sea, roamed over and controlled the earth for a time, and then had their power taken away, the scene changed. He no longer gazed upon a stormy sea and fierce, ugly-looking beasts. His eyes were directed to heaven, where he saw thrones. One of these thrones "was like the fiery flame, and his wheels as burning fire." Upon this throne sat God the Father, the Ancient of Days, "whose garment was white as snow, and the hair of His head like the pure wool. . . . A fiery stream issued and came forth from before Him: thousand thousands ministered unto Him, and ten thousand times ten thousand stood before Him: the Judgment was set, and the books were opened. . . . And, behold, One like the Son of man came with the clouds of heaven, and came to the Ancient of Days, and they brought Him near before Him."

2. The Investigative Judgment. What a scene! In the most holy apartment of the heavenly sanctuary, the great court room of heaven, God the Father, the supreme Judge of all the earth, is seated on His glorious throne of mercy — the heavenly mercy seat. Be-

---
References Used: E. W., pp. 52, 251; 1 Peter 4:17; G. C., pp. 480-482.

neath His throne, forming its foundation, is His holy law. Before Him lie all the great record books of heaven, opened — opened before the law which has been transgressed, and by which every deed will be judged. Round about Him stand ten thousand times ten thousand, and thousands of thousands, of loyal angels, every eye fixed upon the Judge. Here, in sublime silence, in almost breathless expectation, they wait — wait for Jesus, the heavenly High Priest, the sinners' Advocate, or Attorney, Him who is to plead the cases of those whose records are in the open books. Where is He? Officiating in the holy place, the first apartment. Now He comes!

"The Judgment was set, and the books were opened."

Clouds of bright angels bring Him near before the Ancient of Days. Surrounded by angels and in a flaming chariot He passes within the second veil. It is the great day of atonement in the heavenly sanctuary,— the day when the cases of all who are written in the books will be investigated and decided, to know whether they will be retained as members of God's family or cut off from among His people. The Investigative Judgment begins.

3. The Book of Life. One of the books that lie open before the Judge is the book of life. This book contains the names of all the people on earth who since the days of Adam have been adopted into the family of God and have entered His service. It is these only whose cases are to be considered at this time. The judgment of those who have never accepted Christ is another work, and takes place at a later time.

4. The Book of Remembrance. Another book is called "the book of remembrance." In this book have been recorded the good deeds of "them that feared the Lord, and that thought upon His name." Every generous and thoughtful deed, every kind word, every tender, loving thought, has been carefully registered. Every prayer offered, every temptation resisted, every evil overcome, has been faithfully recorded. Every little act of self-sacrifice made for Jesus' sake, every trial endured for Him — every one has been written, and all will come up in remembrance before the Father when our name is called.

5. The Book of Sins, or the Book of Death. There is also another book. This book contains the record of our sins. Opposite each name in this book has been entered with terrible exactness every wrong and idle word, every selfish act, every unfulfilled duty, every secret sin, with every attempt to deceive. Unheeded warnings, neglected reproofs, wasted moments, unimproved opportunities, the influence of our example, with its far-reaching results, all have been written by the recording angel.

How to Study: After reading the lesson narrative, answer the following questions, looking up the references given. Notice that five references are in Daniel 7 and three in Revelation. "Bookmark" these places.

A Scene in the Heavenly Court Room

1. Who sits upon the throne as Judge? Dan. 7:9.
2. Where is this divine court room?
3. To what does it correspond in the earthly sanctuary?
4. What indicates that the Judge will show mercy?
5. What is the foundation of His throne?
6. Who are present as witnesses? Dan. 7:10.
7. Whose arrival is necessary before any cases can be investigated? Dan. 7:13.
8. What part does Jesus act? 1 John 2:1.

The Judgment

1. What is this work called? Dan. 7:10, last part.
2. According to what will everyone be judged? Rev. 20:12.
3. By what standard is every act judged? James 2:12.

THE BOOKS

1. Where have the records in heaven been kept? Dan. 7:10, last part.
2. What is the name of one of the books? Rev. 20:12.
3. What is written in this book? Rev. 3:5.
4. What is another book called? What is written in this book? Mal. 3:16.
5. What other records are kept? Matt. 12:36, 37; *Eccl. 12:14.

Memory Work: Memorize Ecclesiastes 12:14.

---

11. EXAMINATION OF CASES

Dan. 7:14, 22

"Judgment must begin at the house of God." 1 Peter 4:17.

1. Those Who Are Accepted. The examination of the records begins with the righteous who first lived upon the earth. Adam's name heads the list. Then generation after generation comes in review before God. Last of all, the cases of those who are now living will be investigated. As a name is called by the great Judge, the interest of the angels is intense to know what decision will be rendered. Name after name is mentioned and every case carefully considered. Some are accepted, others rejected.

When the judgment begins on the living, our cases will be tried. We are all criminals. The death sentence hangs over our heads. But Christ is our Advocate, and He never lost a case that was committed to Him. When a name is called by the Judge, the angels produce the witness from the records which they have made of deeds and words and thoughts and feelings that they by personal observation know about us. If our sins have all been confessed and have gone "before to judgment," Jesus, the Attorney, says: "Father, these sins have all been confessed and I have forgiven them. This boy, this girl, stood for Me, firm for the right down on earth — at home, at school. Now I stand for them." Then, lifting His hands, He continues: "They are Mine, Father. I have graven them on the palms of My hands. For My sake blot out all their sins, and retain their names in the family record book, the book of life. They are My brother, My sister — members of the royal family. I will that they also be with Me where I am."

References Used: John 17:24; Matt. 25:41; Mark 13:35, 36; 1 Thess. 5:4, 6.

As Jesus confesses us before the Father and before the holy angels, the Judge accepts the plea of our heavenly Attorney, and we are accepted as joint heirs with Him, to sit with Him on His throne. Our sins are blotted out of the book, and we have the promise that none of the sins that we have committed shall be mentioned to us.

2. Those Who Are Rejected. Those who have upon the record book sins that have not been repented of, are not accepted. They do not have on "the wedding garment," the garment of Christ's righteousness, and they cannot be retained in the heavenly family. Of such Jesus says: "I never knew them. They are none of Mine." Then the Father erases their good deeds from the book of remembrance and blots their names out of the book of life, but their unconfessed sins still remain on the books. "The righteousness of the righteous shall not deliver him in the day of his transgression. . . . If he trust to his own righteousness, and commit iniquity, all his righteousnesses shall not be remembered; but for his iniquity that he hath committed, he shall die for it."

3. The Work Finished. We are now living during this time of the investigation of the heavenly records — the Investigative Judgment. The examination of the vast multitude who have lived and died upon the earth during the past ages is nearly finished. Soon the work will be begun upon the living. When that work is all finished, the Judge will announce: "He that is unjust, let him be unjust still: and he which is filthy, let him be filthy still: and he that is righteous, let him be righteous still: and he that is holy, let him be holy still. And, behold, I come quickly; and My reward is with Me, to give every man according as his work shall be." Then the mystery of God is finished.

4. Christ as King (7: 14, 22). In the vision, Daniel not only saw this work in progress, but looking beyond our time, he saw it closed. He saw the Son of man receive "dominion, and glory, and a kingdom, that all people, nations, and languages, should serve Him: His dominion is an everlasting dominion, which shall not pass away, and His kingdom that which shall not be destroyed." At last, "judgment was given to the saints of the Most High; and the time came that the saints possessed the kingdom."

5. "Watch Ye Therefore." When the work of the Investigative Judgment closes, all cases will be decided for eternal life or eternal death. But the righteous and the wicked will still be living upon the earth. People will be planting and building, eating and drinking, just the same as now, not knowing that the work of our High Priest has been finished in the heavenly sanctuary. The exact hour when this work closes will come as a thief in the night. That is why Jesus says, "Watch ye therefore: . . . lest coming suddenly He find you sleeping,"—find you careless and thoughtless, more interested in selfish pleasure than in the service of Jesus. Those who earnestly watch have the assurance that that day shall not overtake them as a thief, for they will be ready.

How to Study: After reading the lesson narrative, answer the following questions. "Bookmark" Ezekiel 33; Revelation; Matthew 10.

THE FAITHFUL

1. Whose cases are considered in the Investigative Judgment? 1 Peter 4:17.
2. What decision is given in the case of those who have turned away from their sins? Eze. 33:14-16.
3. What does the Advocate do and say in their behalf? Isa. 49:16; Matt. 10:32.
4. What then becomes of their sins? *Acts 3:19.
5. What about their names? Rev. 3:5.

THE UNFAITHFUL

1. What decision is given in the case of the righteous who have at last turned away from the right? Eze. 33:12, 13.
2. What does the Advocate say of these? Matt. 10:33; 7:23.

CLOSING EVENTS

1. What decree announces the close of the Judgment? Rev. 22:11.
2. What event comes after the Judgment is over? Rev. 22:12; Dan. 7:14.
3. What reward is given to the saints? Dan. 7:22, last part.

Memory Work: Memorize Acts 3:19.

Chapter to Remember: What vision is given in Daniel 7?

REVIEW OF DANIEL 7

Test Questions: Recite starred texts from memory.
1. Of what is the sea a symbol in prophecy? the wind? a day?
2. Describe the lion in Daniel's first vision.
3. What did the lion represent? its wings? the man's heart?
4. Describe the bear in Daniel's first vision.

5. What did the bear represent? its rising up on one side? the three ribs?
6. Describe the third beast in Daniel's first vision.
7. What did the leopard represent? its wings? its four heads?
8. Describe the fourth beast in Daniel's first vision.
9. What did the fourth beast represent? its ten horns?
10. Describe the little horn of the fourth beast.
11. What power does the little horn represent?
12. What three things did the angel say the little horn would do? *Dan. 7:25.
13. How has the papacy spoken great words against the Most High?
14. How has it worn out the saints of the Most High?
15. How has it thought to change the law of the Most High?
16. How long was it to continue? How many years is this? When did this period of time begin? When did it end? What event marked its beginning? its end?
17. What will become of this power?
18. Describe the scene now in the heavenly sanctuary. *Dan. 7:9, 10.
19. What three books are used in the Judgment? What does each contain?
20. What is Christ's work in heaven? When His work is finished, what decree will go forth? Rev. 22:11.
21. What will God bring into judgment? *Eccl. 12:14.
22. If we repent and are converted, when will our sins be blotted out? *Acts 3:19.

12. DANIEL'S SECOND VISION OF THE GREAT CONTROVERSY

Dan. 8:1-8, 16, 20-22

"Thus saith the Lord God; Remove the diadem, and take off the crown."
Eze. 21:26.

1. The "Ram Which Had Two Horns" (8:3, 4). It had now been more than twenty years since the great king Nebuchadnezzar had passed away. Since then the government had been in the hands of wicked kings, and every year troubles were increasing. As prime minister, Daniel carried heavy responsibilities. On this occasion he was down by the River Ulai, whither he had withdrawn doubtless to be alone with God, and to seek wisdom for his perplexing duties. While he sat by the river, suddenly he saw a ram standing on the bank of the river. The ram "had two horns: and the two horns were high; but one was higher than the other, and the higher came up last." As Daniel looked, he saw "the ram pushing westward, and

References Used: Esther 1:1, 2; Ezra 6:14.

northward, and southward; so that no beasts might stand before him, neither was there any that could deliver out of his hand; but he did according to his will, and became great."

2. What the Ram Represented (8: 16, 20). As Daniel prayed for an understanding of the vision, Gabriel appeared before him, and he heard a voice from above the river which said, "Gabriel, make this man to understand the vision." Then the angel said, "The ram which thou sawest having two horns are the kings of Media and Persia." From this explanation it is plain that this beast represented the same kingdom as the breast and arms of silver in the image shown to Nebuchadnezzar, and the bear that raised itself up on one side, as shown to Daniel in his first vision. All these represented the same kingdom, Medo-Persia. The higher horn, which came up last, was Persia, and, though it came into power later than Media, yet it was the stronger.

In this vision Babylon is not represented at all. And why? Because Babylon was soon to be taken captive by the Medo-Persian kingdom. Babylon, the head of gold, was about to be succeeded by the breast and arms of silver. The dominion of the lion was to be taken by the bear. The Medes and the Persians were already on the warpath. In their conquests, they pushed westward as far as the Mediterranean Sea, northward as far as the Caspian Sea, and southward as far as Egypt, taking in all the strong nations of the then civilized world.

Ahasuerus, who chose Esther for his queen, was one of the kings of the Medo-Persian kingdom. During his reign, Medo-Persia ruled over 127 provinces. Three other important kings were Cyrus, Darius, and Artaxerxes. These three kings were the ones who issued the decree permitting the Jews to return to Jerusalem at the end of the seventy years' captivity. It was at the very place where this vision was given to Daniel, at one of the royal residences, the palace at Shushan, that a little later King Ahasuerus was to sit on the throne, and Queen Esther was to live.

3. The He-Goat and What He Did (8: 5-8). As Daniel was watching the ram pushing in various directions, "behold, an he-goat came from the west on the face of the whole earth." So rapidly did he come that he "touched not the ground." Daniel noticed especially that the goat was headed directly toward the ram. "And he came to the ram that had two horns, . . . standing before the river, and ran unto him in the fury of his power, . . . and smote the ram, and brake his two horns, and . . . cast him down to the ground, and stamped upon him: and there was none that could deliver the ram. . . . Therefore the he-goat waxed very great: and when he was strong, the great horn was broken; and for it came up four notable ones toward the four winds of heaven."

4. What the He-Goat Represented (8: 21, 22). The angel explained to Daniel: "The rough goat is the king of Grecia: and the great horn that is between his eyes is the first king." The first king of Grecia, represented by the "notable horn," was Alexander the Great. In the vision, Daniel saw the ram on one side of the

The rough goat   The ram

river, and he saw the he-goat run into him in the fury of his power. One writer, referring to this prophecy, says, "One can hardly read these words without having some image of Darius's army standing and guarding the River Granicus, and of Alexander on the other side, with his forces plunging in, swimming across the stream, and rushing on the enemy with all the fire and fury that can be imagined."

Three years after this first victory, the last engagement took place between the Medo-Persians and the Grecians. On the eve of this last battle, Darius sent representatives to Alexander to ask for peace. Alexander sent back the word, "Tell your sovereign . . . that the world will not permit two suns or two sovereigns." And so, in the year B. C. 331, Alexander became master of the world. It is interesting to know that about two hundred years before the time of Daniel, the Grecians were called *Ægeadæ*, a word that means "the goats' people." The goat was their national emblem. The city of Ægæ was the usual burying place of their kings, and Alexander's son was named Alexander Ægus, or the son of the goat.

5. The Four Notable Horns (8:8, 22). But Alexander, after ruling the world for only two years, in the very height of his power, died,— a victim to strong drink. "When he was strong, the great horn was broken; and for it came up four notable ones toward the four winds of heaven." Explaining this, the angel said, "Four kingdoms shall stand up out of the nation, but not in his power." And this was true. After years of strife, the great kingdom of Alexander was divided among four of his generals, each taking a different section of the kingdom, represented by "the four winds of heaven,"— one, Asia Minor, to the north of Palestine; another, Babylon, to the east; another, Egypt, to the south; and another, Greece, to the west. But none of these possessed the power of the original kingdom of Alexander.

6. God's Overruling Power (8:7). Thus it is again shown that "the Most High ruleth in the kingdom of men, and giveth it to whomsoever He will." Every king, or kingdom, has full opportunity to coöperate with God and do that which is right. But if he refuses, the time will surely come when his cup of iniquity will be full. Then God will say, "Remove the diadem, and take off the crown." Gabriel and Michael had both stood to help and strengthen the kings of Media and Persia, but these kings had resisted the divine influence. For this reason they were at last left to their own ways. Then the prince of Grecia came, and because God's protection was withdrawn, "there was none that could deliver the ram out of his hand."

How to Study: Be able to describe the ram and the he-goat, and tell what each did. Tell what kingdoms are meant by each of these beasts, and what they correspond to in the great image and in Daniel's first vision. Review the dates of the rise and fall of these kingdoms. Tell what the following symbols represent: the two horns of the ram; the higher horn that came up last; the pushing westward and northward and southward; the notable horn of the goat; its four notable horns. Why were these great kingdoms overthrown?

Map Work: Locate the Medo-Persian and Grecian kingdoms; the river where Daniel had this vision. Trace the campaign of the Medes and Persians as described under topic 2. Locate the city where at this time was one of the king's palaces; the river where the Medo-Persians and Grecians fought an important battle; the four divisions of Alexander's kingdom.

For Your Workbook: On diagram No. 6 place the ram and the he-goat.

13. SATAN'S MASTERPIECE OF DECEPTION
The Little Horn That Waxed Exceeding Great — Dan. 8: 9-27

"The mystery of iniquity doth already work." 2 Thess. 2:7.

1. Conquests of the Little Horn (8: 8, 9). In the second vision that God gave to Daniel, he saw a little horn coming out of one of the "four notable ones" which came up on the head of the he-goat after the first notable horn had been broken. This little horn represented both pagan and papal Rome, the same as the terrible beast with ten horns, three of which were finally plucked up. But this little horn did not long remain little. It "waxed *exceeding* great." Its greatness was first shown in the countries it conquered. It "waxed exceeding great, toward the south, and toward the east, and toward the pleasant land." The Roman Empire began in Italy at the city called Rome. Through war, it conquered all the territory to the east, first Greece in Europe, then that part of the Grecian Empire located still farther east in Asia. It also extended its conquests south into Egypt, and conquered Judea, "the pleasant land." At last every civilized nation was captured by Rome, the little horn that "waxed exceeding great." When Jesus came to Bethlehem the whole civilized world was ruled by Rome.

Out of one of the four notable horns "came forth a little horn, which waxed exceeding great."

2. Destruction of "the Holy People" (8:10, 24). But this little horn did more than conquer *earthly* kingdoms. "It waxed great, even to the host of heaven; and it cast down some of the host and of the stars to the ground, and stamped upon them." We have already seen how cruelly this wicked power persecuted the church of Christ and "stamped upon them" with its feet having nails of brass, and how it wore out the saints of the Most High. Had not God prevented, it would have stamped His people out of existence. When the angel explained the work of the little horn, he called it "a king of fierce countenance" who "shall destroy wonderfully," who "shall destroy the mighty and the holy people." No other power that has ever existed on this earth has done such a work of destroying God's people as has Rome — both pagan and papal Rome.

3. **God's Truth Cast Down** (8: 12, 24). "And his power shall be mighty," said the angel, "but not by his own power." No merely human power could do what this little horn would do. It was Satan's masterpiece of cruelty and deception,— of cruelty in destroying God's people, of deception in leading the world to believe false teachings. With fiendish satisfaction Satan has seen this little horn obey his dictates, and make the breach in God's holy law, which only the death of Jesus could restore. He has seen the little horn tear out of God's law the sacred Sabbath, the sign or seal of God's authority, and in its place establish a day of his own appointment as a mark or seal of *his* authority.

The prophecy says of this little horn, "It cast down the truth to the ground; and it practiced, and prospered." This was the same work that was done by the little horn that Daniel saw in his first vision, that power which should think to change the law of the Most High. The world knows how Rome has changed God's law, and Rome herself boasts of her blasphemous accomplishment. Urged on by Satan, she even speaks of it as proof that her authority is greater than the authority of God.

Through one of her priests, the papacy says: "There is but one church on the face of the earth which has the power . . . to make laws binding on the conscience, binding before God. . . . For instance, the institution of Sunday. What right has any other church to keep this day? . . . Sunday is not the Sabbath. Any schoolboy knows that Sunday is the first day of the week. I have repeatedly offered $1,000 to anyone who will prove to me from the Bible alone that I am bound to keep Sunday holy. There is no such law in the Bible. It is a law of the holy Catholic Church alone. The Bible says, 'Remember that thou keep holy *the Sabbath day*.' The Catholic Church says, 'No! By my divine power I abolish the Sabbath day, and command you to keep holy *the first day of the week*.' And lo! the entire civilized world bows down in reverent obedience to the command of the holy Catholic Church." This shows how fully the papacy has "prospered" in daring to change God's divine law.

4. The Prince of Princes Slain (8: 11, 25). But the little horn did even worse, for "he magnified himself even to the Prince of the host," or as the angel said, "He shall also stand up against the Prince of princes." And Rome did this when by her consent Jesus was put to death on the cross. "He shall magnify himself in his heart," the angel said. Surely this sounds like the * "man of sin . . . who opposeth and exalteth himself above all that is called God, or that is worshiped"— the "mystery of iniquity" which Paul tells about. It sounds like Satan's boast, "I will exalt my throne above the stars of God: . . . I will be like the Most High."

5. Daniel's Distress. When Daniel saw all these things and the terrible experiences through which his people would pass, and especially when he saw Jesus the Saviour put to death, it made him sick at heart. Already the people of God were in captivity; already their country had been laid waste; already Jerusalem, that beautiful city, and the sacred temple, were in ruins. And now the Lord shows him that still greater evil is to follow. Daniel knows that they have sinned; he knows that God is just. But how can he bear all this! How long, O how long, must these things continue?

6. How Long Shall These Things Be? (8: 13, 14, 26). In his distress he hears angel voices. He listens. They seem to be talking the very thoughts of his own heart. "How long" shall these things be? This is what they are talking about. And then, turning to Daniel, one of them says: "Unto two thousand and three hundred days; then shall the sanctuary be cleansed. . . . The vision of the evening and the morning which was told is true: wherefore shut thou up the vision; for it shall be for many days."

7. Effect on Daniel (8: 27). And so, thought Daniel, must the beautiful sanctuary at Jerusalem lie waste 2300 years? He had supposed that seventy years was the time, and he knew this time had nearly passed. Was he mistaken? Had he been building on wrong ideas? Had he been holding out a false hope to his people? What could it all mean? Overcome with grief and disappointment, Daniel fainted, and for days he was sick. When he recovered he left Shushan and went to Babylon to attend to business for the king.

How to Study: Show on the map what territory was conquered by the little horn. Be able to tell how he destroyed the holy people, how he cast the truth down to the ground, how he stood up against the Prince of princes, and what was the cause of Daniel's distress. Tell also with what previous prophetic symbol this little horn corresponds.

Use of Concordance: Find the starred verse under topic 4.

Memory Work: Memorize Daniel 8:14. This is the last reference to enter in the center point of the "crown" on the "Service Flag."

Chapter to Remember: Daniel 8 tells Daniel's vision of the ram, the he-goat, and the little horn that "waxed exceeding great;" also about the 2300 days.

For Your Workbook: On diagram No. 6 add the little horn that "waxed exceeding great."

REVIEW OF DANIEL 8

Test Questions:

1. What nation is left out in Daniel's second vision? Why?
2. What nations are represented?
3. What represented Medo-Persia? What represented the twofold nature of this nation? Dan. 8:3. How was this characteristic represented in the bear of Daniel 7?
4. Name four of the Medo-Persian kings.
5. What represented Grecia? the rapidity of its conquests? the first king? the division of the kingdom into four parts? Dan. 8: 5-8.
6. Why does it seem fitting that the Grecians are represented by a goat?
7. Into what four parts was Alexander's kingdom divided?
8. What represented Rome in this vision? Dan. 8: 9.
9. In what four ways did this little horn wax exceeding great? Dan. 8: 9, 10, 11, first part, 12, last part.
10. How has the papacy, the "king of fierce countenance," "stamped upon" "the host of heaven"?
11. How has the papacy "cast down the truth to the ground"?
12. How has the papacy magnified himself "against the Prince of princes"?
13. Compare this prophecy with the great image; with Daniel 8.
14. Locate the four world kingdoms on the map.
15. Give the dates of the rise and fall of each of these kingdoms.
16. What story or prophecy is told in Daniel 1? 2? 3? 4? 7? 8?

Verse-Finding Drill: Practice until you can find in three minutes or less the verses containing the following statements:

1. Unto two thousand and three hundred days.
2. Gabriel, make this man to understand the vision.
3. He shall speak great words against the Most High.
4. The Ancient of Days did sit.

5. The four winds of the heaven strove upon the great sea.
6. O king, . . . break off thy sins by righteousness.
7. Our God . . . is able to deliver us from the . . . furnace.
8. A stone . . . smote the image upon his feet.

14. THE DOWNFALL OF THE FIRST WORLD EMPIRE

B. C. 538 — Daniel 5

"Thou art weighed in the balances, and art found wanting." Dan. 5:27.

1. Babylon's Departure from God. Over twenty years have passed since Nebuchadnezzar sat on the throne of Babylon. During these years different kings have ruled. They knew of the strange dream which Nebuchadnezzar had had, of the failure of the wise men to interpret it, and of the God of Daniel who had revealed its hidden meaning. They knew of the golden image that Nebuchadnezzar had set up in the plain of Dura, of the decree that he had made against any who refused to worship the image, of the fiery furnace, and the wonderful deliverance which God had wrought for the three Jews who in the face of death had remained true to their conscience. They knew also of Nebuchadnezzar's dream of the great tree; of that terrible seven years when the king, because of the hardness and pride of his heart, had dwelt with the beasts of the field until he learned that "the Most High ruleth in the kingdom of men, and giveth it to whomsoever He will." They knew of the decree which Nebuchadnezzar, after the return of his reason, sent out to all the world, in which he acknowledged God as supreme, the only source of peace and safety. But, though they knew all this, they had failed to profit by Nebuchadnezzar's experience.

2. God's Mercy Disregarded. Nevertheless God had been merciful to Babylon. He had left Daniel within its boundaries to assist in the affairs of the government, and to hold up the gospel light. Through him they might have known of the dangers that threatened the kingdom; they might have sought refuge in Him in whose hands are the destinies of nations as well as of men. Had they done this, God "would have healed Babylon." But they felt no need of divine protection. In their own power and pride they felt secure.

3. Rebellion of the Medes and Persians. As a result of Babylon's departure from God, only a short time after the death of

Nebuchadnezzar, the Medes and Persians, under Darius, assisted by Cyrus, his nephew, rebelled against the rule of Babylon. They decided to overthrow Babylon and themselves rule the world. Victory after victory followed their efforts, until at last Babylon was the only city in that part of the empire which held out against them.

4. The Siege of Babylon. And now Cyrus was sent to besiege Babylon. For days the siege continued, but without success. And

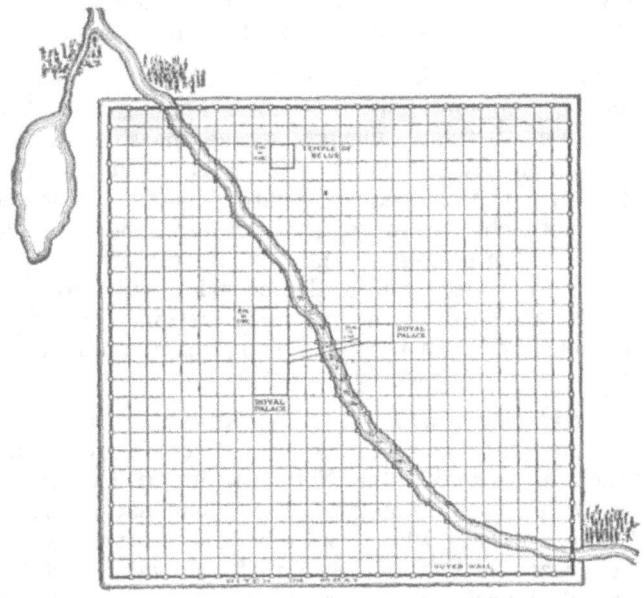

DIAGRAM No. 7

Plan of the city of Babylon, showing wall, moat, river, streets, gates, royal palaces connected with tunnel under the river bed, temple of Belus, and the three divisions of Darius's besieging army.

with the weapons then in use, it would seem as if no amount of battering could ever tear down those walls three hundred fifty feet high and eighty-seven feet thick, with their immense two-leaved gates of solid brass. Cyrus thought! Force would never conquer. He could not starve them out, for within those walls was provision enough to last a lifetime. He must resort to stratagem. He knew of an idolatrous feast which was soon to be celebrated within the city, and he chose that occasion as the time when he would undertake its capture. In order to do this he planned to turn the waters of the Euphrates into an artificial lake just above the city. While one division of soldiers was busy at this task, another was stationed at a point where the river flowed under the city wall into the city, and a third division at a point on the opposite side, where the river flowed under the wall out of the city. These two divisions were directed to watch the river, and as soon as the water was low enough, they were to wade along the river bed and make their way to the palace, capture or slay the king, and take possession of the city.

5. The Feast of Belshazzar (5:1). It was the last night for the kingdom of Babylon. But the people knew it not. Some were wrapped in quiet slumber. Others passed the time in thoughtless gayety. In the royal palace all was mirth and revelry. Music sounded through the brilliantly lighted halls. Decorated tables were spread with choice dainties. A thousand lords attended the royal banquet. Men of genius and education were there. Beautiful women richly robed graced the occasion with their presence. Belshazzar the king led in the riotous feasting. He "drank wine before the thousand." In response, the guests drank to the health of the king.

6. The Fatal Deed (5: 2-4). The fatal hour had come. Half intoxicated, the king "commanded to bring the golden and silver vessels which his grandfather Nebuchadnezzar had taken out of the temple which was in Jerusalem." The sacred vessels were brought — those vessels which had been made after the divine pattern, and consecrated to the worship of Jehovah. But Belshazzar would prove that nothing was too sacred for him to handle. The golden goblets were filled with sparkling wine. Then "the king, and his princes, his wives, and his concubines, drank in them. They drank wine, and praised the gods of gold, and of silver, of brass, of iron, of wood, and of stone." O thou impious Belshazzar! Little do you dream what awaits you!

7. The Handwriting on the Wall (5: 5, 6). Again the king fills the golden goblet with the crimson liquid. He lifts it to his lips. But — What is that? From the opposite wall, in the direct light of the candlestick,— perhaps the very candlestick that had once lighted the sacred temple of God,— there is reflected a blaze of daz-

Doré

"In the same hour came forth fingers of a man's hand, and wrote upon the wall of the king's palace."

zling light which reveals a man's hand ready to write. Paralyzed with fear, the king gazes at the spot. Every eye in that vast throng is turned in the same direction. The loud laughter ceases. The music dies away. Then the bloodless hand silently traces strange letters as with a pen of fire. No one understands the writing. The king's countenance expresses deep anxiety. His whole body shakes with fear. Some fearful judgment seems about to fall on the fated palace. But who knows what it is?

8. The Wise Men Called In (5:7-9). Then in tones of wild distress that are easily heard throughout the company, Belshazzar cries out, "Bring in the astrologers, the Chaldeans, and the soothsayers!" All the wise men hurry in. The king promises great rewards to the one who will read the writing. In blank amazement the wise men look at the burning letters. They do not know the meaning of a single word. The anxiety of the king increases. The whole company of lords is seized with fear.

9. Daniel Called In (5:10-17). Just then the queen-mother enters the banquet hall. Approaching the king, she reminds him of Daniel, who more than once had revealed secrets to Nebuchadnezzar. "Let Daniel be called," she urged, "and he will show the interpretation." Then Daniel was brought in before the king. Belshazzar endeavors to compose himself, that he may speak calmly.

"Art thou that Daniel, which art of the children of the captivity of Judah, whom the king my grandfather brought out of Jewry?" he asks. "I have even heard of thee, that the spirit of the gods is in thee, and that light and understanding and excellent wisdom is found in thee. And now the wise men . . . have been brought in before me, that they should read this writing: . . . but they could not show the interpretation of the thing. . . . Now if thou canst read the writing, and make known to me the interpretation thereof, thou shalt be clothed with scarlet, and have a chain of gold about thy neck, and shalt be the third ruler in the kingdom."

The anxious, terror-stricken company bend forward to catch every word. Before them stands Daniel in calm dignity, not to speak words of flattery, hoping for the king's reward, but to speak the words that God shall give him. "Let thy gifts be to thyself, and give thy rewards to another," he said to the king; "yet I will read the writing."

10. The King Reproved (5: 18-23). With a silent prayer, Daniel looked at the blazing letters, and as their meaning was impressed on his mind, he turned to the king with a look of terrible censure. "O thou king," he began, "the most high God gave Nebuchadnezzar . . . a kingdom, and majesty, and glory, and honor. . . . But when his heart was lifted up, and his mind hardened in pride, he was deposed from his kingly throne, . . . till he knew that the most high God ruled in the kingdom of men. . . . And thou, . . . Belshazzar, hast not humbled thine heart, though thou knewest all this; but hast lifted up thyself against the Lord of heaven; and they have brought the vessels of His house before thee, and thou, and thy lords, thy wives, and thy concubines, have drunk wine in them; and thou hast praised the gods of silver, and gold, of brass, iron, wood, and stone, which see not, nor hear, nor know: and the God in whose hand thy breath is, and whose are all thy ways, hast thou not glorified."

11. The Writing Explained (5: 25-29). Without a word, the guilty king listened to this public exposure of his sins. Then, pointing to the writing on the wall, Daniel read slowly and with terrible distinctness, as the people, breathless, listened: "MENE; God hath numbered thy kingdom, and finished it. TEKEL; Thou art weighed in the balances, and art found wanting. PERES; Thy kingdom is divided, and given to the Medes and Persians." Only three words, but they sealed the doom of the most glorious kingdom this earth has ever seen. Belshazzar did not forget his promise, and at his command Daniel was clothed with scarlet, a chain of gold was put about his neck, and he was proclaimed third ruler in the kingdom.

12. Babylon Captured (5:30, 31). Scarcely had this been done when the tramp of soldiers and the clash of weapons was heard in the very vestibule of the palace. The army of Cyrus, under the direction of Darius, had succeeded in entering the city by way of the river bed, the gates along the bank of the river having in that night of drunken revelry carelessly been left open, and the soldiers had found their way to the palace without the least opposition. "In that night was Belshazzar the king of the Chaldeans slain. And Darius the Median took the kingdom."

Thus was fulfilled the prophecy given by Isaiah more than a century before: "Thus saith the Lord . . . to Cyrus; . . . I will . . . open before him the two-leaved gates; and the gates shall not be shut; . . . I will break in pieces the gates of brass; . . . and I will give thee the treasures of darkness." Will Cyrus prove worthy of the responsibility intrusted to him by God?

How to Study: Be able to tell why Babylon was overthrown, and how Cyrus took the city. Then, from topics 5-12, try to tell connectedly the story of Belshazzar's feast. What lesson do you think this story should teach us? In what year was Babylon taken by the Medo-Persians?

Use of Concordance: Find the prophecy quoted under topic 12. Key word: Cyrus.

Chapter to Remember: Daniel 5 tells the story of Belshazzar's feast and the fall of Babylon.

For Your Workbook: On the plan of Babylon indicate, in appropriate colors, the Euphrates River, the two royal palaces, the temple of Belus, the gates of brass, the outer wall, the underground passages connecting the two palaces, and where Cyrus stationed his soldiers. Diagram No. 7.

15. THE PLOT TO DESTROY DANIEL
Daniel 6

"My God hath sent His angel, and hath shut the lions' mouths, that they have not hurt me." Dan. 6:22.

1. Daniel Prime Minister of Medo-Persia (6:1-3). Medo-Persia now ruled the world; and Darius, the uncle of Cyrus, was its king. In arranging the affairs of his newly acquired kingdom, King Darius divided the responsibility among one hundred twenty princes, each prince to have command of a section of the kingdom. Over these princes he placed three presidents. These presidents were

Daniel "kneeled upon his knees three times a day, and prayed, as he did aforetime."

to protect the interests of the king, that "the king should have no damage." Because there was "an excellent spirit" in Daniel, the king decided "to set him over the whole realm." He therefore made Daniel the first of the three presidents. More than a thousand years before this, Pharaoh, king of Egypt, had said to Joseph, "Only in the throne will I be greater than thou;" and now Daniel held the same position in Medo-Persia. He was the king's prime minister.

2. The Plot Against Daniel (6:4-7). When Daniel was honored with the first position in the new kingdom, Satan was angry. Because of this man's faithfulness and loyalty to God, the plans of the enemy had more than once been defeated under Babylonian rule; and now he is placed at the very head of affairs in the new government. Satan knew there was little opportunity to promote his de-

---
References Used: P. K., pp. 539-548.

signs so long as this Daniel held control. He determined to get rid of him. He therefore stirred the other presidents and princes with a spirit of wicked jealousy. "Why should he, a Hebrew captive, be thus honored above us?" they said to one another. As they talked the matter over, they decided if possible to destroy the king's confidence in Daniel. To do this they first "sought to find occasion

"These men assembled, and found Daniel praying and making supplication before his God."

against Daniel concerning the kingdom." But in this they were disappointed, for Daniel faithfully attended to every detail of his work for the king. Though they sought diligently, they could find no error or fault in him.

Again they consulted together, and at last they agreed: "We shall not find any occasion against this Daniel, except we find it against him concerning the law of his God." They knew that

Daniel was frequently in prayer with God. So in order to accomplish their wicked designs, they decided to ask the king "to make a firm decree" that whosoever should ask a petition of any god or man for thirty days save of the king should be cast into the den of lions. The plan delighted them all, for they felt sure that in this way Daniel would soon be disposed of.

3. The Decree Signed (6: 6-9). Then these presidents and princes "came tumultuously" to the king as if on important business that required haste. They presented the decree for him to sign. With great satisfaction they urged that a decree of this kind would add to his honor and authority. The king felt flattered that these great men should be so zealous for his honor. He never dreamed of their real purpose. So King Darius signed the decree.

4. Daniel's Attitude Toward the Decree (6: 10). Daniel knew nothing of what was going on, until he learned that the decree had been signed. He read the writing carefully. He knew that, according to the laws of the Medes and Persians, whatever the king signed could not be altered. Should he pray to God as usual? If he did, he would disobey the king's law, and in that case but one thing awaited him — he would be cast to the hungry lions. But Daniel was not afraid of the king's decree, nor was he afraid of the lions. He knew that God could save from the lions as well as from the fiery furnace, and whether He did or not, he would serve God faithfully. To Daniel it was more important to hold up the light of life to others than to try to save his own life. "He went into his house; and his windows being open in his chamber toward Jerusalem, he kneeled upon his knees three times a day, and prayed, and gave thanks before his God, as he did aforetime." No doubt at this very time Daniel was praying to understand the vision about the 2300 days, for this was still weighing heavily on his heart.

5. Daniel Is Reported to the King (6: 13-17). The princes kept watch all one day, and when they saw Daniel in prayer to God, they reported to the king: "That Daniel, which is of the children of the captivity of Judah, regardeth not thee, O king, nor the decree that thou hast signed, but maketh his petition three times a day." They tried to make the king believe that Daniel was disloyal to the government. As soon as the king heard this report, he realized what he had done in signing the decree. He saw now that it was not zeal for his honor, but jealousy against Daniel, that had led the princes to urge the decree. He knew that Daniel was not disloyal to the best interests of the kingdom. Daniel was his most honored and trusted counselor. There was not another man in all his realm whom he so greatly respected and loved. "Why, O why," he thought, "did I sign the writing!" All day long he labored, "till the going down of the sun," to deliver Daniel. The princes observed the king's effort to save Daniel, and they reminded him that a law signed by the king could not be changed.

There seemed no way out except to trust God to deliver His servant. So the king commanded, and they brought Daniel, now an old man nearly ninety years of age, and cast him into the den of lions. The king's last words to Daniel were, "Thy God whom thou servest continually, He will deliver thee." Then "a stone was brought, and laid upon the mouth of the den; and the king sealed it with his own signet," so that no one would dare to open the den.

6. A Night of Anxious Suspense (6: 18-24). Then the king went to his palace, but not to feasting and merriment as usual. He refused the food that was brought him and he sent away the musicians. In his distress he wanted to be alone. As the night dragged wearily along, his thoughts were of Daniel. Was God protecting him? Was he still alive? Or had the hungry lions devoured him? The king could not sleep, and how long the night seemed! At the first dawn of day, he went in haste to the den of lions. In a voice of anxious distress, he called out, "O Daniel, servant of the living God, is thy God, whom thou servest continually, able to deliver thee from the lions?"

Back from that den came the triumphant answer: "O king, live forever. My God hath sent His angel, and hath shut the lions' mouths, that they have not hurt me." How good it seemed to the king to hear Daniel's voice! "Exceeding glad," he commanded that Daniel be taken out of the den. So Daniel was taken out, "and no manner of hurt was found upon him, because he believed in his God." Then those men who had accused Daniel were cast among the lions, and the lions seized them and tore them in pieces before they reached the bottom of the den.

7. Darius's Decree Honoring God (6: 25-28). Nebuchadnezzar had several times written a decree of honor to God; and now a decree was written by Darius, another heathen ruler, proclaiming the God of Daniel as the only true God. It was sent to "all people,

"My God hath sent His angel, and hath shut the lions' mouths, that they have not hurt me.

nations, and languages, that dwell in all the earth," and read: "Peace be multiplied unto you. I make a decree, that in every dominion of my kingdom men tremble and fear before the God of Daniel: for He is the living God, and steadfast forever, and His kingdom that which shall not be destroyed, and His dominion shall be even unto the end. He delivereth and rescueth, and He worketh signs and wonders in heaven and in earth, who hath delivered Daniel from the power of the lions."

Thus again Satan was caught in his own trap, and the name of God was made known throughout the world. As a result "Daniel prospered in the reign of Darius, and in the reign of Cyrus," who succeeded Darius.

How to Study: Ask your father to read Daniel 6 for family worship. After reading the lesson carefully, try to tell the whole story. Copy the topics as a guide, if this will help you to get all the points in their proper order.

Chapter to Remember: Daniel 6 tells the story of Daniel in the lions' den.

For Class Discussion: How was Medo-Persia represented in the great image? in Daniel's first vision? in his second vision?

---

16. GABRIEL SENT TO ANSWER DANIEL'S PRAYER
Dan. 9: 1-3, 20-24

"O our God, . . . cause Thy face to shine upon Thy sanctuary, that is desolate, for the Lord's sake." Dan. 9:17.

1. Daniel Studying the Prophecies (9: 2). In spite of the many anxious cares and heavy burdens that came to Daniel as prime minister to the king, he did not neglect prayer or the study of God's word, not even in the face of death. Over and over again since his second vision he had thought of the angel's words, "Unto two thousand and three hundred days; then shall the sanctuary be cleansed." Day after day he studied the messages God had sent His people, to find what the prophets had written about the release of Israel from captivity, and their return to Jerusalem to restore the sanctuary that had been desecrated and laid waste.

References Used: Jer. 25: 11, 12; 29: 10.

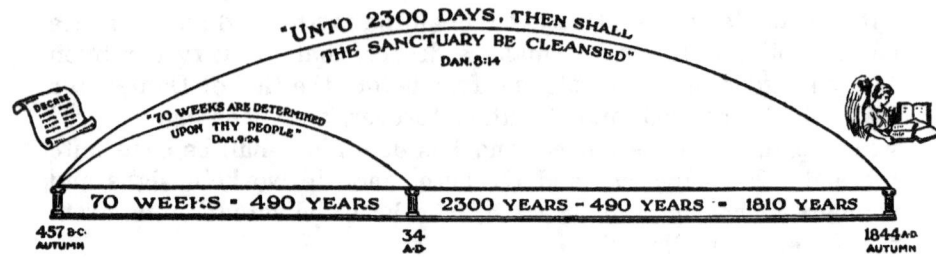

DIAGRAM NO. 8. The 2300 days

But the only message Daniel could find said plainly that the captivity would end, not after 2300 days, but "when seventy years are accomplished." In the writings of Jeremiah, he read: "This whole land [Judah] . . . shall serve the king of Babylon seventy years. And it shall come to pass, when seventy years are accomplished, that I will punish the king of Babylon, and that nation, saith the Lord, for their iniquity." And again, "Thus saith the Lord, that after seventy years be accomplished at Babylon I will visit you, and perform My good word toward you, in causing you to return to this place." Nothing could be plainer than these words. What could the angel have meant by saying that the sanctuary would not be cleansed for 2300 days, or years?

To Daniel the sanctuary meant the temple at Jerusalem, which had been destroyed by unholy hands of heathen warriors. How could it be 2300 years before *that* would be cleansed or restored? He could not harmonize the words of Jeremiah with what the angel had told *him*. Could it be that Israel's sins had been so great that long, long years must still pass before they would be permitted to return to their beloved Zion and restore the sanctuary?

2. Daniel in Prayer (9: 1, 3). Daniel was sad and perplexed. But he knew where to find help in time of trouble. He was acquainted with the One who could reveal secrets and give understanding. And to Him he went. Since God had given him the vision, he had doubtless often prayed for wisdom; for the seventy years were drawing to a close, and he felt that he must have help. He set his face "unto the Lord God, to seek by prayer and supplications, with fasting, and sackcloth, and ashes."

3. Arrival of Gabriel (9: 20-23). While Daniel was still praying, Gabriel, the very angel who had talked with him in the vision, the one to whom God had said, "Make this man to understand the vision," flew swiftly to him and gently touched him. Gabriel knew the burden on Daniel's heart; he knew that Daniel had not understood the vision, and he had come to give him skill and understanding. "O Daniel," he said, "at the beginning of thy supplications the commandment came forth, and I am come to show thee; for thou art greatly beloved: therefore understand the matter, and consider the vision."

4. The Seventy Weeks (9:24). As Gabriel explains the vision, let us follow step by step.

Gabriel's Words	*Their Meaning*
"Seventy weeks	Four hundred ninety days, or years,
are determined	are cut off from the 2300 days,
upon thy people and upon thy holy city,	for the Jews and for Jerusalem,
to finish the transgression,	to fill up their cup of iniquity or to repent,
and to make an end of sins,	to make an end of sin offerings, because Jesus would become the great sin offering,
and to make reconciliation for iniquity,	to make atonement for sin by the sacrifice of Jesus,
and to bring in everlasting righteousness,	to bring in the righteousness of Jesus' life on earth,
and to seal up the vision and prophecy,	and thus — by these events coming to pass — seal up or make sure that the other events of the vision and prophecy would come to pass,
and to anoint the most holy."	and to anoint the heavenly sanctuary for the work of Jesus our heavenly High Priest.

5. Jesus' Work in the Holy Place. In this one verse Gabriel told the whole future of the nation which God had set apart as His special missionary nation. As God's chosen nation they were to have 490 years, either to repent and do the work God wanted them to do, or to fill up their cup of iniquity and be forever rejected. During this time Jesus would come to this earth, live a perfect life among them, and be crucified as an offering for the sins of the whole world. After that the work in the earthly sanctuary would be at an end and no more sin offerings would be accepted. Then the heavenly sanctuary would be anointed, and Jesus, the true High

Priest, would begin His work in the holy place, the first apartment on high. This was the great event of the seventy weeks — the event that would seal up, or make sure, this vision and all other prophecies. It is one of the greatest events in all the history of this world.

How to Study: What was troubling Daniel's mind, and what was he praying for? How long did it take Gabriel to come to his assistance? The most important thing in this lesson is to be able to explain each step of Daniel 9:24. Study this verse very closely. What was the greatest event of the seventy weeks? When did it occur? What verse in the Bible proves that a day in prophecy represents a year?

Perhaps Daniel's prayer could be read for family worship at your home. When it is read, notice particularly verses 3, 5, 8-11, 15-18. They show Daniel's unselfish desire to honor God and see His work prosper.

Memory Work: Memorize Daniel 9:24. Review Daniel 8:14.

Chapter to Remember: Daniel 9 records Daniel's prayer to understand the 2300 days, and Gabriel's explanation.

For Your Workbook: Begin the diagram of the 2300 days, indicating its two main divisions — the 70 weeks, or 490 years, and the remainder of the time. How many years would be left after cutting off 490?

17. GABRIEL'S EXPLANATION OF THE 2300 DAYS
Dan. 9:25-27

"Unto two thousand and three hundred days; then shall the sanctuary be cleansed." Dan. 8:14.

1. Divisions of the Seventy Weeks (9:25-27). After explaining that the 2300 days had two main divisions, Gabriel further explained that the first of these divisions, the seventy weeks, was made up of three smaller divisions — seven weeks, threescore and two weeks, and one week. Find out how many literal years there are in each division, and mark off these three divisions on the diagram you began in the last lesson.

2. The Seven Weeks (9:25). The event to take place at the beginning of the seven weeks he said would be "the going forth of the commandment to restore and to build Jerusalem." In Ezra 6:14, this commandment of God is called "the commandment of Cyrus, and Darius, and Artaxerxes," because it was issued by all three of these kings. Mark this event on your diagram.

References Used: Ezra 6:14; 7:8; Acts 8:1, 4; 10:38; Matt. 3:16.

"The going forth" of this commandment meant when it should be put into effect. Ezra was the one chosen by Artaxerxes to see that this decree was carried out and that Jerusalem was restored. According to Ezra 7:8, he reached Jerusalem in B. C. 457, in the fifth Jewish month, which in our time would be in the autumn — about the middle of the year. This of course would be 456½ years B. C. Mark this time on your diagram. You now have both the event and the time marking the beginning of the seven weeks.

"The street [of Jerusalem] shall be built again, and the wall, even in troublous times." This was the event that Gabriel said

THE 70 WEEKS. The time of Jesus' baptism and crucifixion definitely foretold.

should mark the end of the seven weeks. Indicate this event on your diagram. Indicate also the date.

3. The Threescore and Two Weeks. Gabriel said that threescore and two weeks more would reach "unto the Messiah the Prince." "Messiah" means "anointed," and Christ was anointed with the Holy Spirit at the time of His baptism. The baptism of Christ occurred in the autumn of 27 A. D., or 26½ years after Christ. This is just "seven weeks, and threescore and two weeks," or 483 years, after the autumn of 457 B. C. You can prove this by adding 456½ years B. C. to 26½ years A. D., which equals 483 years. On your diagram mark the date and the event at the end of the sixty-two weeks.

4. The One Week (9:27). Gabriel further said, "And He [the Messiah] shall confirm the covenant with many for one week." This period of seven years, which you have already marked, will extend seven years after the autumn of 27 A. D., or to the autumn of the year 34 A. D. "And in the midst [middle] of the week [which would be the spring of A. D. 31] He shall cause the sacrifice and the oblation to cease [by His death]." Jesus was crucified at the time of the last Passover He attended, in the spring of 31 A. D. Mark this event on your diagram with a cross. Mark also the date.

5. Jesus' Work During the One Week. How earnestly Jesus worked during this last "week" to "confirm the covenant" with His chosen people! For three and one half years He went from place to place, teaching and working miracles. But in spite of all that He could do, they refused to repent. And at last with wicked hands they nailed His sacred body to the cross of Calvary. But even after this, mercy for the Jewish nation still lingered a little longer. For three and one half years more, God worked mightily by the Holy Spirit, which Jesus sent when He ascended to heaven. On the day of Pentecost three thousand were won to Christ. But this only aroused Satan's anger still more, and God's own chosen nation became the most bitter persecutors of those who accepted Christ. At last, in 34 A. D., they stoned Stephen to death, and terrible persecution followed. The limit of God's forbearance was then passed, and the chosen nation was at last rejected. This event marked the end of the seventy weeks.

6. The End of the 2300 Days. You have already learned that if you subtract 490 years [the seventy weeks] from 2300 years, 1810 years remain. This is the rest of the 2300 years. On your diagram add 1810 years to the autumn of 34. To what time does it reach? At this time, the autumn of 1844, "then," said the angel, "shall the sanctuary be cleansed." Then the wicked work of the little horn would be exposed. Its true character would be made known. No longer would God's people be deceived by this blasphemous power. No longer would God's law be cast down to the ground. At that time God would send "to every nation, and kindred, and tongue, and people" a message that would expose the deceptive character of the little horn, and help all to understand the work of Jesus in the heavenly sanctuary. The message which began to be preached at this very time is called the *third angel's message*.

7. Cleansing of the Sanctuary Explained. You have already learned that the earthly sanctuary was cleansed on the day of atonement, which always came in the autumn, after the harvest was past and the summer was ended. The exact time was the tenth day of the seventh month. The cleansing of the heavenly sanctuary is the antitype of the day of atonement. This work is called the Investigative Judgment, because at this time the record of every child of God is investigated, or examined, and God, the great Judge, decides whether he is worthy or unworthy of eternal life.

8. Jesus' Work in the Most Holy Place. The cleansing of the heavenly sanctuary began in the autumn of 1844, on October 22, the date on which the day of atonement would have come that year in the earthly sanctuary had that work not been transferred to heaven. On that day Jesus entered the second apartment of the heavenly sanctuary, and began His work before the Ancient of Days and in the presence of all the angels of heaven. Then "the books were opened" which Daniel saw in his first vision. When the Investigative Judgment is finished, probation will close, and Jesus will come the second time. May no one who reads these lessons be compelled to say, when his record is investigated, "The harvest is past, the summer is ended, and I am not saved."

How to Study: As you read this lesson, continue, step by step, the drawing of the diagram which you began in the last lesson. You should be able to understand every event, and figure out every date for yourself. After you have once drawn it from the lesson, you should be able to draw it from memory, giving all the dates, and the events for each date. Where is Daniel's vision of the Investigative Judgment recorded? How many years since it began?

Memory Work: Memorize Daniel 9: 25, 26, first part, and 27, first part. Enter this reference in the first star on the left point of the "crown" on the "Service Flag." Review Daniel 9: 24.

For Your Workbook: Finish the diagram of the 2300 days. On diagram No. 1 indicate where this period of time belongs.

For the Ambitious Student: The "commandment" which Gabriel told Daniel marked the beginning of the 2300 days is recorded in Ezra 7: 11-26. You will enjoy reading it.

Where are these events told in the Bible? — Crucifixion of Christ, three thousand converted on the day of Pentecost, Stephen stoned and persecution following, the third angel's message.

REVIEW OF DANIEL 5, 6, 9

Test Questions and Exercises: Memory verses are starred. Numbers refer to preceding lessons.

14. Why was Babylon overcome by Medo-Persia? By what stratagem did Cyrus take Babylon? What was the last of Belshazzar's wicked acts?

What three words told the doom of Babylon? What is the meaning of each? What prophecy was fulfilled in the capture of Babylon by Cyrus? Give reference. In what year was this?

15. What position was given to Daniel in the Medo-Persian kingdom? What did Satan lead the other rulers to do? Why? How was he defeated and God honored?

16. Why did the 2300 days perplex Daniel? Where is Daniel's prayer to understand the vision recorded? What six events did the angel say would take place at the close of the seventy weeks? *Dan. 9:24. How was each fulfilled? Into how many parts did Gabriel divide the seventy weeks, and what events marked these divisions? *Dan. 9:25, and first part of 26 and 27. What event did the angel say would occur at the end of the 2300 days? *Daniel 8:14.

17. Explain your diagram of the 2300 days, telling:
   a. The entire period — Bible reference; number of literal years.
   b. Beginning of 2300 days — event; date.
   c. 70 weeks — Bible reference; number of literal years.
       7 weeks — number of literal years; event and date at end.
       62 weeks — number of literal years; event and date at end.
       1 week — number of literal years; event and date at end.
       Midst of week — event; date; number of years in each half.
   d. Number of years left of the 2300.
   e. End of 2300 years — event; date.

18. PREPARATIONS TO RETURN TO JERUSALEM

B. C. 536 — Daniel 10, 11

*"When the Lord turned again the captivity of Zion,
We were like them that dream." Ps. 126:1.*

1. Cyrus and His Relation to God's Work. Only about two years after Darius captured Babylon, he died. Then Cyrus became king. Cyrus regarded Daniel as a great man. He knew of his deliverance from the lions, and God used this circumstance to increase the king's regard. Any man who would refuse to do wrong even when threatened with a horrible death is worthy of the esteem of any king. It had now been seventy years since Judah was taken captive by Nebuchadnezzar. The year of deliverance had at last come. Daniel was familiar with the prophecies that Isaiah had written nearly two hundred years before, foretelling the return of his people to Jerusalem. In these prophecies, God had spoken of Cyrus, calling him by name more than one hundred years before he was born. * "Cyrus," He said, "is My shepherd, and shall perform all My

---

References Used: P. K., pp. 551, 552, 557, 560; G. C., pp. 470, 471; D. R. on lesson text; Ezra 1:4, 7, 11; 6:4, 14.

pleasure: even saying to Jerusalem, Thou shalt be built; and to the temple, Thy foundation shall be laid." * "I have raised him up in righteousness, and I will direct all his ways: he shall build My city, and he shall let go My captives."

2. **The Decree of Cyrus.** Through Daniel, Cyrus learned of these prophecies. His heart was deeply impressed as he realized that the great King of the universe had thought about *him*. He at once issued a decree proclaiming liberty to all the Jews throughout his world kingdom. This decree provided not only that the people might go, but that they be helped "with silver, and with gold, and with goods, and with beasts" for their long journey across the desert, "beside the freewill offering for the house of God that is in Jerusalem. . . . Also Cyrus the king brought forth the vessels of the house of the Lord, which Nebuchadnezzar had brought forth out of Jerusalem, . . . five thousand and four hundred" vessels of gold and of silver. These were to be taken back to Jerusalem, the temple was to be rebuilt, and "the expenses be given out of the king's house." This decree was the beginning of "the commandment to restore and to build Jerusalem"—"the commandment of Cyrus, and Darius, and Artaxerxes king of Persia."

3. **Effect on the Jews.** This decree was sent to every part of the kingdom, and before long all the Jews had learned about it. Many, like Daniel, had been earnestly studying the prophecies and praying to God for deliverance. And now their prayers were answered, and there was great rejoicing. To these faithful ones it seemed like a beautiful dream.

> "When the Lord turned again the captivity of Zion,
> We were like them that dream.
> Then was our mouth filled with laughter,
> And our tongue with singing:
> Then said they among the heathen,
> The Lord hath done great things for them."

But while some were glad to return, a much larger number preferred to remain among the heathen. Here they had built their homes, and they were more interested in comfortable living than in sacrificing to promote God's work in the earth.

4. **Cyrus' Disappointment; Effect on Daniel.** Cyrus was disappointed because so many of the Jews did not appreciate his generous offer. He could not understand why they should hesitate to carry

out the plain directions of God, in whom they professed to believe. These conditions gave Daniel deep sorrow. He feared that Cyrus would become discouraged, and lose interest in the return of his people to Jerusalem. He thought about the visions God had given him, and he wondered if his people, by refusing to follow God's plan, would, after all, suffer the persecutions that had been shown him. He wondered if by their sins they would bring still further distress to the heart of God and reproach upon His work.

5. Daniel's Three Weeks of Prayer (10:1-9). For months Daniel carried this burden upon his heart. Then he determined, if possible, to understand these matters more fully. With a few trusted companions he withdrew to a quiet place on the banks of the river, and here for three whole weeks he fasted and prayed and studied the inspired prophecies. At the end of that time Christ Himself came to Daniel. The prophet saw by the river "a certain man clothed in linen, whose loins were girded with fine gold. . . . His body also was like the beryl, and His face as the appearance of lightning, and His eyes as lamps of fire, and His arms and His feet like in color to polished brass, and the voice of His words like the voice of a multitude." This man clothed in linen was the Son of God. Those who were with Daniel were terrified and fled, leaving Daniel alone with Jesus. Even Daniel's strength left him, and he fell "in a deep sleep" with his face to the ground.

6. Gabriel with Daniel (10:10-13). The next that Daniel knew, Gabriel touched him, and said, "O Daniel, a man greatly beloved, understand the words that I speak unto thee, and stand upright: for unto thee am I now sent." Daniel stood trembling. The angel said gently, "Fear not, Daniel." Why should Daniel fear the angel who, in answer to his earnest prayer and because he was greatly beloved, was sent to help him? It is the joy of the angels to minister to those who shall be heirs of salvation. Gabriel explained to Daniel that his prayer was heard from the very first day, and he would have come at once had he not been delayed twenty-one days by Cyrus, the king of Persia. At last, to prevent further delay, Michael Himself came to his help, and he was released. God was working to prevent Cyrus from becoming discouraged in his effort to help the Jews rebuild Jerusalem.

7. A Glimpse of "the Great Conflict." How little do we realize what, all unseen by human eyes, is going on in this conflict between good and evil, between Christ and Satan! Here the curtain is lifted and we catch a glimpse of the struggle. Daniel prays. God hears. Gabriel is sent to answer the prayer. But Cyrus must act before Daniel's prayer can be answered. So Gabriel goes first to Cyrus. Satan is there to oppose. They meet in the king's palace. Satan appeals to selfish ambition and worldly interests to influence the king against yielding to God. Gabriel appeals to his sense of right and duty. One moment Cyrus almost decides to yield to the angel. Then his selfish nature rises. He hesitates. He delays. Day after day passes. Daniel still prays on. Three weeks pass. Then Jesus Himself comes, pausing by the way to speak a word of encouragement to Daniel. The victory is won. Gabriel is released and flies swiftly to the beloved Daniel. And all this is the result of prayer. The same privilege is ours to-day. Victory awaits the one who will pray without ceasing.

8. The Future Revealed (10:14). After assuring Daniel that Cyrus would do his part, and that his people would return and rebuild Jerusalem and restore the temple, Gabriel said, "I am come to make thee understand what shall befall thy people in the latter days." Twice Daniel nearly fainted and had to be strengthened before Gabriel could continue. Twice the angel repeated, "Thou art greatly beloved." Then he unfolded before him another line of prophecy, the third one revealed to Daniel. This long prophecy is recorded in the eleventh and twelfth chapters of Daniel. The eleventh chapter covers about the same ground as his first two prophecies. It reaches from the Medo-Persian kingdom in Daniel's day to the very last events that will take place on this earth. It is a prophecy of crime and wickedness, of wars and revolutions, of the making and breaking of treaties; yet through it all God shows His overruling providence in the working out of His great plan.

How to Study: Be able to tell about the decree of Cyrus — what it was, what influenced him to issue it, and its effect on the Jews. Tell also why Daniel spent three weeks in prayer. Describe the appearance of the Son of God. Describe the glimpse of the struggle between Christ and Satan given us in the events of this lesson.

Use of Concordance: Find the two texts starred in paragraph 1. Key words: shepherd, direct.

Chapters to Remember: Daniel 10 tells about Daniel's three weeks' prayer and his vision of Christ. Daniel 11 and 12 contain Daniel's third prophecy.

For Class Discussion: In what year did Cyrus issue his part of the decree? When did the decree finally "go forth"? Of what long-time prophecy does it mark the beginning? What Bible book records "the commandment of Cyrus, and Darius, and Artaxerxes" "to restore and to build Jerusalem"?

19. THE SECOND COMING OF CHRIST FORETOLD
Dan. 12:1-3

"At that time shall Michael stand up, the great Prince which standeth for the children of thy people." Dan. 12:1.

1. Michael Shall Stand Up (12:1). When Gabriel had finished showing Daniel the events that would take place on this earth down to the end of time, he directed his attention to the heavenly sanctuary. "At that time shall Michael stand up," he said, "the great Prince which standeth for the children of thy people." The work of examining the records in the books that Daniel had seen in the first vision was finished. The last case was decided. The last sin was blotted out. God's great family was at last fully made up and their names were all in the book of life. Then Jesus stands up and with a loud voice proclaims, "It is done." The angel of mercy on earth responds, "It is done," and leaves the earth to Satan and its fate. All the angels lay off their crowns while Jesus slowly and solemnly announces, "He that is unjust, let him be unjust still: and he which is filthy, let him be filthy still: and he that is righteous, let him be righteous still: and he that is holy, let him be holy still."

When Jesus stands up, He lays aside His priestly garments and puts on His royal robe. How it must have cheered Daniel's heart to know that at the last, when the struggle is all over, the children of *his people* would be the special objects of Jesus' thought; that, come what might, the great Prince would "stand up" for them!

2. The Time of Trouble (12:1). When Jesus finishes His work with "the books," and stands up to leave the heavenly sanctuary — "at that time," said Gabriel, "there shall be a time of trouble, such as never was since there was a nation even to that same time." This time of trouble is caused by the withdrawal of the Spirit of God from the earth after Christ has finished His work as our Advocate. It is then that we shall have to stand without an In-

---
References Used: G. C., pp. 613, 637, 643; Isa. 25:9; 59:16; Jer. 30:7; Rev. 1:7; 22:14; Matt. 26:57-68; Ps. 111:10.

tercessor. It is then that the seven last plagues will be poured out. We are told that already the angel of mercy is folding her wings, ready to depart from the earth.

When God showed Jeremiah the time of trouble, He said: "All faces are turned into paleness. Alas! for that day is great, so that none is like it: it is even the time of Jacob's trouble; but he shall be saved out of it." It is called "the time of Jacob's trouble" because just as Jacob was threatened with death by his angry brother, influenced by Satan, so the people of God will be threatened with death by angry mobs who, urged on by Satan, are seeking to destroy them. And just as Jacob wrestled all night with the angel for the assurance of protection from Esau, so God's people will cry to Him day and night for deliverance from their enemies. If Jacob had not previously repented of his sin against his brother, God could not have heard his prayer and protected him. So in this time of trouble, if we have unconfessed sins, God cannot protect us. Satan leads many to think that God will overlook little sins; but no sin is small in God's sight. Now is the time for us to make sure that our record in the books of heaven is perfectly clear before God.

3. God's People Delivered (12:1). As Jacob was delivered from Esau, so, "at that time thy people," said Gabriel, "shall be delivered, every one that shall be found written in the book,"—the book of life. Though they are left in this world after undisputed freedom has been given to Satan, and though they are without an Intercessor in heaven, yet at that time God fulfills His promise:

> *"Because thou hast made the Lord, which is my refuge,
> Even the Most High, thy habitation;
> There shall no evil befall thee,
> Neither shall any plague come nigh thy dwelling.
> For He shall give His angels charge over thee,
> To keep thee in all thy ways."

4. The Resurrection (12:2). Gabriel continued, "And many of them that sleep in the dust of the earth shall awake, some to everlasting life, and some to shame and everlasting contempt." This is not the general resurrection of *all* the righteous, which takes place *after* Jesus comes, and of the wicked, which takes place at the end of the thousand years. This is a special resurrection, not of *all* but of *"many."* Who are these? Those who awake "to everlasting life" are God's people who have died keeping all His commandments. These are raised to receive the blessing which God will pronounce upon those who have kept His law. "Blessed are they that do His commandments, that they may have right to the tree of life, and may enter in through the gates into the city." Those who awake "to shame and everlasting contempt" are those "which pierced Him" and others who have most violently opposed His truth and persecuted His people. These are raised that they may understand more fully the greatness of their sins, and know that their punishment is just.

5. The Punishment of the Wicked (12:2). When those who had to do with the crucifixion of Jesus see the cloud in the distance, they know it is the sign of the Son of man. Their guilty consciences remind them of the time when they led Him to Caiaphas to be tried. They remember how, in response to the high priest's demand, "Tell us whether Thou be . . . the Son of God," He answered, "Thou hast said; nevertheless I say unto you, Hereafter shall ye see the Son of man . . . coming in the clouds of heaven." And it was for this saying that He was pronounced guilty of death. Yes, this is the very Jesus whom they smote and spit upon, the very One whom they mocked, the very One whom they crucified. And now He is the King of glory. As they recall these things, they see their sin. They acknowledge that their punishment is just. They are unable to bear His glory. They cannot look upon His face. In their agony they call for the mountains and rocks to fall upon them and hide them from His presence. They are given over to shame and everlasting contempt.

6. The Reward of the Righteous (12:2, 3). The righteous are raised "to everlasting life." They are filled with unspeakable joy as they hear the voice of God proclaim: "Blessed are they that do His commandments. These shall have right to the tree of life. These may enter in through the gates into the city." Soon Jesus appears, surrounded by a cloud of shining angels. The base of the cloud is like glowing fire. Above the cloud is a glorious rainbow. It is impossible to imagine the splendor of that scene. The whole heavens are aglow with heavenly light and glory. Then, said Gabriel, "they that be wise shall shine as the brightness of the firmament; and they that turn many to righteousness as the stars forever and ever." Who are the "wise"? Those who fear the Lord, for "the fear of the Lord is the beginning of wisdom." While the wicked plead for destruction, the righteous look up and joyfully exclaim, "Lo, this is our God; we have waited for Him, and He will save us."

How to Study: Read this lesson in Daniel 12:1-3. Be able to tell when and where Michael shall "stand up" and the events that take place at that time. When will be the "time of trouble," and what will it be like? Who will be delivered? What two classes are raised from the dead at this time? Why? What experience do the wicked have? the righteous?

Use of Concordance: Find the verses starred under topic 3. Key word: plague.

Memory Work: Memorize Daniel 12:1-3.

20. DANIEL'S WORK ENDED
Dan. 12:4-13

"Go thou thy way till the end be: for thou shalt rest, and stand in thy lot at the end of the days." Dan. 12:13.

1. The Book Sealed (12:4-9). "But thou, O Daniel," said Gabriel, "shut up the words, and seal the book, even to the time of the end." Why were these wonderful words to be shut up? Why was God's book to be sealed? Daniel could not understand. Anxiously he looked again. Then he saw two more angels, "the one on this side the bank of the river, and the other on that side of the bank of the river." They were talking to Christ Himself, "the man clothed in linen." What were they saying to Him? Daniel listened. One of them asked, "How long shall it be to the end of these wonders?" That was the very question that was in Daniel's mind. Holding up His right hand and His left hand to heaven, Christ answered, "It shall be for a time, times, and an half, . . . when he shall have accomplished to scatter the power of the holy people." Daniel heard the words, but he did not understand their meaning. Then he pleaded, "O my Lord, what *shall* be the end of these things?" But the answer still was, "Go thy way, Daniel: for the words are closed up and sealed till the time of the end."

2. "The Time of the End" (12:7-10). From Daniel's first vision we have learned that "a time, times, and an half" are 1260 years. We have learned that this period of time began in 538, when the power of the papacy, represented by the little horn, was established, and that it ended in 1798, when this power was broken and the pope was taken captive. During this long period of persecution he "accomplished to scatter the power of the holy people." During this time "many," by their persecutions and sufferings for Christ's sake, were "purified, and made white, and tried." During all this time the truth of God's word was "sealed" and "shut up." And especially were the prophecies of Daniel sealed and shut up.

Missionaries sailing for the Orient. Hundreds of missionaries "run to and fro" throughout the world every year preaching the gospel of God's great plan.

The papal power forbade the reading of the Scriptures by any except the priests. Besides, it was not until 1535 that the first complete Bible was printed in English. Up to this time it was in Latin, a language that but few could understand. And even when Bibles began to be printed in a language that could be understood by the common people, the priests burned them whenever they could get hold of them. This wicked power saw to it that these prophecies were sealed, for if the people understood them, its own sinful character would be exposed.

3. **Increase of Knowledge (12:4).** But at "the time of the end," said Gabriel, "many shall run to and fro, and knowledge shall be increased." And the man clothed in linen said, "The wise shall understand." And so at the time of the end the book would be unsealed, and those who feared the Lord and studied His word, would understand it. When the power of the papacy was at last broken (in 1798), Bible societies began to be organized, and by them the word of God was rapidly published and sent into all parts of the world. And now the Bible is printed in hundreds of languages, so that everyone may read God's word in his own tongue, and millions of copies are distributed every year. When the time of the end was reached and people were able to secure Bibles of their own, devoted men and women began to study God's word as they had never studied it before. And as they studied, God began to unseal the great truths of His great plan. Then He placed upon the hearts of some of these men and women the burden to go as missionaries and teach others to read and understand the word of life. And now not only do people "run to and fro" through the prophecies as they study the Bible, but hundreds of missionaries "run to and fro" throughout the world every year, preaching the gospel of God's great plan.

4. **"The Wise Shall Understand" (12:10).** During this "time of the end," there was to be a reform in education. A "wise" people were to be developed who would "understand" God's word. For this purpose schools were to be established like the schools of the prophets. These schools would make the Bible the greatest of all textbooks. The truth of God's word would be the foundation of all teaching. In these schools the written book of God would be studied in connection with His great book of nature. The errors of evolution would thus be exposed—Satan's scheme to turn people's minds away from the Creator. In these schools history would be taught, not as a series of events that once upon a time took place, but in its study the students, like Daniel, would see God's hand overruling in all the affairs of nations as He works out His great plan for man's salvation. Physiology would be taught, not that boys and girls might know how many bones there are in the body, or other similar facts, important enough in themselves, but that they might realize that their bodies are the temples of God's Holy Spirit, and as such should be kept in health, that they

may be prepared to do valiant service for Him. These schools were to teach manual training, that the students might understand the practical duties of life and thus be fitted to be practical missionaries for God. And so on down the list of subjects to be taught. Everything was to be done with reference to accomplishing God's work in the earth. Will the boys and girls in these schools do their part in carrying out God's great plan?

5. **Daniel's Last Days (12:13).** And now the vision has faded. Christ has departed. Gabriel has gone. The other two angels have

Pacific Union College. For the training of missionaries, schools were to be established like the schools of the prophets.

disappeared. And Daniel finds himself by the side of the river whither he had withdrawn for prayer. The last words of the Saviour were still lingering in his ears: "Thou shalt rest." He returned to the king's palace, and as nothing more is told us about him, it is probable that he went to his long rest soon after — a noble veteran of the great Prince. He had lived during the reign of nine kings. He had seen the head of gold succeeded by the breast and arms of silver. He had traced the hand of the Most High ruling in the kingdom of men and giving it to whomsoever He would. He had seen his people taken captive and at the end of the time released. In all these events he had watched the unfolding of God's great plan to save man. Through all these changes

Daniel's first concern had been God's people and God's work. He had been faithful to earthly kings, and above all he had been true and loyal to the King of heaven. And now his work is ended, and he rests with the sweet assurance, "Thou shalt . . . stand in thy lot at the end of the days."

How to Study: After carefully reading the whole story once, read it again, locating the quotations in the Bible. They are all found in Daniel 12: 4-13. Be able to explain "a time, times, and an half." Tell when this period of time began, when it closed, and what took place during these years. Explain also *how* God's word was sealed during that time. Tell how knowledge was increased, and the result. What is God now doing so that we may be among "the wise" who "shall understand"?
Was Daniel's life a success? Why?
Memory Work: Memorize Daniel 12: 4. Review Daniel 12: 1-3.
Chapter to Remember: Daniel 12 tells about the second coming of Christ.
For Your Workbook: On diagram No. 1 review the location of the period of time called "a time, times, and an half." Show the date when "the time of the end" began.

21. THE NATION'S SECOND OPPORTUNITY FOR SERVICE

"Awake, awake; . . . put on thy beautiful garments, O Jerusalem, the holy city. . . . Shake thyself from the dust, . . . O captive daughter of Zion."
Isa. 52: 1, 2.

1. The Decree of Darius. After Daniel and Cyrus were both gone, the Lord saw trouble ahead for His people. But before the trouble came, He influenced Darius, the king then ruling in Medo-Persia, to make another decree, which provided a second opportunity for the Jews to return to Jerusalem. Through the prophet Zechariah also He warned them to flee from Babylon. But most of them failed to listen to the warnings or take advantage of the opportunity offered.

2. Through Esther God Protects His People. At last the trouble came. Through Haman, an unprincipled man who held a high position in the kingdom, Satan planned to destroy all the people of God. Haman was jealous of Mordecai, an accomplished, earnest, trustworthy Jew who sat in the gate of the king; but "he thought scorn to lay hands on Mordecai alone," so he laid a plot to destroy

---

References Used: P. K., p. 618; Esther 8: 17; 9: 2; Ezra 6: 14; 8: 22; 9: 6, 10, 13, 14; Neh. 2: 20; 6: 3; Dan. 9: 25; Isa. 52: 1, 2, 7, 9.

every Jew throughout the kingdom. To carry out his wicked plan, he secured from the king a decree that on a certain day this work of destruction should be done. The story of Haman's plot, and how, through earnest prayer and fasting by the Jews, it was defeated, is told in the book of Esther. God had brought Esther to the kingdom for this very time, and she proved brave enough and true enough for the occasion. As a result, Haman was hanged on the very gallows which he had prepared for Mordecai. The decree that Haman had influenced the king to make for the destruction of the Jews could not be altered, so the king issued another decree,

Through Haman, Satan planned to destroy all the people of God; but through Queen Esther, God defeated his plans.

allowing the Jews to fight for their lives on the day set for them to be slain. But the word had gone out through all the kingdom, that Haman had been hanged and that Queen Esther was a Jew; so when the day came, "the fear of them fell upon all people," and "no man could withstand them." Angels were sent to protect God's people, and when their enemies saw how wonderfully God worked for them, "many of the people of the land became Jews." Thus Satan suffered another defeat.

    3. **The Decree of Artaxerxes.** It was now nearly eighty years since the first company had returned from captivity. The temple had been restored and dedicated, but much still remained to be done. So many difficulties had attended the work, that the people were well-nigh discouraged. It was at this time that Artaxerxes came to the throne of Medo-Persia. He issued the third and last decree

to rebuild Jerusalem. This decree completed "the commandment of Cyrus, and Darius, and Artaxerxes," "to restore and to build Jerusalem," which the angel had told Daniel would mark the beginning of the 2300 days.

The decree provided silver and gold and freewill offerings for the finishing of the work at Jerusalem. It also provided that Ezra should return with the people and act as their priest and teacher.

4. **Ezra's Journey to Jerusalem.** When the people who desired to return had assembled, there were only a few thousand, including women and children, for by far the larger number chose to remain

Artaxerxes issuing the last of the decree "to restore and to build Jerusalem."

among the heathen. This company, with Ezra as leader, now prepared for their long and perilous journey. The freewill offering which they took with them amounted to six hundred fifty talents of silver and one hundred talents of gold, besides a number of silver and gold vessels for the temple. Gladly would the king have furnished soldiers to protect them from robbers on their way; but Ezra said: "I was ashamed to require of the king a band of soldiers and horsemen to help us against the enemy in the way: because we had spoken unto the king, saying, The hand of our God is upon all them for good that seek Him." So, before leaving, they gathered together for fasting and prayer, seeking the Lord for *His* protection. God honored their faith, and after a journey of four months they reached Jerusalem in safety.

5. **Reformation Begun by Ezra.** When Ezra arrived in Jerusalem he was told that the people, and even some of the priests, had disobeyed God's explicit command, and by marriage had again

joined themselves to the heathen. This was the very sin that in years past had led the people into idolatry, and had finally resulted in the captivity of their fathers and the destruction of their nation.

Ezra was deeply stirred. After all that God had done for them, how could Israel be so false to Him! He called the people to prayer, and before them he unburdened his heart to God. "O my God," he prayed, "I am ashamed and blush to lift up my face to Thee, my God: for our iniquities are increased over our head, and our trespass is grown up unto the heavens." Then after a most humble confession, he continued: "And now, O our God, what shall we say after this? for we have forsaken Thy commandments, which Thou hast commanded by Thy servants the prophets. . . . And after all that is come upon us for our evil deeds, and for our great trespass, seeing that Thou our God hast punished us less than our iniquities deserve, and hast given us such deliverance as this; should we again break Thy commandments, and join in affinity with the people of these abominations?" When the people realized their great sin, they repented and there was a great reformation.

6. Nehemiah's Assistance. As time passed, Nehemiah heard that his brethren in Jerusalem were in need of help and encouragement in their heavy task of rebuilding the city. Nehemiah was loved and trusted by Artaxerxes, and he readily obtained permission to visit his people and lend them assistance. When he reached Jerusalem, he saw what was needed, and at once set to work to rebuild the city wall. By his faith in God and his unceasing labors he encouraged the workers, meeting difficulties with the cheering words, "The God of heaven, He will prosper us." Time after time, the heathen round about tried to hinder the work, and many a plot was laid for Nehemiah. But he kept perseveringly at his task. Nothing could turn him from the straight path of duty. On one occasion when he was working on the wall they desired him to leave his work, pretending that they wanted to counsel with him, but with the real intention of killing or imprisoning him; but he sent messengers to them, saying, "I am doing a great work, so that I cannot come down." The angel had said to Daniel, "The street shall be built again, and the wall, even in troublous times." And this was indeed true. But at last, under Nehemiah's unwavering faith, after only fifty-two days of energetic effort, the wall was completed. The city was then safe from outside enemies.

7. The Last Prophet. Malachi was the last of the prophets before the coming of the Saviour. He faithfully gave God's messages to the people. Then the voices of the prophets ceased. And for four long centuries God's people were left without a living messenger to reveal to them His will. But they had the scrolls of all the prophets from the days of Moses — the entire Old Testament. By studying these sacred writings — the Scriptures — they could know God's plan concerning them. They could know that

When Nehemiah reached Jerusalem, he saw what was needed, and at once set to work to rebuild the city wall.

Jesus, the long-expected Messiah, the One in whom "all families of the earth" were to be blessed, was soon to come. They could know all the important particulars regarding His coming — the time when He was to come, where He was to be born, His ministry, and His sacrifice for sin. God expected His people to study these writings, that they might be prepared to welcome the coming Saviour.

8. God's Purpose in Restoring Israel. But God expected more of His people than merely that they themselves should be prepared for the Saviour's coming. He expected them to prepare others for the great event. Now, as never before, they were to heed the message: "Awake, awake; put on thy strength, O Zion; put on thy beautiful garments, O Jerusalem, the holy city. . . . Shake thyself from the dust, . . . O captive daughter of Zion. . . . How beautiful upon the mountains," He said, "are the feet of him that bringeth good tidings, that publisheth peace; that bringeth good tidings of good, that publisheth salvation; that saith unto Zion,

Thy God reigneth! . . . Break forth into joy, sing together, ye waste places of Jerusalem: for [for this purpose] the Lord hath comforted His people, He hath redeemed Jerusalem."

God had comforted His people, He had redeemed Jerusalem, not that a handful of Israelites might again enjoy the pleasure of their own homes in their own land, but that they might extend the "good tidings" of a coming Saviour — that they might publish peace and salvation to the nations living "upon the mountains" round about. If God's people would do this work, many would accept the message, and a royal welcome would await Jesus when He should come — a welcome worthy of the King of heaven. What a privilege was theirs to prepare a reception for the Saviour of men! Did they appreciate their privilege? Did they carry out God's plan? A future lesson will tell.

How to Study: As you study this lesson, remember who issued "the commandment to restore and to build Jerusalem;" when the last part of it was given; and what relation it had to the 2300 days of Daniel's prophecy. Remember also how Ezra and Nehemiah helped in the work; who the last prophet was; and be able to explain *why* God restored His people to Jerusalem.

On diagram No. 1 locate the 400-year period when there were no prophets.

Use of Concordance: Find the quotations given in paragraph 8. They are all in one chapter. "Publisheth" is a good key word.

For Class Discussion: What three Bible books were written by people mentioned in this lesson? How much of the Bible did the people now have?

What was the value in our money of the gold and silver that Ezra took with him to Jerusalem?

REVIEW OF DANIEL 10, 12

Questions and Exercises: Numbers refer to preceding lessons.

18. Who became king of Medo-Persia after Darius died? Why was Cyrus interested in the prophecies? What did this interest lead him to do? Why did Daniel pray for three weeks?

19. When shall "Michael stand up"? When He stands up what work in heaven is finished? What decree then goes forth? Rev. 22:11. What takes place after Michael stands up? What occurs during the time of trouble? What takes place at the end of the time of trouble?

20. How long was this prophecy to be sealed? How was it unsealed? When did "the time of the end" begin? How has Bible knowledge increased since that time? Who did the angel say would understand these prophecies? How is this part of the prophecy now being fulfilled?

21. What three kings issued "the commandment to restore and to build Jerusalem"? In what book in the Bible is it recorded? Who was the last prophet of Old Testament times? What was God's purpose in restoring Israel?

Familiar Sayings: Who spoke the following words, to whom were they spoken, and under what circumstances?

1. "We shall not find any occasion against this Daniel, except we find it against him concerning the law of his God."
2. "Thy God whom thou servest continually, He will deliver thee."
3. "My God hath sent His angel, and hath shut the lions' mouths."
4. "O Daniel, a man greatly beloved, understand the words that I speak unto thee."
5. "From the first day that thou didst set thine heart to understand, . . . thy words were heard, and I am come for thy words."
6. "Shut up the words, and seal the book, even to the time of the end."
7. "They that be wise shall shine as the brightness of the firmament."
8. "I am doing a great work, so that I cannot come down."
9. "I am ashamed and blush to lift up my face to Thee, my God."
10. "The hand of our God is upon all them for good that seek Him."

GENERAL REVIEW

Important Dates to Remember: (See diagrams Nos. 1, 7, 8.) What events occurred on these dates, and what prophecy did they fulfill? B. C. 606, 457, 538, 536, 331, 168; A. D. 27, 31, 34, 476, 538, 1798, 1844.

Chapter Drill: The following is a chapter outline of the book of Daniel. Be able to find quickly any of these topics. Be able also to give in order the subject of each chapter.

1. Daniel in the king's school.
2. Nebuchadnezzar's dream of the image.
3. The golden image set up. Daniel's companions delivered from the fiery furnace. Nebuchadnezzar's first decree.
4. Nebuchadnezzar's dream of a tree. The king's insanity. His second decree.
5. Belshazzar's feast. Handwriting on the wall. Capture of Babylon.
6. Daniel in the lions' den. The decree of Darius.
7. Daniel's vision of a lion, a bear, a leopard, and a ten-horned beast. The Investigative Judgment. The little horn.
8. Daniel's vision of the ram and the he-goat.
9. Daniel's prayer to understand the 2300 days.
10. Daniel's three weeks' prayer. Daniel's vision of Christ.
11. Daniel's third great world prophecy.
12. The prophecy of the second coming of Christ.

Memory Work for the Period: Ps. 111: 10; 76: 10; Eccl. 12: 14; Acts 3: 19; Dan. 7: 9, 10, 25; 8: 14; 9: 24, 25, first part of 26 and 27; 12: 1-4.

What truth is taught in Numbers 14: 34? in Revelation 17: 15? in Jeremiah 25: 32, 33?

Fourth Period—Chapters V and VI *

OUTLINE OF CHAPTER V

Topics —	A. D.
Preparing for the Coming Redeemer	
The Reception of Jesus	
The Messiah Anointed for Service	27 Autumn
Satan's Effort to Destroy the Prince of Peace	
Jesus Rejected by Priests and Rulers	
Jesus Rejected at Nazareth	
Jesus Rejected by the Galileans	
Jesus Rejected by the Samaritans	
Priests and Rulers Rejected by Jesus	
The Birthday of the Christian Church	
Satan Cast out of the Councils of Heaven	
Jesus Securing the Keys of Satan's Prison House	31 Spring
Review	

---

*To the Teacher: Chapters V and VI constitute the test work for period four. Following the test, several lessons from chapter VII, given before the close of the six weeks, will balance the work for period five.

CHAPTER V

The Man Christ Jesus Working Out God's Plan

1. PREPARING FOR THE COMING REDEEMER

"Prepare ye the way of the Lord, make straight in the desert a highway for our God." Isa. 40: 3.

1. The Saviour Promised to the Patriarchs. When in the garden of Eden Adam and Eve were told that the Saviour would come to this earth and suffer and die that they might be delivered from the bondage of Satan and once more live with God, they thought that He would come soon. "They joyfully welcomed their firstborn son, hoping that *he* might be the Deliverer." But in this they were sadly disappointed. Though day after day at the gates of Eden they offered the sacrifice that showed their faith in the coming Redeemer, yet the fulfillment of the promise tarried. They lived for nearly a thousand years, but at last they died without seeing Him of whom their sacrifices were a type. To Seth, to Enoch, to Methuselah, to Noah, to Shem, and to other patriarchs the promise was repeated. Again and again to Abraham, Isaac, and Jacob God said, "In thee shall all families of the earth be blessed." And yet the Saviour did not come. Still the hope of seeing the Son of God walk among the children of men did not die out of the hearts of God's faithful ones. As they offered the sacrifices, which pointed to His coming, they studied the writings of the prophets, to learn more about that event.

2. His Coming Foretold by the Prophets. Isaiah, Jeremiah, and other prophets instructed the descendants of Jacob — the nation whom God chose — about the Messiah to come. Micah said that the coming Redeemer would be born in Bethlehem. Isaiah said

---

References Used: D. A., pp. 31, 115; P. K., pp. 685, 686, 701, 709; "Practical Lessons," pp. 688-690; Micah 5: 2; Isa. 7: 14; 60: 2; Jer. 31: 15-17; Dan. 9: 25; Luke 10: 31; Mal. 3: 8; Matt. 23: 23; Ps. 2: 8, 9; Eze. 12: 22.

that His name should be Immanuel. Jeremiah told about the terrible slaughter of the little children of Bethlehem and of the "bitter weeping" of the mothers who "refused to be comforted." And Daniel foretold the exact time when Messiah should come. Not only the experiences of His birth and childhood, but His baptism, His later ministry, His triumphal entry into Jerusalem, His betrayal, persecution, and trial, His crucifixion, death, and burial, His

As God's faithful ones offered the sacrifices, they studied the writings of the prophets to learn more about the coming Saviour.

resurrection and ascension — all were clearly written in the scrolls of the prophets hundreds of years before He came. Finally the voices of the prophets ceased.

3. Satan Determines to Defeat God's Plan. It was God's plan that Israel, after being released from captivity, should faithfully study the scrolls of the prophets, and tell the world about the first advent of Christ, just as He expects His people now to tell the world about His second advent. Satan is a diligent student of the prophecies, and from these he learned when Jesus was to come. For the Son of God to live in his kingdom among his subjects caused him to fear greatly for his dominion, and he determined to do all in his power to cause Israel to misunderstand the real meaning of the prophecies. He hoped that in this way the world and God's own chosen people would be led to reject the Saviour when He came.

4. A False Idea of Separation from the World. How did Satan go about his deceptive work? The captivity had fully cured Israel of the worship of graven images, and of marrying among idolaters. Satan now took advantage of this by leading them to shut themselves so completely away from the world that instead of making their religion a blessing to others, they made it a wall of partition that shut the world away from the light of God. They soon began to think they were better than others, and that God's plan was for them alone. They would not eat with anyone who was not a Jew. Like the priest who refused to help the wounded man by the roadside, so they "passed by on the other side." When they passed a gentile on the street, they drew their garments about them, lest by contact with others they should become defiled.

5. Selfish Tithe Paying. As the people shut themselves away from the nations around, their own hearts became proud and selfish. They failed to return to God His own in tithes and offerings. Especially was this true in Malachi's day. God sternly rebuked this spirit of selfishness. "Will a man rob God?" He asked. "Yet ye have robbed Me." In self-defense they asked, "Wherein have we robbed Thee?" He answered, "In tithes and offerings." Because of this, the curse of God was upon their fields, and a lack of prosperity followed. Then Israel carefully measured out the tithe, even to "mint and anise and cummin." But this selfish obedience made their hearts barren of the love of God, barren of the weightier matters of justice, mercy, and faith. All this pleased Satan.

6. Man-Made Burdens upon God's Law. A mere form of religion was rapidly taking the place of true heart devotion and unselfish service for others. God's holy law, instead of being a law of liberty, was burdened with many foolish requirements. Especially was this true in the observance of the Sabbath, the day which God had made the most enjoyable of all. For instance, some of the rabbis said that an egg laid on the Sabbath must not be eaten. No soap was to be used in washing the hands, as this they claimed was unnecessary labor. In going to the synagogue one must empty his pockets of everything, even to a pocket handkerchief, for this would be an unnecessary burden. The distance allowed to be walked on the Sabbath was carefully defined, and if one should take a step farther, he would be subject to a flogging for Sabbath breaking. Every one of the Ten Commandments was burdened with hundreds and even thousands of similar laws — so many that it would be impossible for anyone to remember them all.

7. Meaningless Sacrifices. Even the sacrificial offerings lost their sacred meaning, and the temple, especially at the time of the great yearly feasts, became a scene of buying and selling and making money. That which should have been a place of prayer for all nations became a den of thieves. As priests and people wandered away from God, it was easy to lose sight of Jesus as the real Sacrifice for their sins. Then as they read the Scriptures that told of His coming, they could not understand their meaning. They did not desire redemption from sin — they felt that they were already holy. They were not interested in the Saviour who was to come to this earth to die — they desired a Saviour who would free them from the power of Rome and make them a great nation, as they had been in the days of Solomon. The prophecies that referred to Jesus' second coming they applied to His first coming. They looked for Messiah to come as a great conqueror who would break the nations "with a rod of iron" and "dash them in pieces like a potter's vessel"— a Messiah who would exalt Israel to dominion over all nations.

8. Will Satan Succeed? Satan exulted as he saw how well he had succeeded. He was preventing many from obtaining a knowledge of God, of Jesus, and of the future life. Multitudes were without hope. Darkness covered the earth, and gross darkness the people. It was the darkest, darkest time that this world had ever seen. Many were ready to throw away their faith in God. When Ezekiel in vision saw this time, he heard the people say in tones of discouragement, "The days are prolonged, and every vision faileth."

But we know that the enemy, though sometimes seeming to succeed, will surely be defeated in the end. For do you not remember how, when under his influence Pharaoh pursued Israel, God opened the Red Sea and let His people pass through, while Pharaoh's army was drowned? Do you not remember how, when he thought to destroy Daniel with the wise men of Babylon, God used that very occasion to give Daniel the highest position,— next to the king of the world? And again when he caused Daniel to be thrown into the den of lions, only to have God's name exalted throughout the whole world? Do what he may, Satan can do nothing against the truth, but for the truth.

How to Study: From this lesson you should understand how from the first God's people had looked for the coming of Jesus, and why Satan tried to keep the people from preparing for that event; also what different means he used to accomplish this — four are described. Where is the first promise of His coming given? In which prophecy did Daniel tell the time of Jesus' coming? On diagram No. 1, and on the 2300-day diagram, locate the time of this lesson.

Memory Work: Memorize Malachi 3: 10.

---

2. THE RECEPTION OF JESUS

*"Glory to God in the highest,
And on earth peace, good will toward men." Luke 2:14.*

1. The Angels' Interest in Jesus' Life. The angels knew that the Son of God had met and overcome Satan in heaven. They knew that time after time in His *divine* nature He had prevailed in man's behalf on this earth. Now "the fullness of the time was come" when He was to lay aside His divine power, and, taking upon Himself the weakness of sinful flesh, He was to battle with the enemy. Will He still succeed? Will Satan still be defeated? Every angel in heaven watched with the deepest interest to see how their Commander would be received here in Satan's dominion.

2. Preparations to Welcome Jesus. The angels knew the exact time when Christ should come to this earth; and "when the great clock of time pointed to that hour," Jesus, the King of glory, was born in Bethlehem. The arrival of an innocent baby is a great event in any home. Angels watch with loving interest over each one. But never, never had they been so deeply interested as when this tiny Baby opened His bright eyes in the manger in Bethlehem. All heaven was astir with preparations to give Him a royal welcome.

It was God's design that His people on earth should share with the angels the joy and honor of announcing the Saviour's arrival. The prophecies of Daniel had foretold the time of His coming, and more than a year before He was born, an angel was sent to the temple in Jerusalem to tell the priest Zacharias that His coming was near. But when the time came, not a single preparation had they made to welcome Him. Their hearts were absorbed in selfish interests. It is true that morning and evening they offered at the

---

References Used: D. A., pp. 32, 43-47, 60, 61, 64, 67; Gal. 4:4; Luke 1:13-31; 2:9-16; Num. 24:17; Matt. 2:8-15, 23; Rev. 12:4, 5, 9; Hosea 11:1.

temple the sacrifices which foretold His coming, but this service was to them only a meaningless form.

3. The Welcome of the Shepherds. The angels were amazed at the indifference of the very ones whom God had chosen to tell the world of the Saviour. They were amazed that the One who had come to save them must find His cradle in a manger of a stable.

H. Lerolle
Angels were amazed that the Saviour of men must find His cradle in a manger of a stable.

But though priests and rulers were indifferent, there were those among the common people who were longing and praying for the Messiah. Through the silent hours of the night, while watching their flocks, the shepherds talked together about the promised Saviour, and anxiously looked for His coming. For this reason, when the angels came to make known the Saviour's arrival, they passed by the proud leaders in Jerusalem and hovered over the fields on the hills near Bethlehem. Here they waited the signal to tell the glad tidings.

When the hour of Jesus' birth arrived, "lo, the angel of the Lord came upon them, and the glory of the Lord shone round about them." At first the shepherds were afraid; but the angel said: "Fear not: for, behold, I bring you good tidings of great joy, which shall be to all people. For unto you is born this day in the city of David a Saviour, which is Christ the Lord." As this announcement was made, the heavens seemed full of shining angels, and the whole plain was lighted with their glory. Then upon the still night air the shepherds heard the sweetest music as the angelic choir made the heavens ring with the anthem:

"Glory to God in the highest,
And on earth peace, good will toward men."

Soon the angels disappeared, the light faded away, and once more the plain and the hills were wrapped in the darkness of night. Quickly the shepherds went to find the Lord, and they "found Mary, and Joseph, and the Babe lying in a manger." Then with great joy they spread the news among the people even to Jerusalem.

4. Wise Men Led to Jerusalem by the Star. As the light of the angels faded, a brilliant star appeared and lingered in the sky just above the place where Jesus lay. This star was a multitude of shining angels in the distance. Far away in the East the star was seen by a company of wise men. These men were not Jews, but they had studied the prophecies, and they believed that the Saviour was soon to come. In the books of Moses they read, "There shall come a Star out of Jacob." They understood something about astronomy, and they knew that this star was not like the other stars. Could it be that it had been sent to direct them to the coming King?

As this thought came to them, they were told in a dream to go in search of the newborn Prince. This they were delighted to do. So, gathering together some of the richest gifts they could secure, they set out on their long but happy journey. The star led them to Jerusalem. As they came in sight of the city, they saw it above the temple, and then it faded from their sight. Eagerly they hastened forward, expecting to hear the whole city talking about the Messiah's birth. "Where is He that is born King of the Jews?" they asked. They were disappointed to find that no one seemed

The angel said, "Unto you is born this day in the city of David a Saviour, which is Christ the Lord."

to know anything about the great event. Even the priests, although they had heard the report of the shepherds, appeared utterly indifferent.

5. Herod's Anxiety. The people of the city soon heard about the wise men and why they had come, and they became greatly excited. When the news reached the ears of King Herod, his suspicions were aroused. He thought the priests were plotting with the wise men to put another king in his place. He called the priests and asked them what the prophecies said as to where the Messiah was to be born. Having been told, he secretly called the wise men to his palace and questioned them as to when they had first seen the star. When they told him, he pretended to be much interested and pleased, and said, "Search diligently for the young Child; and when ye have found Him, bring me word again, that I may come and worship Him also."

6. The Wise Men Welcome Jesus. As the wise men left Jerusalem, to their "exceeding great joy," they again saw the star. It directed them toward Bethlehem. They had no difficulty in finding Jesus, for when they reached Bethlehem the star "stood over where the young Child was." Though they found Him in a humble dwelling, yet they knew that He was the Son of God, their own Saviour. Falling down before Him, they worshiped Him, and then "they presented unto Him gifts; gold, and frankincense, and myrrh."

7. Satan's Plans Defeated. "The great dragon, . . . that old serpent, called the devil, and Satan," knew very well when and where the Son of God was to be born, and through Herod he stood "before the woman . . . for to devour her Child as soon as it was born." But the wise men did not know of Herod's evil intentions, so after they had found Jesus they prepared to return to Jerusalem. Immediately they were "warned of God in a dream that they should not return to Herod." Therefore "they departed into their own country another way." God's people had failed to tell the world of Jesus' coming, but God's work did not fail. Through these wise men, He sent to the heathen His message of salvation.

8. Prophecies Fulfilled. After the visitors had gone, the angel of the Lord appeared to Joseph in a dream and warned him to flee to Egypt; "for," said he, "Herod will seek the young Child to destroy Him." The gifts of the wise men provided the means necessary for the journey, and Joseph and Mary, protected by an angel,

Joseph and Mary, protected by an angel, soon found a safe retreat for Jesus in the land of Egypt.

Plockhorst

soon found a safe retreat for Jesus in the land of Egypt. This was another evidence to the Jews and to the world that He was the Son of God, for the prophecy had said, "Out of Egypt have I called My Son."

When the angel directed Joseph to return to the land of Israel, he was told to go to Nazareth. This, too, was a fulfillment of prophecy, which said, "He shall be called a Nazarene." Thus evidence after evidence was given that Jesus was really the Messiah for whom the world had so long waited.

Such was the Saviour's reception when He came to the land of the enemy. His life was constantly in danger, even from the leaders of God's own chosen nation. From the cradle to the cross it was necessary for angels to protect Him till His mission on earth should be finished.

How to Study: Observe in this lesson how Satan tried from the first to destroy Jesus. Notice also the angels' interest, how God's providences provided for Jesus, and how each event was a fulfillment of prophecy.

Oral Composition: As you study, copy the paragraph topics, with any subtopics that you need, and from this outline be able to tell any part of or all the story. You may use your Bible to read any quotations given.

For Class Discussion: Name some instances that have been related in past lessons when Jesus in His divine nature worked for man against Satan.

How do you suppose a knowledge of God's word had reached the wise men? Name the books of Moses.

---

3. THE MESSIAH ANOINTED FOR SERVICE

Autumn of 27 A. D.

"Thou art My beloved Son, in whom I am well pleased." Mark 1:11.

1. Jesus' First Passover Visit. Jesus lived a simple, uneventful life in His humble home at Nazareth. "And the Child grew, and waxed strong in spirit, filled with wisdom: and the grace of God was upon Him." The only event recorded in the Bible that marked these years was His visit to Jerusalem at the age of twelve, to at-

---

References Used: D. A., pp. 71-79, 109, 111, 112; Luke 2:40, 49, 52; Matt. 3:2, 14, 15; John 1:29, 32-34.

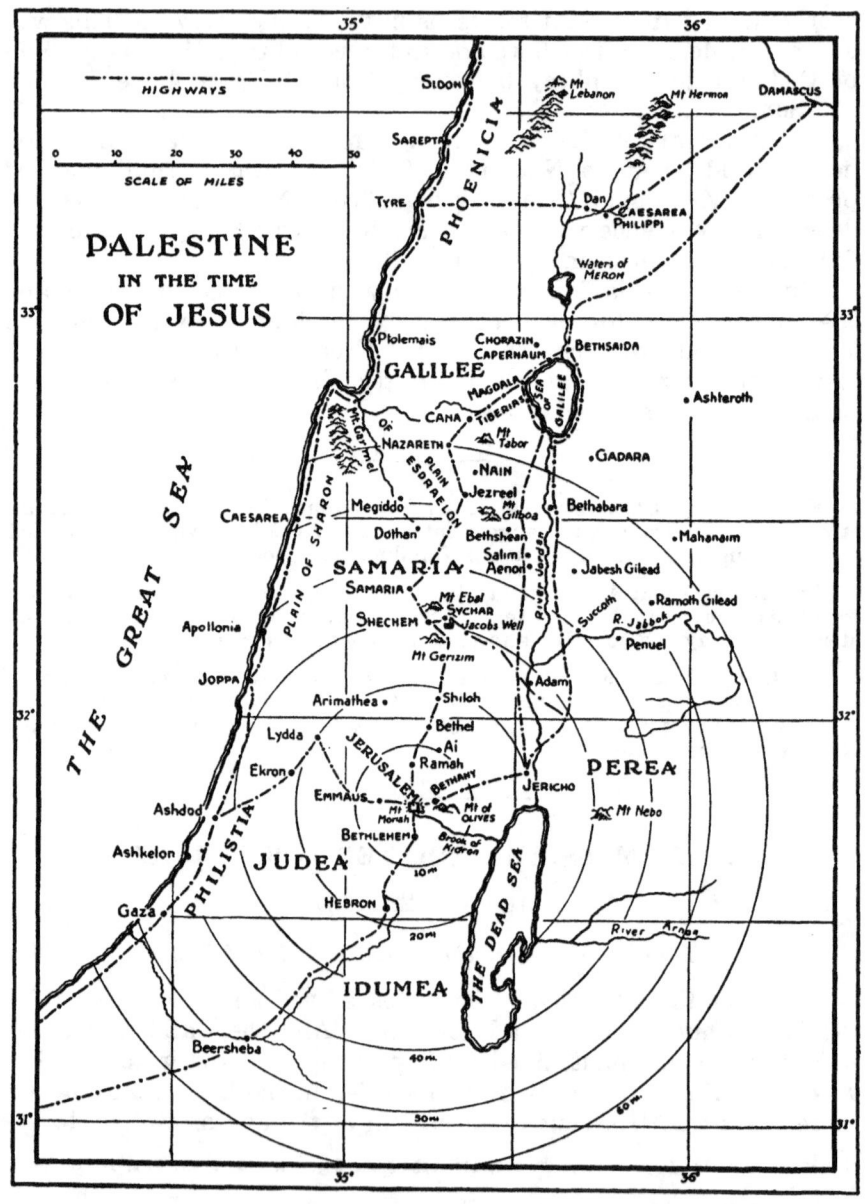

tend the Passover. Among the Jews, the twelfth year marked the division between childhood and youth. At this age children were expected to attend the feasts and take part in the services.

This was the first time that Jesus had ever seen the temple, or the priests dressed in their white linen garments, offering the sacrifices. With the closest attention He watched everything they did. As He saw the innocent lamb slain, and its bleeding body placed on the altar of sacrifice, His heart seemed to stand still. He recalled the lessons His mother had taught Him from the writings of Moses about the sacrifices and their meaning. Now the Holy Spirit more fully interpreted these things to His heart. Never before had He witnessed so impressive a service. Day after day during the Passover week, as He, thoughtful and quiet, attended the services, He understood more and more clearly their heavenly meaning and their relation to His own life. "Silent and absorbed, He seemed to be studying out a great problem. The mystery of His mission was opening to the Saviour."

2. Jesus with the Teachers. As these solemn truths came home to His heart, He wanted to get away from the crowd and be alone. Wandering aside, He entered a room connected with the temple, where He found a few priests teaching the Scriptures. But their teaching was lifeless and uninteresting. Jesus, His heart burning within Him, began to ask them questions. The Holy Spirit was directing the questions. God was trying to reach the hearts of these teachers through the simple words of this Child. They recognized the unusual character of the Child, but they closed their proud hearts against the influence of the Holy Spirit.

3. The Youth Jesus About His Father's Business. As Jesus returned to Nazareth, a new life opened before Him. "Wist ye not," He had said to His mother, "that I must be about My Father's business?" He was beginning to understand that from now on He must make definite preparation to do the work given Him by His heavenly Father. During the eighteen years that followed, Satan never ceased his efforts to overcome the Youth of Nazareth. He had failed to destroy Him at His birth, and now with the bitterest hatred he determined if possible to destroy Him by causing Him to sin. In every way he could think of he tried to ensnare Him. No other child or youth will ever be tempted so severely as Jesus was. Yet His entire life was free from every trace of wrong.

Jesus acted His part in the home duties. As He worked with Joseph in the carpenter's shop, He was about His "Father's business" just as much as when later He was working miracles for the multitude, for He did His work accurately and thoroughly. "He did not use His physical powers recklessly, but in such a way as to keep them in health, that He might do the best work in every line." Thus "Jesus increased in wisdom and stature, and in favor with God and man." Jesus is our example, and the approval of God rests upon children and youth who, like Him, cheerfully share the burdens of father and mother, and who accurately and thoroughly and faithfully do the work assigned them.

As Jesus worked with Joseph in the carpenter's shop, He was about His "Father's business," for He did His work accurately and thoroughly.

4. Jesus Hears the Preacher in the Wilderness. One day, when Jesus was thirty years of age, the report reached Nazareth that a prophet in the wilderness of Judea, near the Jordan River, was preaching about the coming of the Messiah. "Repent ye: for the kingdom of heaven is at hand." This was his message. Many prophets had told of a Messiah *to come,* but this man declared that He was *at hand.* Everywhere people were talking about his wonderful message. Multitudes flocked to the wilderness to listen to him, and many believed, repented, and were baptized. When Jesus heard these reports, He knew that this was His Father's call to

Him to begin His work of explaining to the world God's great plan to save them. Bidding farewell to His mother, He went with others to hear this great preacher. And with others Jesus presented Himself for baptism.

5. Jesus Baptized. Although Jesus was John's cousin, yet John had never seen Him. He had heard about Him, and believed Him to be the Messiah. It had been revealed to him that Jesus would come to be baptized, and that then a sign of His divinity would be given. As soon as Jesus asked to be baptized, John recognized His divine character, and he believed that this was the Messiah of whom he was preaching. It seemed to him that he, himself a sinner, could not baptize the sinless One. "I have need to be baptized of Thee," he said to Jesus, "and comest Thou to me?" But, that Jesus might be our example in this as in other things, He answered, "Suffer it to be so now: for thus it becometh us to fulfill all righteousness." Then John led Jesus down into the Jordan, and buried Him beneath the water.

6. Jesus' Prayer for Help. "Coming up out of the water, Jesus bowed in prayer on the river bank." He knew that He was entering upon the conflict of His life. He knew that the kingdom He had come to establish was entirely different from that which the Jews desired. He knew that, although He had Himself given them the service of the sanctuary, they would look upon Him as its destroyer. He knew that, although with His own voice He had spoken God's law upon Sinai, they would accuse Him of breaking the law. He knew that, although He had come to destroy the power of Satan, they would accuse Him of working miracles by means of Beelzebub, the prince of the devils. He knew that Satan would use every possible means of deceiving the people and defeating the work God had sent Him from heaven to do. He knew, too, that in the terrible conflict, the very people whom He had come to save would reject Him; that in the hour of His deepest need, even His own chosen disciples would desert Him; and that at last He would suffer a cruel death. But He knew also that upon Him depended the salvation of God's family on earth. As these thoughts flashed across His mind, He pleaded that the Father would give Him power to conquer the enemy, and deliver the people from his temptations.

7. The Voice of God to His Son. As the angels listen to the cries of their loved Commander for help, they are eager to carry

As John saw the form of a dove, and as he heard the voice from heaven, he knew that the One whom he had baptized was the world's Redeemer.

Him a message of encouragement. "But no; the Father Himself will answer the petition of His Son. Direct from the throne issue the beams of His glory." And Jesus "saw the heavens opened, and the Spirit like a dove descending upon Him." "Of the vast throng at the Jordan, few except John discerned the heavenly vision." Yet a feeling of solemnity rested upon them as they gazed silently upon Jesus. "His upturned face was glorified as they had never before seen the face of man. From the open heavens a voice was heard saying, 'This is My beloved Son, in whom I am well pleased.'"

As John looked upon Jesus, as he saw the form of the dove, as he heard the voice from heaven, he recognized these things as the sign that had been promised him. He knew that the One whom he had baptized was the world's Redeemer. Pointing to Jesus, he cried out to the multitude, "Behold the Lamb of God, which taketh away the sin of the world."

How to Study: Observe in this lesson how Jesus was prepared for the work God had for Him to do — first as a child, then as a youth, and finally as a man. Notice especially the different reasons why He prayed for help. What does the word "Messiah" mean? How was Jesus anointed? Why?

What was the sign that was given John? John 1:33. What prophecy was fulfilled when Jesus was baptized? Dan. 9:25.

Memory Work: Mark 1:10, 11.

---

4. SATAN'S EFFORT TO DESTROY THE PRINCE OF PEACE

"Resist the devil, and he will flee from you." James 4:7.

1. Satan's Fears. At the baptism of Jesus, Satan saw the glory that descended upon the Saviour. He heard the voice from heaven declaring Him to be the Son of God. It was the first time since the days of sinless Eden that the Father had directly spoken to humanity. Before this, Christ had spoken to man for the Father; now Jesus had come "in the likeness of sinful flesh," and the Father Himself spoke. Can it be, thought Satan, that my power over man is after all to be destroyed? Can it be that God is to win the human

---

References Used: D. A., pp. 114, 116, 118, 119, 129, 131; P. P., p. 366; Matt. 4:1-11.

family back to Himself? This thought filled him with anxiety and fear. Ever since that first sin in Eden, Satan had claimed that he was the prince of this world, and here he had determined to establish his empire. Now God had sent His Son to prove that Satan's claim was false, that all who desire may be set free from his power, and the earth be won back to its rightful Owner. Satan knew this. His dominion was in danger. Something must be done to make it more secure.

2. Jesus in the Wilderness. Immediately after His baptism, Jesus, led by the Holy Spirit, went to the wilderness, where, alone with God, He could prepare for the work He had come to do. Satan decided that this was his opportunity to overthrow Him. He well knew that Christ had held the highest position in heaven next to the Father. But now that He had come to this earth as a man, he hoped to defeat Him. Had he not defeated every other man who had ever entered his dominion? Even Adam in the strength of sinless manhood he had overcome. Surely he could easily overcome Jesus, bearing in His body the sins and weaknesses of the whole world. But to make still more sure of his victim, he waited until, at the end of a forty days' fast, Christ was weak from hunger, and worn with the long and difficult study He had been giving to the work that lay before Him.

3. The First Temptation. "If Thou be the Son of God, command that these stones be made bread." This was Satan's first attack. "*If* Thou be the Son of God." The words from heaven, "This is My beloved Son," were still sounding in the ears of Satan. Would God leave His Son in the desert, "without food, without companions, without comfort?" he insinuated. "Would God treat His own Son thus?" In this way he tried to destroy Christ's confidence in the truthfulness of the Father's word. Although Satan appeared as an angel of light, Jesus recognized him, and He would not discuss with him a question which had already been answered by the word which had proceeded out of the mouth of God. Quietly but firmly He replied, "It is written, Man shall not live by bread alone, but by every word that proceedeth out of the mouth of God." The Father had already said, "This is My beloved Son." No further proof was needed. The first Adam had fallen on the point of appetite. Christ, the second Adam, stood the test.

4. The Second Temptation. "Then the devil taketh Him up into the holy city, and setteth Him on a pinnacle of the temple, and saith unto Him, If Thou be the Son of God, cast Thyself down: for it is written, He shall give His angels charge concerning Thee: and in their hands they shall bear Thee up, lest at any time Thou dash Thy foot against a stone."

In this temptation Satan tried to lead Jesus to place Himself in danger just to prove, or *test,* God's willingness or ability to keep Him from harm. If He would cast Himself down and God would send angels to protect Him, then it would be safe to trust God, Satan suggested; but if God did not protect Him, that would be evidence that God could not be depended on in time of need. Jesus would surely need God many times in His conflict with Satan. Could He really depend on His Father? Would it not be well to "test" God so as to be *sure* on this point at the outset? O Satan! How cunning your temptations are! But Jesus knows you too well to be deceived. He knows that you are putting God's promise in a false light. He knows that the Spirit of God has led Him into the wilderness to be tempted of the devil, and He knows that God will keep Him. He knows, too, that it is Satan and not God who has told Him to cast Himself down from the temple, and if He obeys Satan, He has no promise of God's protection. To go to places where God does not lead, and then expect Him to protect us, is presumption — Satan's counterfeit of faith.

To Satan's cunning falsehood Jesus answered, "It is written again, Thou shalt not tempt [or test] the Lord thy God." To do so would be to distrust God's word, which says, "Fear thou not; for I am with thee." We do not need to test God to see whether He means what He says.

5. The Third Temptation. Satan now shows himself in his true character. As the god of this world he places Jesus upon "an exceeding high mountain," and like a panorama he "showeth Him all the kingdoms of the world, and the glory of them." Jesus had come to this earth to win back this very dominion. In His effort to accomplish this, God had placed before Him a path of sorrow and grief, of pain and death. Satan insinuates that God is a hard master. *He* presents a smooth, easy way of gaining the world. In his most persuasive tones, in his most deceptive manner, he says, "All these things will I give Thee, if Thou wilt fall down and worship *me*."

Away back in heaven, when sin first entered the heart of Lucifer, that was what he desired — that Christ should worship *him*. He wanted to be supreme. He wanted to be God. For Christ to yield to this temptation would be to let Satan have the victory. Then man would be forever lost, and this world would be ruined.

Jesus chose the rough and thorny path that led to the cross of Calvary.

With a power that put the foe to flight, Jesus commanded, "Get thee hence, Satan: for it is written, Thou shalt worship the Lord thy God, and Him only shalt thou serve."

6. Help from Heaven. Immediately Satan left Him, and Jesus, exhausted with the struggle, fell to the earth like one dying. With the deepest interest angels had watched the conflict. With inexpressible joy they had seen the victory. And now they hasten to minister to Him on every point where Satan had tempted Him. First they strengthen Him with food. Then they comfort Him with the message that God loves Him and will care for Him in all the dangers that He must meet. And third they assure Him that all heaven triumphed when He refused to acknowledge Satan as the rightful ruler of this world.

How to Study: Study to understand the real force of each temptation of Satan in the wilderness. Be able to state each temptation and the scripture by which Christ overcame. Are we ever tempted in any of these ways?

Memory Work: Memorize Isaiah 41:10.

Chapter to Remember: The temptation chapter,— Matthew 4.

5. JESUS REJECTED BY PRIESTS AND RULERS

"From that day forth they took counsel together for to put Him to death." John 11:53.

1. John's Message Rejected. Among the Jews it was well known that the seventy weeks of Daniel's prophecy, during which time the Messiah was to come, were nearly ended. Yet the leaders were unwilling to believe the message of John. They looked for Messiah to come, not as a humble man going about to do good and at last to become a sacrifice, but as a conquering king. When Jesus returned from His conflict with Satan in the wilderness, John again announced to the multitude: "Behold the Lamb of God!" "This is the Son of God." During the weeks that followed, and especially after Jesus performed His first miracle at the marriage at Cana, the priests and the elders searched with new interest the prophecies relating to Christ's coming. Could it be that this plain, humble man was the Messiah?

2. How Jesus Announced His Mission. The following spring Jesus went to Jerusalem to attend the Passover. This was the first Passover after His baptism. As He came to the temple, He saw the courts filled with people from all parts of the world. In the outer court, animals were being sold for sacrifices, and the foreign money was exchanged for the coin of the sanctuary. Those who sold the sacrifices charged exorbitant prices. At the time of

---

References Used: D. A., pp. 150, 157, 161, 202-206; John 1:34, 36; 2:16; 5:1-16; Isa. 42:21.

the Passover the sales were very many. In all these transactions there was great confusion, which took away the sacredness of the temple of God. Among the people who came to the Passover many were sick and in trouble. They longed for help, but the priests were not interested in these unfortunate ones.

When Jesus saw the sharp bargaining, the buying and selling in the temple courts, when He saw the poor and the sick neglected,

In the outer court, animals were being sold for sacrifices, and the foreign money was exchanged for the coin of the sanctuary.

He was deeply grieved. Standing before the people as One in authority, He cried out in clear, ringing tones that every one could hear, "Take these things hence; make not My Father's house an house of merchandise." No one seemed to dare to disobey His command. People, priests, and rulers alike fled from the temple and its courts. Soon everything was quiet. Only the poor and the sick remained in the courts with Jesus. He looked upon them with love and sympathy. They came close to Him and besought Him to help them. Jesus not only spoke words of comfort, but He healed them all. "In the cleansing of the temple, Jesus was announcing His mission as the Messiah, and entering upon His work." He was announcing His mission to cleanse the temple of the soul from every unholy thing.

3. Priests and Rulers Reject Jesus. When Jesus drove the priests and the rulers from the temple, Satan's anger was aroused. He could see that *his* influence over them was endangered. From that very day he planted in their hearts a hatred which increased more and more, and which finally resulted in their rejection of the Saviour. But many of the common people were impressed that Jesus was the Son of God. They were glad that the greedy priests had been rebuked.

4. Jesus Accused of Sabbath Breaking. "After this there was a feast of the Jews; and Jesus went up to Jerusalem" again. As He passed by the pool of Bethesda, He saw the place crowded with sufferers, waiting for the moving of the waters, that they might be healed. Jesus longed to heal them all, though He knew that to do so on the Sabbath would arouse the prejudice of the Jews. Nevertheless, He had come into the world to teach the people the truth regarding the Sabbath, and this was His opportunity.

There was one man who especially attracted His attention. He had been a helpless cripple for thirty-eight years, and although he had often tried to reach the water, some one stronger than he would plunge in first. Over and over again he had been disappointed. Jesus looked tenderly upon him, and asked gently, "Wilt thou be made whole?" The man answered, "Sir, I have no man, when the water is troubled, to put me into the pool: but while I am coming, another steppeth down before me." Then Jesus said, "Rise, take up thy bed, and walk." Immediately his ankles became strong and he sprang to his feet. Then, rolling up his blanket, he hurried away praising God.

After Satan failed to overcome Christ in the wilderness, he combined all his forces to destroy His work. But in spite of his greatest efforts, he seemed to be making little progress. This only increased his wrath. In the healing of the impotent man he saw his opportunity to increase the opposition of the leaders. The priests were becoming more and more jealous of Jesus, because His work of healing and sympathy had more influence over the people than they themselves had. When they heard that Jesus had healed the man and had told him to carry his bed, they condemned Him as a Sabbath breaker. Then He was brought before the Sanhedrin to be tried.

5. Jesus Accused of Blasphemy. Jesus had not come to destroy the law of God. He had come to "magnify the law, and make it honorable." He had come to free the Sabbath from the burdens that the Jews had put upon it, and make it "a delight, the holy of the Lord, honorable." He explained to the priests how His own heavenly Father did good upon the Sabbath, and that in healing the man He was doing the work of God.

Because Jesus healed the sick man on the Sabbath, He was tried by the Sanhedrin for Sabbath breaking.

When Jesus called God His Father, the priests were furious. They said He had not only broken the Sabbath, but He had blasphemed by making Himself equal with God. If they had not feared the people, they would gladly have put Him to death then and there. They sent messengers all over the country to warn the people against Him. They also sent spies to watch Him and report what He said and did. They were determined to take His life as soon as they dared to do so. Jesus knew their hearts and their plans, but He was not afraid of them. He was in the care of His heavenly Father, and He continued to do the work He had been sent to this earth to accomplish.

How to Study: Gather from this lesson why the priests feared that Jesus might be the Messiah; how Jesus announced His mission; how Satan aroused prejudice and jealousy in the hearts of the priests and how he led them to reject the Saviour. Of what sins did the priests accuse Jesus? On what grounds? Why were these accusations unjust? What was Jesus trying to teach the people in the events told in this lesson?

6. JESUS REJECTED AT NAZARETH

"No prophet is accepted in his own country." Luke 4:24.

1. Why Jesus Left Jerusalem. The Jewish leaders had the first opportunity of carrying to the world the gospel of Christ. But when the Sanhedrin rejected Jesus and set about to kill Him, He left Jerusalem. He did not attend another Passover until the time when He was crucified. In the meantime, His work was almost entirely among the people of Galilee.

2. "The Time Is Fulfilled." As He began His work in Galilee His message was, "The time is fulfilled, and the kingdom of God is at hand: repent ye, and believe the gospel." The "time" to which Jesus referred was the seventy weeks, which Gabriel had explained to Daniel. That part of the time reaching to "the Messiah," Jesus' baptism, was now past. About two years more would reach to "the midst of the week," when "the sacrifice and the oblation" should cease — when Jesus, the Lamb of God, would be sacrificed. Jesus knew how short His time was, and He longed to finish His work and do it acceptably to God. Not one thing did He want to leave undone.

3. In the Synagogue at Nazareth. When Jesus returned to Galilee He visited His own home town, Nazareth. This was the first time He had been in Nazareth since His baptism. Do you not think He was glad to be at home again after an absence of about a year and a half? The people had heard of His work, and everyone was anxious to see Him. On the Sabbath He attended service at the synagogue. As He entered, all eyes turned upon Him. He was asked to take part in the service, and the scroll of Isaiah was handed to Him. He opened the scroll and read from the sixty-first chapter:

> "The Spirit of the Lord is upon Me,
> Because He hath anointed Me to preach the gospel to the poor;
> He hath sent Me to heal the broken-hearted,
> To preach deliverance to the captives,
> And recovering of sight to the blind,
> To set at liberty them that are bruised,
> To preach the acceptable year of the Lord."

References Used: D. A., pp. 236, 268, 271; Mark 1:15, 35; 2:10-12; Luke 4:18-31; 5:16; 6:12; Matt. 9:2-6; John 5:30; 14:10.

"And He closed the roll, and He gave it again to the minister, and sat down."

Then He began to explain the scripture He had read. "This day," He said, "is this scripture fulfilled in your ears." The people looked at one another, amazed that He should claim to be the One of whom the scripture had told. "Is not this Joseph's son?" they whispered among themselves. They believed that the Messiah would come as a great conquering king. When Jesus tried to explain, they "were filled with wrath, and rose up, and thrust Him out of the city, and led Him unto the brow of the hill whereon their city was built, that they might cast Him down headlong." But suddenly He disappeared from among them. Angels protected Him from the frenzied mob and took Him to a place of safety.

4. How Jesus Proved that He Was Messiah. Jesus had been rejected by the Sanhedrin at Jerusalem, now He was rejected at Nazareth. But His work was not yet finished. He continued to preach and teach and heal. He traveled throughout Galilee, seeking every opportunity to explain to the people the mercy and love of the Father, and His great plan to save them. As evidence that He was the Messiah, He cast out devils, He gave sight to the blind, He caused the dumb to speak and the deaf to hear. He spoke to the wind and the sea, and they obeyed Him. He miraculously fed the multitude, He cleansed the lepers, He even raised the dead to life.

Doré
When Jesus said to the sick man, "Thy sins be forgiven thee," the priests accused Him of blasphemy.

5. Jesus Forgives Sin. But, though the common people heard Him gladly, spies were constantly on His track. On one occasion Jesus was teaching in the house of Peter. A man who was a paralytic had heard about the work He had done for the lepers and others as helpless as he. He longed to be healed, but he longed even more to have his sins forgiven. If he could only see Jesus! He begged his friends to carry him into the presence of the great Healer. They consented, but when they reached the house of Peter, the crowd was so great that they could not come even within hearing of His voice. At last they took him to the top of the house, and, opening up the roof, they let him down at the very feet of Jesus. The Saviour looked with pity into the longing eyes of the helpless man. He understood his heart. Then in words that to the poor man sounded like sweetest music, He said, "Son, be of good cheer; thy sins be forgiven thee."

6. Accused of Blasphemy. In their hearts the spies, who were rabbis, said, "This man blasphemeth." "Who can forgive sins but one, even God?" Jesus read their hearts, and said, "Wherefore think ye evil in your hearts? For whether is easier, to say, Thy sins be forgiven thee; or to say, Arise, and walk? But that ye may know that the Son of man hath power on earth to forgive sins," He said, turning to the paralytic, "Arise, take up thy bed, and go unto thine house." "And immediately he arose, took up the bed, and went forth before them all; insomuch that they were all amazed, and glorified God, saying, We never saw it on this fashion."

Hofmann
His strength was in prayer.

The spies did not dare to say a word. They knew they were defeated. They knew that Jesus had done a work that was beyond mere human skill. But they were too proud and stubborn to confess Him, and they went away to invent new schemes to entrap Him.

7. Source of Jesus' Power. And so Jesus was hunted from place to place. Satan, working through wicked men, did everything he could think of to make His life miserable and to discourage Him. No other person ever lived whose life was so burdened for others. But His strength was in prayer. Again and again it is said of Him: "Rising up a great while before day, He went out . . . into a solitary place, and there prayed." "And He withdrew Himself into the wilderness, and prayed." "And . . . He went out into a mountain to pray, and continued all night in prayer to God." Only by this constant dependence upon divine power was He able to accomplish the work He had been sent here to do. This is why He said: "I can of Mine own self do nothing." "The Father that dwelleth in Me, He doeth the works."

How to Study: Notice in this lesson the ways in which Jesus tried to convince the people that He was the Messiah, and to keep them from rejecting salvation. When Jesus was rejected at Nazareth, was He defeated? What was the secret of His success?

7. JESUS REJECTED BY THE GALILEANS

"From that time many of His disciples went back, and walked no more with Him." John 6:66.

1. Planning to Make Jesus King. Another year has gone. Another springtime has come. It is time to attend the Passover. People expect to find Jesus there. But He knows that the scribes and Pharisees have laid a trap for Him, and He decides not to attend this gathering. With His disciples He went away to a quiet place to rest. But the people soon found Him, and Jesus ministered to their needs. Companies of travelers on their way to the Passover stopped to hear His wonderful words, until there were five thousand besides women and children in the assembly. They seemed in no hurry to continue their journey, and when night came, Jesus miraculously fed that vast multitude with five barley loaves and two small fishes.

As the people sat upon the grass in the twilight of that spring evening eating the food that Christ had provided, they talked over the words that He had been speaking to them. They knew that from five barley loaves and two small fishes no human power could create enough food to feed so many hungry people. "Of a truth," they said one to another, "this is . . . that Prophet that should come into the world." As they talked, their hopes rose. Since He can do such miracles, they reasoned, He can make Judea an earthly paradise. "He can satisfy every desire. He can break the power of the hated Romans. He can deliver Judah and Jerusalem. He can heal the soldiers who are wounded in battle. He can supply

References Used: D. A., pp. 377, 419, 421; John 6:14, 48; Matt. 17:2, 5, 7.

whole armies with food. He can conquer the nations, and give to Israel the long-sought dominion." They determine to crown Him king at once. Jesus, they think, is too modest to claim His rights. They will take Him by force and place Him on the throne.

2. How and Why Jesus Defeated Their Plans. Jesus understood their plans. He knew that if these were carried out, the priests and rulers would kill Him. But His work on earth was not yet finished. He saw that something must be done quickly. He sent His disciples away across the Sea of Galilee, and then in tones of authority which the people could not resist, He dismissed the multitude, while He Himself went alone into the mountain to pray to God.

Jesus miraculously fed that vast multitude with five barley loaves and two small fishes.

3. Jesus Rejected by the Galileans. This was the crisis in the work of Jesus in Galilee. The people were so disappointed that their love was turned to hatred. Jesus tried to explain to them that His kingdom was not of this world. He tried to explain that if they desired to become subjects of His kingdom they must live lives of self-sacrifice. He tried to explain that the true bread of life was to give their lives in helping others, just as He was doing. "I am the Bread of life," He said to them. But they were unreconciled. They were not interested in the strange spiritual kingdom of which He spoke. They wanted to be freed from disease and suffering, they wanted to receive gifts from Him, but they did not want to devote their lives unselfishly to others. If He would not free them from the Romans, they decided to have nothing more to do with Him. "From that time many of His disciples went back, and walked no more with Him." Jesus had been rejected by the Sanhedrin, He had been rejected at Nazareth, and now He was rejected by the people of Galilee.

4. One More Year of Service. But the Saviour was not discouraged. He knew that Satan was working hard to turn the world against Him, but He knew too that His heavenly Father would give the victory. Though many would reject Him, others would accept Him, and His family on earth would at last be fully made up. And so He continued to work and pray. Only one more year remained for Him to work for His people. The next Passover will mark "the midst of the week" prophesied by Daniel, when "the sacrifice and the oblation" shall cease. O, how anxious He is that His work every day shall meet His Father's approval!

5. How Jesus Encouraged His Disciples. One evening, with Peter, James, and John, Jesus went once more to a mountain to pray. At first the disciples prayed with Him, but as night came on, they became weary and fell asleep. Jesus had told them of the suffering that awaited Him, and now, lest they too become discouraged and desert Him, He prayed that God would show them the glory He had with the Father in heaven. His prayer is heard. Suddenly the heavens open, the gates of the city of God are thrown wide, and the light of heaven shines upon Him. Rising from prayer, "Christ stands in Godlike majesty." His countenance shines "as the sun," and His garments are "white as the light."

The bright light awakens the sleeping disciples, and in fear they gaze upon the scene. Soon they see that Jesus is not alone. Beside Him are two heavenly beings talking with Him. One of these is Moses, the other Elijah. This scene represented the future kingdom of glory,— Christ the King, Moses representing the righteous who shall be raised from the dead at the second coming of Christ, and Elijah representing those who shall be translated without seeing death.

This experience proved beyond a doubt to the disciples that Jesus was indeed the Messiah. While they were still gazing, "a bright cloud overshadowed them; and behold a voice out of the cloud,

The transfiguration represented the future kingdom of glory.

which said, This is My beloved Son, in whom I am well pleased; hear ye Him." As they heard the voice of the Father, they fell to the earth and hid their faces from the sight. Soon Jesus touched them and said, "Arise, and be not afraid." They arose. The heavenly glory had disappeared, Moses and Elijah had gone, and they were alone with Jesus.

How to Study: After studying this lesson see if you can tell *why* the Galileans wanted to make Jesus king, and *why* they at last rejected Him. Do we ever feel like "walking no more with Him" when things do not go our way? Why was Jesus transfigured before His disciples?

Chapter to Remember: Matthew 17 tells about the transfiguration.

8. JESUS REJECTED BY THE SAMARITANS

"They . . . entered into a village of the Samaritans, to make ready for Him. And they did not receive Him. . . . And they went to another village."
Luke 9: 52, 53, 56.

1. At the Feast of Tabernacles. Though Jesus did not attend the Passover in the spring of 30 A. D., He did go to Jerusalem in

---
References Used: D. A., pp. 580-582, 609, 638, 639; John 7: 31, 45, 46, 59; Luke 9: 51, 52.

the autumn of that year to attend the Feast of Tabernacles. Jews from all parts of the world were present, and Jesus was the chief topic of conversation. Many thought He was the Messiah, while others thought He was an impostor. All the time He was there priests and rulers as spies were watching Him. Ever since He healed the cripple at the pool of Bethesda they had been plotting His death. When the people heard Him teaching, many of them were convinced that He was the Son of God. "When Christ cometh," they said, "will He do more miracles than these which this man hath done?"

2. Plans to Arrest Jesus. When the spies heard these expressions of confidence, they hurried away to the chief priests to lay plans for His arrest. But the officers who were sent to arrest Him came back without Him. Angrily the priests demanded, "Why have ye not brought Him?" The officers had been so impressed with the words they had heard Him speak, that all they could say was, "Never man spake like this Man." The priests were enraged at this unexpected failure, and after expressing their anger, they again laid plans to arrest Him. And again they were defeated.

3. Protected from Mob Violence. This failure to arrest Him only made them the more determined. In their discussions Jesus plainly told them that He came forth from God, that He was the I AM, and that He was from the days of eternity. Again priests and rabbis called Him a blasphemer, and many of the people, siding with them, took up stones to cast at Him. But Jesus, unseen by them, "going through the midst of them," "went out of the temple." Thus again their plans were made of no effect. After this, Jesus returned to Galilee.

4. The Last Journey to Jerusalem. As the following spring drew near, when Jesus should be crucified, He "steadfastly set His face to go to Jerusalem." When He went to the Feast of Tabernacles, He went alone and secretly. But now He went in the most public manner and by the longest route, passing first through Samaria and then through Perea. He even "sent messengers before His face: and they went, and entered into a village of the Samaritans, to make ready for Him." But when the Samaritans learned that He was going to Jerusalem, their hatred for the Jews at that place and their bitter prejudice led them to refuse to receive Him. They would not even give Him a place to rest for the night. Little did they realize that they had turned away the Saviour of the world. In spite of their rude treatment, Jesus had only thoughts of love for them. He commended the good Samaritan who helped the injured man by the roadside; and among the ten lepers whom He healed, the one who returned to give Him thanks was a Samaritan. In these experiences Jesus has left us a most beautiful example of generous good will and kind feelings toward all.

5. **Jesus' Interest in Children.** It was on this, Jesus' last journey to Jerusalem, that He received the children and blessed them. When they were brought to Him, Peter and the other disciples were annoyed and desired that He send them away. But God's great plan is for the children as well as for men and women. Jesus understands their trials and temptations, for He has Himself been a child. He knows that childhood and youth is the time to form right habits, the best time of all to begin service for Him. John the Baptist was filled with the Holy Spirit from his birth. Jesus loved to be with children. He is interested in their progress, and He will be their Helper. His heart is drawn out, not only to the best-behaved children, but to those who are struggling with evil traits of character. In every child who gives his heart to Jesus, He sees a man or a woman who, if faithful, will be a subject of His heavenly kingdom — a member of God's great family.

6. **Decisions of the Sanhedrin.** It was about this time also that Lazarus was raised from the dead. As

Hofmann

In every child who gives his heart to Jesus, He sees a man or a woman who, if faithful, will be a member of God's great family.

soon as the news of this wonderful miracle reached Jerusalem, a meeting of the Sanhedrin was called to decide what should be done to put a stop to Christ's work. The Sadducees, who did not believe in a resurrection, now joined the Pharisees in their hatred against the Life-giver. Jesus had repeatedly been accused of breaking the Sabbath and of blasphemy. He had been accused of trying to incite insurrection against the Roman government. But, so far, every attempt to condemn Him had failed. His work of teaching and healing still went on, and many continued to believe in Him.

In desperation the Jews had passed a law that any man who professed faith in Jesus should be cast out of the synagogue. And now in the council which they had called they determined to silence His voice forever. In this council angels were present pleading with the hearts of these cruel men, to help them to see what an awful deed they were planning. Satan was also there urging them that if they hoped to preserve their own power over the people, they must put Jesus out of the way. At last the decision was reached. They voted to put Him to death at their first opportunity. Thus the terrible conflict was nearing its end.

How to Study: In this lesson, notice how God tried again and again to help the priests and rulers see the true nature of Christ's work. Write a list of as many such instances as you can find. The only reason they did not accept Him was because they *would* not. On what occasion were angels sent to protect Him? Why did the Samaritans refuse to receive Jesus?

Map Work: Trace the last journey of Jesus to Jerusalem through Samaria and Perea. The map is on page 24 of your workbook.

For Class Discussion: What were the three yearly feasts? When were they held? What did they commemorate?

9. PRIESTS AND RULERS REJECTED BY JESUS
31 A. D.

"The kingdom of God shall be taken from you, and given to a nation bringing forth the fruits thereof." Matt. 21:43.

1. The Last Week. The last week of Jesus' life on earth had come,—a week filled with events that meant much in the working out of God's plan. Jesus knew that on Friday of that very week

---
References Used: D. A., pp. 557, 571, 620, 624, 625; Mark 14:8; Matt. 21:13, 40, 41; 23:37, 38; John 12:21, 28, 29.

He would be crucified. But He was not afraid of death. His anxiety was for His disciples. Would *they* stand the test? He had told them plainly that He would be betrayed and put to death, and that He would rise again the third day. But their hopes were so fixed upon a temporal kingdom that they had not comprehended His words.

Plockhorst

The purpose of Christ's triumphal entry into Jerusalem was that many would be led to search the prophecies and be convinced that He was really the Messiah.

2. The Last Sabbath. Sabbath evening before the Passover, Jesus reached Bethany, the home of Lazarus. Here He rested over the Sabbath. During the day He with His disciples and a few friends were eating at the house of Simon, whom Jesus had healed of leprosy. Mary Magdalene, the sister of Lazarus, was there, her heart overflowing with gratitude because Jesus had forgiven her sins, and He had also raised her brother to life. As an expression of her feelings, she poured a box of costly ointment upon the head and feet of Jesus. Then, as her tears of love and gratitude fell upon His feet, she wiped them with her hair. Jesus used this event as another occasion to remind the disciples of His death. He said, "She is come aforehand to anoint My body to the burying." Still the disciples did not understand.

3. Events of Sunday. On Sunday Christ made His triumphal entry into Jerusalem. In this procession were those out of whom He had cast devils, the blind whom He had restored to sight, the dumb and cripples whom He had healed, lepers whom He had cleansed, while Lazarus, whom He had raised from the dead, led the beast upon which Jesus rode. People spread their garments in the way, and children strewed the path with palm branches. Shouts of joy from hundreds of voices echoed through the air. The people expected at this time to crown Him king. But after the procession was over, Jesus quietly withdrew and returned to Bethany, where He again spent the night at the home of His friend Lazarus.

The purpose of this occasion was to direct the attention of all to Jesus, so that during the days to follow they would watch closely every event connected with His trial and crucifixion, and afterward as they recalled these events many would be led to search the prophecies and be convinced that He was really the Messiah.

4. Events of Monday. On Monday Jesus again went to Jerusalem. Already preparations were being made for the Passover. In the outer court of the temple were hundreds of animals, while people were engaged in buying and selling, and exchanging money. On every side were heard angry voices disputing about prices and trying to drive sharp bargains. The very symbols that represented the spotless Lamb of God were made a means of getting gain.

Just as, three years before, at the beginning of His work, Jesus had announced the nature of His mission by driving from the temple those who defiled it with their unholy traffic, so now He closed His work on earth by a similar act. Thus He tried to teach the priests the kind of fruit God expected from them. As He entered the temple, all eyes were fastened upon Him. For a time the bargaining ceased. Then, in a voice that made them feel a deep sense of guilt, He said: "It is written, My house shall be called the house of prayer; but ye have made it a den of thieves." "Take these things hence."

When the traders had left the court, the sick and afflicted crowded about Him and He healed them all. But even this act of mercy had no effect on priests and rulers, for when they ventured back to the temple they were offended, and tried to put a stop to the shouts of praise.

5. Events of Tuesday. The next morning Jesus was back again in the temple. In the meantime, the Sanhedrin had held a meeting, and they decided to question Him as to His authority and then find in His answer something by which they might condemn Him. But the more they tried, the more entangled they became. They had received evidence upon evidence that Jesus was the Messiah, but they were too proud to accept Him and acknowledge that He was greater than they.

As another means of opening their eyes, Jesus told them the parable of the man who planted a vineyard, and let it out to husbandmen, and then went into a far country. But when he sent his servants and at last even his own son to gather the fruit, the husbandmen beat one, and killed another, and stoned another, and his son they cast out of the vineyard and killed. After Jesus had told the parable, He asked, "When the lord therefore of the vineyard cometh, what will he do unto those husbandmen?" The priests and rulers promptly answered, "He will miserably destroy those wicked men, and will let out his vineyard unto other husbandmen, which shall render him the fruits in their seasons."

Then Jesus, looking upon them with pity, said, "The kingdom of God shall be taken from you, and given to a nation bringing forth the fruits thereof." The parable represented the Jews who had so miserably failed to give to others a knowledge of God's plan to save men. They were the husbandmen, and the Father had sent His Son to gather the fruit. And now they were planning to kill Him. The priests themselves had declared their own doom, and the nation chosen by God to cultivate His vineyard was about to be forever rejected.

All through that long meeting Jesus tried to help them see the wicked course they were taking, but they would not yield. At last, with a breaking heart, He exclaimed, "O Jerusalem, Jerusalem, thou that killest the prophets, and stonest them which are sent unto thee, how often would I have gathered thy children together, even as a hen gathereth her chickens under her wings, and ye would not!"

Then, with His disciples, Jesus left the temple, never again to enter it. His last sad words as He looked back were, "Behold, your house is left unto you desolate." From that day God's presence was withdrawn from the temple, and the services were but a meaningless mockery.

As Jesus left the temple, He met in the outer court some Greeks, who said to one of His disciples, "Sir, we would see Jesus." It was an encouragement to Jesus to find some who were earnestly seeking Him. The Jews, as a nation, were ready to kill Him, but here were people outside of the Jewish nation who were longing for truth.

As Jesus talked with them, a strange cloud seemed to surround Him. At first He looked sad and pale. He was thinking of God's great plan that had been laid in eternity to save man, and how near was the time when His life which He had then promised was to be sacrificed. Only three more days! For a moment it seemed as if He could not bear the reproach, the shame, the cruelty, the public exposure as if He were the worst of criminals, and above all, the desertion of His disciples and of His own heavenly Father. Then, willing to suffer anything that would save man, willing to do anything that would glorify God, He said as if in prayer, "Father, glorify Thy name."

As He spoke these words a voice out of the cloud said, "I have both glorified it, and will glorify it again." "As the voice was heard, a light darted from the cloud, and encircled Christ, as if the arms of Infinite Power were thrown about Him like a wall of fire. The people beheld this scene with terror and amazement. No one dared to speak. With silent lips and bated breath all stood with eyes fixed upon Jesus." Then the cloud disappeared. Some who heard the voice said it thundered. Others said an angel spoke to Him. But the Greeks had the desire of their hearts. They saw Jesus, the Son of God, and accepted Him. After this, Jesus slowly and sadly left the temple courts forever.

He then went with His disciples to the Mount of Olives, where He told them many things regarding His second coming in glory with all the holy angels. He also told them many signs of the end of the world — among others the darkening of the sun and the moon, and the falling of the stars. This prophecy is recorded in Matthew 24. And then, as the busy day drew to a close, He turned

His weary steps once more toward Bethany. It was the last time He was in Jerusalem until the night of His betrayal.

How to Study: Follow closely the events of each day. See how Jesus tried again and again to win those who were plotting against Him, and save them from rejecting their only means of salvation. Notice also how He tried to prepare His disciples to meet the trials that were coming. Write a list of the events that occurred on each day — Sabbath, Sunday, Monday, and Tuesday.

Why did Jesus allow the procession to accompany Him to Jerusalem?

This lesson tells the third time that the Father spoke directly to His Son. On what occasions were the other two times?

Chapter to Remember: Matthew 24 gives Jesus' own prophecy of His second coming.

Make an outline of the daily events of this last week as far as this lesson gives them.

---

10. THE BIRTHDAY OF THE CHRISTIAN CHURCH
Spring of 31 A. D.
Lesson 1, Topics 1-5; Lesson 2, Topics 6-10

"As often as ye eat this bread, and drink this cup, ye do show the Lord's death till He come." 1 Cor. 11:26.

1. Thursday Evening in the "Upper Chamber." Jesus remained with His friends in Bethany the last two days before His betrayal. What a comfort it must have been to spend these two days with those whom He could trust! The next we hear of Him He was in an upper chamber of a dwelling at Jerusalem with His disciples. It was Thursday evening, the beginning of Friday. They had come together to celebrate the Passover. Jesus knew that the Passover lamb represented Himself. He knew that before this day ended He would be nailed to the cross. His heart was heavy, and sorrow rested upon His countenance. But it was not because He was about to die, for He knew that when this short period of suffering was over He would return to heaven. The prayer of His heart was that He might not fail, and that His disciples, who would be left in the world to suffer and be tormented by Satan, would be able to stand the test.

References Used: D. A., pp. 643, 644, 646, 654, 656, 679, 680; Matt. 26:26-29; 28:18, 20; John 6:35, 53, 63; 13:4-17, 37; 14:16, 17, 27; 17:1, 4, 11; Mark 14:27, 29, 31; Gal. 6:14; 1 Cor. 11:27.

2. Between the Old and the New. Jesus was standing at the end of the time when the sacrifices pointed forward to the sacrifice of Christ; He was standing at the beginning of the time when His people were to look back upon that event. When on the morrow He should present Himself as a sin offering, all the types and sacrifices that for four thousand years had pointed forward to His death, would come to an end. Now He was about to begin another service, which would point backward and commemorate His death — a service that would take the place of the sacrifices, and especially of the Passover.

3. In Memory of His Death. The Passover supper commemorated the deliverance of Israel from the bondage of Egypt. The Lord's Supper was given to commemorate our deliverance from sin through the death of Christ. The Passover lamb was eaten with unleavened bread. In the Lord's Supper the unleavened bread represented His broken body, His life free from the leaven of sin. "As they were eating [the Passover supper], Jesus took bread, and blessed it, and brake it, and gave it to the disciples, and said, Take, eat; this is My body." This was hereafter to be the bread of the Lord's Supper. Then, taking the cup which contained the juice of the vine, He "gave thanks," and gave it to them, saying, "Drink ye all of it; for this is My blood." No longer was the blood of animals to be shed to represent the Sacrifice for sin. Jesus the true Sacrifice was to shed His own blood, which He represented by the wine.

4. A Pledge of Our Loyalty. Jesus said: "I am the bread of life. . . . Except ye eat the flesh of the Son of man, and drink His blood, ye have no life in you. . . . The words that I speak unto you, they are spirit, and they are life." As we partake of the emblems of the Lord's body, which contain the elements to nourish our daily physical life, by that act we pledge with God to partake daily of the bread of life, His holy word, and to receive daily of His Spirit, that we may be the spiritual light that He expects us to be as His true followers. As we partake of the emblems of His broken body, we pledge ourselves to be "crucified . . . unto the world."

5. A Pledge of His Return. The Lord's Supper points not only backward to the death of Christ, but forward to His second coming. When He gave them the wine, He said, "I will not drink henceforth of this fruit of the vine, until that day when I drink it new with you in My Father's kingdom." "As often as ye eat this bread, and drink this cup, ye do show the Lord's death *till He come.*" And so in their struggles they were to find comfort in the hope of their Lord's return.

6. Jesus Washing the Disciples' Feet. When the disciples came to the upper chamber, they were unprepared to partake of the Passover supper or to appreciate the emblems of the Lord's Supper. Among them there was a strife as to which of them should have the highest place in the earthly kingdom, which even yet they hoped

A pledge of loyalty; a pledge of humble, faithful service.

Jesus would establish. They all wanted it. James and John had already asked for it. But Judas was determined to have it. So when they took their places at the table, Judas pressed next to Christ. There was no servant present to wash their feet as was the custom at a feast. The disciples knew that under these circumstances it was their duty to act the part of a servant. But because of the strife that was in their hearts they were unwilling to humble themselves. Jesus waited a moment. Then, quietly rising from the table, He Himself acted the servant's part. What a rebuke to the haughty disciples! They felt guilty and ashamed. As Jesus gently bathed their feet, their hearts were touched, and their pride and jealousy were washed away.

7. A Pledge of Humble Service. "Know ye what I have done to you?" Jesus asked. "Ye call Me Master and Lord: and ye say well; for so I am. If I then, your Lord and Master, have washed your feet; ye also ought to wash one another's feet. For I have given you an example, that ye should do as I have done to you. . . . If ye know these things, happy are ye if ye do them." This service was not for the purpose of physical cleansing. "Ye are clean, but not all," He said. The physical washing was a type of the spiritual cleansing. Their hearts needed to be cleansed from sin. This service was a pledge that they would not strive for the highest place, but with true humility of heart would give their lives in unselfish service to others. Without this preparation of heart, the disciples would partake of the Lord's Supper "unworthily," and like Judas, "be guilty of the body and blood of the Lord." They would then look forward to His second coming, not to be saved, but to be destroyed with those "which pierced Him."

8. The Christian Church Organized. In these services Jesus completed the organization of the Christian church, which He began when He called His first disciples. As the first Passover was the birthday of the missionary nation, so the last Passover was the birthday of the Christian church. Jesus pledged Himself to be their personal Helper in the work they were to do for Him. "All power is given unto Me in heaven and in earth," He said. "And, lo, I am with you alway, even unto the end of the world."

9. The Holy Spirit Promised. This was Jesus' last opportunity to talk with His disciples, for even now Judas, who had left the room, was completing arrangements with the priests to betray Him. The disciples knew that trouble was ahead. Jesus had told them that He was to leave them. How could they get along without Him? They were sad and perplexed. Jesus comforted them with the promise, "I will pray the Father, and He shall give you another Comforter, that He may abide with you forever; even the Spirit of truth." Then Jesus explained to them what the Holy Spirit would do for them.

10. Jesus' Last Words to His Disciples. It was getting late in the evening, and Jesus knew that He would soon be betrayed into the hands of an angry mob. But He did not talk with His disciples about His own sufferings. Among His last words before leaving the room were: "Peace I leave with you, My peace I give unto you. . . . Let not your heart be troubled, neither let it be afraid." Then as He lifted His voice in song, they joined in the hymn and went out.

Slowly and silently they passed through the city streets toward the Mount of Olives, at the foot of which was Gethsemane. At last Jesus spoke. "All ye shall be offended because of Me this night," He said. Peter was shocked. "Although all shall be offended," he answered, "yet will not I." "I will lay down my life for Thy sake." "Likewise also said they all." But Jesus knew. With strong, hopeful words, He tried to prepare them for the trial and disappointment they would have to meet, to stand true even when everything looked dark. He knew Satan's plans, but He knew also that when Satan should put Him to death, all heaven would triumph, for in that very act, "the knell of Satan's empire would be sounded."

Then, surrounded by His anxious disciples, Jesus lifted His eyes to heaven and prayed for them. "Father," He said, "the hour is come. . . . I have finished the work which Thou gavest Me to do. . . . And now I am no more in the world, but these are in the world, and I come to Thee. Holy Father, keep through Thine own name those whom Thou hast given Me, that they may be one, as We are." When He had finished His prayer, He went forth to His last battle with Satan.

How to Study: In this lesson try to understand what it *means* for a Christian to partake of the bread and the wine, and to take part in the ordinance of humility.

Memory Work: Memorize 1 Corinthians 11:26. This verse completes the left point of the "crown" of the "Service Flag."

Chapters to Remember: The Lord's Supper is recorded in Matthew 26; the ordinance of humility, in John 13; Jesus' last prayer with His disciples, in John 17.

For Class Discussion: Which would be worse, for the Jews to offer meaningless sacrifices, or for us to go through the form of the Lord's Supper without appreciating its real meaning? Why, do you think, did Jesus use grape juice to represent His spilled blood? John 15:1; Isa. 63:3.

11. SATAN CAST OUT OF THE COUNCILS OF HEAVEN

"Now shall the prince of this world be cast out. And I, if I be lifted up from the earth, will draw all men unto Me." John 12:31, 32.

1. On the Way to the Garden. The garden of Gethsemane was less than a mile beyond the wall of the city. The disciples had often gone with Jesus to this quiet spot for prayer. But never before had they seen Him so utterly sad and silent. He was bearing the sins of the whole world, and it seemed to Him that they would forever shut Him away from His Father's face, and that He would die. "My soul is exceeding sorrowful unto death," were the words that at last escaped His lips.

2. Satan's Effort to Overcome Jesus. When they reached the garden, Jesus left His disciples, and going a little distance from them, He fell upon the ground. Here Satan met Him for the last terrible struggle. Satan knew that everything was at stake with him. "If he failed here, his hope of mastery was lost; the kingdoms of the world would finally become Christ's; he himself would be . . . cast out." But if he could overcome Christ, the earth and its inhabitants would forever be in his power.

In the wilderness, Satan had offered Jesus all the kingdoms of the world if He would only acknowledge him as the supreme ruler. Now he suggested to Christ: "Your own people have rejected You, one of Your disciples will betray You, and the rest of them will all forsake You. Besides, if You take upon Yourself the sins of the world, the Father will forever separate Himself from You. In that case You will after all belong to my kingdom. You might as well give up."

As Satan whispered these thoughts to Jesus, it seemed to Him that He could not endure the test. "O My Father," He cried out, "if it be possible, let this cup pass from Me: nevertheless," He added with complete submission, "not as I will, but as Thou wilt." Three times Satan renewed his temptations. Three times Jesus prayed the same prayer. The pressure of the enemy became so great that at last Jesus' "sweat was as it were great drops of blood falling down to the ground." Still He refused to yield. "Not as I will, but as Thou wilt," He repeated with every prayer.

References Used: D. A., pp. 687, 690, 694, 734, 753, 756, 760, 761; Mark 14:34; Matt. 26:39-44; 27:19, 46; Luke 22:43, 44; 23:28, 34, 42-44, 46; John 19:6, 26, 30; Ps. 119:89.

3. The Victory of Jesus. Angels in heaven saw the agony of the Saviour. They saw Satan with all his forces trying to overcome Him. They saw the Father in silent grief, turn His face away from His Son. Not a word was spoken. Not a harp was touched. Unfallen worlds also watched the scene with intense interest to see what answer the Father would give to the prayer of His Son. Angels longed to bring Him relief — to tell Him as they told Abraham when he was about to sacrifice Isaac, "It is enough; You need

Then Gabriel came to Jesus, not to take the cup from Him, but to strengthen Him to drink it.

not drink the cup." But no; they were not permitted to bear this message.

At last the decision is made. Jesus will save man at any cost to Himself. He will not turn from the work God has sent Him to do. He does not now pray that the cup pass from Him, but, "If this cup may not pass away from Me, except I drink it, Thy will be done."

4. Jesus Strengthened. Then Gabriel, the angel who took Lucifer's place in the presence of the Father, came to Jesus,— not to take the cup from Him, but to strengthen Him to drink it. "And there appeared an angel unto Him from heaven, strengthening Him." He assured Him of His Father's love. He reminded Him that the Father was greater than Satan, that His death would result in Satan's complete defeat, and that through His sacrifice a multitude of the human family would be saved, eternally saved.

5. In the Hands of the Mob. In the strength which the angel had brought, Jesus rose, calm and serene. He heard the footsteps of the mob in search of Him. He stepped forward to meet them. As He did so, the angel who had strengthened Him passed between Him and the mob. Priests, soldiers, and even Judas, fell as dead men to the ground. Then the angel disappeared and the light faded away. It was past midnight. As soon as the mob recovered from the shock, they bound Jesus, and hurried Him back to the city to be tried. Heaven beheld Him dragged to and fro from palace to judgment hall, brought twice before the Sanhedrin, twice before Pilate, and once before Herod, mocked and scourged, and — that which was the hardest of all to bear — deserted by every one of His disciples.

6. Condemned to Death. When He was brought before Pilate for the last time, the Roman governor, hoping to satisfy the clamors of the mob, said that he would chastise Jesus. But they demanded the life of the Prisoner. Just at this time a messenger pressed through the crowd and handed Pilate a letter from his wife, which read, "Have thou nothing to do with that just Man: for I have suffered many things this day in a dream because of Him." If Pilate had been a conscientious judge with courage to do what he knew to be right, he would have released Jesus at once. But having yielded to wrong by chastising Him, he continued to yield to the unjust demands of the mob, so that when they with mad fury cried, "Crucify Him!" he cried out, "Take ye Him, and crucify Him: for I find no fault in Him." Then they dragged Him away to crucify Him.

7. On the Cross. "Satan led the cruel mob in its abuse of the Saviour. It was his purpose to provoke Him to retaliation if possible, or to drive Him to perform a miracle to release Himself, and thus break up the plan of salvation." But Jesus patiently submitted as they nailed Him to the cross. He was not thinking about Himself. Though suffering the most intense agony of body and mind,

The dream of Pilate's wife. "Have thou nothing to do with that just man."

He thought only of others. To the women who stood by weeping, He said, "Weep not for Me, but weep for yourselves, and for your children." To the penitent thief, He granted forgiveness of sin. Looking upon His grief-stricken mother, and then upon John, who supported her, He said, "Woman, behold thy son!" and to John, "Behold thy mother!" For His murderers, as He thought of the terrible punishment that they would finally suffer, He prayed from the depths of a breaking heart, "Father, forgive them; for they know not what they do."

8. The Final Struggle and Victory. As Jesus hung upon the cross, Satan pressed the weight of sin upon Him until He felt that He would be forever separated from His Father. He felt the same terrible anguish that the sinner will feel when he is forever lost. Although it was midday, a thick darkness rested upon the earth "until the ninth hour." Lightnings occasionally flashed forth from the cloud, revealing the dying Saviour. The Father's presence was in the darkness, but Jesus did not know it. At the baptism, at the transfiguration, and again just before the betrayal, the Father spoke to His Son from heaven, but now that voice was silent. Angels could no longer look upon the awful scene. Then from the

"When the angels saw Jesus breathe His last, they clearly understood Satan's character, and the last link of sympathy between him and the heavenly world was broken."

darkness Jesus with a loud voice cried out, "My God, My God, why hast Thou forsaken Me?" Still His sufferings continued until He drained the last drop from the cup of human woe.

In these dreadful hours, though He had no present evidence of His Father's care, He remembered His word, "This is My beloved Son," and in that word He trusted. He knew that His Father was a God of justice, mercy, and love; and when He cried out, "It is finished," He rested in that love, saying, "Father, into Thy hands I commend My spirit." As Jesus thus submitted Himself to God, then it was that He realized the presence of His Father, and He died a conqueror.

9. God's Word Settled in Heaven. When the angels saw Jesus breathe His last, they had no further need of evidence that Satan was a murderer. Then was fulfilled those words: "Forever, O Lord, Thy word is settled in heaven." "And I heard a loud voice saying in heaven, . . . The accuser of our brethren is cast down, which accused them before our God day and night." The angels now clearly understood Satan's character, and the last link of sympathy between him and the heavenly world was broken. Henceforth his work was to be confined to this world. Never again was he allowed to meet in the councils at the gate of heaven.

How to Study: Write a topical outline of this lesson, writing several subtopics under the main topics here given. Do not omit any important point.

Jesus was rejected by the Jewish priests, by the people of His own home town, by Galileans and Samaritans, deserted by His own disciples, and at last shut away from His Father's face. Yet He was so sure of His Father's love and His great plan to save man that none of these things could overthrow Him. Is our confidence as firm in God's love, and in the work He has given us to do for Him?

Memory Work: Memorize Revelation 12: 10, and enter the reference on the right point of the "crown" of the "Service Flag."

Complete your outline of the events of this last week.

---

12. JESUS SECURING THE KEYS OF SATAN'S PRISON HOUSE

"I am He that liveth, and was dead; and, behold, I am alive forevermore; . . . and have the keys of the grave and of death." Rev. 1: 18.

1. Jesus Resting on the Sabbath. Before the last rays of the setting sun had announced the beginning of God's holy rest day, Jesus lay quietly in Satan's prison house. With hands folded peacefully upon His breast, He rested through the sacred hours of the Sabbath. On the seventh day God rested from the work of creation, and now on the same day Jesus rested from the work of redemption. In the beginning, "God blessed the seventh day, and sanctified it:

References Used: D. A., pp. 780, 782, 785-787, 829-831, 833, 834; Isa. 42: 21; Heb. 2: 14, 15; John 10: 17, 18; 11: 25; Matt. 27: 53, 62-65; 28: 2; 1 Cor. 15: 55; 1 Peter 5: 8; Acts 1: 9; Psalm 24.

because that in it He had rested." By the death of Jesus the Sabbath day is made doubly sacred. Thus Jesus not only in His life but in His death fulfilled God's word, "He will magnify the law, and make it honorable." The claims of God's broken law, and the authority of its seal, were at last fully confirmed.

2. Joy in Heaven. When Jesus was laid in the tomb, there was disappointment and grief among those who loved Him on earth, but among the angels in heaven there was great joy. God and angels knew that Jesus, God's beloved Son, the Commander of the heavenly host, was no longer to be tormented and insulted and abused by Satan and his agents. They knew that the salvation of man was now made sure, for Jesus had suffered death that He might "destroy him that had the power of death, that is, the devil; and deliver them who through fear of death were all their lifetime subject to bondage." The conflict was at last over, and Jesus was victorious. No wonder there was rejoicing in heaven.

3. Fears of the Jews. Now that the terrible deed was done and Jesus was out of the way, the priests and Pharisees did not seem to enjoy their victory as they had thought they would. They were more troubled than ever. He had raised others from the dead; what if He Himself should come back to life! They remembered that He had said: "I lay down My life, that I might take it again. No man taketh it from Me, but I lay it down of Myself. I have power to lay it down, and I have power to take it again." They trembled for fear of what might happen. They could not rest. The patient, calm face of Jesus kept coming up in their minds. The events of the trial and the crucifixion came back to them with a force that seemed to say to their guilty consciences, "He was indeed the Son of God." What if He should come back to life and demand that they should answer for His murder!

4. The Grave Guarded. Something must be done to hold Him in the grave. A council was called. "The chief priests and Pharisees came together unto Pilate, saying, Sir, we remember that that deceiver said, while He was yet alive, After three days I will rise again. Command therefore that the sepulcher be made sure until the third day, lest His disciples come by night, and steal Him away, and say unto the people, He is risen from the dead." Pilate was as anxious as they were not to have any more trouble about Jesus, so he answered, "Ye have a watch: go your way, make it as sure as ye can." Then the tomb was sealed with the Roman seal, and a guard of one hundred soldiers was stationed at the sepulcher to see that no one meddled with it.

5. The Prison House Opened. When Jesus was laid in the grave, Satan dared to hope that he could hold Him in his prison house. But his hope was vain. In the darkest hour of the night, just before the dawn on the first day of the week, Gabriel, "the angel of

Satan's hope that he could hold the Son of God in his prison house was vain. Jesus came forth declaring, "I am the resurrection, and the life."

the Lord," the one who took the place that Lucifer had held in heaven, descended and "rolled back the stone from the door" of the sepulcher. Then, while angels from the courts above sang, "Death is swallowed up in victory. O death, where is thy sting? O grave, where is thy victory?" Jesus removed the graveclothes, and came forth declaring in tones of triumph, "I am the resurrection, and the life."

6. The Real Wave Sheaf. When Jesus at His death cried out, "It is finished," there was a great earthquake, which opened many graves. When He arose there was another earthquake. Then those whose graves had been opened came forth with Jesus. They were those who had been martyrs for the truth. They were raised to everlasting life. As Jesus appeared first to Mary and then to the other disciples in Jerusalem, those whom He had brought from the grave also "went into the holy city, and appeared unto many," declaring that Christ had risen from the dead and that they were risen with Him.

Like the wave sheaf, the first fruits of the harvest, which in the services of the earthly sanctuary was waved before the Lord as a thank offering, looking forward to the harvest to come, so Jesus brought from the grave these captives of Satan, as the first fruits of His victory over death and the grave. They were His thank offering looking toward the final resurrection of all the righteous. The death of Jesus took place on the very day and at the very hour when the Passover lamb was slain; His resurrection took place on the very day when the wave sheaf was to be presented before the Lord.

Biermann
"All heaven are waiting to welcome the Saviour."

7. Satan's Defeat. When Satan saw Christ unlock the doors of his prison house and come forth in triumph, bringing with Him "the keys of the grave and of death," he knew that his kingdom was lost. He knew that he was a conquered foe. He knew that he would never again be admitted to the councils of heaven. He knew that he could have no further influence with the angels. He knew that finally he must die. With baffled rage he set himself to do everything in his power to discourage and defeat and destroy Christ's representatives on earth, the people who would dare to be loyal to God's law and endeavor to spread throughout the world a knowledge of God's great plan. From that time to the present "your adversary the devil, as a roaring lion, walketh about, seeking whom he may devour."

8. Jesus Going Home. After the resurrection of Jesus, He remained on this earth for forty days, that His disciples might fully understand that He was a risen Saviour. Then, ten days before the Pentecost, He with His disciples made His way leisurely toward the Mount of Olives, at the base of which was Gethsemane. Jesus led the way across the summit of the mount till they were near Bethany. Here they paused. This was to be the last time He would talk with them as He had so often done before. How happy they were to have Him alive and with them! How eagerly they listened to every word He spoke! But, behold, while He was speaking, He slowly ascended from among them. As He passed upward, "a cloud [of angels] received Him out of their sight." With straining eyes they gazed after Him, anxious to catch the last glimpse of their Lord. As they watched the cloud, "there floated down to them the sweetest and most joyous music from the angel choir."

9. The "Welcome Home" Song. All heaven are waiting to welcome the Saviour. Not only the angels but the representatives of unfallen worlds are there — "the heavenly council before which Lucifer had accused God and His Son, the representatives of those sinless realms over which Satan had thought to establish his dominion — all are there to welcome the Redeemer." As Jesus and the angels cry out to those within the city,—

> "Lift up your heads, O ye gates;
> And be ye lift up, ye everlasting doors;
> And the King of glory shall come in!"

the angels within joyfully ask,

> "Who is this King of glory?"

Back comes the answer from those who attend Jesus:

> "The Lord strong and mighty,
> The Lord mighty in battle.
> Lift up your heads, O ye gates;
> Even lift them up, ye everlasting doors;
> And the King of glory shall come in!"

Again the angels within ask,—
> "Who is this King of glory?"

And the answer comes ringing back,—
> "The Lord of hosts;
> He is the King of glory."

And so they sing back and forth until all heaven rings with their joyous music. As the Father receives His Son and accepts the sacrifice He has made, He clasps Him in His arms and proclaims, "Let all the angels of God worship Him."

How to Study: As you read this lesson, keep these thoughts in mind:
 1. The Sabbath is doubly blessed and sanctified and magnified by the death of Jesus. It is not done away by His death, as many claim.
 2. By putting Jesus to death, Satan sounded his own death knell.
 3. By Christ's resurrection Satan's prison house is forever unlocked.
 4. Those who were raised with Him were the antitype of the wave sheaf of the sanctuary service.
 5. Where is the "Welcome Home" song recorded in the Bible?

Memory Work: Memorize the text at the head of the lesson.

REVIEW OF CHAPTER V

Test Questions: The numbers refer to previous lessons.

1. How did Satan try to prevent Jesus from receiving a welcome to this earth?

2. How did he try to destroy Jesus at His birth?

3. How did he try to overcome the youth Jesus? How did Jesus gain the victory?

4. How did Satan try to defeat Jesus after His baptism? How did Jesus conquer the enemy?

5. What led the priests and rulers to reject Jesus? Of what did they accuse Him? Why?

6. Why did the people of Nazareth reject Him? How was He protected from their wrath? By what different acts did Jesus prove that He was the Messiah? What was the source of His power?

7. On what occasion and why was Jesus rejected by the Galileans? What wonderful vision did Jesus ask the Father to show the disciples so that they might be kept from rejecting Him?

8. Why did the Samaritans reject Jesus? On what occasion did the priests begin to lay plans to arrest Him? How was He at this time protected from violence? What circumstance caused the Sadducees to unite with the Pharisees against Jesus? Following what miracle did they vote to put Him to death?

9. What was the purpose of Jesus' triumphal entry into Jerusalem? What parable did Jesus tell the priests, to help them to see their sin of planning to kill Him?

10. When was the Christian church fully organized for gospel service? Besides commemorating Jesus' death, of what are the bread and the wine a pledge on our part? Of what is the ordinance of humility a pledge?

11. Where did Satan meet Jesus for the last struggle? Who was sent to strengthen Him? When was Jesus deserted by His disciples? Who else seemed to forsake Him at the last? What at this time was forever settled in heaven?

12. How is the Sabbath made doubly sacred since the death of Jesus? How did Jesus get the keys of Satan's prison house? What was the antitype of the wave sheaf?

What were the three yearly feasts of the Jews? When was each held? What did each commemorate? On what three occasions did the Father speak directly to His Son?

Familiar Sayings: Who said, to whom, and on what occasion? —

1. "Fear not; for, behold, I bring you good tidings of great joy."
2. "Where is He that is born King of the Jews?"
3. "Herod will seek the young Child to destroy Him."
4. "I have need to be baptized of Thee."
5. "This is My beloved Son, in whom I am well pleased."
6. "Thou shalt not tempt the Lord thy God."
7. "Behold the Lamb of God."
8. "Is not this Joseph's son?"
9. "Never man spake like this Man."
10. "She is come aforehand to anoint My body to the burying."
11. "My house shall be called the house of prayer."
12. "Behold, your house is left unto you desolate."
13. "Not as I will, but as Thou wilt."
14. "Father, forgive them; for they know not what they do."
15. "It is finished."
16. "Have thou nothing to do with that just Man."
17. "Who is this King of glory?"
18. "Command . . . that the sepulcher be made sure until the third day."
19. "I am the resurrection, and the life."
20. "Let all the angels of God worship Him."

Chapter Drill: Find the chapter that tells about

1. The "Welcome Home" song
2. The baptism of Jesus
3. The temptation of Jesus
4. The transfiguration

What is recorded in each of these chapters? — Matthew 26, Matthew 24, John 13, John 17.

Memory Verse Review: Mal. 3: 10; Mark 1: 10, 11; Isa. 41: 10; Rev. 12: 10; 1 Cor. 11: 26; Rev. 1: 18.

OUTLINE OF CHAPTER VI

Topics —
    The Church of Christ to Be God's Missionaries
    Born of the Spirit into God's Family
    The First Step Homeward
    The Second and Third Steps Homeward
    "Of the Household of God"
    The Adoption Ceremony
    A Bible Study on Baptism
    Review

CHAPTER VI

Christian Missionaries

1. THE CHURCH OF CHRIST TO BE GOD'S MISSIONARIES

"Go ye into all the world, and preach the gospel to every creature."
Mark 16:15.

1. The Jewish Nation Rejected. When Jesus cried, "It is finished," as He died on the cross, the priests at the temple were offering the evening sacrifice, the Passover lamb. Suddenly the inner veil of the temple, between the holy and the most holy place, was torn from top to bottom by an unseen hand, and the most holy place, which up to this time had never been entered except by the high priest on the day of atonement, was now thrown wide open. It was as if a voice had spoken, saying: "Of no more value are all these sacrifices and offerings for sin. Henceforth Jesus Himself will be 'our Passover.'" The services in the earthly sanctuary were at an end. The services in the heavenly sanctuary were about to begin. The nation whom Jesus had chosen two thousand years before had rejected Him, and now He is compelled to reject them.

2. The Church to Be God's Missionary. Shortly before His ascension, Jesus explained to all the believers the work that He had given His church on earth to do. "Go ye into all the world," He said, "and preach the gospel to every creature." All the inhabitants of earth must know of God's great plan to save them. The Jewish nation, which He had chosen to do this work, had failed. Now the work is taken from them and given to others. Everyone who hears and accepts the gospel is to become a missionary to give the good news to some one else. "Let him that heareth say, Come." The church of Christ is now God's missionary to finish His work in the earth, and gather together those who shall be counted as members of His great family.

References Used: D. A., pp. 756, 818; 1 Cor. 5:7; Rev. 22:17; 6:2; Acts 1:8; 2:1, 4-6, 12, 37-41, 45-47; 8:1, 4; 12:2; 13:46; Heb. 7:25; 9:24; John 14:13; Ex. 40:9-16.

3. The Need of the Holy Spirit. But the church could not accomplish this work without the aid of the Holy Spirit, the Comforter whom Jesus had promised to send in His place. So in His last talk with them on the Mount of Olives, He told them not to depart from Jerusalem until they should receive the gift of the Holy Spirit. "After that the Holy Ghost is come upon you," He

When Jesus cried, "It is finished," the inner veil of the temple was torn from top to bottom by an unseen hand.

said, "ye shall receive power, . . . and ye shall be witnesses unto Me both in Jerusalem, and in all Judea, and in Samaria, and unto the uttermost part of the earth."

4. Christ's Work in Heaven. Having told the disciples to wait for the gift of the Holy Spirit, Jesus left them and was received into heaven. "Christ is not entered into the holy places made with hands, which are the figures of the true; but into heaven itself, now to appear in the presence of God for us." After the royal welcome above was over He began His work as our High Priest in the first apartment of the heavenly sanctuary, where "He ever liveth to make intercession" for us. Before He left this earth He said, "Whatsoever ye shall ask in My name, that will I do." It is His work to receive every sincere, unselfish prayer. Then to the Father, at whose right hand He sits, He presents our requests with the incense of His own righteousness, pleading His own blood for us. And the Father is pledged to answer every request presented by His Son. But if we ask amiss, merely to bestow it upon ourselves, Jesus cannot present such a request to His Father,— He cannot add His righteousness to selfishness.

5. The Heavenly Sanctuary Anointed. When at Sinai the earthly sanctuary was finished, it was anointed with holy anointing oil before the priests began their work in it. So in heaven, before Jesus began His work as High Priest, the heavenly sanctuary, "the most holy," was anointed with the Holy Spirit. "To anoint the most holy" was one of the events prophesied to take place during the seventy weeks. That part of the prophecy was now fulfilled.

6. The Disciples on Earth Anointed. When the heavenly sanctuary was anointed, the Holy Spirit descended upon the disciples on the day of Pentecost here on earth, to prepare them to be co-workers with Christ in heaven. This was why they were told to *wait* for the Holy Spirit. Jesus and His church were to be true yokefellows. As the Holy Spirit had been present in mighty power when Jesus spoke the Father's law at Sinai fifty days after the first Passover, so now fifty days after the last Passover the Holy Spirit was present to prepare the disciples to explain to all the world the eternal sacredness of that law. This event was the antitype of the feast of Pentecost.

"And when the day of Pentecost was fully come, . . . they were all filled with the Holy Ghost, and began to speak with other tongues. . . . And there were dwelling at Jerusalem Jews, devout men, out of every nation under heaven. . . . And . . . every man heard them speak in his own language." When the people heard these plain, unlearned Galileans speak with ease and accuracy every known language, they were astonished, and they said to one another, "What meaneth this?" The disciples knew what it meant. Jesus had told them to preach the gospel "to every creature," and now the Holy Spirit was preparing them to do this work.

Jesus had told the disciples to preach the gospel "to every creature," and now the Holy Spirit was preparing them to do this work.

They could not have learned all these languages in a lifetime. This miraculous gift was proof to all, that God was with the disciples.

The priests and rulers began to feel that, though they had slain Jesus, His work could not be stopped. They gave vent to their rage by circulating the report that the disciples were drunk. But most of the people refused to believe their words. When Peter heard the report, he stood up before the people, and, after explaining the work of the Holy Spirit, he preached Christ to them. It was a powerful sermon, and the people, deeply convicted of sin, inquired of the apostles, "Men and brethren, what shall we do?" Peter answered, "Repent, and be baptized every one of you in the name of Jesus Christ for the remission of sins, and ye shall receive the gift of the Holy Ghost." And the same day about three thousand were added to the church.

7. The Work of the Christian Church. The work of the Christian church was now fairly begun. The disciples gave all "their possessions and goods" to promote the gospel. "With gladness and singleness of heart" they went "from house to house" teaching the people. "And the Lord added to the church daily such as should be saved." The impulsive Peter and the ambitious John, now fully consecrated to God, devoted their entire lives to faithful service. And the Holy Spirit worked through them, making the lame to walk, healing the sick, and winning thousands to Christ. The apostolic church went forth in the power of the Holy Spirit, "conquering, and to conquer."

8. Satan's Opposition. It would be too much to expect that Satan would give up the struggle, even in the face of defeat. No, indeed! He rallied his forces, and more than once these disciples were put in prison and cruelly treated. But they rejoiced for the privilege of suffering for the One who had suffered for them, and they sang praises as heartily while in prison as when preaching to the multitudes. One of Satan's chief agents was a young man whose name was Saul. But when Jesus appeared to him and showed him how blind he was, Saul was converted, and from that time to the end of his life, he traveled from place to place teaching Jesus and telling everyone of God's great plan.

Portraits of Peter and Paul. From a gilded glass cut found in the catacombs of Rome.

9. The Gospel to the Gentiles. It was just about this time, 34 A. D., that Stephen suffered martyrdom at the hands of the Jews. "And at that time there was a great persecution against the church; . . . and they were all scattered abroad. . . . Therefore they . . . went everywhere preaching the word." Everything that Heaven could do had been done for the Jewish nation, and now, as Paul said to them, "It was necessary that the word of God should first have been spoken to you: but seeing ye put it from you, and judge yourselves unworthy of everlasting life, lo, we turn to the gentiles." This event marked the close of the seventy weeks allotted to the Jews.

10. The Last of the Apostles. We are told that every one of the twelve apostles suffered martyrdom, except John. Peter was crucified. But he, who had once denied his Lord, felt so unworthy to suffer death as did his Master, that at his request he was crucified with his head downward. James the brother of John was put to death by the sword. John outlived all the others. The last we hear of him was near the end of the first century, when, banished for the word of God to work in the mines in the lonely isle of Patmos, he gave to the church that wonderful book of prophecy — the Revelation.

How to Study: From this lesson get a clear idea of the end of the sacrificial services in the earthly sanctuary, the beginning of Christ's work in the first apartment of the heavenly sanctuary, and what His work is, also of the transfer of His work on earth from the Jewish nation to the Christian church; the anointing of both the holy place in heaven and the church on earth; the antitype of the feast of Pentecost; and the devotion and success of the first or apostolic church. Why was this church so successful?

Dictionary Work: witnesses. (*Wit* means *to know*. What does *ness* mean?) The ordinary meaning of "witness" is "a person who has seen or known something." But it has a deeper meaning, for it comes from a word that means "martyr." We may witness for Christ by our words or by our godly life, but the highest witness would be to give our lives as a sacrifice for the truth, as did the apostles.

Memory Work: Memorize Jesus' commission to His church, recorded in Matthew 28: 19, 20.

Chapter to Remember: Which is the Pentecost chapter? What book in the Bible is devoted largely to comparing the earthly with the heavenly sanctuary?

2. BORN OF THE SPIRIT INTO GOD'S FAMILY

"Except a man be born of water and of the Spirit, he cannot enter into the kingdom of God." John 3: 5.

1. The Privileges of God's Family. The true church is God's family on earth, those who will finally be the subjects of His kingdom. To them only is given the honor of being workers together with Christ and the angels to tell others about God's great plan to save men. They have the privilege of rescuing from the ruin of sin all who desire to have a home in the kingdom of God. Do we want a part in this great work? Then we ourselves must become children of God's family.

References Used: D. A., p. 669; "Questions and Answers," Vol. 1, p. 181; Luke 1: 19; Rev. 22: 17; Ps. 80: 3; 1 Cor. 2: 10; 2 Cor. 4: 6.

2. **Strangers in the Enemy's Land.** Sometimes a child so grieves and disgraces his father and the family by an evil course of action that the father disowns him. He refuses to recognize him as a member of his household. The child by this act is disinherited; he has no further right to any of the privileges of the family or to any of the father's possessions. His share of the property and his privileges as a member of the family are given to some one else in the family. This was Lucifer's experience. When he disgraced all heaven by his wicked rebellion, he was cast out of the heavenly family, and his position and privileges were given to Gabriel, another angel.

Since "all have sinned" we have all been separated from God. Our sins have hid His face from us. We have all been disowned by our heavenly Father. We have all been disinherited. Without Christ we are strangers in a strange land, "having no hope, and without God in the world." We are aliens, or foreigners, in the land of an enemy.

3. **Returning to the Father's House.** But though without Christ we have no hope, yet in Him there is hope. He is "the way" back to the homeland. He is "the door" of mercy to the Father's house. At the threshold of this open door stands our Father with outstretched arms to welcome back "whosoever will." "The Lord's hand is not shortened, that it cannot save; neither His ear heavy, that it cannot hear." But if like Lucifer we refuse to seek forgiveness for our sins, the position and privileges in God's family that might have been ours will be given to some one else.

4. **Born of the Spirit.** The experience of returning to our Father's house is referred to in the Bible as being "born again"—"born of the Spirit"—born into God's family. "Except a man be born of water and of the Spirit, he cannot enter into the kingdom of God," he can never be adopted into the heavenly family. When, on that memorable night in Jerusalem, the ruler Nicodemus sought Jesus to talk with Him about the miracles He had performed, Jesus saw in his heart a longing for a new experience, and said, "Nicodemus, you must be born again." But Nicodemus could not understand how this could be. Do *we* understand it? If you study the Bible earnestly and prayerfully, the Holy Spirit will "teach you all things." No other teacher can enable you to understand in reality what it is to be born again.

5. The Work of the Holy Spirit. Like the Father and the Son, the Holy Spirit knows all things, "yea, the deep things of God." "The Holy Spirit is the mighty energy of the Godhead, the life and power of God flowing out from Him to all parts of the universe, and thus making living connection between His throne and all creation." The Holy Spirit is the representative of the Father and the Son, "but divested of the personality of humanity, and independent

Jesus said to Nicodemus, "Ye must be born again."

thereof." This explains how God by His Spirit can be everywhere present to help us. The psalmist says:

> "Whither shall I go from Thy Spirit?
> Or whither shall I flee from Thy presence?
> If I ascend up into heaven, Thou art there:
> If I make my bed in the grave, behold, Thou art there.
> If I take the wings of the morning,
> And dwell in the uttermost parts of the sea;
> Even there shall Thy hand lead me,
> And Thy right hand shall hold me."

No matter where we are, the Holy Spirit of God, like a powerful X ray, penetrates everything that would separate us from God's kind watch-care. It is as if to Him all substances were transparent. His vision is stronger than the most powerful telescope, bringing near by that which is far distant. His gentle whispers are more far-reaching than the voice of a friend many miles away conveyed over the telephone wire, or than a message sent by wireless, or radio.

The Spirit of God knows not only all we do and say, but He knows all our thoughts; He knows them "afar off," even before we express them. Just as He brooded over the troubled waters in the beginning when God commanded light to shine out of darkness, so now the Spirit broods over our hearts and lives, gently wooing us away from the troubles and darkness of sin to the light and joy of obedience. He knows just how to help every one in need.

How to Study: After studying the lesson, answer the following questions by reading the texts from the Bible:
1. How many of God's family on earth have sinned? Rom. 3: 23.
2. How does sin affect our connection with God? Eph. 2: 12.
3. How only can we again become connected with God's family? Isa. 59: 1; John 3: 3.
4. What did Christ tell Nicodemus was the only way to be born again? John 3: 5.
5. Where can we find the Holy Spirit? Ps. 139: 7-10.
6. How much does the Spirit of God know about us? Ps. 139: 1-4.

Chapter to Remember: John 3 tells about Nicodemus and the second birth.

3. THE FIRST STEP HOMEWARD

"What must I do to be saved?" Acts 16: 30.

1. Returning to the Father's House. When the prodigal son left his father's house, he wandered about from place to place, vainly looking for pleasure and fame. But at last, disappointed and dissatisfied, he turned his weary steps homeward. When his father saw him, though "he was yet a great way off," it was but a short time till they met. Just so, the wandering away from God is like a long, tangled maze that winds round and round, back and forth, until we seem hopelessly lost. But the journey back to the Father's house is short and direct, provided we enter upon it with our whole hearts. It has but four steps.

References Used: Luke 15: 18, 20; Acts 2: 37; 9: 5, 6; 1 Kings 19: 11, 12; John 14: 16.

2. Examples of Conviction. The first step is *conviction*. On the day of Pentecost, after Peter, standing before the amazed multitude, had preached that powerful sermon on the outpouring of the

Doré

When his father saw him, though "he was yet a great way off," it was but a short time till they met.

Holy Spirit, the multitude "were *pricked* in their heart." They were convicted of sin, and they anxiously said to Peter and the rest of the apostles, "Men and brethren, what shall we do?" When Saul on his way to Damascus saw the bright light from heaven that suddenly shone round about him, and heard a voice say, "It is hard for thee to kick against the pricks," he, trembling and astonished, said, "Lord, what wilt Thou have me to do?" When the keeper of the prison saw the results of the earthquake which had opened the prison doors, behind which Paul and Silas were praying and singing praises to God, he came trembling, and, falling down before Paul and Silas, said, "Sirs, what must I do to be saved?" All these are examples of the *conviction* of sin.

3. The Work of the Holy Spirit. It is the work of the Holy Spirit to convict, or convince, the world of sin. It was the Holy Spirit that brought conviction to the hearts of the multitude, to the heart of Saul the persecutor, and to the heart of the jailer. These occasions were all unusual manifestations of the work of the Holy Spirit, first, on the day of Pentecost, in the "rushing mighty wind" which filled the house, and in the tongues of fire which the multitude had just seen, and which had called forth Peter's Spirit-filled sermon; then, in the firelike light which caused Saul to fall to the earth, resulting in his temporary blindness; and again, in the earthquake which unlocked all the prison doors where Paul and Silas were confined.

4. The "Still Small Voice." But it is not always that the Holy Spirit comes to men in these startling ways. He came to Elijah not in the wind, not in the fire, not in the earthquake; He came to him as He will doubtless come to us, in "a still small voice." This voice whispers to our consciences and tells us that we have done wrong. The Holy Spirit urges us to turn away from wrong. "Cease to do evil; learn to do well," are His words. When He speaks to us we should open the door of our hearts by saying as did the prodigal son, "Father, I have sinned." We should ask as did the jailer, "What must I do to be saved?"

5. Importance of the Spirit. Without the Spirit, we should never have one good impulse nor the least sorrow or regret for our sins. Whenever we sincerely desire to do right, whenever we are truly sorry for wrong that we have done, we may know that the Holy Spirit is near us. It is His "still small voice" speaking to our hearts. If we listen to His voice, He will sympathize with us in our temptations and struggles; He will help us to get away from sin. He will come to us as a Comforter; He will encourage us not to be weary in well-doing. God has promised His presence. In fact, our heavenly Father is more willing to give us the Holy Spirit than our earthly parents are to give us good things. Daily should we pray for the presence of the Holy Spirit, for we are never safe without Him. And never, never should we grieve Him away by refusing to listen and obey. It is only by opening the door of our hearts and letting the Holy Spirit in that we can be born again. In this way only can we have "the fellowship of the mystery" and be "sealed unto the day of redemption."

How to Study: After reading the lesson, answer the following questions, looking up the given Bible texts:
1. How does God convict us of sin? John 16:8, first part, margin.
2. Give three striking examples of the convicting power of the Holy Spirit.
3. How did the Holy Spirit come to Elijah?
4. What does the "still small voice" say to our hearts? Rev. 22:17; Isa. 1:16, last part, 17, first part.
5. How willing is God to send His Spirit to us? Luke 11:13.
6. Why should we never grieve away the Holy Spirit? *Eph. 4:30.
7. When Lucifer finally grieved away the Holy Spirit, who took his place in the presence of God? What will be the result if we refuse the salvation God offers us?

Memory Work: Memorize Ephesians 4:30.

4. THE SECOND AND THIRD STEPS HOMEWARD

"If we confess our sins, He is faithful and just to forgive us our sins, and to cleanse us from all unrighteousness." 1 John 1:9.

1. Contrition, the Second Step. If we listen to the voice of the Holy Spirit, He will lead us the second step toward our Father's house — *contrition*. True contrition is a godly sorrow for our sins, a sorrow that "worketh repentance." There are many who do not understand the true nature of this sorrow. They sorrow because they fear that their wrongdoing will bring punishment. They are sorry for the suffering instead of for the sin.

Esau had this sorrow when he saw that he had lost his birthright inheritance. Balaam, terrified by the angel standing in his pathway with drawn sword, acknowledged his guilt, not because he was sorry for his sin, but for fear he should lose his life. Judas, not because of his sin, but because of the awful judgment that he knew awaited him, was sorry that he had sold his Lord. Pharaoh's

---
Reference Used: "Steps to Christ," pp. 26, 27.

repentance was only that the plagues might be stayed. But in such sorrow there is no genuine repentance.

True sorrow for sin abhors the evil itself even though no punishment should follow. It comes because we have grieved our Saviour. Some sins are never found out, no one knows them but ourselves and God, and these often cause our hearts the bitterest sorrow of all. If like David we long for a pure, clean heart, that we may rightly represent our sinless Saviour, God will not despise our contrition. "The Lord is nigh unto them that are of a broken heart; and saveth such as be of a contrite spirit."

2. The Third Step Homeward. The third step to our Father's house is *confession*. If we are not willing to confess our sins, we are not truly sorry for them,—we have not taken the *second* step toward our Father's house. If we have wronged others, we should go to them, not only to tell them that we are sorry and to ask their forgiveness, but true confession will make restoration. If we have stolen, we will return even more than we took. If we have wronged some one by making false statements about him or in any way injuring him by talking in a critical way, we will do all we can to undo the influence of our unkind, cruel remarks. It is a very difficult matter to gather up the influence of evil speaking; and for this reason we should ask the Lord to set a watch at the door of our lips, that we speak only that which is kind and true and pure. If our sins have been public, our confession should be public. Those sins which we have committed against God alone and which have not wronged anyone but ourselves and God, we should confess to Him alone.

3. Covering Sins. If we have been untruthful or deceitful, attempting to cover our sins or hide them in any way, God says to us, "He that covereth his sins shall not prosper: but whoso confesseth and forsaketh them shall have mercy." When we attempt in any way to shield ourselves under a deceitful cover, we not only forfeit God's mercy, but we lose the confidence of our friends and our own self-respect. No one can respect a person who covers sin with a cloak of righteousness. Such a course is detestable hypocrisy.

4. What Is Hypocrisy? Satan often tries to take us away from God by giving us a wrong idea of what hypocrisy really is. Perhaps after we have started to be a Christian, we make some mistake. Then he whispers to us, or perhaps he speaks to us through some thoughtless boy or girl: "You profess to be a Christian, yet you do wrong. You are a hypocrite." Do not be deceived by the enemy. He is only trying to drag you back to be his bond servant. Tell him that David sinned, but because he *confessed* his sin he was "a man after God's own heart." Tell him that Abraham sinned, but because he *forsook* his sin he was called "the friend of God." Humbly, sincerely *confess* and *forsake* your wrong — never, never please

"If we confess our sins, He is faithful and just to forgive us our sins."

Satan by trying to cover it — and God will help you. Then, in time, even those who once thought you were a hypocrite will trust and respect you. They will see your good works, and they too may be won to God.

5. Forgiveness. When we have sincerely confessed to God all our known sins, we can claim His precious promise, "If we confess our sins, He is faithful and just to forgive us our sins, and to cleanse us from all unrighteousness." True confession carries with it forgiveness not only on God's part, but on our part. If some one has wronged us we are to forgive him. If we do not forgive those who trespass against us, God cannot forgive us when we trespass against Him.

How to Study: After reading the lesson, answer the following questions, looking up the given texts:
1. What kind of contrition, or sorrow, leads to repentance? 2 Cor. 7: 10, first part.
2. How is sorrow for sin often misunderstood? Give example.
3. How does the Lord regard the broken, contrite heart? Ps. 34: 18.
4. What will be the result if we try to cover sin? If we confess our sins? *Prov. 28: 13.
5. What will be the result of letting our light shine by honest confession? Matt. 5: 16.
6. When we pray, how fully can we ever ask God to forgive us? Matt. 6: 12.

Dictionary Work: Contrite, contrition.

Memory Work: Memorize Proverbs 28: 13.

Chapter to Remember: Matthew 6 records the Lord's Prayer. Of what famous sermon is this a part?

---

5. "OF THE HOUSEHOLD OF GOD"

"There is joy in the presence of the angels of God over one sinner that repenteth." Luke 15: 10.

1. Conversion. The fourth step toward our Father's house is *conversion*. Conversion means a turning squarely about and walking in the opposite direction. "Let him that stole steal no more." "Let no corrupt communication proceed out of your mouth." "Obey . . . not with eyeservice, as men pleasers; but . . . as to the Lord." This is God's instruction to us. If we are truly converted we do not *want* to do wrong. Even that which we once found pleasure in doing, we now turn away from. God's word will grow more and more precious to us as we become better acquainted with it, and our greatest pleasure will be found in helping others to know the joy that we have learned.

2. Evidence of Conversion. Like the wind, which we cannot see, but whose works are plainly visible, so the presence of the Holy Spirit in our hearts will be known by the way we talk, by

---

References Used: Col. 3: 22, 23; John 3: 8; Matt. 5: 16; Ps. 51: 5; 1 Peter 1: 23; 1 John 3: 1-3; Micah 7: 19; 2 Tim. 3: 12; Phil. 4: 7.

the way we dress, by what we read, by where we go, by the way we treat our associates, by our actions at home, at school, at church, on the street; in fact, by all we do and say, by what we think about, and even by the feelings in our heart. If we are truly converted, our whole life will be changed, for our heart has been re-created. Then others, seeing our good works, will glorify our Father who is in heaven.

3. God's Image Restored. When a child is born into a family, he resembles his parents, both in features and in disposition. At creation, when man was made in the image of God, he was like his Creator Father both in outward appearance and in character. When he became a servant of Satan, he lost the divine nature and became a partaker of Satan's nature. David said, "I was shapen in iniquity; and in sin did my mother conceive me." We have been born of corruptible seed, the seed of sin. We have inherited tendencies to evil. That is why we find it so hard always to do exactly right.

But when we are converted, we are "born again, not of corruptible seed, but of incorruptible, by the word of God." Because of the love which the Father has bestowed upon us, we are "called the sons of God." Then we shall be like Him, for "as far as the east is from the west, so far hath He removed our transgressions from us." He has cast our sins "into the depths of the sea." Once more we become "partakers of the divine nature," and if we are faithful, the image of God will at last be fully restored.

4. The Christian's Joy. "All that will live godly in Christ Jesus shall suffer persecution." But as Christians we shall "count it all joy," for we know that the trying of our faith "worketh patience." Though storms rage without, yet in our heart is "the peace of God, which passeth all understanding." The word of God hidden daily in our heart will keep us from yielding to temptation. The Holy Spirit will be in us a power to overcome all the sinful tendencies that we have inherited by birth and those we have ourselves cultivated. We shall be "more than conquerors through Him that loved us."

5. Joy in Heaven. Conviction, contrition, confession, conversion,— these are the steps back to our Father's house. These are the steps that make us "no more strangers and foreigners, but fellow citizens with the saints, and of the household of God." Whenever one sinner repents and is converted, "there is joy in the presence of the angels of God,"—joy because one more star is added to Jesus' crown of victory, one more child is adopted into the royal family, one more step is traveled toward the end of this reign of sin.

How to Study: After reading the lesson, answer the following questions, looking up the given texts:
1. What change will be seen in the life of a person who has experienced conversion? Eph. 4: 28, 29.
2. Whom do children resemble? Whom did Adam and Eve resemble when created? What character do we now inherit?
3. When we become the sons of God, of whose nature shall we be partakers? 2 Peter 1: 4.
4. When we give Jesus our heart, what becomes of the sin? Ps. 103: 12.
5. Why can the Christian "count it all joy" when tempted? James 1: 2, 3; Rom. 8: 37.
6. When we have been converted, to whose household do we belong? Eph. 2: 19.
7. How do the heavenly family feel when one person is won back to God's family?

Memory Work: Memorize Luke 15: 10. This completes the right point of the "crown" on your "Service Flag."

6. THE ADOPTION CEREMONY

"Behold, what manner of love the Father hath bestowed upon us, that we should be called the sons of God." 1 John 3: 1.

1. Steps to Adoption. When we have listened to the voice of the Holy Spirit as it convicts us of sin, when we have felt true contrition of heart, when we have whole-heartedly confessed our sins and turned away from them, we have become truly converted. We have returned to our Father's house. We are now ready for the important ceremony that adopts us into God's family on earth.

2. The Adoption Ceremony. What is this ceremony? When Jesus was about to ascend to heaven, His last words of instruction to His disciples regarding the gathering together of His family on earth were, "Go ye therefore, and teach all nations [margin:

References Used: Acts 2: 37, 38; 8: 38; 16: 33, 34; Matt. 3: 16; Eph. 4: 24; 2 Peter 1: 4; Ps. 51: 10.

make disciples, or Christians, of all nations], baptizing them in [into] the name of the Father, and of the Son, and of the Holy Ghost." Baptism, then, is the adoption ceremony.

3. The Form of Baptism. There is but one true form of Christian baptism. When the Ethiopian was baptized, both he and Philip went down into the water and came up out of the water. Baptism is God's way of giving us an opportunity to show to the

The adoption ceremony. "Baptizing them into the name of the Father, and of the Son, and of the Holy Spirit."

world that we have accepted Jesus, the great Sacrifice for our sins, and that hereafter we intend to be His children instead of servants of Satan. By this act we say that we now leave the ranks of Satan and enlist as soldiers under the bloodstained banner of Prince Emmanuel.

4. Relation of Baptism to the Crucifixion. Conversion and baptism correspond to three great events in the life of Jesus — His crucifixion, His burial, His resurrection. They also represent three corresponding events in our lives — the crucifixion and burial of sin, and the resurrection to a new life of righteousness. It would be a terrible thing to bury a person alive. But it is more terrible to bury a person with Christ by baptism into death before he is really dead to sin. Before we are baptized, we should know that our sins, or as Paul says, our "old man," is crucified with Christ, "that the body of sin might be destroyed." Conviction of sin by the Holy Spirit, contrition, or godly sorrow for sin, and honest, humble confession, which involves sincere repentance, or turning away from sin,—these experiences crucify "the old man" of sin. We are then converted—we have turned squarely about, determined to walk a better life. The sharp, two-edged sword of God's word in the hands of the Holy Spirit is the weapon that crucifies the man of sin.

5. **Baptism the Burial and Resurrection.** When sin is crucified, then, and not till then, are we ready for baptism—the burial of the body of sin. When the *Holy Spirit* has led us through the crucifixion, we are buried with *Christ* "by baptism into death"—not sprinkled with a few drops of water, nor wet with a little water poured on our heads—these could not possibly represent a burial. No; we are buried in the water just as Jesus was buried in the earth—covered out of sight. We are then raised to a new life "by the glory of the *Father*." So the Father, the Son, and the Holy Spirit all have a part to act in adopting us into the royal family.

6. **The Welcome into the Royal Family.** The act of baptism is in itself but a form. But it is a necessary form. "He that believeth and is baptized shall be saved." Baptism corresponds to the adoption papers which would be necessary if your father were to adopt a child into his family. By it we are received into God's adopted family, and become His children. But adoption papers would be worthless unless they were sealed by the proper authority, and baptism is worthless without the royal seal. The Holy Spirit is the seal that makes baptism genuine. He "beareth witness with our spirit, that we are the children of God." When that seal is received into the heart, Jesus is not ashamed to call us brethren, and God the Father announces in heaven, "This is My beloved son, in whom I am well pleased." Then we have the assurance that He loves us just as He loves His Son Jesus.

We have been baptized into the full name of the Deity—the Father, the Son, and the Holy Spirit; and we now bear this royal name. May we never take God's name in vain! Then the heavenly scribe enters our new name in the great family record book above — the book of life. Blessed is he whose name, once entered, is never blotted out of this great family record.

7. The New Life. When we come up out of the water, it is not the old man that comes up. "Ye have put off the old man with his deeds," "anger, wrath, malice, blasphemy, filthy communication out of your mouth." As we rise from the watery grave, we are "freed from sin," that "like as Christ was raised up from the dead by the glory of the Father, even so we also should walk in newness of life." Thus we are "in the likeness of His resurrection."

Having "put off the old man," "ye put on the new man, which after God is created in righteousness and true holiness." Then the image of God is restored —"the image of Him that created him"— and we are "partakers of the divine nature." A new creation has taken place in our hearts,— God has done for us that for which David prayed, "Create in me a clean heart, O God."

8. The Character of the New Man. What is the character of this new man which we have put on? "Put on therefore . . . mercies, kindness, humbleness of mind, meekness, long-suffering; forbearing one another, and forgiving one another, if any man have a quarrel against any: even as Christ forgave you, so also do ye. And above all these things put on charity, which is the bond of perfectness. And let the peace of God rule in your hearts, . . . and be ye thankful. Let the word of Christ dwell in you richly in all wisdom. . . . Children, obey your parents in all things: for this is well pleasing unto the Lord." "For as many of you as have been baptized into Christ have put on Christ."

Then we can pray "Our Father," but when we do this we must practice "our brother." Thus we are prepared to be workers for God, true missionaries for Jesus. The jailer gave evidence of having this experience when he washed the stripes of the disciples whom he had cruelly treated, and when he brought them into his house and set food before them. Those who accepted the words of Peter had this experience, for when they were "pricked in their heart" by the sword of the Spirit, they repented, were baptized, and received the gift of the Holy Spirit.

How to Study: The following arrangement of the lesson thoughts will help you to see the threefold relationship of one who is baptized "into the name of the Father, and of the Son, and of the Holy Ghost." Keep this outline before you as you read the lesson. Read from left to right, also from top to bottom.

Experience of Christ	Crucifixion	Burial	Resurrection
Experience of the Christian	Crucifying the old man	Putting off the old man	Putting on the new man
The work of the Deity	Crucified by the Holy Spirit	Buried with Christ	Raised by the Father
Adoption into God's family	Receive the Holy Spirit	Put on Christ	This is My beloved son
The royal welcome	The Spirit's witness	Jesus calls us brethren	The Father loves us as His Son
The family name	The Holy Spirit	The Son	The Father

Dictionary Study: baptize.

---

7. BIBLE STUDY ON BAPTISM

1. What step follows believing? Mark 16: 16.
2. What experiences show the only true form of Christian baptism?
3. To what threefold experience in the life of Jesus do conversion and baptism correspond? Rom. 6: 3, 4.
4. In our experience what is crucified? Rom. 6: 6.
   By whom is the old man crucified? John 16: 7, 8.
   What weapon does the Spirit use? Eph. 6: 17.
5. What is buried in the water by baptism? Col. 3: 9, last part.
   With whom is the man of sin buried? Rom. 6: 4, first part.
   From what are we then freed? Rom. 6: 7.
6. Who raises us to walk in newness of life? Rom. 6: 4.
   What do we put on as we come up out of the water? Col. 3: 10.
   Who is this "new man" that we put on? Gal. 3: 27.
   What will this new man do? Col. 3: 12-16, 20.
7. To what does baptism correspond in the adoption of a child?
   What is necessary to make adoption papers legal?
   What is the seal that makes baptism genuine?
   When the Holy Spirit seals the adoption in baptism, what announcement does the Father make? Matt. 3: 17.

8. Into what family name are we baptized? Matt. 28:19.
   When are our names written in the book of life?
   On what condition will our names not be blotted out of the book of life? Rev. 3:5.
9. How does the Holy Spirit welcome us into God's family? Rom. 8:16.
   How does Jesus feel toward us? Heb. 2:11, last part.
   How does the Father treat us? John 17:23, last part.
10. Who witnesses the joy of the Deity when a sinner repents? Luke 15:10.

REVIEW OF CHAPTER VI

Test Questions: The numbers refer to preceding lessons.

1. What event indicated that the work in the earthly sanctuary was at an end? How was the heavenly sanctuary prepared for the service of Christ? Of what prophecy was this a fulfillment? What occurred at the same time on earth? Why? When? What is the work of Jesus in heaven? Heb. 7:25. Describe the work of the apostolic church. When was the Jewish nation finally rejected? What was the command given to the Christian church? *Matt. 28:19, 20.

2. How may we have a part in the work of the Christian church? How have we been separated from God's family? How only can we again become connected with it? What person of the Deity wins us back?

3. What does the Holy Spirit first do to win us back to our Father's house? How can we know that He is convicting us? Why is it dangerous for us to refuse to listen to His "still small voice"? *Eph. 4:30.

4. What goes with true confession? What will be the result of trying to cover sin? *Prov. 28:13. How can we meet Satan's accusation of hypocrisy? What has Jesus taught us about forgiveness?

5. How may we know that we are truly converted? How will God's image be restored in us? Recite *Luke 15:10. Why is there joy in heaven when one sinner repents?

6, 7. Show from the Bible that immersion is the only true form of baptism. Explain the outline of the baptismal ceremony, showing how conversion and baptism correspond to Christ's threefold experience, what part each of the three persons of the Deity has to act in our adoption, our threefold welcome, and our threefold family name.

Chapters to Remember: What special subject is found in these chapters?— John 3; Matthew 28; Romans 6; Colossians 3; Acts 2; Matthew 6.

Memory Verse Review: Matthew 28:19, 20; Ephesians 4:30; Proverbs 28:13; Luke 15:10.

INTRODUCTORY OUTLINE OF GOD'S GREAT PLAN AS GIVEN IN "THE REVELATION"

Revelation

I. God's Plan Revealed Through His True Church . 1; 2; 3
    Symbols — The seven churches
    Time   — The Christian era
    Result   — The church an overcomer

II. Satan's Opposition Through the Apostate Church   4; 5; 6; 7
    Symbols — The seven seals
    Time   — The Christian era
    Result   — Satan defeated
              The apostate church destroyed

III. Satan's Opposition Through the Nations of Earth 8; 9; 10; 11
    Symbols — The seven trumpets
    Time   — The Christian era
    Result   — Satan defeated
              The nations of earth destroyed

IV. The Opposition of Three Persecuting Powers in Union of Church and State 12; 13
    Symbols — The great red dragon
                 The leopard beast
                 The two-horned beast
    Time   — The Christian era
    Result   — Satan defeated
              Persecuting powers destroyed

V. God's Last Appeal to Man 14
    Symbols — The first angel's message
                 The second angel's message
                 The third angel's message
    Time   — The last generation
    Result   — A loyal, obedient people
              Separation of the just from the unjust

VI. The Climax of Satan's Destructive Reign . . 15; 16; 17; 18
    Symbols — The seven last plagues
    Time   — "One day," the last year of the reign of sin
    Result   — Destruction of the whole earth
              Satan cast into the lake of fire

VII. The Triumph of God's Plan 19; 20; 21; 22
    Subject — A new heaven and a new earth
                 God's great family "home coming"
    Time   — A thousand years; then eternity
    Result   — No more death, neither sorrow nor crying, nor pain, nor tears, for "The Lord God omnipotent reigneth"

Fifth Period — Complete Chapter VII, Chapters VIII and IX

OUTLINE OF CHAPTER VII

Symbols — The Seven Churches
Time — The Christian Era
Result — The Church an Overcomer

Topics —	Revelation
A Sabbath Day in Exile	1
The Message to the Church of Ephesus	⎫
The Message to the Church of Smyrna	⎬ 2
The Message to the Church of Pergamos	⎪
The Message to the Church of Thyatira	⎭
The Message to the Church of Sardis	⎫
The Message to the Church of Philadelphia	⎬ 3
The Message to the Church of Laodicea	⎭
Review	

CHAPTER VII

God's Plan Revealed Through His True Church

1. A SABBATH DAY IN EXILE

Revelation 1

"I was in the Spirit on the Lord's day." Rev. 1:10.

1. The Beloved Disciple. During the ministry of Jesus on this earth, John was His "beloved disciple." He was one of His closest companions. He was one whom Jesus took with Him on special occasions. He was taken into the chamber where Jesus raised to life the little daughter of Jairus. He was one of those chosen to be with Jesus at His transfiguration. He was with the Saviour in Gethsemane. With anxious sympathy he kept close to Jesus all through His trial. And at the cross it was John to whom Jesus intrusted the care of His mother. John's love for the Master is shown again when, having learned that Jesus was risen, he outran even Peter, in his anxiety to reach the sepulcher.

By nature John was not more attractive than the other disciples. In fact, he was not only proud, and ambitious for honor, but he was bad-tempered. He and his brother James were called "sons of thunder." But beneath all his evil traits of character, Jesus saw a sincere, loving heart and a keen appreciation of every kindness shown him. He was the "apostle of love" not because he was of a mild, yielding disposition naturally, but because by close association with Jesus he had grown more and more into the likeness of Him whom he loved so truly.

2. How John Worked for God. After the ascension, John became one of God's faithful missionaries. Through false apostles, whom Paul likened to grievous wolves, Satan worked to bring evil doctrines into the church. "The mystery of iniquity doth already work," Paul wrote. These things often caused bitterness and trouble. John met these troubles with courage yet with love. The

---

References Used: A. A., pp. 540, 570; 2 Thess. 2:7; 1 John 1:1, 3; 4:1, 7, 8, 11; Matt. 12:8.

letters he wrote to the churches seemed written "with a pen dipped in love." "Beloved," he wrote, "believe not every spirit, but try the spirits whether they are of God: because many false prophets are gone out into the world. . . . Beloved, let us love one another: for love is of God; and everyone that loveth is born of God, and knoweth God. He that loveth not knoweth not God; for God is love. . . . Beloved, if God so loved us, we ought also to love one another."

In trying to help those who brought differences and troubles into the church, John did not enter into controversy. From his intimate association with Jesus, he told what he had seen and heard. "That which was from the beginning, which we have heard, which we have seen with our eyes, which we have looked upon, and our hands have handled, of the Word of life . . . declare we unto you." Because of his loyalty to the cause of Christ, the rulers of the Jews hated John. They felt that so long as he kept preaching about that which he had seen and heard of Christ, their efforts to destroy the work of Christ would amount to nothing.

3. Tried for His Faith. At last, through the influence of the Jews, John was taken to Rome to be tried for his faith. The Roman emperor bitterly hated the Christians, and he determined to put an end to John's preaching. So, we are told, he caused him to be put into a great caldron, or kettle, of boiling oil. But the Lord preserved him from harm as He preserved the three Hebrews in the fiery furnace, and the very men who cast him in were compelled to take him out.

4. Banished to Patmos (1: 9).* After this, John was again condemned "for the word of God, and for the testimony of Jesus Christ." This time he was banished to Patmos, a small island about eight miles long and one mile wide, located in the Ægean Sea. John was now an old man, probably nearly one hundred, and his enemies thought that on this lonely, barren isle, he would never again be able to preach Christ, and that soon he must die. But as we have so often seen in the past, the very means that Satan used to defeat God's plan became a power to promote it.

5. John's Vision; Its Importance (1:3). On Patmos, John saw in vision the most complete and vivid view of God's great plan

---

* Note: From now to the end of the book the figures in parentheses after paragraph titles refer to chapter and verse in Revelation.

that has ever been revealed to man. It is a revelation of the gospel for the Christian church to give to the world. One writer has called these visions "a panorama of the glory of Christ." When they were shown to John, he was commanded to write them in a book. This book is called "The Revelation." So interesting and so important is the instruction it contains, and so shortly were the things written to come to pass, that a special blessing is pronounced on those who study its wonderful words. "Blessed is he that

"What thou seest, write in a book, and send it unto the seven churches."

readeth," said the angel, "and they that hear the words of this prophecy, and keep those things which are written therein: for the time is at hand."

6. On the Lord's Day (1:10). It was on "the Lord's day" that God gave John his first vision. This was the Sabbath, for Jesus Himself said, "The Son of man is Lord even of the Sabbath day." Tradition tells us that about halfway up the mountain in the southern part of Patmos is a rocky cave or grotto in which John had this vision. Whether or not this be true, John had doubtless sought out some quiet, sheltered spot where, undisturbed, he could spend the day alone with God. Though his surroundings were desolate, yet with the Holy Spirit as his comforter, the great sea spread out before him would remind him of the One who holds its waters in the hollow of His hand, the rugged rocks about him would speak to his heart of the Rock of Ages, while the blue heavens bending over him would direct his mind to the beautiful home of the angelic host — the home where we hope some day to live. Do you think he was lonely? Ah, no! Never before had he spent such a glorious Sabbath. Satan could banish him from the presence of earthly friends, but he could not banish him from the presence of heavenly friends.

7. The Great Voice (1:10, 11). As John was meditating on his favorite theme, the love of God, suddenly he heard behind him "a great voice, as of a trumpet." The voice said, "I am Alpha and Omega, the first and the last: and, What thou seest, write in a book, and send it unto the seven churches which are in Asia; unto Ephesus, and unto Smyrna, and unto Pergamos, and unto Thyatira, and unto Sardis, and unto Philadelphia, and unto Laodicea."

8. The Vision of Jesus (1:12-16). John turned to see who spoke. What a scene met his eye! No longer was the hillside barren and desolate. There before his astonished gaze stood Jesus, not as He had looked in Gethsemane, not as John had seen Him in the hands of the Roman soldiers, wearing an old purple robe and a crown of thorns, not as he had seen Him on the cross of Calvary, not even as he had seen Him after His resurrection. No! "His head and His hairs were white like wool, as white as snow; and His eyes were as a flame of fire; and His feet like unto fine brass, as if they burned in a furnace; and His voice as the sound of many waters. . . . And His countenance was as the sun shineth in his strength." The long, flowing garment which reached to His feet was held in place with a golden girdle. "And He had in His right hand seven stars: and out of His mouth went a sharp two-edged sword." About Him were seven golden candlesticks, and Jesus was walking among them — the very same Jesus whom John so dearly loved.

9. Effect on John (1:17, 18). When Jesus appeared to Daniel after he had spent three weeks in prayer, the glory of the divine presence caused him to fall to the ground. So John, being unable to bear the glorious sight, fell at His feet as dead. Then Jesus laid His strong right hand tenderly upon him, saying, "Fear not; . . . I am He that liveth, and was dead; and, behold, I am alive forevermore, . . . and have the keys of the grave and of death." What a message of comfort to this aged disciple who would himself soon be laid to rest in the lowly grave! He had seen Jesus unlock the grave even while here on earth. Now he is assured that He holds the master key to the grave of every sleeping saint.

10. The Stars and the Candlesticks (1:20). "The seven stars which thou sawest in My right hand," Jesus explained, "are the angels of the seven churches: and the seven candlesticks . . . are the seven churches."

How to Study: The references with the topics refer to the text in Revelation. Read these from the Bible as you study. In this lesson be able to describe John's character, his work for God, why he was banished. Give a clear description of Jesus as He appeared to John. Remember the interpretation of the stars and the candlesticks. Be able to recite the names of the seven churches in their order.

What verses of Revelation 1 give the description of Christ?

Map Work: Locate Rome, the isle of Patmos, the Ægean Sea, the seven churches. See map, page 69; also map in your workbook, page 33.

Dictionary Work: Alpha; Omega.

Chapter to Remember: Revelation 1 — John on Patmos one Sabbath day.

For Class Discussion: What five books of the Bible were written by the apostle John?

---

2. THE MESSAGE TO THE CHURCH OF EPHESUS

Period of the Early Apostles — First Century A. D. — Rev. 2: 1-7

"To him that overcometh will I give to eat of the tree of life, which is in the midst of the paradise of God." Rev. 2:7.

1. Why Jesus Sent Messages to the Church (1:1). When Jesus went back to heaven, He did not forget His struggling people whom He had left on this earth. He knew they would have a long, hard battle with Satan and his forces, before the work of salvation would be finished and God's family be fully gathered out of the wreckage. He wants "His servants" to understand the "things which must shortly come to pass," so that they will not become discouraged and think that He is never going to fulfill the promise He made just before He left them,—that beautiful promise: "I

References Used: John 14:2, 3; 16:12, 13.

go to prepare a place for you. And . . . I will come again, and receive you unto Myself; that where I am, there ye may be also." When Jesus was here with His disciples He wanted to tell them many more things than He did, "but," He said, "ye cannot bear them now. Howbeit," He added, "when He, the Spirit of truth, is come, He will guide you into all truth. . . . And He will show

you things to come." And now, in these messages to the church, He was about to fulfill His word.

2. How and Why Satan Opposes the Prophecies. Satan did not like to have the future made plain to God's people. He knew that if they understood all his plans to deceive and destroy them, they would be on their guard, and he would be defeated. But he could not prevent Jesus from sending the truth to His church. He knew that so far as his relation to Jesus was concerned, he was already a conquered foe. It was no longer possible for him to trouble Jesus personally, but with hateful determination he resolved to make His followers miserable, and, so far as possible, destroy them. So, while he could not prevent Jesus from giving the Revelation to John, he could do this: he could make people think that it could not be understood. If he could only keep people from studying this great book of truth, he would be just as successful as if he had prevented Jesus from giving it to us.

3. How We May Defeat Satan (1:3). Jesus knew Satan's scheme, and that is why at the very beginning He told John to write, "Blessed is he that readeth, and they that hear the words of this prophecy, and keep those things which are written therein." It is Satan's business to deprive God's children of as many blessings as he possibly can, but may he not thus rob any of us. As we begin the study of these prophecies, let us defeat him by studying earnestly every lesson. If we do this, and if we "hear the words" and "keep" them — that is, if we obey — we shall surely have the promised blessing.

4. Divisions of "the Revelation." The events told in "the Revelation" reach from the time of Jesus' first coming until His throne shall be established on the earth made new. (See diagram No. 1.) Not only are some of the prophecies of this book in seven parts, such as the seven churches, the seven seals, the seven trumpets, and the seven last plagues, but the entire book may be divided into seven sections, or, we may say, seven visions. The first four of these visions cover in general the full time, each one giving a different view of the "things which must shortly come to pass." It is as if God would show us this great pillar of truth "foursquare." First He shows us one side. This side He calls "The Seven Churches." Then He turns the pillar around, and shows us the next side. This He calls "The Seven Seals." Then He turns the pillar again and shows us the third side, which He calls "The Seven Trumpets." When He turns the fourth side of the pillar to our view He shows us three strange-looking beasts. The last three of the seven visions refer to events which take place during "the time of the end."

5. First Prophecy in Revelation. The first prophecy in "the Revelation," called the seven churches, tells the story of God's great plan as He is working it out in His true church on earth. During this time the church passes through seven distinct periods of experience. To each period a special name is given, a name that corresponds with the nature of the special experience through which the church is passing at that time. But, while seven names are given to the church, it is one church — the church of God. This church has its trials; it makes its mistakes; but in every case it is at last victorious, and at the end receives the reward of the overcomer.

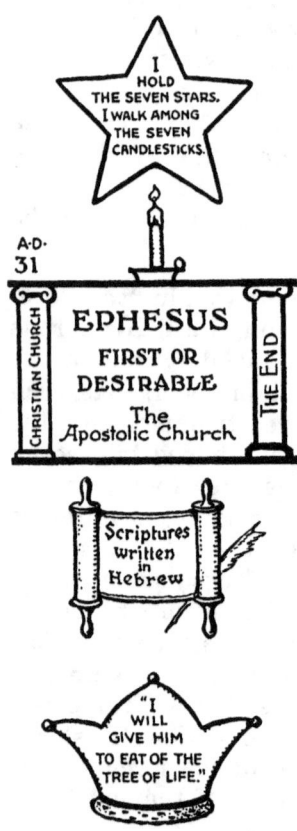

6. Message to the Church of Ephesus (2:2, 3). The first message was sent to the church of Ephesus. "I know thy works, and thy labor, and thy patience, and how thou canst not bear them which are evil: and thou hast tried them which say they are apostles, and are not, and hast found them liars: and hast borne, and hast patience, and for My name's sake hast labored, and hast not fainted."

The word "Ephesus" means *first*, or *desirable*. And truly the condition of the church during its first period, when the apostles were still living, was "desirable." The Holy Spirit worked with great power through Paul and Peter and Philip and Stephen and James and John and others, and thousands were converted in a day. These noble men were noted for their "works," their "labor," and their "patience." They were faithful to the true principles taught by Christ. They could not bear those who were evil. They tried false apostles and exposed their evil teachings. They fainted not before persecution and trial, but bore all with Christlike patience.

7. The One Sin of Ephesus (2:4, 5). Only one accusation is brought against the church at this time: "Thou hast left thy first love." After the disciples were all gone, the earnestness, the fervor, the devotion which they had shown in their work began to diminish. They had walked and talked with Jesus as a personal friend, while those who lived later were acquainted with Him only through others. But the church is not excused on this ground. Our love for Jesus should be just as real, our zeal for Him just as earnest, as if we could see Him face to face from day to day. "Thou God seest me" should be our motto in our everyday duties. If this be not true, He will at last remove our candlestick, and our light as Christians will go out in darkness.

8. Jesus and His Reward (2:1, 7). To this first church Jesus represented Himself as "He that holdeth the seven stars in His right hand, who walketh in the midst of the seven golden candlesticks." This He had really done when He was here on earth. With His own right hand He had kept and led the apostles, and from day to day He had walked among His people.

The promise to this church is, "To him that overcometh will I give to eat of the tree of life, which is in the midst of the paradise of God." This first church had just been separated from their Lord. Before He left them He told them that He was going to prepare a place for them. And now He repeats the promise. Nothing could so fill the longing of their hearts as the privilege of being with Jesus in the paradise of God, where they could eat of the tree of life and live with Him forever.

9. Time Covered by Ephesus. The Ephesus period of the church is sometimes called the apostolic church, because it existed during the days of the early apostles. It began when Jesus Himself founded the Christian church in 31 A. D. About the end of the first century, when the work of John, the last of the apostles, was ended, the church entered upon the second period of its experience.

How to Study: Find in the Bible the message to the church of Ephesus. Be able to state clearly why Jesus gave the Revelation, and why Satan opposes it. Get a clear idea also of the seven divisions of the Revelation, what period of time the seven churches cover, and how much of that is covered by the Ephesus church. What was the character of the church during the Ephesus period? Why does the reward promised seem specially fitting? On page 335 notice the seven sections into which the book of Revelation is divided.

Memory Work: Recite the reward promised to the overcomer, found in Revelation 2: 7. This is part of the first memory section leading to the memory certificate in your workbook.

For Your Workbook: Begin diagram No. 9, "The Seven Churches," representing on it the church of Ephesus. The blank diagram to be filled out is a page in "Bible Workbook" for the eighth grade. The pictures needed are also in the workbook.

3. THE MESSAGE TO THE CHURCH OF SMYRNA

Pagan Persecution — Beginning About 100 A. D.— Rev. 2: 8-11

"He that overcometh shall not be hurt of the second death." Rev. 2:11.

1. The Christians Persecuted (2:10). The second step in the working out of God's great plan through His true church is revealed in His message to the church of Smyrna. The word "Smyrna" means *myrrh*, or *sweet-smelling perfume*, as the perfume of a plant that becomes more fragrant when crushed, or as the perfume from burning incense. The early disciples who belonged to the Ephesus period suffered persecution; but during the Smyrna period, the second and third centuries A. D., the persecutions were more general, more frequent, and more terrible. The Roman government permitted all religions, so long as the believers worshiped the statues of the Roman emperors. But the Christians refused to do this. Therefore they were accused of being unpatriotic and disloyal to the government, and they were often tried for treason. If, when tried, they refused to worship the Roman statues they were cruelly tortured, and if they persisted in refusing they were put to death.

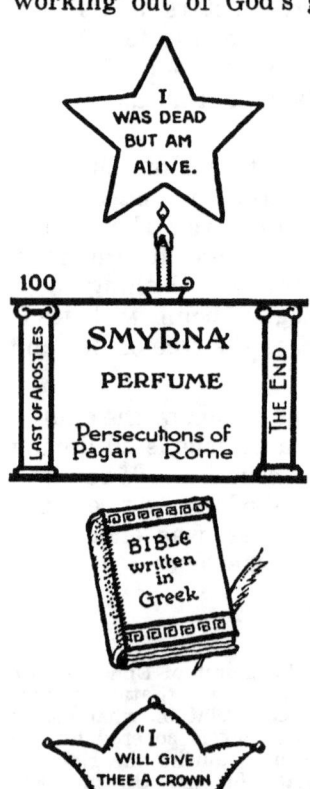

Often when a great calamity occurred, such as a famine, a pestilence, or an earthquake, the Christians were said to be the cause of it. Because of these things some Roman emperors did their best to stamp out the Christian religion out of existence. The Christians were cast into dungeons, thrown to the wild beasts in the amphitheater, burned over a slow fire, and put to death by every other mode of torture that Satan could think of. But they remembered the promise, "Be thou faithful unto death, and I will give thee a crown of life." Jesus had been put to a cruel death, and why should they expect better treatment? Their loyalty to their Master and their willing sacrifice came up before God as a "sweet-smelling perfume."

2. "The Synagogue of Satan" (2:9). Among the members of the Smyrna church was a class of people described as "them which say they are Jews, and are not, but are the synagogue of Satan."

Christians were thrown to the wild beasts in the amphitheater.

These disloyal followers gave up their faith when persecution came to them. Thus the fires of persecution served to purify the church from those who were untrue, and to increase the devotion and loyalty of those who were true. The blood of the martyrs was like seed sown, for their death only led many others to accept Christ. As a result, instead of being stamped out of existence, the church grew stronger and better.

3. "Tribulation Ten Days" (2:10). "Fear none of those things which thou shalt suffer," was the message of the Spirit to this church. "Behold, the devil shall cast some of you into prison, that ye may be tried; and ye shall have tribulation ten days." These ten days represent ten years. The persecution here referred to was the last but most savage and bloody persecution carried on by pagan Rome. It lasted just ten years, from 303 to 313 A. D.

4. Religious Liberty Proclaimed. When Satan saw that the more he persecuted the church, the stronger and purer it became and the more rapidly it increased in numbers, he became rather discouraged, and for a time ceased his cruel efforts. In 313 an edict, called the Edict of Milan, was issued by Constantine the Great, emperor of Western Rome, proclaiming religious liberty to the whole world. This ended the long period of pagan persecution. But do not think for a moment that Satan had given up. Oh no! He was simply laying another plan, which he carried out in the next period of the church, and which he hoped would be more successful.

5. Jesus and the Reward (2: 8, 9, 11). The Holy Spirit represented Jesus to this church as He "which was dead, and is alive." Jesus always comes to us in just the way we most need Him. To these faithful Christians who were suffering the martyr's death, He said, "I also suffered the martyr's death, yet now I am alive forevermore, and have the keys of the grave and of death." This was an assurance to them that they too should live again. Jesus understood all about their trials. "I know thy works," He said, "and tribulation, and poverty, (but thou art rich)." Jesus always knows and cares. The world may look upon us as in poverty, but He knows that the true Christian is rich, for he is an heir of heaven. To the Smyrna church He says, "He that overcometh shall not be hurt of the second death." Though they suffered the first death, the second death, from which there is no resurrection, shall not touch them.

How to Study: Find in the Bible the message to the Smyrna church. What text shows that a day in prophecy represents a year?

After studying the lesson carefully, review it a topic at a time and on each topic write one or two questions that can be answered by what is told under the topic. Write at least five questions in all. Bring them to class and see if your classmates can answer them. Be sure that you know the answers yourself, so that you can correct a wrong answer.

Compare the Smyrna and Ephesus churches on the following points:
 1. Meaning of the name
 2. Experience of the church
 3. Period of time covered
 4. How Christ represents Himself
 5. The reward to the overcomer

Memory Work: Memorize the promise to the overcomer as found in Revelation 2: 11. Remember also the date of the ten days' persecution, and of the edict proclaiming religious liberty to the world.

For Your Workbook: Add the Smyrna church to your diagram of the seven churches.

---

4. THE MESSAGE TO THE CHURCH OF PERGAMOS

The Great Apostasy in Constantine's Time — Beginning 313 A. D.

Lesson 1: Topics 1-7; Rev. 2: 12, 13
Lesson 2: Topics 8-13; Rev. 2: 14-17

"To him that overcometh will I give to eat of the hidden manna, and will give him a white stone, and in the stone a new name written, which no man knoweth saving he that receiveth it." Rev. 2:17.

1. Satan's Plot for the Pergamos Church (2: 12, 14). The third step in the working out of God's great plan through His true church is described in His message to the church of Pergamos. The word "Pergamos" means *height,* or *exaltation.* During the Smyrna period, Satan had shown himself in his real character as a bitter enemy of the followers of Jesus, and through the most cruel persecution, he had tried to destroy them. In this he had failed. Many, seeing the Christlike spirit of the martyrs, left his ranks and joined the forces of Jesus. Satan saw that this would not do, so he next decided to favor the church, to pretend to be its friend, and by gifts and rewards lead the people unconsciously back to himself. Just as Balaam for the sake of money taught Balak to cast a stumblingblock before the children of Israel, so Satan determined to bring into the church worldly prosperity, popularity, and a spirit of pride that would be a stumblingblock to them. He hoped that God would then be displeased with them and reject them.

2. How the Church Became "Exalted." In the year 313, as we have learned, Constantine the Great, emperor of Western Rome, proclaimed throughout the empire the privilege to adopt any religion, while he professed to be a convert to Christianity, though from his life it is evident that he was not truly converted. He doubtless accepted Christianity merely for the sake of gaining

---

References Used: P. P., p. 441; B. R., new ed., pp. 15, 16, 282; S. B., pp. 490, 491, 535, 536; D. R. on Rev. 2:17; Hist. of Sab., fourth ed., pp. 389-391; Heb. 4:12.

the influence and support of the Christians. He was just the one for Satan to use to accomplish his purpose. Constantine began at once to enrich the church with large donations of money from the imperial treasury. With this money beautiful churches were built and high salaries were paid to the clergy. These and other favors brought into the church a spirit of "exaltation" which placed it in far greater danger than when it was followed with prison, fire, and sword. Of course, as soon as the emperor placed himself on the side of the Christians, Christianity became fashionable, and many joined the church who were not Christians at heart. After a while Christianity became a part of the law of the empire, and the names of thousands of unconverted pagans were added to the church. Some writers have called this period the "death blow to paganism," but in reality paganism under a cloak of Christianity walked into the church and took possession. The result was that the church reached a great "height" in numbers as well as in popularity.

3. God's True Church (2:13). There is nothing so dear to the heart of Jesus as His true church on earth. They are as "the apple of His eye." As He looked down upon them at this time, He saw among the large numbers who merely professed to be His, a few who were true. To these He said, "I know thy works." Jesus always notices and appreciates what we do for Him. Then He added, "I know . . . where thou dwellest, even where Satan's seat is." This was as if He had said, "I know you are in a hard place, right where Satan has placed his seat, or throne." But, He added with deep satisfaction, in spite of all this, "thou holdest fast My name, and hast not denied My faith, even in those days wherein Antipas was My faithful martyr, who was slain among you."

4. **"Satan's Seat" (2:13).** Where did Satan place his seat, or throne? You remember how under the "head of gold" he built up his throne in Babylon, the capital of the Babylonian Empire; but that was destroyed long ago. Now under the "legs of iron" he tries again, and this time he chooses as his seat the capital of the Roman Empire, which was the city of Rome. His throne in Babylon was destroyed in 538 B. C.; his throne in Rome was established in 538 A. D. The next paragraph explains how he came to establish his seat in Rome.

5. **How There Came to Be a Pope.** Not long after the days of the apostles the Christian churches in different places bound themselves together in order to be an encouragement and help to one another. They called themselves the Catholic Church. The word "catholic" means *universal*, or the *whole*, and at that time it merely meant that in this organization *all* the churches were included.

Constantine and his wife Fausta

Gradually certain leaders that were over these churches were recognized as greater than others, and finally the one that was over the church at the city of Rome came to be regarded as being the greatest of all and having the most authority. Gradually he, instead of Jesus, was looked to as the head of all the churches, the one to say what others should do. This leader was then called the *pope*, a word that means *father*. This was the beginning of the papacy.

6. **Creeds and Heretics.** As these churches drifted away from Jesus, their true Leader, they drifted away from the Bible, the true guidebook. Instead of making God's word their guide, they wrote out creeds, which named the points of religion in which they believed. Then these creeds were voted upon and adopted by the councils. Those who had different ideas from what were expressed in the creeds, even though their ideas might be in harmony with the Bible, were called *heretics*. At last the pope became so "ex-

alted" that he began to think that, as he was the great leader, everyone else ought to think just as he thought about religious matters. This you will recognize as "that man of sin" who *"exalteth* himself,"—the "mystery of iniquity," that Paul mentioned. This was the "little horn" that Daniel saw, having "eyes like the eyes of man, and a mouth speaking great things."

7. "Antipas . . . My Faithful Martyr" (2:13). But God's faithful ones knew that Jesus and not the pope was the real Head of the church. They knew that God's word was the only true creed, and they believed that every man should be free to obey God according to his own conscience. These opposed the authority of the pope, and they were the ones who in the prophecy are called "Anti-pas," a word which means *opposed to the pope*. But as this so-called Christianity had been made a law of the land, if these people would not willingly obey, they must be forced to do so. It was about this time that the Roman Empire was broken up and divided into ten parts. Three of these divisions so strongly opposed the pope that their power was destroyed by Roman armies, and many of the people who refused to submit were martyred. These three divisions were the three horns, or kingdoms, that the little horn "plucked up" in order to establish himself.

8. How Satan Changed the Second Commandment. As we already know, it was and still is Satan's one great purpose to overthrow God's law and set up a government of his own, and he himself be God. We shall now see how He tried to do this. The pagans who had joined the church did not want to give up the worship of their idols. So Constantine tried to please them by placing "Christian" pictures and images before them. They had been accustomed to do penance to appease the anger of their gods, so now they were taught to make pilgrimages to Palestine and to the tombs of the martyrs, or do other things that would give pain to their bodies or humble their pride. Relics were brought from places where Jesus had lived. These were said to be sacred, to possess healing properties, and were sold at enormous prices. All this was a violation of the second commandment of God's law.

9. How Satan Changed the Fourth Commandment. The chief god of the pagans was the sun god. Baal was a name given the sun god in the Old Testament. In the New Testament he was called Beelzebub, the prince of the devils. At Rome and other parts of the Roman Empire this god was represented by a snake under a name which means "the serpent that taught mankind,"— the one that taught them "the knowledge of good and evil." This was the great god, supreme over all the other gods, the source of light and heat and joy and all good things. It was hard for the pagans to give up this worship, though it was purely the worship of Satan, the prince of the devils, and with it were connected some of the most debasing practices.

But Constantine wanted the good will and influence of his pagan subjects, so he made a law for the church, recognizing Sunday, "the venerable day of the sun," as a day free from care and work, and to be given to pleasure. This law was passed in the year 321, and is called an edict of Constantine. No one claimed or thought that it had to do with the fourth commandment of *God's* law. It was simply an edict of a heathen emperor. For hundreds of years true Christians had kept the seventh day of the week as the Sabbath of God's law.

But Satan hates God's law as he hates nothing else, because he knows that it is the foundation of God's throne, the very basis of His government. He particularly hates the fourth commandment, because it is this that teaches all mankind that the God above is the great Creator of all things. He, and not the sun, is the one supreme God. The Sabbath was given to commemorate creation and to honor the Creator. It reads, "Remember the Sabbath day, to keep it holy." Why? "For in six days the Lord made heaven and earth, the sea, and all that in them is." Only on the seventh day can creation, the birthday of the world, be commemorated, just as your birthday can be commemorated only on the day on which *you* were born. So long as men worship God as the Creator, Satan will fail to accomplish his purpose to have them worship him.

But, though at first Sunday was only a heathen holiday, after a while it was recognized by the church as a holy day,—a day for worship, and *Christian* worship at that. Still, although the people met for worship in the morning, in the afternoon they went about their usual duties. One law after another was made in an effort to establish the sacredness of this "venerable day of the sun." Gradually Sunday came to be observed quite generally as "the

Lord's day," and the true Sabbath was spoken of in contempt as "Jewish." Laws were made requiring that all labor be laid aside on this day, and punishments were inflicted on those who disobeyed. At last, "the Christian Sabbath," as Sunday began to be called, actually took the place of the true Sabbath of the Lord. This, then, was the way the little horn that Daniel saw in his first vision should "think to change the times and the law" of the Most High. Little by little, Satan had succeeded in turning the minds of the people away from the word of God, away from the great fundamental law of God's government, and substituting in its place a law of his own.

10. How Baptism Was Perverted. The perversion of baptism, like that of the Sabbath, in the backsliding church followed the path of expediency rather than the vital principle of being true to God's word. When the unbaptized became too ill to be immersed, water was sprinkled or poured upon them. Doubtless others who joined the church thought that if this form of baptism was sufficient for the sick, it was sufficient for them. Certain it is that in the following period of the church, when the Scriptures were almost unknown among the common people, the practice of baptism by immersion largely disappeared, while sprinkling or pouring was substituted. Many other errors also crept into the church during these times.

11. Why People Were Led Away from the Bible. To us it may seem strange that people could so easily be led away from the plain words of the Bible. But we must remember that in those days they did not have access to the Bible. There were only a few copies in all the world. These were written by hand on parchment or papyrus, and they were too expensive to be owned by the common people. It was more than a thousand years after the time of Constantine before printing from type was invented. And even then it was a long time before the Bible was translated into a language that the people could read.

12. Jesus and the "Two-Edged Sword" (2:12). Jesus saw the hard place in which His followers had to live at this time. He saw that they were deprived of His word, and so He addressed Himself to the Pergamos church as "He which hath the sharp sword with two edges." This sharp "two-edged sword" is the word of God.

And this was just what they needed. But that which was a defense and protection to His true followers was the weapon which He said He would use to fight against those who would not repent. In the next period of the church we shall see how effectively He used this sharp sword.

13. The Overcomer's Reward (2:17). Here, as in all periods of the church, God's eye is upon the overcomers, and to them He says, "To him that overcometh will I give to eat of the hidden manna, and will give him a white stone, and in the stone a new name written, which no man knoweth saving he that receiveth it."

In ancient times there were not the conveniences for traveling that we have to-day, and for this reason strangers were often entertained in private homes. This sometimes resulted in the formation of lasting friendships. Among the Greeks and the Romans there was a beautiful custom of giving the guest as a parting token of the friendship thus formed, a small white stone, cut in half. Upon each half the host and the guest engraved their names, and then interchanged with each other — a sort of "calling card," you see. These stones were handed down from father to son, as a pledge of hospitality and friendship whenever they should be presented to the proper person. To avoid their being used by some one who had no right to the favors they secured, these stones were secretly kept.

So Jesus promises to the overcomers of the Pergamos church His personal friendship. In this life they have been largely deprived of His word, the bread of life, the true manna, but in the future life He will give them "to eat of the hidden manna," the living Word. What a feast to spread before these faithful ones!

Lesson 1, Topics 1-7

How to Study: Be able to explain: (1) "Satan's seat," verse 13; (2) "Antipas, My faithful martyr," verse 13. Be able also to tell the meaning of "Pergamos"; when this period of the church began and closed; how the "height" and "exaltation" came into the church; how there came to be a pope; and why Jesus was pleased with the few who were true.

For Your Workbook: Locate the Pergamos church on your diagram of the seven churches.

Lesson 2, Topics 8-13

How to Study: Explain: (1) "a white stone" and "the hidden manna," verse 17; (2) "the sharp sword with two edges," verse 12. Be able also to tell how the second and fourth commandments of God's law were changed, and why; how baptism was changed; also how the people of that age were so easily deceived.

Dictionary Work: anti-pas; papyrus. What common word has its root in "papyrus"?

Memory Work: Memorize the promise to the overcomer, Revelation 2:17.

---

5. MESSAGE TO THE CHURCH IN THYATIRA

Period of Papal Supremacy — Beginning 538 A. D.

Lesson 1: Topics 1-5; Rev. 2:20
Lesson 2: Topics 6-9; Rev. 2:18-29

"He that overcometh, and keepeth My works unto the end, to him will I give power over the nations." "And I will give him the morning star." Rev. 2:26, 28.

1. The Fourth Period of the Church. The next period through which God's true church was to pass was shown to John under the name of the Thyatira church. This church is the middle one of the seven. It occupies the middle of the Christian era. In history this period is called the Middle Ages. It is also known as the Dark Ages, because during this time the light of God's word was almost extinguished. This experience of the church began when, in 538 A. D., the papacy became supreme. It extended to 1517, when the Reformation arrested the progress of the papacy. This period of nearly a thousand years has been called the noon of the papacy, but the midnight of the world.

2. Satan's Plan. During the Pergamos period, Satan had succeeded in drawing into the church all classes of pagans, from the nobility to the slaves. He had succeeded in bringing all the churches together under one head, and this head he himself controlled and directed. He had established the seat of his government at Rome— "Satan's seat." He now determined to banish God's word from the face of the earth, for this Book he well knew would show men his deceptions and lead them to rebel against him. He determined that God should have nothing to do with this earth, and if any of His followers should dare to oppose his scheme, he would unhesitatingly put them to death. When this should be accomplished, his govern-

---

References Used: G. C., pp. 51-53, 55, 57, 65, 72, 577; 2 Thess. 2:3, 4; Dan. 8:12; Matt. 24:21, 22.

ment would be fully established, and he would be absolute ruler of this earth. What a clear photograph this is of "that man of sin . . . who opposeth and exalteth himself above all that is called God"! Will Satan's plan succeed? Will "that man of sin" be absolute monarch?

3. The Bible Disregarded and Forbidden. When this period of the church was shown to Daniel, he saw the papacy (the little horn) "cast down the truth to the ground." This work began during the Pergamos period, when the papacy was getting a start. During the Thyatira period, the worship of images became more general. Satan did not dare openly to reject Christ and God's law, so the images were "Christian" images of Jesus, Mary, and the saints! Candles were burned before them, and prayers were offered to them. Sunday, "the day of the sun," was not at first set up in opposition to the Lord's Sabbath, but at Satan's cunning suggestion it came to be celebrated in *honor* of the resurrection of Christ! As if Jesus by His resurrection could destroy the law which He died to restore! Surely this was but satanic mockery, as great an insult to Christ as when pagan Rome, urged on by this same Satan, dressed Jesus in a purple robe, placed a crown of thorns on His head, and cried out, "Hail, king of the Jews!"

The people were taught that the pope was the vicegerent of God on earth and that God had put him here to save them. They were taught to confess their sins to him, and to trust him, instead of Christ, for forgiveness. They were also taught that the pope had power to punish those who disobeyed; and combined with this was the doctrine of eternal torment. For hundreds of years no one was allowed to circulate the Bible. The people were forbidden to read it or to have it in their houses, so of course they did not know how wrong all this was. How do you think the loyal, trusting angels of heaven felt when they saw the one who once was the leader of their choir engaged in this blasphemous work? How do you think the unfallen worlds felt?

4. "That Woman Jezebel" (2:20). In His message to the Thyatira church, Jesus likens all this departure from God's truth to "that woman Jezebel." Jezebel was the daughter of Ethbaal, the sun-worshiping king of Sidon. Contrary to God's law, King Ahab married this licentious sun-worshiper. She killed the prophets of

"God's holy word was prized when 'twas unsafe to read it."

the Lord, led her husband into idolatry, and fed the prophets of Baal at her own table. Under her influence Israel was utterly separated from God. Her name is used here because the deeds of this wicked woman fitly represent the deeds of the papal church. Any church that departs from the teachings of the Bible and unites with the ungodly world, is said to have committed fornication.

5. The Church Persecuted. During this long dark period, the papacy not only "cast down the truth to the ground," but it wore out the saints of the Most High. In the great prophecy that Jesus gave His disciples just before He left them, He told them about this very time. He said it would be a time of "great tribulation, such as was not since the beginning of the world to this time, no, nor ever shall be." And this was all true. During the Smyrna period, the church of God suffered terrible things from pagan Rome; but no language can ever describe the persecutions of papal Rome. The awful tortures of the Inquisition are too terrible to relate or to read, and historians say that the numbers put to death for standing true to God and opposing the church of Rome will never be fully known. If ever Satan tried to "wear out the saints of the Most High" and utterly destroy them from off the earth, he did at this time through this "mystery of iniquity," the papacy.

"Except those days should be shortened," said Jesus, "there should no flesh be saved: but for the elect's sake those days shall be shortened." And it was the Reformation that at last shortened these days.

6. "The Rest in Thyatira" (2: 24). To the true church at this time Jesus says, There are some—"the rest in Thyatira"—who "have not this doctrine, and which have not known the depths of Satan." While God lives and reigns, Satan can destroy neither God's truth nor His people. There are always some who remain true. And so it was at this time. In the very land where the papacy placed its throne, in the secluded mountains of Italy and France, there lived a people who refused to yield to the pope. These people were called *Waldenses*.

7. "None Other Burden" (2: 21, 24, 25). To those who remained true, Jesus said: "I will put upon you none other burden. But that which ye have already hold fast." To hold fast what they already had was the only burden that the true church could bear during this period. And this the church in Thyatira did. Although in those days Bibles were few, and although the pope had forbidden the people to have them, yet the Waldenses had the Bible in their own language. And they studied it. Through all the Dark Ages they held fast to God's word. They denied that the pope was God on earth, they refused to worship images, and some of them kept the true Sabbath. They understood the plan of salvation, and believed in the second coming of Christ.

And they not only studied the Bible for themselves but they taught it to others. Many accepted their teachings, but only to find a martyr's grave. Through these faithful missionaries God gave Rome "space to repent, . . . and she repented not." The sacrifices which the Waldenses made and the sorrows they endured surely entitle them to be among the true church of Thyatira, a name which means "sacrifice of contrition."

The Waldenses not only studied the Bible themselves, but they taught it to others.

8. Jesus' Care for His Flock (2:18, 19, 25). "The Son of God, who hath His eyes like unto a flame of fire," was able to penetrate the thick darkness. Nothing could hide His persecuted but loyal church from such eyes as His. "I know thy works," He says. Then He adds, "I know thy . . . charity, and service, and faith, and thy patience." And then, to emphasize His genuine sympathy and appreciation, He repeats, I know "thy works; and the last to be more than the first." To His church at this time He is represented as having not only eyes like a flame of fire, but feet like fine brass. These are the feet that walked with His people through the fiery affliction and persecution. As a parting word of encouragement, He says, "Hold fast *till I come.*" These people believed in the second coming of Christ, and this hope gave them comfort, for then they would be delivered from Satan's oppression.

9. **The Reward (2:26-28).** "He that overcometh," said Jesus, "and keepeth My works unto the end, to him will I give power over the nations: and he shall rule them with a rod of iron; as the vessels of a potter shall they be broken to shivers. . . . And I will give him the morning Star." This church had been oppressed by the nations, but Jesus assures them that the time is coming when all this will be changed. Then these very nations will themselves "be broken to shivers," and the church, which has lived through "the midnight of the world," will live with Jesus, "the bright and morning Star."

How to Study: After studying the lesson carefully, explain:
  1. How Satan planned to complete the work he began under the Pergamos church.
  2. What the papal church did to merit the name "that woman Jezebel." Rev. 2:20.
  3. Who "the rest in Thyatira" were. Verse 24.
  4. What was the only "burden" that Jesus placed upon the true church during this period. Verse 24.
  5. Why Jesus addressed Himself to this church as One "who hath His eyes like unto a flame of fire, and His feet . . . like fine brass." Verse 18.
  6. Why the reward promised would be specially prized by Thyatira.
  7. The meaning of "Thyatira," and how it applies to this church.
  8. The beginning of the Thyatira period.

Memory Work: Memorize the promise to the overcomer. Rev. 2:26, 28.

Chapter to Remember: Revelation 2—the messages to the first four churches—Ephesus, Smyrna, Pergamos, and Thyatira.

For Your Workbook: Locate the Thyatira church on your diagram of the seven churches.

6. THE MESSAGE TO THE CHURCH IN SARDIS

The Reformation Period — Beginning 1517

Lesson 1: Topics 1-7; Rev. 3:1-4
Lesson 2: Topics 8-14; Rev. 3:5

"He that overcometh, the same shall be clothed in white raiment; and I will not blot out his name out of the book of life, but I will confess his name before My Father, and before His angels." Rev. 3:5

1. Condition of the Sardis Church (3:1). After the Dark Ages, the church entered upon the next great period of her experience— the Reformation, which began in 1517. In the prophecy this period is called, "the church in Sardis." The word Sardis means *that which remains, prince of joy,* or *song of joy.* At the time when the Reformation began, the truths of the Bible seemed nearly suffocated under the errors and evils of the papacy. The church seemed to be alive only in name. "Thou hast a name that thou livest, and art dead," said Jesus. He addressed Himself to this dying church as "He that hath the seven Spirits of God." He assures them that He still holds "the seven stars." The church has stood the terrible test. To the angels and the unfallen worlds, Satan has demonstrated his character. Now Jesus, with the full power of the Holy Spirit, for He had "the seven Spirits of God," stands ready to revive the church and bring it back to life.

2. "The Things Which Remain" (Rev. 3: 2, 3). Some truths still "remain" even after the long period of the Dark Ages, and there still "remain" some who are true to God. "Be watchful," said Jesus, "and strengthen the things *which remain,* that are ready to die: for I have not found thy works perfect before God." Was it any wonder that even the true church of God living in a time of such universal apostasy should not be "perfect before God"? But Jesus understood. "I know thy works," He said, "Remember therefore how thou hast received and heard, and hold fast, and repent."

3. Why the Church Was "Ready to Die." One great cause of spiritual death to a church or to an individual is the neglect of Bible study. With the exception of the Bible among the Waldenses, the only copies at this time were written in Greek or Latin, and there were but few of these in all the world.

The first book printed from movable type was the Bible in Latin. It was printed by John Gutenberg, at Mainz, Germany, in 1456, about seventy-five years after Wyclif's task of translating the Bible into English. In 1926 a copy of this Bible was sold in New York for $106,000, the highest price ever paid for a single book.

For more than a thousand years, even these few copies were securely hidden from the people. And even if they had had access to them, they could not have read them, for the Greek and Latin languages were not at this time generally understood. The word of God is the bread of life, the spiritual food, and without it the church was literally starving to death,—"ready to die."

4. The Bible Translated into English. Over in England there lived a man whose name was John Wycliffe. More than one hundred years before the Reformation began, the Lord put it into the heart of Wycliffe to translate the Bible into English, and thus provide the bread of life for His starving church. To do this was a dangerous undertaking, for the pope and the priests did not want the Bible to be read by anyone but clergy. They said the common people could not understand it; and to place it in their hands would be to cast the gospel pearls before swine. But in spite of all their protests and threats, Wycliffe kept at his work until it was accomplished. This indicated the dawn of a better day for all mankind. Copies of his translation were written by hand and circulated among the people. For the great work which this courageous man did, he is called "The Morning Star of the Reformation." But we must remember that printing was still unknown, and copies of the Bible existed only in handwriting. Copying by hand was a very slow, laborious, and expensive process. But it all helped, and the light of a new and glorious day was beginning to dawn.

JOHN WYCLIFFE
translated the Bible
into English in 1382.

MARTIN LUTHER
translated the Bible
into German in 1534.

5. "A Few Names Even in Sardis" (3:4). "Thou hast a few names even in Sardis which have not defiled their garments; and they shall walk with Me in white: for they are worthy." There were at this time a few great men "even in Sardis" who most nobly and bravely stood for God and His word. And these "few names" have been enrolled in the record books both on earth and in heaven, "for they are worthy."

6. Martin Luther. Martin Luther was one of these noble men. One day when he was looking through the library at the university he was attending, he discovered a complete copy of the Bible written in Latin. Although he was twenty years of age, he had never before seen God's Book. Reverently he took it in his hands, and with a thrill of joy he murmured, as he turned its sacred pages, "O God, could I but have one of these books, I would ask no other treasure." Luther belonged to the Roman Church, but like many others, he longed to be a true child of God. He had been taught that the path to a holy

life lay through the monastery, so he became a monk. In the monastery he found a Bible chained to the wall, and this he delighted to study.

Later in life, he visited Rome. Up to this time he had supposed that the priests studied and taught the pure truth of God's word. He was disappointed and horrified to find extravagance, dissipation, and profanity instead of humility and heart devotion to God among these church leaders. While in Rome he learned that the pope had promised special favors to all who should ascend "Pilate's staircase" upon their knees. The pope claimed that Jesus descended this staircase when He left the judgment hall at the time of His trial, and that it was afterward miraculously brought to Rome. Anxious to do anything that would strengthen his spiritual life, Luther began to creep up the staircase. Suddenly a voice seemed to shout in his ears, "The just shall live by faith!" He sprang to his feet in shame, and from that moment he saw the Bible in a new light. He saw that man cannot earn salvation by his own works. He saw that the teachings of Rome were contrary to the word of God.

Luther's room in Wartburg castle, where he translated the New Testament into German.

7. The Bible Translated into German. Luther longed to help the church, and when he returned home he began to study and teach the truth of God as he found it in the Bible. "The Bible and the Bible only," he said, "is my creed." Thousands who listened to his words of life and hope were filled with joy. Satan's anger was aroused. Luther was declared a heretic. His life was constantly in danger. But he bravely continued to preach God's word, and God protected him. To guard his life on one occasion, his friends seized him and concealed him in Wartburg castle for nearly a year. Here he translated the New Testament into the German language. This was published (for printing had been invented by this time) and given to the people who were starving for the bread of life. Then Luther translated the Old Testament.

8. "Song of Joy." The Bible was translated not only into the German language, but, within the short period of about twenty years, it was translated also into Danish, Dutch, French, and other European tongues. And for the first time in their lives, the common people were able to read the word of God in their own language. A great "song of joy" went up from all Europe as the people received God's word, and from it they learned of a loving Saviour, One who forgave their sins "without money and without price." No longer were they compelled to pay money to the pope in order to be saved.

Satan was furious as he saw his cherished plan crumbling to ruin. On different occasions all the Bibles that could be found were gathered together and publicly burned. Thousands, yes, millions of believers were put to death; but they went to the stake with a "song of joy" upon their lips. The sharp two-edged sword, the word of God, was converting the people. And God's great work went on.

9. "Prince of Joy." Only twelve years after Luther began opposing the errors of the church, the Christian princes of Germany wrote out a solemn statement, protesting against the pope or any earthly power claiming the right to compel any man's conscience in religious matters. The day when this famous protest was presented to the German emperor has been called, "the great day of the Reformation, and one of the most glorious in the history of Christianity and of the world." This was the origin of *Protestants,* and this event makes the year 1529 worthy to be remembered. Luther, because he had been pronounced a "heretic," had been forbidden to appear before the emperor, but he accompanied the princes part way. On this journey he composed the words and music to the famous hymn, "A Mighty Fortress Is Our God." This "song of joy" inspired hope in the hearts of the princes and made each one of them a "prince of joy." Many another "song of joy" was written by this great Reformer. The Roman Church declared that "the whole German people were singing themselves into Luther's doctrines, and that his hymns destroyed more souls than all his writings or sermons." After the protest was presented, Luther wrote, "I thrill with joy that I have lived until this hour, in which Christ has been publicly exalted by such illustrious confessors, and in so glorious an assembly."

10. Revival of Church Song. For many years before this time, the voices of the congregation were never heard praising God in church song. The singing was done by choirs alone, and even then in a dead language which could reach neither the understanding nor the hearts of the people. But as the people learned of the gospel from the word of God, they could not remain silent. The deep emotion of their souls burst forth in sacred song. Many of the Psalms were translated, set to music, and published. This was the beginning of some of our first hymnbooks.

WILLIAM TYNDALE
1492-1536

JOHN BUNYAN
1628-1688

"The Psalms soon displaced the meaningless ballads which till then had been sung by the choirs. They were heard in the castles of nobles as well as at the firesides of the common people. Wherever the gospel advanced, it was amid the sounds of melody and praise."

The historian tells us that when the gospel came to Malmö, a city at that time belonging to Denmark, "it was signalized by a mighty outburst of singing. The people, filled with joy at the clear light that shone upon them after the long darkness, poured forth their gratitude in thundering voices in the Psalms of David, the hymns of Luther, and in other sacred canticles."

"In a little while," the historian continues, "all France fell to singing the Psalms. These songs charmed the ears, heart, and affections of court and city, town and country. They were sung by ladies, princes, and even by the king himself. All ranks and degrees of men practiced them in the temples and in their families. No gentleman professing the Reformed religion would sit down at his table without praising God by singing. It was an especial part of their morning and evening worship in their several houses to sing God's praises."

How fitting that the prophecy should name this period of the church "Sardis"— meaning "prince of joy" or "song of joy"!

11. William Tyndale and John Bunyan. While John Wycliffe was the first to translate the Bible into the English, it remained for William Tyndale to perfect his work and see that it was printed so that the people might have copies of their own. His desire that everyone should have this Book was so great that he said, "If God will spare my life, I will cause the boy that drives the plow to know more of the Scriptures than the priests themselves know."

Another of the great men that might be mentioned is John Bunyan. He was among the later English Reformers. He was cast into a loathsome dungeon for his faith, but here he wrote "Pilgrim's Progress," that wonderful book which has helped so many in the Christian life.

In 1620 the persecuted Pilgrims left Europe and found refuge on the shores of free America, where they could have "a state without a king, and a church without a pope."

12. The Pilgrim Fathers. A hundred years after Luther began his work, the persecuted Pilgrims left Europe and found a refuge on the shores of free America, a land whose glory has always been the principles of the great Reformation—civil and religious liberty. Here again went up a "song of joy" for freedom to worship God.

13. The 1260 Days Ended. The power of the pope over the members of the Catholic Church was still very great, but he was no longer allowed to persecute mankind. And his power over the governments of the world was taken from him when, in 1798, at the end of the 1260 years, he was taken prisoner by the French. Satan's plan was badly shattered, but he has not yet given up. A future lesson will tell us what further plans he had to destroy God's people.

14. The Reward of Sardis (3:5). "He that overcometh, the same shall be clothed in white raiment; and I will not blot out his name out of the book of life, but I will confess his name before My Father, and before His angels." The great lesson that the church of Sardis learned was that they could never earn salvation by their own righteousness or by deeds of penance. Salvation is the gift of God, and when we receive this gift, He clothes us with the "white raiment" of His righteousness. For the joy of wearing this garment and having their names written in the book of life they have suffered untold persecution, and even laid down their lives. Many of the church of Sardis were publicly branded as heretics, but some day Jesus will confess their names before His Father and the angels. Could any other reward be more gratefully appreciated by the church of Sardis?

How to Study: After studying the lesson, you should be able to answer the following questions:
1. Why did Jesus address Himself to Sardis as "He that hath the seven Spirits of God"? As He that holds the "seven stars"?
2. Why was the church "ready to die"?
3. How did God save the life of the church?
4. Who were some of the "few names" in Sardis that were worthy?
5. What great work did John Wycliffe do? Martin Luther? William Tyndale? John Bunyan?
6. What was "the famous protest"?
7. What was the origin of "Protestants"? In what year did they originate?
8. What reward is promised to Sardis? Why?
9. Why was the church of this period given a name that means "That which remains"? "Song of joy"? "Prince of joy"?

Memory Work: Memorize the promise to the overcomer in Revelation 3:5.

For Your Workbook: Locate the Sardis church on your diagram of the seven churches.

Dictionary Study: protest; Protestant.

7. THE MESSAGE TO THE CHURCH IN PHILADELPHIA

A Great Missionary Awakening — Beginning About 1792

Lesson 1: Topics 1-5; Rev. 3:8
Lesson 2: Topics 6-12; Rev. 3:7-13

"Him that overcometh will I make a pillar in the temple of My God, and he shall go no more out: and I will write upon him the name of My God, and the name of the city of My God, which is New Jerusalem, which cometh down out of heaven from My God: and I will write upon him My new name." Rev. 3:12.

1. The Work of the Philadelphia Church. The great work of the Philadelphia church was to carry the gospel to all the world, to warn the people of the judgment, and to tell them that Jesus was soon coming. The crowning event was the finishing of Christ's work in the holy place of the heavenly sanctuary preparatory to the beginning of His work in the most holy place. This latter work, as you have already learned, was the Investigative Judgment, the opening of "the books" in heaven, and the investigation of the records.

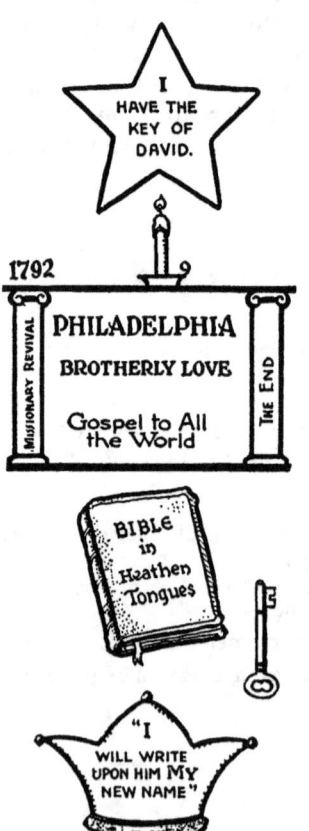

2. A Work of "Brotherly Love" (3:8). Before Christ could come, all must have a chance to know of His plan to save them. There were more Bibles now, but who would go to the ends of the earth and teach the people? The Sardis church had had all it could do to free itself from the shackles of the papacy and bring *itself* back to life by feeding on God's word. It had scarcely thought of the millions of heathen outside of Europe who had never heard of the true God, who did not know of such a book as the Bible, and who knew nothing whatever of the loving Saviour and the plan of salvation. As a result of feeding on His word, the church of God

---

References Used: E. W., pp. 42, 43, 250; G. C., pp. 287, 288, 430, 435; H. Y. M., pp. 70, 91.

had gained "a little strength." And now God expects them to use their strength in carrying to others who are starving the spiritual food that has restored *them* to life. He places before them the great mission field in the regions beyond where their brothers, sitting in the darkness of heathenism, are starving for the bread of life. And He asks the Philadelphia church to carry the word of life to these starving people, to carry the gospel to all the world. Surely, this was a work of true "brotherly love," and the word "Philadelphia" means *brotherly love*.

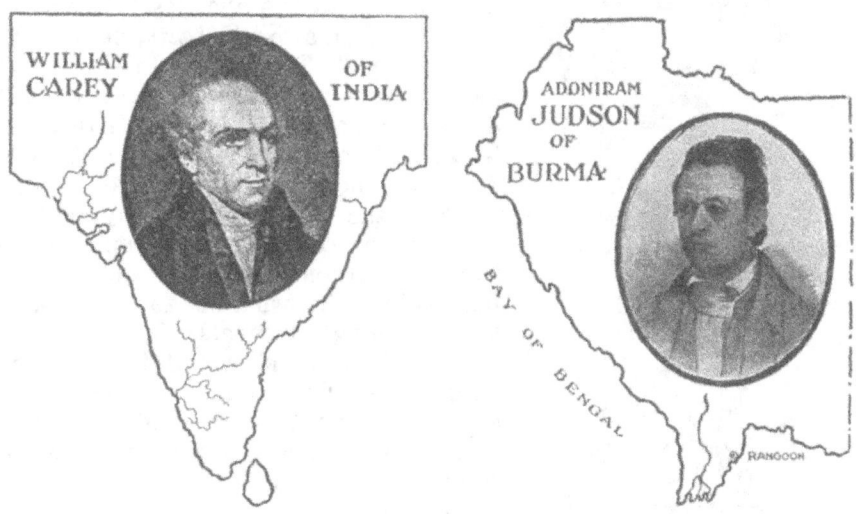

"I know thy works," said Jesus. "Thou . . . hast kept My word, and hast not denied My name." This was as if He had said, "I know I can depend on you to do this work of 'brotherly love.' My church in every period has done the work I have assigned them. You have kept My word. You have not denied My name. I know you will not disappoint Me now." And they did not disappoint Him.

3. Beginning of Modern Missions. In 1780, when the Lord gave the first signs of His coming, and even for many years before that, scarcely a thing had been done to carry the message of His great plan to the heathen. But the prophecy had said that during the "time of the end," many should "run to and fro" to spread a knowledge of

God's word. This time of the end began near the close of the eighteenth century, and at that time God placed upon William Carey the burden to give his life to carry the gospel to the heathen world. Carey is called the "Apostle of Modern Missions."

It was in 1792 that Carey preached his "deathless sermon," which was destined to arouse the religious world to a sense of their responsibility. At a religious meeting, he was called upon to name a subject for discussion, and he asked, "Is not the command given to the apostles to teach *all nations,* given also to *all ministers to the end of time?*" The leader of the meeting looked sternly at him, and said: "Sit down, young man. . . . When God wants to convert the world, He can do it without your help." Others tried to discourage the movement by saying that the idea of converting the millions of savage heathen was unreasonable and impossible. Who would be foolish enough to go among cannibals? Where in all the heathen world would they begin? And who would give money to carry out such wild plans? But though men tried to stop this work, God was in it, and it could not be stopped.

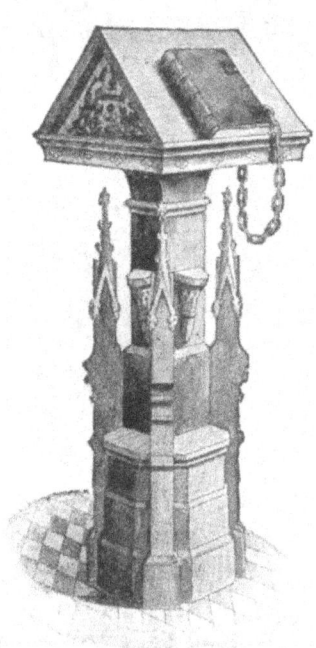

In the year 1539 a copy of the English Bible was chained to the reading desk of every parish church in England.

The historian calls the year 1792 *annus mirabilis,* or famous year, for it was "the beginning of a new epoch for the kingdom of God on earth." Concerning this movement it was written of England: "Christians in every corner of the land are meeting in a regular manner, and pouring out their souls for God's blessing on the world." And again: "You call on the wise and good of every nation to take interest in the work and bear a part. Such a call was never heard before." And another writer says, "It was the beginning of the Lord's preparation." God was about to open the doors of every nation, kindred, tongue, and people that they might hear the gospel message. The hour had indeed struck announcing a new and glorious period of the church, a period which Revelation has most appropriately called "Philadelphia," *brotherly love.*

4. **The First Bible Society.** Although at this time Bibles were more easily obtained than during the Dark Ages, the following true story shows that they were still very scarce: One day as a minister in Wales was returning from church service, he asked a little girl—Mary Jones—if she could repeat the text from which he had preached the preceding week. Mary was silent a moment, then she burst into tears as she said, "The weather was so bad last week that I could not get to the Bible." She had been accustomed to go seven miles every week over the hills to a place where she could have access to a Bible. How many boys and girls to-day would put forth such an effort to learn a memory verse?

This incident deeply impressed the minister with the need of Bibles, and finally led to the organization of the British and Foreign Bible Society, the first of its kind. The friends of this society still hold in loving remembrance the name of Mary Jones. The society was organized not only to multiply Bibles but to give serious thought to the immense undertaking of sending the printed Word to every nation in the world. Its original membership numbered twelve, the same as the number whom Christ chose to go "into all the world, and preach the gospel to every creature." And the offering they made for the world's conversion was £12 2s. 6d., or about sixty dollars—this, only this, for the nearly a billion non-Christian people of the world!

It is true that this was a small beginning, but it was the beginning of "a great change." "From this time the work of foreign missions attained an unprecedented growth."

5. **Bibles Translated for the Heathen.** But though Bibles and money and men for this work were scarce, Carey was not discouraged. He offered himself for India, and there he spent the remaining years of his life. He lived to see a revival in mission work such as had not been since the days of the apostles. Before his death Adoniram Judson had carried the good news of salvation to Burma, Robert Moffat into darkest Africa, and John Williams to the cannibals of the South Sea Islands. Every one of these missionaries translated the Bible into the language of the people for whom he labored. From this time the door to the great mission fields has stood wide open,

and through it tons of Bibles in nearly every spoken language, and millions of dollars, and thousands of missionaries have passed, to carry to the heathen a knowledge of God's great plan. Surely, the prophecy was being fulfilled, "Many shall run to and fro, and knowledge shall be increased."

6. The Prophecies Studied. While Carey, Judson, Moffat, Williams, and other noble missionaries had left the homeland and were translating the Scriptures and carrying the gospel into heathen lands, God moved upon the hearts of others who remained in the homelands, both in America and Europe, to give most earnest study to the truths of His word. More and more the prophecy was being fulfilled, "knowledge shall be increased." These Christian men studied the prophecies of Daniel and the Revelation, especially the one that says, "Unto two thousand and three hundred days; then shall the sanctuary be cleansed." In those days, the subject of the sanctuary had not been very carefully studied, and it was generally supposed that the sanctuary was this earth. Therefore, William Miller with others concluded that the "cleansing of the sanctuary" was the cleansing of this earth by fire.

7. "Behold, I Come Quickly" (3:11). As a result of this study in the early years of the nineteenth century, these Bible students made a thrilling discovery. They found that this prophecy of the cleansing of the sanctuary pointed to the soon coming of Jesus. Their hearts were deeply stirred with the conviction that theirs was the responsibility of telling these truths to the world so that all might prepare for the coming of Christ and the destruction of the earth. God's message, "Behold, I come quickly," kept ringing in their ears.

8. Preaching the Prophecies. Among those who first preached this message were William Miller and Dr. Joseph Wolff. They began in the early thirties, at the very time when, in 1833, God gave another sign of Jesus' coming—"the stars shall fall from heaven." Within a few years, this message of the soon coming of Jesus was preached in all parts of the civilized world. And thousands believed.

As these believers accepted this truth and talked to others about it, many of them were thrust out of the churches they had been attending. But even this did not discourage them. They knew that God was on their side. Their hearts beat in unison and they possessed a fervent love for one another. They were bound together in true "brotherly love." Selfishness and covetousness were laid aside, and all their earthly goods were placed on the altar of sacrifice and service that others might know the glorious truth that meant so much to them.

9. "The Hour of Temptation" (3:8-10). God knew that some would accept His message, not because they wanted to see Him, but because they were afraid of the destruction that would come upon them if they rejected it. At first, those who were preaching the message thought that the 2300 days would end in the spring of 1844, and that Jesus would then come. But the time passed, and He did not come. Then, "the hour of temptation" came "to try them that dwell upon the earth." Some began to doubt. Others rejected the message entirely. But the truehearted believers "kept the word," and God kept them during this "hour of temptation." They studied their Bibles more closely than ever. And they found their mistake,—the 2300 days reached to the *autumn* of 1844. But *that* time came and went, and still Jesus did not come. It was a terrible disappointment to all who were awaiting the advent; but those who did not really want Him to come, who preferred to "dwell upon the earth," made fun of the believers and basely misrepresented them. Jesus says that these were "of the synagogue [or church] of Satan, which say they are Jews [God's people], and are not, but do lie."

10. The "Open Door" in Heaven (3:7, 8, 11). Jesus encouraged His true children by saying, "Hold that fast which thou hast, that no man take thy crown." These patiently continued to pray and study. They then learned that their second mistake was not in the *time* when the 2300 days were to close, but in the *event* that was then to take place. They discovered that the sanctuary was not this earth, but the real sanctuary in heaven. They learned that in the autumn of 1844, Jesus, instead of coming to cleanse this earth, finished His work in the holy place of the heavenly sanctuary, and went into the most holy place to begin the work of cleansing the heavenly sanctuary from the sins recorded in "the books." It was then that "the door" into the holy place was shut, and "the door" into the most holy place was opened.

11. "The Key of David" (3:7). Jesus holds "the key of David," which gave Him the right to open the door and enter into the most holy place, where the throne is. The throne of David, on which Christ is to reign, "is included in the capital of His kingdom, the New Jerusalem, now above, but which is to be located on this earth, where He is to reign forever and ever."

12. The Overcomer's Reward (3:12). The wonderful work that God did through the Philadelphia church in proclaiming the glad tidings of the soon return of the Saviour, entitles them to a place of honor and importance in God's temple. "Him ... will I make a pillar in the temple of My God," said Jesus. And this pillar shall never be broken down by Satan as in the past, but it will stand throughout eternity, for "he shall go no more out."

Those who at this time overcome are ready to take the last step toward their eternal home. The last station on the long journey of the Christian church has been reached. Now the gospel train is waiting to take them to their final destination. To make sure that every passenger reaches his journey's end in safety, Jesus, the mighty Conductor and Owner of the road, says, "I will write upon him the name of My God [to whom they belong], and the name of the city of My God, which is New Jerusalem [the place for which they are bound], which cometh down out of heaven from My God: and I will write upon him My new name [showing that they have gained the victory over sin and have a right to travel on this train]." Thus labeled, and under the care of so able a conductor, they will surely reach their journey's end in safety.

How to Study: See how many of these questions you can answer:

1. Why is this church called "Philadelphia"?
2. How did the church get "a little strength"? How did God direct them to use this strength? What opposition did they meet?
3. How did God express His confidence that this church would do the work He placed upon them? Rev. 3:8.
4. Who is called "The Apostle of Modern Missions"?
5. What great work did those do who went as missionaries to the heathen?
6. What special message did God send this church? Why did "the synagogue of Satan" object to this message? Rev. 3:11, 9.
7. What was "the hour of temptation" which came upon this church? Because they kept His word, what did God promise? Rev. 3:10.
8. What door in heaven was shut at this time? What door was opened? What key opened this door?
9. Explain the reward promised to the overcomer.

Memory Work: Memorize Revelation 3:12.

For Your Workbook: On your diagram of the seven churches, locate the Philadelphia period of the church.

---

8. THE MESSAGE TO THE CHURCH OF LAODICEA

The Investigative Judgment—1844 to the End—Rev. 3:14-22

"To him that overcometh will I grant to sit with Me in My throne, even as I also overcame, and am set down with My Father in His throne." Rev. 3:21.

1. Time and Meaning of Laodicea (3:14). We have now reached the seventh and last period of the church of God. This tells us about the finishing of God's great plan. We ourselves are living in this period, and if we are Christ's we are a part of this church which He is getting ready to take home to the New Jerusalem. The word "Laodicea" means *a judging of the people*. During this whole period of the church, the Investigative Judgment is going on in the heavenly sanctuary. It began in 1844, at the end of the 2300 days; and it will continue until Jesus, "the Amen," says, "It is done."

2. God's Law Seen Through the "Open Door" (3:8). In 1844, when Jesus finished His work in the holy place and went into the most holy place, the ark in which are placed the commandments

---

References Used: James 2:5; Luke 4:18; 12:21; 1 Tim. 6:18; Job 23:10; Isa. 64:6; Matt. 7:3-5; 2 Peter 1:9.

of God was revealed through the door that He opened. God opened this door before His church that they might call the attention of the whole world to His law. He wants all to know that the papacy has taught man to disobey it. Then those who are sincere in their love for God will cease to disobey. They will break every chain of Satan. They will put themselves on God's side by keeping all His commandments. Those who are of "the synagogue of Satan" will not want to look upon that law. They will want to shut the door into the most holy place. But God has opened it, and no man can shut it. Everyone must choose whether he will be on God's side or remain with Satan. The Sabbath, which in the warfare between Christ and Satan has been made the test of loyalty, will be the test of loyalty for every follower of Jesus.

3. The Name of Jesus (3:14). To the Laodicea church Jesus calls Himself "the faithful and true Witness." The work that God has given His church to do is almost finished. The struggle with Satan is almost over. But in all our struggles and temptations we can depend upon Jesus. He will be "faithful and true" to the end. When our names come up in judgment, He will witness to every victory that we have won. And He will be just as true and faithful to witness to sins unconfessed.

Jesus also calls Himself "the beginning of the creation of God." All things in the beginning were created by Him, and when the end comes He will create all things anew. He wants to create in us clean hearts, so that we may be ready to meet the Judgment. And soon He will create "a new heaven and a new earth" free from every trace of sin. Jesus also calls Himself "the Amen." Can you tell why?

4. "Thou Art Lukewarm" (3:16). "Thou art lukewarm, and neither cold nor hot." This is the accusation made against the

Laodiceans. What a terrible condition! Indifferent, self-satisfied, thinking we are all right, when, alas, we really lack that zeal and devotion which would make us like Jesus! God says we are lukewarm. It would be better if we were cold, for then we would realize our condition and fervently pray for a more zealous Christian experience. Simply to have our names on the church record, simply to attend church, simply to say prayers, simply to read the Bible through every year,— these things cannot save us. We cannot excuse ourselves on the ground that some one else is as bad as we are. We cannot lay the blame on another. We must learn to hear the still small voice of the Holy Spirit and always obey, no matter what others do. We must cease to do evil. We must learn to do well. We must see to it that our influence over others is right at all times. We must know that God accepts us every day and every hour.

5. "Rich, and Increased with Goods" (3:17). The Laodiceans proudly say, "I am rich, and increased with goods, and have need of nothing." They think they are all right. They do not know that they are "wretched, and miserable, and poor, and blind, and naked." Think of a person so poverty-stricken that he has no clothing to put on. Besides this he is blind, groping his way about in darkness. He is miserable and wretched. But, strange as it may seem, he does not know it. A drunkard lying in the ditch imagines that he is rich. Poor man! His mind is too clouded to know his own terrible condition.

With the Laodiceans this is not a condition of the body. It is a spiritual condition, which is even worse. Spiritual riches are within their reach, but they do not use them. They have the Bible, they understand its teachings, they are able to interpret the prophecies correctly, they pay a tithe for the support of the gospel, they go to church on the Sabbath, they believe in the second coming of Christ according to His promise. Yet they are poor, because they do not have in their hearts the Christian graces of faith and hope and charity and patience. They do not have the robe of Christ's righteousness, they do not have the Holy Spirit to enlighten their hearts — they are blind, and yet they do not know it. What a wretched, miserable condition for God to find in the very church that is soon to meet Him!

6. "Gold Tried in the Fire" (3:18). God loves this people, and in their inmost hearts, they love Him. But Satan, the great adversary, is trying to ruin them. Nevertheless, he will be defeated if we accept the counsel of the true Witness, who says, "I counsel thee to buy of Me gold tried in the fire, that thou mayest be rich"—"rich in faith." He counsels us to lay up our treasure in heaven, that we may be "rich toward God." He counsels us to be "rich in good works, ready to distribute, willing to communicate." If we bravely and with patience meet the trials and temptations that come to us day by day, we have the promise that we "shall come forth as gold" tried in the fire.

7. "White Raiment" (3:18). Again the true Witness says, "I counsel thee to buy of Me . . . white raiment, that thou mayest be clothed, and that the shame of thy nakedness do not appear." This raiment is the robe of righteousness,— not our own righteousness, which is "as filthy rags," but the righteousness of Christ. If we have traits of character that are unlike Jesus, we must overcome them before we are ready to meet our Saviour.

8. "Eyesalve" (3:18). The true Witness also says, "I counsel thee to . . . anoint thine eyes with eyesalve, that thou mayest see." Jesus called the Pharisees blind because they thought they were more righteous than others. He advised them to take the beam out of their own eye before trying to take a mere speck or mote out of another's eye. If in our own hearts we think we are better than others who are trying to do right, if we criticize their motives, we may be sure that a great beam is in our own eyes, which prevents us from seeing ourselves. Peter says that if we lack patience, brotherly kindness, and charity, we are "blind, and cannot see afar off." Jesus was anointed with the Holy Spirit in order that He might give "sight to the blind." The Holy Spirit is the eyesalve with which He will anoint our eyes and help us to see ourselves as God sees us. Then we shall feel as did Mr. Gough, the great temperance lecturer, when, pointing to a poor drunkard lying in the ditch, he said, "Except for the grace of God, there lies John B. Gough."

9. A Rebuke That Is Love (3:19, 20). "As many as I love, I rebuke and chasten: be zealous therefore, and repent." It is because Jesus loves us that He rebukes and punishes us. He does not want us to be lost, therefore He says, "Be zealous . . . and repent." It is not because Jesus has no friends in heaven that He knocks at the door of my heart and asks to come in. He has a glorious home in heaven where everyone adores Him. Yet He longs for a home in *my* heart. He wants *my* love. And He shall have it. I will open the door and let my Saviour in.

10. The Promise to the Overcomer (3:21). "To him that overcometh will I grant to sit with Me in My throne, even as I also overcame, and am set down with My Father in His throne." We may have made mistakes, we may have failed many times, but we may still be overcomers. In every age since Jesus founded His church, Satan has done his utmost to discourage, to defeat, and to destroy. But in every age, the true church of God has been an overcomer, and to it, all His promises are made.

How to Study: After studying the lesson, you should be able to answer the following questions:
 1. What does "Laodicea" mean? When does this period of the church begin and end?
 2. What was seen through the "open door" of the most holy place?
 3. Why is Jesus called "the Amen"? "the faithful and true Witness"? "the beginning of the creation of God"? Rev. 3:14.
 4. What is meant by saying that the Laodiceans are "lukewarm"? that they are "rich, and increased with goods"? Verses 16, 17.
 5. What did Jesus mean by telling them to buy of Him "gold tried in the fire"? "white raiment"? "eyesalve"? Verse 18.

Memory Work: Recite the promise to the overcomer. Rev. 3:21. If you have learned the promise to the overcomer in each church, and Revelation 12:11, you are entitled to the first star on your memory certificate.

Chapter to Remember: Revelation 3 contains the messages to the Sardis, Philadelphia, and Laodicea churches.

For Your Workbook: Locate the Laodicea church on your diagram of the seven churches.

REVIEW OF REVELATION 1-3

Test Questions: Study these questions with your diagram of the seven churches before you.
 1. Give in order the names of the seven churches, and explain from the meaning of the word how each name fits its period.
 2. In what church was the work of the apostles? the pagan persecutions? the rise of the papacy? the reign of the papacy? the fall of the papacy? the gospel to the heathen? the Judgment? the great apostasy? the Dark Ages? the Reformation? the Middle Ages?

3. Give the date of the beginning of each of the seven periods of the church, and the event marking each.
4. In which church was the Bible on separate scrolls? in unknown languages? a forbidden book? translated into modern languages? translated into heathen languages? best understood? How does this illustrate Proverbs 4:18?
5. How did Satan try in each period to destroy God's church? Rev. 2:4, 10, 13, 14, 20; 3:2, 10, 16.
6. Where was Satan's seat?
7. Who was Antipas?
8. Who were some of the "few names even in Sardis" who were worthy?
9. How and when did Protestants have their origin?
10. What was the open door which no man could shut?
11. Who were some of the first to enter the mission fields?
12. What is the great danger of the last church? Rev. 3:16. What will keep them from this danger? Rev. 3:18. What is the "gold"? the "white raiment"? the "eyesalve"?

Memory Drill: Recite from memory the reward to the overcomer, and tell how it applies to each church. Rev. 2: 7, 11, 17, 26, 28; 3: 5, 12, 21.

Verse-Finding Drill: With your Bible open to Revelation 1, 2, and 3, see how quickly you can find the verse containing each of the following expressions. After you have found them in order, try skipping about.

1. Behold, He cometh with clouds.
2. Every eye shall see Him, and they also which pierced Him.
3. I am Alpha and Omega.
4. I was in the Spirit on the Lord's day.
5. I saw seven golden candlesticks.
6. I . . . have the keys of hell and of death.
7. The seven candlesticks . . . are the seven churches.
8. The seven stars are the angels of the seven churches.
9. These things saith He that holdeth the seven stars in His right hand.
10. Thou hast left thy first love.
11. To him that overcometh will I give to eat of the tree of life.
12. These things saith the first and the last, which was dead, and is alive.
13. Ye shall have tribulation ten days.
14. Be thou faithful unto death, and I will give thee a crown of life.
15. He that overcometh shall not be hurt of the second death.
16. Thou dwellest . . . where Satan's seat is.
17. Antipas was My faithful martyr.
18. These things saith He which hath the sharp sword with two edges.
19. To him that overcometh will I give to eat of the hidden manna.
20. I . . . will give him a white stone.
21. I will give him the morning Star.
22. Strengthen the things which remain.
23. He that overcometh, the same shall be clothed in white raiment.
24. I will not blot out his name out of the book of life.
25. I have set before thee an open door, and no man can shut it.

26. I also will keep thee from the hour of temptation.
27. Hold that fast which thou hast, that no man take thy crown.
28. Him that overcometh will I make a pillar in the temple of My God.
29. These things saith the Amen.
30. Thou art lukewarm, and neither cold nor hot.
31. Buy of Me gold tried in the fire.
32. Anoint thine eyes with eyesalve, that thou mayest see.
33. To him that overcometh will I grant to sit with Me in My throne.

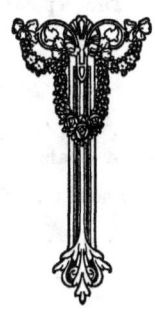

OUTLINE OF CHAPTER VIII

Symbols — A Book with Seven Seals
Time   — The Christian Era
Result — The Apostate Church Destroyed

Topics —   Revelation

At the Throne of God 4
The Book with Seven Seals 5
Opening the First and Second Seals .... ⎫
                                                                          6
Opening the Third, Fourth, and Fifth Seals .... ⎭
The Sixth Seal Opened 6, 7
The Seventh Seal Opened 7, 8
Review

CHAPTER VIII

Satan's Opposition Through the Apostate Church

1. AT THE THRONE OF GOD
Rev. 4; 5:1, 9

"Thou art worthy, O Lord, to receive glory and honor and power: for Thou hast created all things, and for Thy pleasure they are and were created." Rev. 4:11.

   1. **John's Second Vision (5:1; 4:1, 2).** The second vision given to John on Patmos is called the seven seals. It is shown under the symbol of "a book [or scroll] written within, and on the backside sealed with seven seals." Like the seven churches, the events of this prophecy extend over the Christian era. Before the scenes described in this book were shown to John, he was permitted to look into heaven itself. Here he saw a door opened, and "the first voice," the same one that had spoken to him in his first vision, called out in trumpet tones, "Come up hither, and I will show thee things which must be hereafter." "Immediately" he was lost to everything about him. What if he was an exile on a lonely, barren island! What mattered that to him, with the door of heaven opened and the voice of Jesus calling him thither? "Immediately" "in the Spirit" he was in heaven. What a change!

   2. **The Throne of God (4:3).** John has tried to describe what he saw so that we, too, may look into heaven. First, he saw the throne, and the great God Himself seated on it. The royal robe that the Father wore was resplendent purple reflecting light like a jasper stone, mingled with a blood-red color like a sardine stone. When Ezekiel was given a view of heaven, he said the throne was like a sapphire, which is a deep, pure, transparent blue. Upon the throne he saw "the likeness as the appearance of a man." Round

---

References Used: D. A., p. 97; D. R. on lesson text; Eze. 1:26-28; Matt. 27:52, 53; Eph. 4:8; Isa. 6:2; Rev. 7:11.

about he saw "as the color of amber," which poets have tried to describe by comparing it to the sunshine or the rich yellow glow of the morning sky. He also says it looked to him like "the appearance of fire." Round about the throne John saw a gorgeous rainbow "in sight like unto an emerald." Ezekiel says it looked like "the bow that is in the cloud in the day of rain." Perhaps the reason John described it as of a deep, rich, emerald green was because he had already spoken of the other rainbow colors. It was no doubt very difficult for either John or Ezekiel to find language to describe fitly the glory of the scene. We shall understand it better when we see it for ourselves.

3. "The Four and Twenty Elders" (4:4; 5:9). Round about the throne of God John saw "four and twenty seats [or thrones]: and upon the seats . . . four and twenty elders sitting, clothed in white raiment; and they had on their heads crowns of gold." These twenty-four elders once lived as men on this earth. Now their conflict is finished. They have won the victory, for they have on their heads "crowns of gold." They are "clothed in white raiment," which represents a perfected character. They tell us that they have been redeemed "out of every kindred, and tongue, and people, and nation."

When were the twenty-four elders redeemed? Matthew says that when Jesus died on the cross, "graves were opened," and "after His resurrection" "many bodies of the saints which slept arose, and came out of the graves." And Paul says that when Jesus "ascended up on high, He led a multitude of captives." The twenty-four elders were therefore among the captives whom Satan had shut up in his prison house, and whom Jesus released and took with Him to heaven at His ascension. When Daniel was shown the Judgment scene he also saw thrones placed around "the Ancient of Days." In the sanctuary service on earth there were twenty-four courses of priests, each one ministering in the temple one week twice a year. So these twenty-four elders are now priests assisting Christ in the service of the heavenly temple.

4. The Seven Lamps; the Sea of Glass (4:5, 6). John also saw lightnings flashing forth from the throne, and he heard thunderings and voices. The voice of God is often compared to the deep-toned thunder, and as He gives His commands the angels, like flashes of lightning, delight to carry the message of comfort and love to those in need. "Before the throne there was a sea of glass like unto crystal." There were also "seven lamps of fire burning before the throne, which are the seven Spirits of God." In the earthly sanctuary the seven-branched candlestick which was before the ark, was in the first apartment, or holy place. This would indicate that although John had been looking into the most holy place, where the throne of God is, the door into the holy place was open and through it he saw into the first apartment also.

5. "**The Four Living Creatures**" (4:6-8). Looking again in amazement at the wonderful scene, John saw "four beasts," or as some translations read, "four living creatures." These creatures seemed to him to be "full of eyes before and behind." Each one had six wings. The first was like a *lion*, the second like a *calf* or *ox*, the third had a face as a *man*, and the fourth was like a flying *eagle*. These creatures, like the twenty-four elders, were also among the "multitude of captives" whom Christ redeemed from the grave, and took with Him to heaven at the time of His ascension. They were even closer to the throne than were the twenty-four elders. John says they were "in the midst of the throne, and round about the throne." They were not the angels, for "all the angels stood round about . . . the elders and the four living

Living creatures arranged "like a flying eagle"

creatures." These creatures and elders represent the redeemed who will one day reign in heaven. They are the "first fruits," and correspond to the wave sheaf in the earthly sanctuary.

During the war some one made an interesting picture of President Wilson. Viewed at a little distance every feature of his face could be plainly traced. On close examination the picture was found to be made up of hundreds of United States army soldiers, so arranged as to represent the President. This may help us to understand how the living creatures that John saw appeared at a distance — one group resembling a lion, another group resembling an ox, another a man, and another a flying eagle.

If you will look at your diagram of the camp of Israel, it will be easier to understand the sanctuary above; for the earthly sanctuary and everything connected with it was a pattern of heavenly things. In the center is the court, and the sanctuary with its two apartments, containing among other things the ark and the candlestick. Immediately surrounding this are the four divisions of the priests and Levites, corresponding perhaps to the "four living creatures." Next away and surrounding all are the twelve tribes, who were represented in the priestly service by the twenty-four courses of priests — the twenty-four elders — serving in the temple twice a year, one week at a time. The lion, the ox, the man, and the eagle are symbols denoting the kind of service that God desires — the lion representing strength of love, the ox or calf representing perseverance in duty, the man representing ability to understand God's will, and the eagle representing swiftness in obeying. These, you remember, are the same symbols that were pictured on the four standards of the camp of Israel.

6. The Worship in Heaven (4:8-10). As John, spellbound, looked on the scene, he heard the four living creatures saying fervently, "Holy, holy, holy, Lord God Almighty, which was, and is, and is to come." As they thus worship and praise the Father, "the four and twenty elders fall down before Him that sat on the throne, and worship Him that liveth forever and ever." Then casting their crowns before the throne, they join the worship, saying, "Thou art worthy, O Lord, to receive glory and honor and power: for Thou hast created all things, and for Thy pleasure they are and were created."

How to Study: Study this lesson with the diagram of the camp of Israel before you, remembering that the earthly sanctuary was a "figure," or "pattern," or illustration, of things in heaven. It will help you to understand why God was so extremely particular that everything about the earthly sanctuary be made "according to the pattern" which He showed to Moses in the mount. As you study, see how the pattern corresponded to the real sanctuary in heaven. Try to get a clear idea of each part of this heavenly scene,— see the glory of it, and enter into the feelings of those who are there. Notice carefully what each one does and says.

Chapter to Remember: Revelation 4 — the throne of God.

For Class Discussion: On what other occasions has the voice of God been heard as thunder?

---

2. THE BOOK WITH SEVEN SEALS
Revelation 5

"Worthy is the Lamb that was slain to receive power, and riches, and wisdom, and strength, and honor, and glory, and blessing." Rev. 5:12.

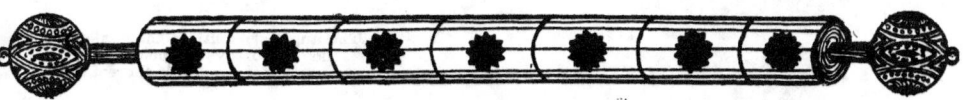

"A book sealed with seven seals"

1. The Book and Its Contents (5:1). Again John's attention was directed to the throne of God. What is that in the hands of the Father? "A book written within, and on the backside sealed with seven seals." This book was a scroll rolled up. When the scroll was unrolled, the writing within was discovered to be a record of the cruelties that Satan would inflict on the church of God to the end of time. When he failed to conquer and destroy the Son of God and was shut out of the councils of heaven, his wrath was aroused, and he turned every power of his being against the followers of Christ. He determined if possible to destroy them from his dominion, and he carefully organized his forces for the conflict. The prophecy of the seals tells how he worked through the apostate church —"the synagogue of Satan"— to defeat God's plan for His people. It is not at all likely that he wanted this seven-sealed book opened and his plans made known to those whom he so bitterly hated.

2. Who Will Open the Book (5:2-4)? As God holds up the book, a mighty angel comes forth as a crier, and with a loud voice utters the challenge, "Who is worthy to open the book, and to loose the seals thereof?" To loose the seals on this book and to read its contents would require some one who could successfully meet the wicked plans of Satan which were written therein, and fully defeat him. Who could do this? Could the living creatures about the throne? Could the four and twenty elders? Could the angels? There is a pause. No one responds. "No man in heaven, nor in earth, neither under

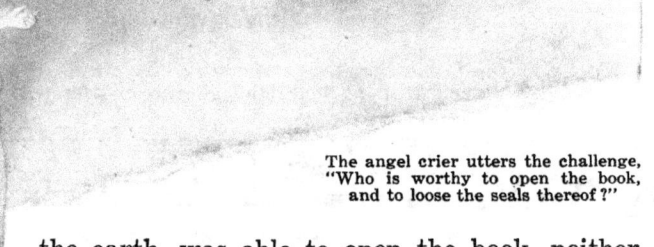

The angel crier utters the challenge, "Who is worthy to open the book, and to loose the seals thereof?"

the earth, was able to open the book, neither to look thereon."

The silence was painful. John wept, and wept much. And no wonder, for unless some one could be found to grapple successfully with the terrible contents of that book, it meant destruction to God's church on earth. Daniel also had been deeply distressed at these very scenes. When he saw the awful experiences through which his people would have to pass, he "fainted, and was sick certain days."

3. One Found to Open the Book (5:5, 6). John was not left long to weep. In an ecstasy of delight, one of the elders said to him: "Weep not. Look! Look! The Lion of the tribe of Judah, the Root of David, hath prevailed to open the book, and to loose the seven seals thereof." John looks up through his tears. What is that he sees? In the open space between the throne and the four living creatures, instead of a Lion there stands "a Lamb as it had been slain," as if just ready for the sacrifice. This represented Jesus, the Lamb of God, who gave His life to break these seals, to conquer Satan and rescue man from his death grip. Because He Himself had gained the victory over Satan, He was able to open the book. The Lamb had "seven horns," representing complete power. He had "seven eyes, which are the seven Spirits of God sent forth into all the earth." From these searching eyes never will Satan be able to conceal his plans. With such eyes never will Jesus lose sight of a single one of His tempted children. "Thou God seest me."

4. The "New Song" of the Redeemed (5: 7-10). Jesus, the Lamb of God, came to the Father and took the book out of His right hand. Then "the four living creatures and four and twenty elders fell down before the Lamb, having every one of them harps, and golden vials full of odors." These odors, or perfumes, in golden bottles represent our prayers that are offered with the righteousness of Christ. Not one true, unselfish prayer is ever lost or left unnoticed. Even if God does not seem to answer at once, the prayer, like precious incense or costly perfume, is sacredly treasured, and sometime it will surely be answered. Then as the living creatures and the elders fell down before the Lamb, they sang a new song. What is this song? It is a song in which the angels do not join, for only those who have been redeemed from sin can sing: "Thou art worthy to take the book, and to open the seals thereof: for Thou wast slain, and hast redeemed us to God by Thy blood out of every kindred, and tongue, and people, and nation; and hast made us unto our God kings and priests: and we shall reign on the earth."

5. The Angels Unite in Praise (5: 11, 12). But, though the angels cannot sing the song of redemption, because they have never sinned, they listen with thrills of joy, and at last "ten thousand times ten thousand, and thousands of thousands" of angels swell the anthem of praise. They were present when Lucifer was conquered in heaven. They saw their Commander break Satan's power over the grave and triumphantly bring forth the keys of death and the grave. Now they give Him sevenfold praise, saying, "Worthy is the Lamb that was slain to receive power, and riches, and wisdom, and strength, and honor, and glory, and blessing."

6. The Universe Joins the Chorus (5: 13, 14). Then "every creature which is in heaven, and on the earth, and under the earth, and such as are in the sea, and all that are in them," John heard saying, "Blessing, and honor, and glory, and power, be unto Him that sitteth upon the throne, and unto the Lamb forever and ever."

The anthem closed with the grand "Amen" sung reverently by the four living creatures.

How to Study: Remember, "the book" is the central theme of this lesson. It is seen in the hands of the Father; then comes the challenge of the angel, followed by a painful silence because no one is found to open the book, the sorrow of John, the elder's joyful announcement, the Lamb with seven horns and seven eyes taking the book, and the song of joy and victory because Jesus the slain Lamb is able to open it,— the song begun by the redeemed of earth, joined in by the angels, and at last by the entire universe.

Read the lesson thoughtfully, then read the same story in Revelation 5, and after that try to describe the scene and just what was said and done. Try to enter into the experiences of the various ones in the story. How do you think the Father felt as He held up the book? How do you think the angel crier felt? Do you think Satan was glad to have this book unsealed? Why not?

Chapter to Remember: Revelation 5 tells about the book with seven seals.

---

3. OPENING THE FIRST AND SECOND SEALS
Revelation 6:1-4

"The Lion of the tribe of Judah . . . hath prevailed to open the book, and to loose the seven seals thereof." Rev. 5:5.

1. The Churches and the Seals Compared. The vision of the seven churches gives the experience of the Christian church in seven successive periods from the close of Christ's life on earth to His second coming. Jesus gave this prophecy to His church to encourage them to look to Him as the One who is able to meet their needs under any and every condition. And to them during all this time He holds out the encouragement of reward to the overcomer.

The vision of the book with seven seals again covers the experience of the church through the same time. The purpose of this prophecy is to make clear the wicked character of the apostasy which came into the church with its subtle and destroying influence. The churches hold up the ideal to be reached; the seals reveal the evils and dangers to be shunned. The churches give the work of Jesus for His church; the seals the work of Satan

---

References Used: Rom. 1:8; Col. 1:23; 2 Thess. 2:7.

against the church. As you study the seals, look for this comparison.

2. **The First Seal Opened (6:1, 2).** With the deepest anxiety John watched to see the Lamb break the seal, open the book, and show him its contents. Satan would gladly keep his wicked plans concealed from God's people, sealed with a sevenfold seal which they cannot break. But Christ is stronger than he, and He at once opened the first seal. Then one of the four living creatures, in a voice like thunder, called out to John, "Come and see." And this is what he saw: "A white horse: and he that sat on him had a bow; and a crown was given unto him: and he went forth conquering, and to conquer."

PURITY AND POWER

PERSECUTIONS OF PAGAN ROME

3. **The Meaning of the First Seal.** The first seal covers the same period of time as the first church. The color of this horse fitly represents the purity of the church in its first period. It is true that even in the days of the apostles Satan persecuted the church and put the apostles to death. Nevertheless the church of God moved victoriously forward, so that Paul could say of the church at Rome, "I thank my God . . . that your faith is spoken of throughout the whole world." After he had been preaching only about thirty years, Paul said that the gospel had been "preached to every creature which is under heaven." And so Satan's first efforts were not very successful. The church of God, wearing the crown of victory, went forth conquering and to conquer.

4. **The Second Seal Opened (6:3, 4).** Then the Lamb opened the second seal, and the second living creature called out to John, "Come and see." With the deepest interest, not only John but the living creatures about the throne watched to see what each part of this book would reveal. This time they saw a red horse, and to

the rider was given a great sword. "And power was given to him . . . to take peace from the earth, and that they should kill one another."

5. The Meaning of the Second Seal. The time covered by the second seal is the same as that covered by the second church. "The mystery of iniquity" which Paul said was already at work even in his day was gaining power. Satan has organized his forces into what Jesus called "the synagogue of Satan." He begins to see that he has a long, hard battle before him if he is to wage successful warfare against the forces of Jesus. Satan's method is to kill with the sword—"to take peace from the earth." And he surely did this in the terrible persecutions that raged under pagan Rome during the second and third centuries. But the blood of the martyrs was like seed sown for an abundant harvest. The weapon that Jesus has given *His* followers is the "sharp sword with two edges," the word of God, which gives peace and hope and life even in times of war.

How to Study: Keep the diagram of the seven churches before you as you study this lesson. Notice that the first and second seals correspond in time to the first and second churches.

Be able to describe the symbols for each seal, and explain their meaning.

For Your Workbook: Fill out the first and second seals on your diagram of the seven seals. The blank for this diagram is a page in "Bible Workbook" for the eighth grade.

---

4. OPENING THE THIRD, FOURTH, AND FIFTH SEALS
Revelation 6: 5-11

"Thou art worthy to take the book, and to open the seals thereof." Rev. 5:9.

1. The Third Seal (6:5, 6). When the Lamb had opened the third seal, the third living creature called out, "Come and see." "And lo a black horse; and he that sat on him had a pair of balances in his hand." Then from among the four living creatures John heard a voice saying, "A measure of wheat for a penny, and three measures of barley for a penny; and see thou hurt not the oil and the wine."

2. The Black Horse. The white horse showed that Satan's influence over the church had hardly begun to be felt. The red horse showed that his cruel power was doing its terrible work. But black is as far as possible from the purity of white. It was during the third or Pergamos period of the church, that the papacy was fully formed, the Bible was almost lost sight of, and state and church became united, bringing in popularity, wealth, and pride.

3. The Man with the Balances. The man with the balances fitly represents that "man of sin" who took it upon himself to

weigh the deeds and motives of men. This symbol may also represent the uniting of religion and the civil power in one person. The emperor Constantine directed not only the affairs of the state but those of the church. But neither Satan nor any of his agents are allowed to touch "the oil" of God's grace or "the wine" of the inner spiritual life. These are in the keeping of Jesus, who alone can truly weigh the motives of our hearts.

Because a voice was heard saying, "A measure of wheat for a penny, and three measures of barley for a penny," this symbol doubtless also represents the ambition for worldly gain, which was manifest by the many unconverted ones who joined the church during this period because it was popular to do so.

4. The Fourth Seal and Its Meaning (6: 7, 8). When the Lamb opened the fourth seal, the fourth living creature said, "Come and see." And what a ghastly sight — a pale, sickly-looking horse, whose rider, Death, was followed close behind by the grave! And power was given to him "to kill with sword, and with hunger, and with death, and with the beasts of the earth." The period of time covered by the events of the fourth seal is the same as that covered by the events of the fourth church. The terrible work of the rider Death is easily recognized as the papal persecutions during the Dark Ages, when so many millions of Christians actually met death "with sword, and with hunger, . . . and with the beasts of the earth."

5. The Fifth Seal Opened (6:9-11). When the Lamb opened the fifth seal, it was not a war horse that John saw. The power of Satan to make war upon the church of God was at last checked. That wicked woman Jezebel no longer ruled. And it was the work of the courageous Luther and other reformers in God's hands that brought about these wonderful results. All honor to the "few names even in Sardis"! But what *did* John see? There, under the altar, he saw "them that were slain for the word of God, and for the testimony which they held." These were the victims who under the rule of the papacy had sacrificed their lives rather than dishonor and disobey God or give up their loyalty to His word.

As the blood of Abel cried to God from the ground, so these martyrs cried with a loud voice — so loud that we can hear them even yet. They cried, "How long, O Lord, holy and true, dost Thou not judge and avenge our blood on them that dwell on the earth?" And the answer came back "that they should rest yet for a little season, until their fellow servants also and their brethren, that should be killed as they were, should be fulfilled." Although the Reformation had begun, the work of persecution did not at once cease. Rome added hundreds of thousands to her already vast throng of victims. But the wicked work at last stopped, and the "little season" came to an end. Since that time all these martyrs have worn "white robes," in the praises that Christians have sung; and in "a little season" they with all others who may still be called to suffer for the word of God, will receive their final reward.

How to Study: As you study this lesson, keep the diagram of the seven churches before you, comparing the seals with the churches.

Be able to describe accurately the symbols of each seal, and explain their meaning.

For Your Workbook: Fill out the third, fourth, and fifth seals on your diagram of the seven seals.

5. THE SIXTH SEAL OPENED
1755 to the end
Lesson 1 — Topics 1-4; Rev. 6: 12, 13
Lesson 2 — Topics 5-7; Rev. 6: 14-17; 7: 1-8

"There shall be signs in the sun, and in the moon, and in the stars; and upon the earth distress of nations." Luke 21: 25.

1. The Sixth Seal Opened (6: 12, 13). The sixth seal covers about the same time as both the sixth and seventh churches. When the Lamb opened this seal, "lo, there was a great earthquake; and the sun became black as sackcloth of hair, and the moon became as blood; and the stars of heaven fell unto the earth, even as a fig tree casteth her untimely figs, when she is shaken of a mighty wind."

2. The Great Earthquake. The great earthquake of November 1, 1755, is the first event of the sixth seal. It is called the Lisbon earthquake, because it began at the city of Lisbon, Portugal, and here its destruction was the greatest, 90,000 people being destroyed and the entire city reduced to ruin. It extended over the most of Europe, Africa, and America, and in all these countries the shock was felt on the same day. Attempting to describe it, one writer says: "The terror of the people was beyond description. Nobody wept; it was beyond tears. They ran hither and thither, delirious with horror and astonishment, beating their faces and breasts, crying, 'The world's at an end! The world's at an end!'" Another writer says: "A great concourse of people had collected on the quay at the water front for safety, as a spot where they might be beyond the reach of falling ruins; but suddenly the quay sunk down with all the people on it, and not one of the dead bodies ever floated to the surface. . . . At a distance of eight leagues from Morocco, a village, with the inhabitants to the number of eight or ten thousand persons, together with all their cattle, was swallowed up. Soon after, the earth closed again over them."

Other earthquakes may have been as severe in certain places, but no other has ever been felt on this earth that was so severe and at the same time so extensive. The sensitive seismographs of

---
References Used: D. R. on lesson text; Amos 8: 9; Isa. 8: 16; 13: 10; Joel 2: 31; Eze. 32: 7, 8; Mark 13: 24; Matt. 24: 29; Acts 2: 20; Jer. 25: 32, 33; Eph. 4: 30; Heb. 8: 10.

to-day would probably have recorded it as universal. God used this great catastrophe to arouse the minds of people, and, by causing them to realize how uncertain is everything earthly, lead them to think of the future life, where there is no destruction.

The Lisbon earthquake, the first event of the sixth seal, occurred November 1, 1755.

3. The Darkening of the Sun. The darkening of the sun spoken of in this prophecy occurred May 19, 1780. The darkness of the following night was so dense that the moon was invisible until after midnight, and when it did appear it was as red as blood. Eight Bible writers mention this sign, four in the Old Testament and four in the New Testament. Amos tells us that it would be darkest at noon, and that this would be on a clear day. Isaiah says, "The sun shall be darkened in his going forth," that is, in the morning. Joel says the moon would be turned into blood. Ezekiel states that a cloud would cover the sun. History tells us of other dark days; but only the one of May 19, 1780, fully meets the description given in the Bible. Jesus Himself told us just *when* to look for this sign: *"in* those days, *after* that tribulation." He was talking about the 1260 days of papal persecution. Those days ended in 1798, but the tribulation, or persecution, ended about

1776. The dark day of 1780 was the only one "*in* those days, *after* that tribulation."

It is known that the darkness on this occasion extended over all the New England States, and it probably extended much farther, though its exact limits were never fully known. The darkness was not caused by an eclipse, for the moon was then at its full. Astronomers have never been able to give a satisfactory explanation of its cause. Thousands of good people were deeply impressed that the day of Judgment was soon to come. The wicked were terrified, for they too felt that the end of all things was near. No doubt the Spirit of God was working on all their hearts, calling them to study the meaning of these signs.

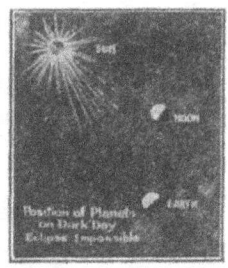

Position of the planets on the dark day of May 19, 1780

4. The Falling of the Stars. This sign occurred November 13, 1833. It was the most extensive and magnificent shower of shooting stars known. We are told that never did rain fall much thicker than the meteors fell toward the earth. For three hours the whole firmament over all North America was in fiery commotion. By many people the day of Judgment was believed to be waiting only for sunrise.

5. The Sealing of God's People (7:1-8). After these signs John saw "four angels standing on the four corners [or sections] of the earth, holding the four winds of the earth, that the wind should not blow on the earth, nor on the sea, nor on any tree." As we have learned in a previous lesson, winds in prophecy denote strife and war among nations. Why were these angels commanded to hold the winds of war? John looked again. Then he saw "another angel ascending from the east, having the seal of the living God: and he cried with a loud voice to the four angels, . . . saying, Hurt not the earth, neither the sea, nor the trees, till we have sealed the servants of our God in their foreheads. . . . And there were sealed an hundred and forty and four thousand."

More than once since these angels were commanded to hold the winds there have been sudden outbursts of war, "like a fitful gust breaking away from the imprisoned and struggling tempest;" and as often have these outbursts been suddenly and unexpectedly checked, that the sealing work might go forward.

6. The Seal of God (14:1). We have already learned that a seal on a legal document gives it authority,— that it corresponds to a signature; and that the seal of God is that part of His law which contains His name, or signature. When a little later John saw this company of 144,000, he said they had the "Father's *name* written in their foreheads." The only part of God's law that contains the name of the true God, the Creator, is the fourth commandment.

The most extensive and magnificent shower of shooting stars known, occurred November 13, 1833

Without this commandment, the heathen has as much right to say that the God mentioned in the other commandments is *his* god as we have to say that He is *our* God. He can obey all the rest of God's law and still worship the sun, the Nile, the sacred bull, or any other creature. But the fourth commandment defines the true God as the Creator, the only One worthy of worship. This is why God calls the Sabbath His sign or signature, His seal or mark. The observance of the Sabbath is a mark that distinguishes and distinctly separates the worshipers of the true God from all others.

During the centuries when Satan ruled the world through "that man of sin," the seal of authority of God's law was cunningly disposed of, and thousands of sincere Christians have never understood about this evil work. In their hearts they have thought they kept God's law, and God no doubt accepts their sincerity. But we have reached the time when Satan's work is to be exposed, and God's law is to be honored and magnified by His people. When God showed Isaiah these last days, He said, "Seal the law among My disciples." As the blood on the doorposts protected Israel that night when the destroying angel passed over the land of Egypt, so before the awful winds of trouble are allowed to blow upon the earth God will seal His own, that they may be protected from the last destructive storm.

But to have this seal in truth means more than laying aside our work and going to church on the seventh day of the week. It means accepting Jesus as our personal Saviour from sin — from any transgression of God's pure and holy law. It means grieving not "the Holy Spirit of God, whereby ye are *sealed* unto the day of redemption." The Holy Spirit alone can place God's seal upon us. He says, "I will put My laws into their mind, and write them in their hearts."

7. **"The Heaven Departed as a Scroll"** (6:14-17). After God's people were all sealed, the angels loosed the winds, and John saw everything in earth and heaven in commotion. He saw the heavens rolled together as a scroll, and "every mountain and island . . . moved out of their places. And the kings of the earth, and the great men, and the rich men, and the chief captains, and the mighty men, and every bondman, and every freeman, hid themselves in the dens and in the rocks of the mountains." All classes of people from the highest to the lowest joined in one despairing cry, calling to the mountains and rocks: "Fall on us, and hide us from the face of Him that sitteth on the throne, and from the wrath of the Lamb: for the great day of His wrath is come; and who shall be able to stand?"

How to Study: Lesson 1. Name the three signs of Christ's coming given in this prophecy, and tell the exact date when each was fulfilled. Be able to tell how these events fulfilled the prophecy in every particular.

Lesson 2. What part of the sixth seal is still future? Be able to explain that the Sabbath is God's seal. Who applies the seal of God to His people? Why is this sealing work a special characteristic of the *last* days? What text shows that winds in prophecy represent war?

Map Work: Locate Lisbon and Morocco. Show also the extent of country affected by each of the signs.

Dictionary Work: Seismograph.

27 — B. L., Eighth Grade

Memory Work: Revelation 6: 12-17 is the memory work for the second star on your memory certificate. The star is granted only when you can recite the entire selection perfectly and without any help.

For Your Workbook: Fill out the sixth seal on your diagram.

For Class Discussion: Notice that in the sealing work, Dan, the backbiter (Gen. 49: 17), is left out. Who is "that old serpent," "the accuser of our brethren"? Rev. 12: 9, 10. Notice also that Joseph has a double portion in that which was given to him and his eldest son, Manasseh.

---

6. THE SEVENTH SEAL OPENED
Rev. 8:1; 7:9-17

"And when He had opened the seventh seal, there was silence in heaven about the space of half an hour." Rev. 8:1.

1. "Silence in Heaven" (8:1). When the sixth seal is past, the work of sealing God's people is finished. Then the angel of mercy proclaims, "It is done," and speeds away to heaven. This is the beginning of the "time of trouble, such as never was since there was a nation." As that time draws to a close, those who have refused to be sealed are wild with anguish and despair. They know that they are lost.

When the Lamb breaks the seventh and last seal of the book, John's attention is turned away from the commotion and trouble on earth to heaven. There all is quiet. Not a voice is heard. Not an angel is to be seen. The Lamb is not there. The Father, too, has disappeared. Silence prevails. Where have they all gone? The wicked ones on earth know. In bitterness of soul, they are calling for the mountains and rocks to fall on them and hide them "from the face of Him that sitteth on the throne, and from the wrath of the Lamb." Jesus "in His glory" and *"in the glory of His Father" has gone to rescue His people from the destruction that threatens them on the earth — He has gone, *"and all the holy angels with Him." The silence in heaven lasts "about the space of half an hour," which in literal time would be about seven days.

2. On the Sea of Glass (15:2; 7:9, 13, 14). Again John looks into heaven. It is not deserted now. There, on the sea of glass, at

---

References Used: E. W., p. 288; G. C., pp. 646-650; Matt. 16: 27; 25: 31, 34; Dan. 12: 1; Rev. 1: 6; 5: 10; 6: 16; 15: 2.

the east side of the city, "before the throne," stand the 144,000, "arrayed in white robes." They are arranged in a hollow square, arranged no doubt just as the twelve tribes in the camp of Israel were arranged about the earthly sanctuary. Jesus stands in the center of this square, His majestic form much taller than the saints or even the angels, so that everyone in the square can see Him. How beautiful He looks as He gazes upon His redeemed family, His face beaming with love! Then angels bring from the city many glorious crowns, a crown for everyone in the square, with his "new name" engraved on it. With His own hand Jesus places the crowns upon the heads of His children. He knows just which crown to place on each head. The angels also bring golden harps,

There is silence in heaven, for all the holy angels are with Christ on His way to this earth.

and Jesus presents to each one a harp and a palm of victory. "Then, as the commanding angels strike the note, every hand sweeps the harp strings with skillful touch," and every voice bursts forth in a triumphant song of grateful praise. Can you imagine the music— 144,000 harps sending forth strains of heavenly harmony, and a chorus of 144,000 voices without one note of harshness or discord?

At first John did not know who these were or whence they had come. But one of the elders explained, saying, "These are they which came out of great tribulation, and have washed their robes, and made them white in the blood of the Lamb." John had seen this company on earth as they were receiving the seal of God. He had seen them passing through the time of trouble. But now they are so changed in their glorified state, and are amid such different surroundings, that for a time he did not recognize them.

Surrounding the 144,000 stand a "great multitude, which no man could number, of all nations, and kindreds, and people, and tongues, . . . clothed with white robes, and palms in their hands." And beyond these are ten thousand times ten thousand, and thousands of thousands of angels.

3. The Triumphal March to the Throne. Next begins the triumphal march into the holy city, in the same order doubtless as the camp of Israel were commanded to march from place to place. Jesus opens wide the pearly gates; they swing back on their glittering hinges, and the redeemed host with their brilliant crowns, their shining harps, and their waving palm branches, march to the throne of God. As they march in, Jesus with a voice richer than any music, says, "Come, ye blessed of My Father, inherit the kingdom prepared for you from the foundation of the world." When they reach the throne, Jesus presents them to the Father, saying, "Here am I, and the children whom Thou hast given Me."

4. The Two Adams Meet. As Jesus turns to welcome His family to the beautiful city, a shout of joy rings out upon the air. "The two Adams are about to meet. The Son of God is standing with outstretched arms to receive the father of our race. . . . As Adam discerns the prints of the cruel nails, he . . . casts himself at His feet. . . . Tenderly the Saviour lifts him up, and bids him look once more upon the Eden home from which he has so long been exiled. . . .

"Transported with joy, he beholds . . . the very trees whose fruit he himself had gathered in the days of his innocence and joy. He sees the vines that his own hands have trained, the very flowers that he once loved to care for. . . . The Saviour leads him to the tree of life, and plucks the glorious fruit, and bids him eat. He looks about him, and beholds a multitude of his family redeemed, standing in the Paradise of God. Then he casts his glittering crown at the feet of Jesus, and, falling upon His breast, embraces the Redeemer. . . . This reunion is witnessed by the angels who wept at the fall of Adam." Now with joy they behold the work of redemption finished.

5. The Mighty Song of Victory (14: 3; 7: 9-12). At first Adam can hardly grasp the truth that what he sees is all a reality; but as it dawns upon his mind, he touches his golden harp, and begins the song of triumph. Then the 144,000 take up the strain. "And they sung as it were a new song before the throne, . . . and no man could learn that song but the hundred and forty and four thousand." It is the song of their experience, and is called the song of Moses and the Lamb.

After that the whole family of Adam, "a great multitude, which no man could number, of all nations, and kindreds, and people, and tongues," join in the chorus with the 144,000, "with a loud voice, saying, Salvation to our God which sitteth upon the throne, and unto the Lamb." Last of all the angels, who stand "round about the throne, and about the elders and the four living creatures," with joy unspeakable, fall "before the throne on their faces," and worship God. Then they, too, join in the closing strains of that wonderful song of sevenfold praise, saying, "Amen. Blessing, and glory, and wisdom, and thanksgiving, and honor, and power, and might, be unto our God forever and ever. Amen."

6. Special Reward of the 144,000 (7:14-17; 14:4). Because of their special experience in receiving the seal of God, and because of their special tribulation on this account, the 144,000 have a special reward. "Therefore," said the elder, "are they before the throne of God, and serve Him day and night in His temple: and He that sitteth on the throne shall dwell among them." Jesus has made them "kings and priests unto God and His Father." "These are they which follow the Lamb whithersoever He goeth." From planet to planet, from world to world, wherever Jesus goes, this special company follow Him. "They shall hunger no more [as they did in the time of trouble on earth], neither thirst any more; neither shall the sun light on them, nor any heat. For the Lamb which is in the midst of the throne shall feed them, and shall lead them unto living fountains of waters: and God shall wipe away all tears from their eyes."

How to Study: Be able to show from the Bible the cause of the silence in heaven; the two starred references in topic 1 tell. Figure out and explain the statement that "about half an hour" of prophetic time represents about seven days of literal time. What text shows that one day represents one year? From your diagram of the camp of Israel locate the 144,000 by tribes. What tribes are omitted? What ones take their places?

Compare Revelation 5:12 and 7:12. How many parts are there to each song? In connection with this lesson, you will enjoy reading "Early Writings," pages 15-20, 285-289; also "Great Controversy," pages 648-650.

Chapters to Remember: Revelation 6—the first six seals opened; Revelation 7—God's people sealed and in heaven. What four chapters tell about the book sealed with seven seals? One more verse completes the description: which verse is this?

For Your Workbook: Fill out the seventh seal in your diagram.

REVIEW OF THE SEVEN SEALS
Rev. 4, 5, 6, 7, 8:1

Test Questions: Hand in written answers to the starred questions. You may use your Bible for this if you desire, but not your Bible lesson book.

*1. What chapters in Revelation tell about the seven seals?
2. Describe the scene in heaven which John saw. How does this scene correspond to "the pattern" which God gave? Point out the comparison in detail.
*3. Describe the book with seven seals. Who held it? Who were unable to break the seals? Who was worthy? Why?
*4. What two texts in the Bible show that some were raised and taken to heaven by Christ when He ascended? Of what offering in the earthly sanctuary are they the antitype? What are these now doing in heaven?
5. Compare the seals and the churches on the following points: entire time covered, divisions of time, and purpose of each.
*6. Which of the seals are given in symbols? What are these symbols? Which seals are literal?
7. Describe and explain the symbols for the first five seals.
*8. What events take place during the sixth seal? Name the signs and tell their dates.
9. Show from the Bible that the Sabbath is God's seal.
*10. What text shows that winds in prophecy represent war? that a day represents a year?
11. Show from two texts in the Bible what causes the silence in heaven under the seventh seal.
12. Describe the song that is sung after the redeemed reach heaven. What are its different parts?

Verse-Finding Drill: Find the chapter and verse in Revelation that tells each of the following facts. After finding them in order, try skipping about.
1. There is a rainbow about God's throne.
2. There are twenty-four thrones round about God's throne.
3. On these thrones twenty-four elders are seated.
4. There is a "sea of glass" in heaven.
5. The Lion of the tribe of Judah prevailed to open the book.
6. The Lamb had seven horns and seven eyes.
7. The living creatures and the elders have harps.
8. Incense in golden vials represents the prayers of saints.
9. There are ten thousand times ten thousand and thousands of thousands of angels.

10. The first seal was represented by a white horse.
11. The second seal was represented by a red horse.
12. The third seal was represented by a black horse.
13. The fourth seal was represented by a pale horse.
14. White robes were given to the martyrs.
15. A great earthquake was the first event of the sixth seal.
16. The sun became black as sackcloth of hair.
17. The stars of heaven fell to the earth.
18. Twelve thousand were sealed from each of the twelve tribes.
19. After God's people are sealed the heavens depart as a scroll.
20. The wicked cry for the mountains to fall on them.
21. The 144,000 serve God in His temple.
22. The 144,000 follow the Lamb wherever He goes.

Memory Drill: Recite from memory Revelation 6: 12-17.

Chapter Drill: See how quickly you can turn to the chapter or chapters that tell about:

1. The throne of God
2. The Philadelphia church
3. The Ephesus church
4. The book with seven seals
5. The seventh seal
6. The Thyatira church
7. The Laodicea church
8. The description of Christ
9. The exile of John
10. The Smyrna church
11. The Sardis church
12. The opening of the sixth seal
13. Satan's seat
14. The Pergamos church
15. The destruction of the wicked
16. The sealing of the righteous
17. The synagogue of Satan
18. The fourth seal
19. Antipas
20. The redeemed in heaven

Give in order the main subject of each of the first seven chapters of Revelation.

OUTLINE OF CHAPTER IX

Symbols — The Seven Trumpets
Time — The Christian Era
Result — The Nations of Earth Destroyed

Topics —   Revelation

Rome Weighed in the Balances 8
    First four trumpets

The Twin of the Papacy ....⎫
    Fifth trumpet, or first woe   ⎬ 9

The Sixth Trumpet, or Second Woe ....⎭

God's Message in "the Little Book" 10

The Mystery of God Finished 11
    Seventh trumpet, or third woe

Review

CHAPTER IX

Satan's Opposition Through the Nations of Earth

1. ROME WEIGHED IN THE BALANCES
The First Four Trumpets — Rev. 8:2-13

"And whereas thou sawest the feet and toes, part of potters' clay, and part of iron, the kingdom shall be divided." Dan. 2:41.

1. John's First Three Visions Compared. John's first vision, the seven churches, shows God's plan for His true church. It was given for the special purpose of encouraging the church of God to be faithful to the end through all the experiences it would have to meet. In every one of its seven divisions, God holds out the promise "to him that overcometh." His second vision, the seven seals, shows the efforts of the apostate church, "the synagogue of Satan," to destroy the true church and defeat God's plan. At the end of this vision the wicked are seen calling for the rocks and mountains to fall on them and destroy them. The third vision is the seven trumpets. This prophecy, like the first two, extends over the Christian era. A trumpet is a symbol of war. The seven trumpets show how Satan, through war among the nations of earth, attempts to cripple God's work and defeat His plan. But God's unseen hand rules even among the nations, bringing victory to His plan when to human eyes defeat seems certain.

2. An Assurance of Victory (8:3, 4, 5). As an assurance of final victory, before John is shown the work of the seven angels with the trumpets, "another angel came and stood at the altar, having a golden censer; and there was given unto him much incense, that he should offer it with the prayers of all saints upon the golden altar which was before the throne. And the smoke of the incense, which came with the prayers of the saints, ascended up before God out of the angel's hand." Thus, through this vision

---

Reference Used: D. R. on the lesson text.

given to John, we are assured that, no matter what troubles come among the nations, God will not forget His people, but He will hear their prayers even in the midst of war. At last "the angel took the censer, and filled it with fire of the altar, and cast it into the earth." When this is done, the work of our heavenly High Priest will be finished. The last prayer of forgiveness will have been answered. The end of all things will be at hand. After that

"I saw the seven angels which stood before God; and to them were given seven trumpets."

"there were voices, and thunderings, and lightnings, and an earthquake,"—events that occur with the second coming of Jesus.

3. The Roman Nation. When the vision of the seven angels with seven trumpets was given to John, Rome was the nation that ruled the world. This kingdom had unusual opportunities to know of God's plan for man. Even Jesus Himself spent His whole life on earth as one of her subjects, offering freely the plan of salvation. But she rejected the light. God bore long with her, but at last the time came when, because of her failure to accomplish His purpose, she, like Babylon of old, was weighed in the balance and found wanting. Then her kingdom was divided and given to others.

The first four of these war trumpets point out the important steps that finally resulted in the breaking up of the Roman Empire into ten parts, corresponding to the feet and toes of the great image which God showed to Nebuchadnezzar. As you have already learned, this was accomplished in 476 A. D. The whole story is told in just six verses in the Bible,— Revelation 8: 7 to 12.

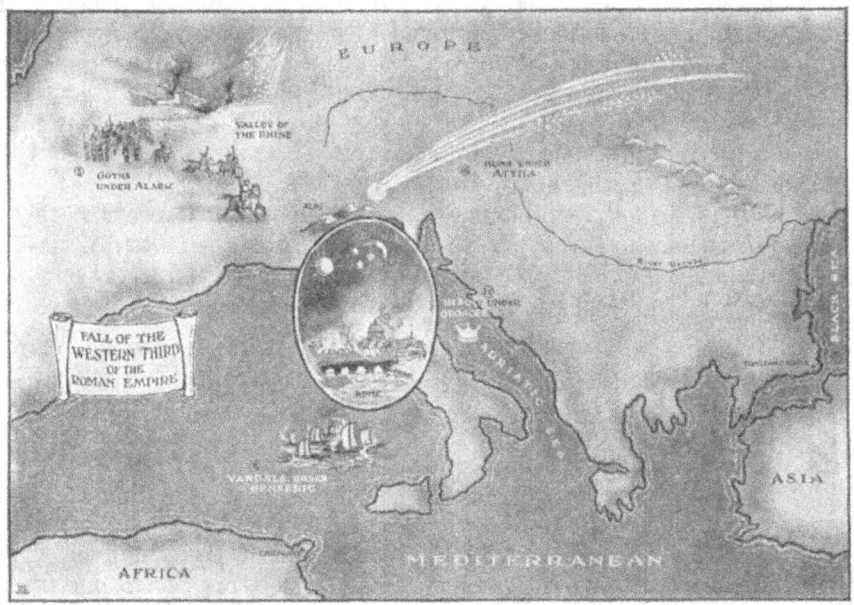

The first four trumpets

The last three trumpets are given much more fully; for they occupy three whole chapters,— Revelation 9, 10, and 11.

4. The First Trumpet (8:7). "The first angel sounded, and there followed hail and fire mingled with blood, and they were cast upon the earth: and the third part of trees was burnt up, and all green grass was burnt up."

In this one sentence God sums up a long series of terrible wars. In the country lying north of the Roman Empire there lived vast tribes of barbarians. The first of these to invade the territory of

Rome was a tribe of bold warriors called Goths. Under their leader Alaric, the historian Gibbon says: "The Gothic nation was in arms at the first sound of the trumpet, and in the uncommon severity of the winter, they rolled their ponderous wagons over the broad and icy back of the river [the Danube]. . . . The pastures of Gaul [now called France], in which flocks and herds grazed, and the banks of the Rhine, which were covered with elegant houses and well-cultivated farms, formed a scene of peace and plenty, which was suddenly changed into a desert . . . of smoking ruins." Alaric led his army even to the city of Rome, burning many of its public and private buildings, and filling its streets with dead bodies. The pride of Rome was humbled by the "hail and fire mingled with blood," which Alaric and his Goths from the frozen regions of the north "cast upon the earth."

The "third part" which is frequently mentioned refers here to the western of the three parts into which Constantine at his death divided the Roman Empire in order to give each of his three sons a throne. Rome was the capital of this division.

5. The Second Trumpet (8:8, 9). "And the second angel sounded, and as it were a great mountain burning with fire was cast into the sea: and the third part of the sea became blood; and the third part of the creatures which were in the sea, and had life, died; and the third part of the ships were destroyed."

This is a fitting description of the invasion of the Roman Empire by a tribe called Vandals, under the leadership of the terrible Genseric. The Vandals had a large navy, and they invaded first Africa and afterward Italy. In order to meet this foe, Rome built three hundred large ships and many smaller ones. But before the fleet was used, Genseric unexpectedly attacked it and many of the ships were sunk or burned. Then Rome fitted out another fleet of more than a thousand ships, which she manned with one hundred thousand men. To meet these Genseric manned his largest ships of war with his bravest warriors, and they towed after them many large barks filled with combustible materials. In the darkness of the night these destructive fire ships were forced against the Roman fleet. The wind quickly carried the flames from one ship to another until the entire fleet was either burned or captured. The scene was "as it were a great mountain burning with fire . . . cast into the sea."

6. The Third Trumpet (8:10, 11). "And the third angel sounded, and there fell a great star from heaven, burning as it were a lamp, and it fell upon the third part of the rivers, and upon the fountains of waters; and the name of the star is called wormwood: and the third part of the waters became wormwood; and many men died of the waters, because they were made bitter."

These verses describe the third invasion of Rome, by a tribe called Huns, under their leader Attila. This brilliant warrior like a blazing star fell upon the empire with the rapidity of a flashing meteor. History tells us that the whole breadth of Europe, extending from the Black Sea to the Adriatic, was at once invaded, and occupied, and desolated, by the myriads of barbarians whom Attila led into the field. The most important operations of this warrior were in the region of the Alps, "the fountains of waters." To proud Rome this star was indeed "wormwood," so bitter were the results of his work. Soon afterward Attila died, and this brilliant meteor disappeared as suddenly as he had come.

7. The Fourth Trumpet (8:12). "And the fourth angel sounded, and the third part of the sun was smitten, and the third part of the moon, and the third part of the stars; so as the third part of them was darkened, and the day shone not for a third part of it, and the night likewise."

The last of the four great invasions which resulted in the breaking up of the Roman Empire into ten divisions was headed by a warrior named Odoacer, king of a tribe called the Heruli. By him the last emperor of Rome was dethroned,— the "sun" of the empire "was smitten" and the power and glory of Rome was gone. The other rulers of the government gradually disappeared. As the poet says:

"She saw her glories star by star expire."

Thus ended the last of the four world empires that were shown to Daniel; and as iron will not mix with miry clay, so the fragments of this great empire will never again be united. This event and the year 476 mark the end of what is called *ancient history*.

How to Study: Keep a map before you as you study, and locate the different places mentioned, as you go along. On the map, locate the western third of the old Roman Empire.

Get a clear picture in your mind of the symbols used to illustrate each of the first four trumpets. Then be able to tell the following about each: (1) Name of invading tribe; (2) Name of leader; (3) How the symbols fittingly represent the invasion.

Why did Rome finally fall? When?

In what respects are the first three visions of John alike? How do they differ? Notice in your Bible in just what chapters each of these three visions is recorded. What relation has each to God's great plan?

For Your Workbook: Begin a diagram of the seven trumpets, locating the first four. The blank outline for this diagram is a page in "Bible Workbook" for the eighth grade.

Pronounce: Goths; Al'a-ric; Van'dals; Gen'se-ric; Huns; At'ti-la; Her'u-li; O-do-a'cer.

2. THE TWIN OF THE PAPACY
Fifth Trumpet, or First Woe — Rev. 9:1-12

"Woe, woe, woe, to the inhabiters of the earth by reason of the other voices of the trumpet of the three angels, which are yet to sound!" Rev. 8:13.

1. The Three Woe Trumpets. The scenes of war and bloodshed that occurred under the first four trumpets, when the barbarian tribes from the northern part of Europe invaded the western third of the Roman Empire and finally crushed it, were terrible enough. But the last three trumpets were so much more terrible that they are called woes. The fifth trumpet is called the first woe; the sixth trumpet is called the second woe; and the seventh trumpet, the third woe. The fifth trumpet describes the troubles that came especially upon the eastern third of the old Roman Empire.

2. Satan's Scheme Through Mohammedanism. After the Roman Empire had ceased to be a world kingdom, and the tribes from the north had taken possession of its western third, another race of people came to the front. These were the Arabs, who lived in the desert peninsula of Arabia. Up to this time the Arabs had not exerted any influence over civilized nations. In scattered tribes they had roamed over the desert, unnoticed by the rest of the world. But, not very long after the pope gained his supremacy in Rome, there appeared a man in Mecca, a town in Arabia, who declared himself to be the prophet of God. This man's name was Mohammed. Mohammed professed to believe in one God, but he rejected the Bible as the word of God and Christ as the Saviour of man. He also re-

---

References Used: D. R. on lesson text; "Seer," p. 168.

jected the Sabbath of the Creator, and put in its place Friday, the sixth day of the week. So, while in the western part of the world Satan, through the papacy, was leading men away from Christ, away from the Bible, and away from the law of God, in the rest of the world he was doing the same thing, only in a somewhat different way, through Mohammedanism. For this reason, Mohammedanism

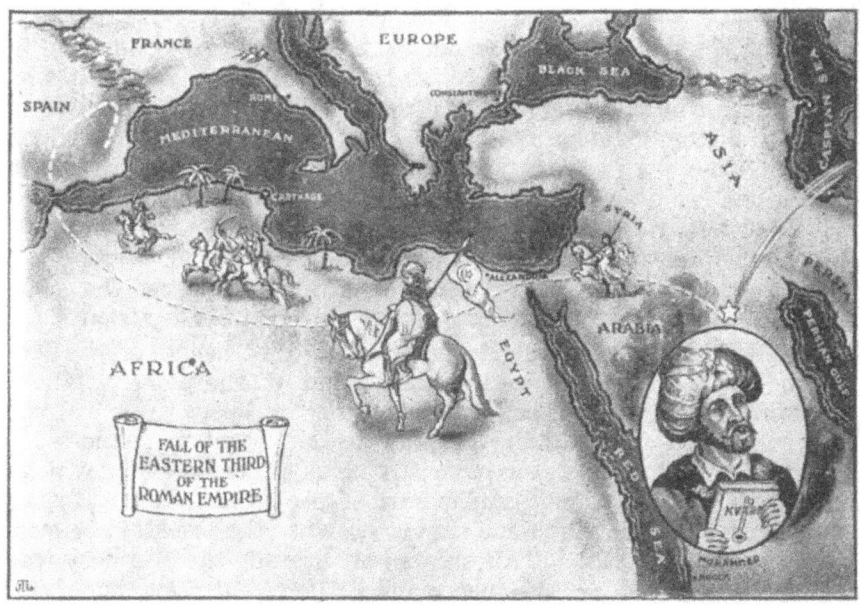

The fifth trumpet

might very fittingly be called Satan's duplicate of the papacy, or the twin of the papacy.

3. Conquests of Mohammedanism (9:1). As Attila was the "star" of the third trumpet, so Mohammed was the "star" of the fifth trumpet. He gradually gained followers, and wherever they went they compelled men to accept the religion of Mohammed or suffer death. At last, Mohammedanism united the scattered tribes of the desert, and they went forth to conquer the world. To those who fell in battle was given the sure promise of a home in Paradise.

4. **Mohammedan Warriors (9:7, 8).** The prophecy speaks of these tribes as having "horses prepared unto battle." Of no place in the world could this be more fitting than of Arabia, which is the home of the horse. The "crowns like gold" which the warriors wore refer evidently to the yellow turbans of the Mohammedans. They also wore long hair, and the prophecy describes them as having "hair as the hair of women." This description makes it very plain that the prophecy here refers to these Arabian warriors.

5. **Effects of Mohammedanism (9:2, 3).** In their conquests, in addition to all the woes of war was the woe of a religion that was without salvation. The gospel of Jesus is called a light from heaven, but the religion of Mohammed is compared to "the smoke of a great furnace," the smoke from "the bottomless pit." Surely no better description could be given of the darkening, suffocating influence of this desolating religion on the lives of men. For hundreds of years these tribes had no general government or king, but in separate bands like "locusts," as the prophecy says, they overspread the countries, and stung men as "a scorpion, when he striketh a man."

6. **Their Hatred for the Papacy (9:4).** The hearts of the Mohammedans were set to destroy the leaders of the papacy, "those men which have not the seal of God in their foreheads." One of the first commands given to the soldiers as they went to battle was: "Destroy no palm trees, nor burn any fields of corn. Cut down no fruit trees. . . . You will find a sort of people that belong to the synagogue of Satan, who have shaven crowns [the priests]; be sure you cleave their skulls." This shows how literally the prophecy was fulfilled which said, "It was commanded them that they should not hurt the grass of the earth, neither any green thing, neither any tree; but only those men which have not the seal of God in their foreheads."

7. **Plan to Capture Rome.** It was the intention of the Mohammedans to conquer all the countries bordering on the Mediterranean, and subjugate the Roman Empire. In a few years Persia, Syria, Egypt, northern Africa, and Spain had surrendered to these merciless warriors, who everywhere compelled the conquered to worship Mohammed, pay tribute, or die. But when they tried to enter France they were driven back into Spain. And so, while they failed to capture Rome, they did bring under their power the whole eastern third of the old Roman Empire.

8. **The Ottoman Empire Founded (9:11).** At last, a great Mohammedan nation was organized, which was called the Ottoman Empire, from its founder, Othman. This is only another name for the Turkish Empire. It is said that this nation came into existence at the expense of fifty thousand cities and towns, and five million lives. No wonder that the prophecy calls the king of such a power "Apollyon," which means *destroyer.*

It was Othman's ambition to gain possession of the middle third of the world and make Constantinople his capital; and we are told that he promised to forgive the sins of the first army that attacked the city. But Othman lived and fought and died, yet he failed to take Constantinople.

How to Study: Turn to your Bible and find where the woe trumpets are described. Notice just which verses tell about the fifth trumpet.
In what ways were Mohammedanism and the papacy alike? How did they differ? What was Satan trying to accomplish through both?
Give the interpretation of these prophetic symbols: smoke of a great furnace; locusts; scorpions; crowns of gold. What command was given to the soldiers as they went to battle? How was this a fulfillment of prophecy? What made the fifth trumpet more terrible than the first four?

Map Work: Locate the country that was swept over by the Mohammedans.

Workbook: Continue the diagram of the seven-trumpets.

---

3. THE SIXTH TRUMPET, OR SECOND WOE
Rev. 9:13 to 11:14

"The word of our God shall stand forever." Isa. 40:8.

1. **Extent of the Sixth Trumpet.** The description of the sixth trumpet begins with Revelation 9:13 and ends with Revelation 11:14. Read these two verses in your Bible. It begins with the downfall of the middle third of the old Roman Empire and reaches to the downfall of the world. This prophecy contains three main divisions: *first,* the experience of the Turkish Empire, beginning with the capture of Constantinople from the Romans, described in chapter 9:13-21; *second,* the war of France against God's people

---

References Used: G. C., pp. 268-273, 276, 287.

and His word, described in chapter 11:2-13; *third,* a message to prepare the world for the coming Redeemer, described in chapter 10. The purpose of this prophecy is to show how, in spite of Satan's strongest efforts to destroy God's word and His people from the face of the earth, "the word of our God shall stand forever."

2. Capture of Constantinople (9:17, 18). Though Othman was dead, the ambition of the Turks to capture Constantinople still lived.

The sixth trumpet

In this vision John was shown a great army on horses. The men who sat on the horses had "breastplates of fire, and of jacinth, and brimstone." This refers doubtless to the principal colors that were used in the dress of the Turkish warriors, fire standing for red, jacinth for blue, and brimstone for yellow. "And the heads of the horses were as the heads of lions,"— a very striking description of the courageous, kingly-looking Arabian horses. "And out of their mouths issued fire and smoke and brimstone." Gunpowder and firearms were first used in the siege of Constantinople. As the Turks, seated on their war horses, discharged their firearms, it appeared to John, looking on at a distance, that the fire and smoke and brimstone came out of the horses' mouths. In this siege cannon also were used for the first time. For more than a thousand years, since the time of Constantine the Great, this city had suffered little from those who attacked it; but now it was captured and the Turks took possession. This was the last of the Constantines.

3. The Papacy's Opportunity to Repent (9:20, 21). The capture of Constantinople is one of the most important events in history. It occurred in the year 1453, and marks the fall of the middle third of the old Roman Empire. By this event the extension of the papacy toward the east was checked, as it had already been checked in the west and the south. God would have used the scourge of these "locusts" and "scorpions" to help the papacy to see the utter folly in false worship,— the worship of "devils, and idols of gold, and silver, and brass, and stone, and of wood: which neither can see, nor hear, nor walk." But they learned no lesson from it. "Neither repented they of their murders, nor of their sorceries, nor of their fornication, nor of their thefts."

4. God's "Two Witnesses" in Sackcloth (11:2, 3). God gave the papal nations "forty and two months," or "a thousand two hundred and threescore days," in which to repent; but during all this time these "gentiles," as they are here called, instead of repenting, continued to "tread underfoot" "the holy city." At no other time in the history of the world has there been such fierce and long continued war against the Bible. Almost the whole world was engaged in this warfare. During this time God's "two witnesses"— the Old and New Testaments — were "clothed in sackcloth." Sackcloth was used in ancient times as an emblem of mourning. Why was the Bible dressed in mourning? Because it was hidden from the people and they were forbidden to read it. Also because God's law had been changed, and the people taught to disobey His commandments, neither was Jesus recognized as the only One who can forgive sin. No wonder God's word, universally disgraced like this, was dressed in mourning.

5. Our Lord "Crucified" (11:8). On one occasion during this time a plot was laid in France to massacre all the Protestants in the country. The signal was given at midnight from the tower of the royal palace in Paris. People sleeping quietly in their homes were dragged forth to death. Anyone who dared to show the least respect for God's word or who was even suspected of being a Protestant was doomed to certain death. The massacre lasted for several weeks, and thousands of aged men, defenseless women, and innocent children were slain. In history this is called the massacre of St. Bartholomew, and it is estimated that seventy thousand were murdered. The prophecy refers to this in these words: "the great city . . . where also our Lord was crucified." Jesus was slain in the person of His followers.

When the news of the massacre reached Rome, the pope's joy was unbounded. Guns gave forth a joyous salute; the bells sounded from every tower; bonfires blazed; and the pope with all his priests formed a magnificent procession to the church, where a hymn of praise was chanted. Eager to show his gratitude to the French king, the pope sent him "the golden rose." This is an ornament of gold beautifully wrought and set with precious gems. Once a year it is blessed by the pope, and then sent as a mark of special favor to some distinguished individual or organization, if some one is considered worthy of such honor. The ceremonies connected with its presentation are intended to represent Christ or the Christian graces. The rose is not always a new and different one; the old one is used until it has been given away.

6. God's Word Witnessing for Him (11:3). Still, though it was "clothed in sackcloth," though warred upon from every quarter, God gave His word power to witness for Him. "I will give power unto My two witnesses," said Jesus, "and they shall prophesy a thousand two hundred and threescore days." During all this long time of mourning, the word of God was loved and obeyed and taught by a few faithful followers of Jesus, a few faithful witnesses for God.

7. The "Two Witnesses" Killed (11:7-10). "And when they shall have finished their testimony [the time when they were "in sackcloth"], the beast . . . shall make war against them, and shall overcome them, and kill them. And their dead bodies shall lie in the street of the great city, which spiritually is called Sodom and Egypt." These words describe perhaps the most terrible experience that any nation on earth has ever passed through. It occurred in the closing part of the 1260-year period, just when these "two witnesses" were finishing their testimony in sackcloth. France was the nation which at this time made open war against the Bible, God's "two witnesses," and overcame them and killed them.

How did she do this? In the French Assembly, that which corresponds to our Congress, a decree was passed forbidding the Bible. This occurred during the time which history calls the French Revolution. After this decree was passed the Bibles were gathered and publicly burned. The Sabbath was set aside, and every tenth day substituted for mirth and wickedness. Baptism and the Lord's Supper were abolished. The very existence of God was denied, and all worship of God forbidden. By legal act the nation declared that "the Goddess of Reason" was the only one worthy of their worship. This "goddess" was a wicked woman who, held aloft on a magnificent throne, was paraded through the streets of Paris to the cathedral to be worshiped in the place of the Deity. France is the only nation in the world that by law has thus openly rejected God. During this time, the streets of Paris literally flowed with the blood of men and women who suffered death.

8. They Ascended to Heaven (11:9, 11-14). The results to the nation in crime and sorrow and want were so terrible that history calls this the Reign of Terror. The prophecy said that it would continue for "three days and an half." Just three and one half years after the decree was issued abolishing the Bible, another decree was passed permitting it. Then "the spirit of life from God entered into them. . . . And they ascended up to heaven in a cloud." This tells how greatly the Bible was exalted after this awful experience in France.

In 1804, only about seven years after the Bible was again tolerated in France, the British and Foreign Bible Society was organized. This was soon followed by other similar societies both in Europe and in America. And from that day to the present, millions of copies of the Bible have been printed in almost every language and scattered throughout the world, even into its darkest corners. And still this good work goes forward. To and fro throughout the earth God's word is being carried by faithful missionaries. Greater and greater light shines upon the truths it contains. More and more carefully and prayerfully are God's true people studying it. Never was there a time when it could more truly be said of these two witnesses, "They ascended up to heaven in a cloud."

"The second woe is past; and, behold, the third woe cometh quickly."

How to Study: Be able to answer these questions: When and by what nation was Constantinople taken? From what nation was it taken? What nation made open war against the Bible? When? How does the prophecy describe the Turkish warriors? How is the use of gunpowder referred to?

Give the meaning of these symbols: God's "two witnesses;" "clothed in sackcloth;" "forty and two months;" the two witnesses "killed;" they "ascended up to heaven;" "three days and an half." What text shows that a day in prophecy represents a year?

Workbook: Continue the diagram of the seven trumpets. On outline map No. 5 indicate the western third, the eastern third, and the middle third of the old Roman Empire, with the capital of each.

---

4. GOD'S MESSAGE IN "THE LITTLE BOOK"
Revelation 10; About 1833-1844

"And I saw another mighty Angel, . . . and He had in His hand a little book open." Rev. 10:1, 2.

1. The Time of the Message. The 1260 years were now past. "The time of the end" had come. God's word was free from the power of the apostate church and from wicked nations. Copies of it could be found in all parts of the world, even in the homes of the most lowly. The time was rapidly approaching when the 2300 days of Daniel's prophecy would end. Then the Judgment would begin. God desired that all the world should know about this prophecy in His word. The tenth chapter of Revelation tells how He called attention to it.

2. The Messenger (10:1). The One who brought this message is described as a "mighty Angel come down from heaven, clothed with a cloud: and a rainbow was upon His head, and His face was as it were the sun, and His feet as pillars of fire: and He had in His hand a little book open." The description given of this mighty Angel corresponds to the description given of Christ in the first chapter of Revelation, His glory clothed with a cloud, as it was when He led Israel out of Egypt.

3. The Book Open. "The little book" in His hand is evidently the book of Daniel, which contained the prophecy of the 2300 days. When Daniel wrote this book, he was told, "Shut up the words, and seal the book, even to the time of the end." No other book in the

Reference Used: G. C., pp. 317-342.

Bible was ever shut up. And now this mighty Angel holds this book open. Jesus has opened the book because it contains an important message for the world at this time. Since the papacy would not repent, God would send a message that would save the honest in heart from being led astray by her deceptions,— a message that would expose the dangerous errors of this "mystery of iniquity." To attract the attention of the people and lead them to realize the importance of this message, the Angel "cried with a loud voice, as when a lion roareth."

4. Eating the Little Book (10:8-10). The experience that God's people had when they began to study this message is illustrated by what the voice from heaven said to John: "Go and take the little book which is open in the hand of the Angel," He said. Then John went to the Angel and said, "Give me the little book." And the Angel said, "Take it, and eat it up; and after you have eaten it, it shall be bitter, but it shall be in your mouth sweet as honey."

"Take the little book which is open in the hand of the Angel, and eat it up."

No words could better express the experience of the people who preached the advent message from 1833 to 1844. After studying the Bible diligently for two full years, sometimes devoting the entire night to comparing scripture with scripture, William Miller reached the conviction that the prophecy of the 2300 days pointed to the second coming of Christ about 1844, and he believed that at that time the world would come to an end. He reached this decision away back in 1818. Then to make absolutely sure that he was right he studied for three years more. But even after all this, it was years before he dared to preach the message, for fear he might be mistaken. That Jesus was soon coming to take His children to the mansions He had been preparing for them seemed too good to be true. Again and again he studied this little book. Lord Bacon once said, in speaking of how books should be read, "Some books are to be tasted; others are to be swallowed; and some few are to be chewed and digested." William Miller "chewed and digested" the little book of Daniel. He "ate it up," and so did many others who believed the message of the coming of Jesus. And in their mouth it was "sweet as honey," for they expected soon to see Jesus and forever live with Him.

5. The Message to All the World (10:2). The Angel "set His right foot upon the sea, and His left foot on the earth." By means of our feet we are able to travel from place to place. The fact that the Angel had one foot on the sea and one on the earth indicates that the message was to go to all the world. And it did. Not only in America, but in different parts of Europe and Asia, God put it into the hearts of earnest men to carry the glad tidings to others. In Sweden, where the laws prevented grown people from giving the message, the Spirit of God came upon the children and they preached it.

6. The Bitter Disappointment. But when the time passed, and Jesus did not come to this earth as they had expected, oh, how bitter was the disappointment! None of us will ever know how hard it was for these devoted Christian people to take up again their daily toil here on this earth, and to meet the insults and scorn of the wicked world. Some of them were almost in despair. What could it all mean? How do you think you would have felt if you had lived at that time?

But the Angel who told them to eat the book had a rainbow of promise about His head; and as they sought comfort in further study of the Bible, light began to break through the cloud of disappointment. They saw their mistake. They learned that the cleansing of the sanctuary at the end of the 2300 days was not the cleansing of this earth by fire, but the blotting out of sins in the heavenly sanctuary, the antitype of the cleansing of the earthly sanctuary on the day of atonement. They learned that the coming of Jesus was not His coming to this earth, but His coming from the holy to the most holy place in heaven. They learned that the Judgment to begin in 1844 was not the Executive but the Investigative Judgment.

They also noticed the words of the Angel in the last verse of Revelation 10: "Thou must prophesy again before many peoples, and nations, and tongues, and kings." The message in its fullness had not yet been preached. Another message must be given to warn the world to prepare for the coming of Jesus in the clouds of heaven. This refers to what is called the "third angel's message," because the Bible represents it as given by the last of three angels who were sent with messages to this world. This message began to be preached soon afterward, and is still being preached to every nation, kindred, tongue, and people. When this has been given to all the world, the "mystery of God" will be finished, and the seventh trumpet will then sound.

How to Study: What message of warning did God send to wake up the world and help them to realize their danger? When was this message given? Notice its location on your diagram.
Describe the Angel of Revelation 10. What was the "little book"? How did the people eat it up? Why was it sweet to the taste? Why was it afterward bitter? What was the message given? When? How extensively? What message was to follow this one before the end? When this message is fully given, which trumpet will sound?

5. THE MYSTERY OF GOD FINISHED
Seventh Trumpet or Third Woe — Rev. 10:7; 11:15-19

"In the days of the voice of the seventh angel, when he is about to sound, then is finished the mystery of God." Rev. 10:7, R. V.

1. Christ Proclaimed King (11:15). When John saw the seventh angel begin to sound, or about to sound, then said the angel, "The mystery of God is finished." Then God's great plan is ended. The gospel of salvation has done its work. "And there were great voices in heaven, saying, The kingdoms of this world are become the kingdoms of our Lord, and of His Christ; and He shall reign forever and ever." This is the time when Jesus lays aside His

---
References Used: G. C., pp. 635-641; Mark 13:35, 36; 2 Thess. 1:7-9.

priestly garments and puts on His royal robe. He is King of kings, and Lord of lords. Everyone whose name has been retained in the book of life is a subject of His kingdom. The work of examining the records of God's people in the books of heaven, to decide who are worthy of a place in the great family of God, is even now going on. Soon this work will be finished. Then the seventh angel will sound, and King Jesus will come to reign forever and ever. Am I ready for Him? Are you?

2. **Rejoicing in Heaven (11: 16, 17).** When the four and twenty elders heard the announcement that Christ was King, they fell upon their faces, and worshiped God, saying, "We give Thee thanks, O Lord God Almighty, which art, and wast, and art to come; because Thou hast taken to Thee Thy great power, and hast reigned." What a time of rejoicing that will be at the throne of God! The long, long struggle between Christ and Satan will then be over. The love of Christ will have conquered. Satan, the foe of man, will forever be deprived of his power to deceive and destroy God's people. He that is righteous will be righteous still, and he that is holy will be holy still. The entire family, which the Deity planned away back "in times eternal," will be numbered and written in the great family record book above.

3. **The Angry Nations of Earth (11: 18).** Nobody on earth will know the day or the hour when Christ's work as High Priest is finished and the censer is cast into the earth. How important, then, that we heed His warning, "Watch ye therefore, . . . lest coming suddenly He find you sleeping."

After probation closes, the time of trouble will begin, the time that the angel told Daniel about. Then the plagues will be poured out. It will be a terrible time on this earth, even more terrible than the Reign of Terror during the French Revolution, for the Spirit of God will be withdrawn from the whole earth. Describing the events then to take place, John says, "The nations were angry, and Thy wrath is come." This is the time when the angry nations of earth all unite in that last great battle, the battle of Armageddon. They are determined to destroy those who persist in obeying God's law instead of the law that Satan will lead the nations to make. After this war, will come the deliverance of God's people from the wrath of Satan and his agents. Jesus will come and take them to heaven, to live and reign with Him a thousand years.

4. **Judgment and Destruction of the Wicked (11:18).** This period of a thousand years is "the time of the dead, that they should be judged." These are the wicked dead, the millions who in every age have rejected salvation. It is also the time, as the twenty-four elders said, "that Thou shouldest give reward unto Thy servants the prophets, and to the saints, and them that fear Thy name, small and great."

When the thousand years are ended and the judgment of the wicked dead is finished, God will "destroy them which destroy the earth." This is the time spoken of by Paul, "when the Lord Jesus shall be revealed from heaven with His mighty angels, in flaming fire taking vengeance on them that know not God, and that obey not the gospel of our Lord Jesus Christ: who shall be punished with everlasting destruction from the presence of the Lord."

5. **Scenes in the Heavens (11:19).** Just before Jesus comes to this earth to deliver His people out of the time of trouble, there will be marvelous scenes in the heavens. Describing these scenes, John said, "The temple of God was opened in heaven, and there was seen in His temple the ark of His testament." In the ark are the commandments of God.

This is but brief mention of these scenes, but doubtless God had good reasons for not telling more to the prophet John. When the time came that the people who were to pass through these experiences lived on the earth, God gave a more complete description through a later prophet in these words:

"The firmament appears to open and shut. The glory from the throne of God seems flashing through. . . . The glory of the celestial city streams from the gates ajar. Then there appears against the sky a hand holding two tables of stone folded together. . . . That holy law, God's righteousness, that amid thunder and flame was proclaimed from Sinai as the guide of life, is now revealed to men as the rule of judgment. The hand opens the tables, and there are seen the precepts of the Decalogue, traced as with a pen of fire. The words are so plain that all can read them. . . . It is impossible to describe the horror and despair of those who have trampled upon God's holy requirements. The Lord gave them His law; they might have compared their characters with it, and learned their defects while there was yet opportunity for repentance and reform; but . . . they set aside its precepts and taught

The wicked "are condemned by that law which they have despised."

others to transgress. . . . Now they are condemned by that law which they have despised. With awful distinctness they see that they are without excuse. They chose whom they would serve and worship. . . . Too late they see that the Sabbath of the fourth commandment is the seal of the living God. Too late they see the

"There were lightnings, and voices, and thunderings, and an earthquake, and great hail."

true nature of their spurious sabbath. . . . They find that they have been fighting against God."

6. Scenes on the Earth (11:19). "And there were lightnings, and voices, and thunderings, and an earthquake, and great hail." These events are more fully described in these words: "In the midst of the angry heavens is one clear space of indescribable glory, whence comes the voice of God like the sound of many waters, saying, 'It is done.' That voice shakes the heavens and the earth. There is a mighty earthquake, 'such as was not since men were upon the earth, so mighty an earthquake and so great.' . . . The mountains shake like a reed in the wind, and ragged rocks are scattered on every side. There is a roar as of a coming tempest. The sea is lashed into fury. . . . The whole earth heaves and swells like the waves of the sea. Its surface is breaking up. . . . Great hailstones, every one 'about the weight of a talent,' are doing their work of destruction. . . .

"Fierce lightnings leap from the heavens, enveloping the earth in a sheet of flame. Above the terrific roar of thunder, voices, mysterious and awful, declare the doom of the wicked. . . .

"The voice of God is heard from heaven, declaring the day and hour of Jesus' coming. . . . Soon there appears in the east a small black cloud, about half the size of a man's hand. . . . The people of God know this to be the sign of the Son of man. . . . The King of kings descends upon the cloud, wrapped in flaming fire." The wicked behold these scenes with unspeakable terror. While they call for the rocks and mountains to fall on them and hide them from the face of God, the righteous exclaim, "Lo, this is our God; we have waited for Him, and He will save us: . . . we will be glad and rejoice in His salvation."

How to Study: After carefully studying this lesson, read Revelation 11:15-19, and try to explain every expression.

If you desire to read more about this wonderful prophecy, you will find a most thrilling description in "Great Controversy," pages 635-641. Perhaps your father will read some of these pages for family worship if you ask him.

Read Daniel's description of Jesus' receiving His kingdom. Dan. 7:13, 14.

For Your Workbook: Locate the seventh trumpet on your diagram. To which of the seals does this trumpet nearly correspond in time?

REVIEW OF THE SEVEN TRUMPETS
Revelation 8, 9, 10, 11

Test Questions
1. What does God want His people to learn from the prophecy of the seven churches? the seven seals? the seven trumpets?
2. What period of time is covered by the seven trumpets? What nation ruled the world at the beginning of this time?
3. Which trumpets tell of the breaking up of the Roman Empire into ten divisions? What tribe is represented by each of these trumpets? Why was the Roman Empire destroyed?
4. What were the last three trumpets called? Why?
5. The history of what people is told in the fifth trumpet? the sixth?
6. What was Satan trying to accomplish through the Mohammedans? Through what two agencies did he try to destroy the Bible from the whole world? What great movement defeated his scheme?

7. What nation made open war against the Bible? What is this period of time called in history? In what part of the 1260-year period did this occur?
8. How did God's "two witnesses" ascend to heaven?
9. What great events are to take place under the seventh trumpet?
10. Dates to Remember: When did the fourth trumpet end? With what event? When was Constantinople captured by the Turks? When did the 1260 days, or 42 months, end? When was the message of Revelation 10 given?

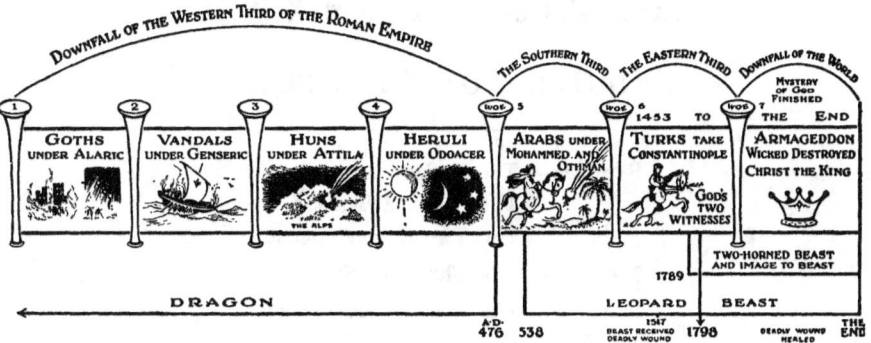

DIAGRAM No. 11. The seven trumpets

Chapter Drill: See how quickly you can turn to the chapter or chapters that contain—
1. The seven churches
2. The seven seals
3. The seven trumpets
4. The Angel with little book open
5. The throne of God
6. The book sealed with seven seals
7. The sealing of God's people
8. God's two witnesses

Give the general subject of each chapter in Revelation 1-11.

Verse-Finding Drill: See how quickly you can find the verse containing each of the following; then try to tell in connection with what prophecy each is found:
1. The angel took the censer, . . . and cast it into the earth.
2. There were voices, and thunderings, and lightnings, and an earthquake.
3. I saw another mighty Angel . . . clothed with a cloud.
4. He had in His hand a little book open.
5. He set His right foot upon the sea, and His left foot on the earth.
6. I took the little book, . . . and ate it up.
7. Thou must prophesy again before many peoples, and nations.
8. The holy city shall they tread underfoot forty and two months.
9. After three days and an half the spirit of life from God entered into them. . . . And they ascended up to heaven in a cloud.
10. The kingdoms of this world are become the kingdoms of our Lord.
11. The temple of God was opened in heaven.

Sixth Period—Chapters X–XIII

OUTLINE OF CHAPTER X

Symbols — The Dragon
  The Leopard Beast
  The Two-Horned Beast
Time   — The Christian Era
Result — The Beasts Destroyed

Topics —
                                                    Revelation
The Wrath of the Dragon 12
The Leopard Beast ....⎤
The Last and Crowning Deception .... ⎬ 13
  An image to the beast   ⎪
The Mark of the Beast ....⎦
Review

CHAPTER X

The Opposition of Three Persecuting Powers

1. WRATH OF THE DRAGON
Revelation 12

"The dragon was wroth with the woman, and went to make war with the remnant of her seed, which keep the commandments of God, and have the testimony of Jesus Christ." Rev. 12:17.

1. John's Fourth Vision. We now begin the fourth and last line of prophecy that reaches from the first coming of Christ to His second coming. The seals show how Satan uses the apostate church to work against God's plan; the trumpets show how he uses the nations of the world to work against God's plan; this prophecy in Revelation 12 and 13 shows how he combines the church and the state to accomplish his purpose. Satan will use every possible means to destroy God's people, for he knows that every person whom he can hold in sin is one less whose sins he will have to suffer for when the final day of destruction comes. Is it any wonder, then, that * "as a roaring lion, [he] walketh about, seeking whom he may devour"?

2. The Two Great Wonders (12:1-6, 14). John first saw in heaven a wonderful woman. The dazzling rays of the sun enshrouded her like a gorgeous garment; under her feet was the waning moon; while upon her head was a crown set with twelve brilliant stars. This woman represents the church of God. The sun represents the gospel of Jesus, "the Sun of righteousness," "the Light of the world." As God made the moon to reflect the light of the sun during the darkness of the night, so in the prophecy, the moon represents the types of the sanctuary service, and other ceremonies of the church, that God has given to reflect the light of the gospel of Christ in this dark world. The twelve stars

---

References Used: P. P., p. 358; "Seer," Ch. 13; Test., Vol. 3, p. 115; B. R., new ed., pp. 264-267; G. C., p. 438.

represent the twelve apostles, the crown of the Christian church. After that, John saw a tiny Child, the Babe of Bethlehem. All this was the first wonder.

Right before this beautiful woman was "another wonder," an immense, ugly-looking, dangerous serpent—"a great red dragon, having seven heads and ten horns, and seven crowns upon his heads. And his tail drew the third part of the stars [or angels] of heaven, and did cast them to the earth." This dragon "stood" before the woman, ready to leap upon his prey. He was watching his chance to spring upon and destroy the little Babe. But he did not succeed, for the "Child was caught up unto God, and to His throne." Then to the terrified woman were given two wings of a great eagle, and she flew "into the wilderness," to a place that God had prepared for her, and there she lived "a thousand two hundred and threescore days."

"A woman clothed with the sun"

3. Who Is This Dragon (12: 7-9)? The meaning of this striking vision seems so plain that it hardly needs explanation. The serpent is the very same who, after drawing the third part of the angels out of heaven to this earth, led astray the innocent woman in the garden of Eden. He is "the great dragon, . . . that old serpent, called the devil, and Satan, which deceiveth the whole world." He is the same who, at the time of the creation of this world, fought in heaven against "Michael and His angels." But he "prevailed not," and at last he "was cast out into the earth, and his angels were cast out with him,"— one third of "the stars of heaven."

The line of prophecy in which this symbol is found speaks of the dragon as standing ready to destroy Jesus as soon as He should be born. It was Satan "that moved upon Herod to put the Saviour to death. But the chief agent of Satan in making war upon Christ

"A great red dragon"

and His people during the first centuries of the Christian era, was the Roman Empire, in which paganism was the prevailing religion. Thus while the dragon, primarily, represents Satan, it is, in a secondary sense, a symbol of pagan Rome."

The ten horns represent the ten divisions of Rome. From the time that Satan was first cast out of heaven, he has persecuted the woman, the church of God. He does not do this in person, but he works through earthly agents, either the nations of the earth or "the synagogue of Satan," his own church, and frequently through both together.

4. Cause of Satan's Wrath (12:10, 12-14). When Satan crucified Jesus, he was forever cast out of the council of God. When he was no longer permitted in the council of God, nor at the gate of heaven, as "the accuser of our brethren," he came back to this earth, "having great wrath, because he knoweth that he hath but a short time." Then, with renewed vengeance and more bitter hatred, he centered his wrath upon the church of God. "He persecuted the woman which brought forth the man Child." The most cruel period of this persecution was the 1260 days, or "a time, and times, and half a time."

5. The Flood Swallowed Up (12:15, 16). When the woman flew into the wilderness, "the serpent cast out of his mouth water as a flood after the woman, that he might cause her to be carried away of the flood. And the earth helped the woman, and the earth opened her mouth, and swallowed up the flood." This was the flood of persecution. The earth "swallowed up the flood," or put a stop to the persecution, by means of the Reformation, which was carried forward by nearly every nation in Europe. At this time America also "helped the woman" by opening her friendly doors as a home of freedom to the persecuted of all lands.

6. Satan's Wrath Against the "Remnant" (12:17; 19:10). Seeing his defeat again, "the dragon was wroth with the woman, and went to make war with the *remnant* of her seed, which keep the commandments of God, and have the testimony of Jesus Christ." The "remnant" of the woman's seed is the last true church of God that will be on this earth. It is the church of God to-day. And this church will be known by two special characteristics — they will "keep the commandments of God, and have the testimony of Jesus Christ." And * "the testimony of Jesus is the spirit of prophecy." These two Satan hates above everything else, because he is trying to overthrow God's law and establish a law of his own, and the spirit of prophecy which God has given to His remnant church clearly reveals his wicked plans. Should we not most carefully study this "spirit of prophecy," that we may not be deceived by the enemy?

7. How to Overcome (12:11). God shows us how we may overcome the evil one. Of ourselves we can never, never conquer this venomous serpent. But Jesus by His death has conquered him for us. We may overcome him "by the blood of the Lamb" and by the word of our testimony. Satan does not like to hear the name of Jesus spoken in prayer or in testimony. But in this way God will give us the victory. In the struggle, we are to love not our "lives unto the death." Are we willing to face death rather than deny our Saviour? We may have to do this; but if we do, let us remember Daniel and his companions. God will deliver us as He did them; but even if He does not, like Daniel, we cannot and we will not disobey God.

How to Study: Read the Bible verses referred to after each topic. Describe exactly the two "wonders" which John saw, and tell what each means. When did the dragon first try to kill the Child Jesus? When was his second great effort? Why is Satan more angry since Christ's death? How are the "ten horns" of the dragon interpreted? What was "the flood"? How did the earth swallow it up? Why does Satan especially hate the "remnant" church? How may we overcome him? Be sure that you can figure out the "time, and times, and half a time" of verse 14.

Use of Concordance: Find the two verses starred under topics 1 and 6. Key words: roaring; testimony.

Memory Work: Memorize Revelation 12:17. Review verse 11.

Chapter to Remember: Revelation 12 — the great red dragon.

For Your Workbook: On your diagram of the seven trumpets show when the "great red dragon," pagan Rome, ruled.

---

2. THE LEOPARD BEAST

Revelation 13:1-10

"And all that dwell upon the earth shall worship him, whose names are not written in the book of life." Rev. 13:8.

1. The Leopard Beast (13:1, 2). This prophecy is a part of the one begun in Revelation 12. As John looked out from Patmos upon the waters of the Mediterranean, thinking perhaps of the two won-

---

References Used: G. C., pp. 579-581.

ders which he had last seen in vision, there, among the waves, he saw the form of "a beast rise up out of the sea." This beast, like the dragon, had "seven heads and ten horns, and upon his horns ten crowns." Like the dragon, he represented one of the powers

A leopard beast, "having seven heads and ten horns, and upon his horns ten crowns"

which Satan uses to persecute the church of God,—the one that followed pagan Rome. And that was papal Rome, or the papacy. "And the dragon gave him his *power*, and his *seat*, and *great authority*." As his full body came into view, John saw that he looked "like unto a leopard, and his feet were as the feet of a bear, and his mouth as the mouth of a lion." This would seem to show that the lion, the bear, and the leopard which Daniel saw in his first vision were really powers through which the dragon worked.

2. A Blasphemous Power (13:1, 5, 6). Upon the heads of this beast was written the name of blasphemy. "And there was given unto him a mouth speaking great things and blasphemies; and power was given unto him to continue forty and two months. And he opened his mouth in blasphemy against God, to blaspheme His name, and His tabernacle [where God's law is], and them that dwell in heaven." This description shows beyond a doubt that this leopard beast is the very same power that Daniel saw,— the little horn that came up among the ten horns, having "eyes like the eyes of a man, and a mouth speaking great things." It is the papacy, which tried to cover the light of God's word all through the Dark Ages, the very one that would "think to change times and laws," the one who Paul said * "opposeth and exalteth himself above all that is called God, or that is worshiped; so that he as God sitteth in the temple of God, showing himself that *he* is God."

3. A Persecuting Power (13:7). John further says of this beast: "And it was given unto him to make war with the saints, and to overcome them: and power was given him over all kindreds, and tongues, and nations." Of the little horn Daniel said, "He . . . shall wear out the saints of the Most High: . . . and they shall be given into his hand until a time and times and the dividing of time," or half a time. This again shows that this leopard beast is the same as the little horn which Daniel saw,— the papacy.

4. "His Deadly Wound" (13:3). After the Lord showed John enough about this leopard beast so that we might be sure that it was the same as the little horn, He showed him some things that were not shown to Daniel. John "saw one of his heads as it were wounded to death." It was the Reformation that dealt the deadly wound. At the end of the period of persecution, in 1798, the pope was taken prisoner, and his power to punish was taken away.

5. The Wound Healed (13:3). But the prophecy says the head was "as it were" wounded to death. For a time he seemed to be dead. But is he really dead? No; for John said, "His deadly wound was healed." Many people in the world think the papacy will never again be a persecuting power; but from this prophecy we know that before the end comes, he will again persecute as he has in the past. This deadly wound, inflicted more than one hundred years ago, has been healing all these years. More and more is the papacy gaining life and power among the nations and churches of the world. The papacy "is silently growing into power. Her doctrines are exerting their influence in legislative halls, in the churches, and in the hearts of men. She is piling up her lofty and massive structures, in the secret recesses of which her former persecutions will be repeated. Stealthily and unsuspectedly she is strengthening her forces to further her own ends when the time shall come for her to strike. . . . Whoever shall believe and obey the word of God will thereby incur reproach and persecution."

Although the papal church will be used by Satan to do this terrible work, we must ever remember that not all who belong to it are evildoers. Among these people are many who conscientiously obey the commands of their church. When these loyal ones understand God's commands, they, like Luther the monk and Saul the persecutor, will gladly place themselves on God's side of this great conflict.

6. **"All the World Wondered After the Beast" (13: 3, 4, 8).** The efforts that Satan is now making to compel people to keep Sunday, the day which the beast has commanded in opposition to the Sabbath of God, is an evidence that this papal beast is still alive. Many Protestants are unconsciously giving their efforts to help the beast do this blasphemous work. The time spoken of in this prophecy will soon come, when "all the world" will wonder "after the beast." And they will worship the beast, saying, "Who is like unto the beast? who is able to make war with him?" "And all that dwell upon the earth shall worship him, whose names are not written in the book of life of the Lamb slain from the foundation of the world."

7. **The End of the Beast (13:10).** After Satan has had full opportunity to show his wicked character, so that not only the inhabitants of the unfallen worlds, but all the people of this world, fully see the results of his evil work, the beast will be slain, "and

his body destroyed, and given to the burning flame." He will reap the fruit of his own sowing, for "he that leadeth into captivity shall go into captivity: he that killeth with the sword must be killed with the sword." These terrible times that are just ahead of us will surely try "the patience and the faith of the saints." And who shall be able to stand?

How to Study: Compare the description given of this beast with the little horn in Daniel 7: 11, 20, 21, 25. Be able to describe the beast; the ten horns. What did he do that made him a blasphemous power? a persecuting power? How many years are forty-two months? When did this time begin? When end? Be able to figure this out. What caused the deadly wound? What will finally become of the beast? In what chapter is this beast described?

Use of Concordance: Find the verse starred under topic 2. Key word: exalt.

For Your Workbook: On your diagram of the seven trumpets show when "the leopard beast" ruled.

---

3. THE LAST AND CROWNING DECEPTION
Rev. 13: 11-14

"And I beheld another beast coming up out of the earth; and he had two horns like a lamb, and he spake as a dragon." Rev. 13: 11.

1. The Beast with Lamblike Horns (13: 11). After John had seen the leopard beast persecuting the people of God, speaking blasphemous words, then worshiped by all the world, he saw "another beast." This beast was coming up out of the earth, not out of the sea, from which all the other beasts had come. Beasts that rose out of the water represented nations that became world powers by conquering some other nations. They came out from "peoples, and multitudes, and nations, and tongues." But this beast did not conquer some other nation in order to make a place for itself. It came up where nations had not existed before. The Bible does not say what the body of this beast was like, but it had two horns like a lamb, and it appeared on the earth near the end of the forty-two months.

References Used: B. R., new ed., pp. 271-279; G. C., pp. 588-590, 612; Dan. 4: 19; Rev. 19: 20; 1 Kings 18: 17, 38; 2 Thess. 2: 10.

2. The Beast Interpreted. The only great and independent nation in the world that was coming into existence about 1798 was the United States of America. This nation declared its independence in 1776, and in 1789 it adopted its constitution. Since then the whole history of its growth has been one of annexation and natural extension, not of conquest. The United States government has adopted as one of its symbols the American buffalo, which has two horns like a lamb. This symbol is found on the back of a nickel. It may have been this beast which God showed to John, though of course John would not know its name, because the American buffalo was not known to the world in John's day.

"And I beheld another beast coming up out of the earth."

3. The Two Horns (13:11). The beast had two horns. A horn represents a kingdom or a government, or some important part of a kingdom or government. Lamblike horns represent a government that is youthful, innocent, and gentle—a government having Christlike principles. The two great principles that caused the United States to be settled and to desire an independent government were freedom to worship God and freedom to develop its own resources as a nation. The people did not want to be ruled by a king. They wanted a republican government, a government "of the people, by the people, and for the people." They did not want to be ruled by a pope, nor did they want the government to tell them how to worship. They wanted "a church without a pope, and a state without a king." They wanted each citizen to have the privilege of worshiping God in his own way. In short, they wanted *civil* and *religious liberty*. And these are the principles of Christ, the Lamb of God. These are the two horns of this great, liberty-loving nation. These two horns are the secret of the nation's power and prosperity.

4. "He Spake as a Dragon" (13:11, 12). "The great dragon, . . . that old serpent, called the devil, and Satan, which deceiveth the whole world," has been the cause of the downfall of all the great nations of the past. And as long as time shall last he will continue his destructive work. In these last days it is his scheme to involve our own nation. How does he plan to do this? The prophecy says he "causeth the earth and them which dwell therein to worship the first beast, whose deadly wound was healed." As we have already learned, the beast whose deadly wound was healed represents the papacy — the very same power through which Satan has wrought such ruin in the past, the very same power that would "think" to change God's law. This shows us that the closing conflict with sin on this earth is but a continuation of the same old controversy that Satan started in heaven. God has made the Sabbath the "seal" or sign of His authority; Satan denies God's authority, and through the papacy he has substituted the first day of the week as the sign or "mark" of *his* authority.

5. Satan's Plot Against Our Nation. With jealous eye Satan has watched this glorious nation of ours from its beginning. He has seen the Christlike principles of the Reformation on which it was founded. He has seen all that it has given of civil and religious liberty to its people. He has seen the influence for good that it has exerted on the rest of the world. He knows that in these last days, if these principles are allowed to continue, many will be led to understand and obey God's law, instead of marching under *his* banner. He is determined that this shall not be.

To accomplish his purpose he will first use force. As in papal Rome he used the civil law to compel heretics, so now, through Protestants who have proved false to their original principles, he is working for the same power. Everyone knows that for many years our government has been constantly besieged by religious bodies to pass laws that will compel all its people to disregard God's law, to trample underfoot the true Sabbath and honor a false sabbath. But in His word God has warned us of this evil, that we may be on our guard. Every true American, every lover of civil and religious liberty, for which the "Stars and Stripes" have waved so long and so gloriously, should in every way possible help this nation to escape the wicked snare that Satan has laid to destroy it.

6. Satan's Last Great Deception (13 : 13, 14). What Satan fails to accomplish by force, he will do by deception. He will deceive "them that dwell on the earth by the means of . . . miracles." He will work "with all power and signs and lying wonders." "He will appear in the character of an angel of light. Through the agency of spiritualism, miracles will be wrought, the sick will be healed, and many undeniable wonders will be performed. And as the spirits will profess faith in the Bible, and manifest respect for the institutions of the church, their work will be accepted as a manifestation of divine power." Jesus warned His disciples about this very thing, saying, * "There shall arise false Christs, and false prophets, and shall show great signs and wonders; insomuch that, if it were possible, they shall deceive the very elect."

But "while appearing . . . as a great physician who can heal all their maladies, he will bring disease and disaster. . . . Even now he is at work. In accidents and calamities by sea and by land, in great conflagrations, in fierce tornadoes and terrific hailstorms, in tempests, floods, cyclones, tidal waves, and earthquakes, in every place and in a thousand forms, Satan is exercising his power. . . . Then the great deceiver will persuade men that those who serve God are causing these evils, . . . that men are offending God by the violation of the Sunday-sabbath, that this sin has brought calamities which will not cease until Sunday observance shall be strictly enforced." Those who continue to obey God by observing the Sabbath of His law will be called troublers of Israel, as Ahab called Elijah. Then to prove his point Satan will make "fire come down from heaven on the earth in the sight of men," just as Elijah did to prove to Ahab the power of the true God. All will be deceived who have "received not the love of the truth, that they might be saved." The Bible will be our only safeguard in that trying day. If we stand on that, our feet will be on the solid rock, and we need not fear Satan's power.

How to Study: Study to recite from the given topics. What three features prove that this symbol represents the United States government? Rev. 13: 11,

12. In how many ways will he show the dragon's voice? Verses 12-14. Be able to explain how he will speak in each of these ways. How should every true American show his loyalty to his country? In what chapter in Daniel is the reference under topic 4? On what occasion did Elijah make fire come down out of heaven?

Use of Concordance: Find the reference starred under topic 6. Key word: elect.

Memory Work: Begin to memorize Revelation 13: 11-17 for your memory certificate.

Chapter to Remember: Revelation 13 — the leopard beast and the lamblike beast. In what chapter does Paul describe "the mystery of iniquity"?

For Your Workbook: On your diagram of the seven trumpets show when the nation represented by "the two-horned beast" began its career.

4. THE MARK OF THE BEAST
Rev. 13: 15-18; 14: 1-5

"He causeth all . . . to receive a mark in their right hand, or in their foreheads." Rev. 13: 16.

1. Making an Image to the Beast (13: 13, 14). The plot that Satan is laying in these last days is called in the prophecy the making of "an image to the beast"—to that beast "which had the wound by a sword, and did live;" that is, the papal beast. Just as the papal beast was the papal church using the civil law to compel people to obey its doctrines, so an image to this beast will be another church or combination of churches using the power of the state to enforce religious observance. And this is just what many Protestant churches are now endeavoring to do. Many of these people through whom Satan is thus working to accomplish his purpose are no doubt conscientious in their efforts. They do not see that he is the power behind this work. Satan has deceived them. When these honest ones understand the truth, they like Paul will immediately place themselves on God's side.

That a work of this kind could be done on the shores of liberty-loving America seemed a wild idea fifty years ago; but to-day, in the efforts to enforce Sunday observance by law, we see evidences on every hand showing us that this image will soon be finished. Just as strongly as possible every true American Christian should oppose to the very last this wicked work of Satan, and protect our beloved land from so foul a stain, that our beautiful

---
References Used: G. C., pp. 578, 579, 584, 607, 608, 614, 615, 625, 626, 629, 631, 635; Isa. 49: 16.

flag may ever stand for that freedom which our forefathers purchased at so great a cost. The great principles upon which this nation was founded have a sacred claim on everyone who is truly loyal to his native land.

2. God's Law Said to Be Unnecessary. Even now many so-called Christian people have been led to believe that we are not required to obey God's law, that it is a "burden" no longer necessary. How foolish this is! "Every nation has its laws, which command respect and obedience; no government could exist without them; and can it be conceived that the Creator of the heavens and the earth has no law to govern the beings He has made? Suppose that prominent ministers were publicly to teach that the statutes which govern their land and protect the rights of the citizens were not obligatory,— that they restricted the liberties of the people, and therefore ought not to be obeyed; how long would such men be tolerated in the pulpit? But is it a graver offense to disregard the laws of states and nations than to trample upon those divine precepts which are the foundation of all government? It would be far more consistent for nations to abolish *their* statutes, and permit the people to do as they please, than for the Ruler of the universe to annul *His* law, and leave the world without a standard to condemn the guilty or justify the obedient." France tried the experiment, and the world knows the terrible result.

3. Beginning of Persecution (13:16). When this image to the beast is made, "both small and great, rich and poor, free and bond," will be required "to receive a mark in their right hand, or in their foreheads,"— in their right hand by laboring on the Sabbath, in their forehead by acknowledging with their minds that Sunday is God's appointed day for worship. If they refuse to receive this mark, they will be accused of disloyalty to the government. Those who persist in refusing "will be threatened with fines and imprisonment [as many have already been]. . . . Some of them will be thrust into prison, some will be exiled, some will be treated as slaves." The persecution will be terrible, and "a large class who have professed faith in the third angel's message . . . [will] join the ranks of the opposition."

4. Not Allowed to "Buy or Sell" (13:17). When these troublous times come, the Bible says that no man can "buy or sell, save he that had the mark, or the name of the beast, or the number of his name." It would seem as if God's children would die of starvation and neglect. But the same God who cared for Elijah in time of famine will care for His persecuted people in the time of trouble. His promise will not fail—*"Bread shall be given him; his waters shall be sure."

5. **The Death Decree (13:15).** At last, it will be decided that the only way to save the world from the troubles into which it has been plunged will be to destroy commandment keepers from the face of all the earth. Then the image of the beast will "cause that as many as would not worship the image of the beast should be killed." Like the law given by Medo-Persia in the days of Esther, so this decree will allow anyone, after a given time, to put to death whoever still persists in obeying the fourth commandment of God's law. Then they will flee from cities and villages, and, like the Waldenses, hide for safety among the mountains or in other solitary places.

6. **Deliverance (14:1-5).** Will the Lord forget His people in these terrible times? Did He forget the lad Joseph in prison? Did He forget the helpless baby Moses? Did He forget Daniel in the lions' den, or his companions in the fiery furnace? Did He forget Paul and Silas and Peter in prison? Jesus has promised: "I will not forget thee. Behold, I have graven thee upon the palms of My hands." If we "have been diligent students of the Scriptures," and "have received the love of the truth," we will be shielded in that dreadful day.

As these terrible scenes in the vision pass away, another scene comes before John. What is it? "A Lamb stood on the Mount Sion, and with Him an hundred forty and four thousand, having His Father's name written in their foreheads." These are the ones who have refused to receive the mark of the beast in their foreheads, and because they have remained loyal they have the name of God in their foreheads. They belong to God and He has delivered them. They are "the first fruits unto God and to the Lamb." Then John heard this great throng "harping with their harps," and down to his listening ears were wafted strains of heavenly music as they joined in the song of the redeemed—free forever from oppression.

How to Study: Read the Bible verses given with each topic, and study to recite from these topics. Be able to explain what the image to the beast will be, and how this image is now being made. In what book in the Bible is the Medo-Persian law that is referred to under topic 5? See how many of the experiences referred to under topic 6 you can locate in the Bible.

Use of Concordance: Find the verse starred under topic 4. Key word: bread.

Memory Work: Finish memorizing Revelation 13:11-17. When you can recite it all perfectly, you are entitled to the third star on your memory certificate.

Chapter to Remember: Revelation 13 — The leopard beast and the beast with two horns.

REVIEW OF REVELATION 12 AND 13

Test Questions and Exercises: What is the interpretation of the following symbols?

1. A Woman —
   - Clothed with the sun
   - A crown of twelve stars
   - The moon under her feet
   - In the wilderness 1260 days
   - *Remnant of her seed

2. Great Red Dragon —
   - Ten horns
   - Accuser of our brethren
   - Third of stars cast down
   - The flood from the dragon's mouth
   - *The earth swallowed up the flood

3. The Leopard Beast —
   - Ten horns
   - A mouth speaking blasphemies
   - One head wounded to death
   - Made war with the saints
   - The deadly wound healed
   - Continued forty-two months
   - Killed by the sword

4. Another Beast —
   - Came up out of the earth
   - Causeth the earth to worship the first beast before him
   - Had two horns like a lamb
   - Spake as a dragon
   - Maketh fire come down from heaven
   - Doeth miracles

5. An Image to the Beast
6. The Mark of the Beast

Dates to Remember: (1) End of the great red dragon. (2) Beginning and end of the forty-two months, 1260 days, or "a time, and times, and half a time." (3) When the lamblike beast came up out of the earth.

Chapter Drill: What prophecy is found in Revelation 1, 2, 3? in Revelation 4, 5, 6, 7? in Revelation 8, 9, 10, 11? in Revelation 12 and 13? Give in order the general subject of each chapter from 1 to 13.

See how quickly you can turn to the chapter or chapters that contain the prophecy of:

1. The dragon
2. The leopard beast
3. The lamblike beast
4. The mark of the beast
5. The United States
6. Pagan Rome
7. Papal Rome

Verse-Finding Drill: See how quickly you can find the verse containing each of the following; then try to tell from memory in which chapter each one is found and in connection with what prophecy:
1. His tail drew the third part of the stars of heaven . . . to the earth.
2. The woman fled into the wilderness . . . a thousand two hundred and threescore days.
3. The great dragon was cast out . . . into the earth.
4. The accuser of our brethren is cast down.
5. The devil . . . knoweth that he hath but a short time.
6. The earth . . . swallowed up the flood.
7. The dragon was wroth with the woman, and went to make war with the remnant of her seed.
8. All the world wondered after the beast.
9. The beast . . . opened his mouth in blasphemy against God.
10. As many as would not worship the image of the beast should be killed.
11. No man might buy or sell, save he that had the mark . . . of the beast.
12. A Lamb stood on the Mount Sion, and with Him 144,000.
13. These are . . . the first fruits unto God and to the Lamb.

Memory Drill: Review your memory verses on the promises to the overcomer, including Revelation 12:11; on the United States in prophecy, Revelation 13:11-17.

OUTLINE OF CHAPTER XI

Symbols — The First Angel's Message
　　　　　　The Second Angel's Message
　　　　　　The Third Angel's Message
Time　　— The Last Generation
Result　— A Loyal, Obedient People Developed
　　　　　　The Just Separated from the Unjust

Topics —

　　　　　　　　　　　　　　　　　　　　　　　Revelation
The Hour of God's Judgment ....⎫
"Babylon Is Fallen" ....⎬ 14
Satan's Plot Unmasked ....⎭
Review

CHAPTER XI

God's Last Appeal to Man

1. THE HOUR OF GOD'S JUDGMENT
The First Angel's Message — Rev. 14: 6, 7

"Fear God, and give glory to Him; for the hour of His Judgment is come."
Rev. 14: 7.

1. John's Fifth Vision. Each one of the first four visions which John saw on Patmos — the churches, the seals, the trumpets, and the three beasts — describes events covering the time from about the first advent of Jesus to His second advent. The vision which we now begin to study covers only the last generation of people who live on this earth before the end. When Jesus was speaking of this time, He said, * "This generation shall not pass, till all these things be fulfilled." And we ourselves are a part of this generation.

The vision is represented under the symbol of three angels flying one after the other, each one giving a message of warning to the people on the earth. For this reason it is usually called the three angels' messages. Sometimes it is called simply the third angel's message, because the messages of the first and second angels really go with that of the third angel.

The purpose of this message is to make plain to all, the deceptive plans of Satan, and to turn people away from him to God, who alone can save them. It will result in separating the just from the unjust, and in developing a people who will "keep the commandments of God, and the faith of Jesus." It is God's last appeal to man.

2. Message of the First Angel (14: 6, 7). Said John: "I saw another angel fly in the midst of heaven, having the everlasting gospel to preach unto them that dwell on the earth, and to every nation, and kindred, and tongue, and people, saying with a loud voice, Fear God, and give glory to Him; for the hour of His Judgment is come: and worship Him that made heaven, and earth, and

---
References Used: S. A. M., pp. 99, 105, 140, 141; G. C., pp. 357-362; Test., Vol. 6, pp. 202, 203.

"Fear God, and give glory to Him; for the hour of His judgment is come."

the sea, and the fountains of waters." This is the same message that was given to the Philadelphia church. It is the same message that was contained in the "little book" which John was told to eat up. It is the same Judgment message that was revealed to Daniel, when he saw the Son of man brought before the Ancient of Days, and "the books were opened,"— events that took place, as we have already learned, in 1844, at the end of the 2300 days. The symbol used was not a wild beast, nor a war horse, nor a trumpet of war, but a mighty angel from heaven with the gospel of peace and salvation. This indicates that the message is of a high character and of great importance. In his rapid flight the angel quickly gave the message to all the world. He announced that the hour of God's Judgment *is come.*

Joseph Wolff

3. **"To Every Nation."** This message was not confined to America, nor were William Miller and his associates the only ones who preached it. In different parts of the earth, at about the same time, men went forth to proclaim this truth, without knowing about one another's work. It was preached with great power by Dr. Joseph Wolff in more than twenty different nations — in Egypt and other parts of Africa; in Palestine, Syria, Persia, India, and other parts of Asia; in Greece, Holland, Scotland, Ireland, and other parts of Europe. He also visited the United States, where he preached the message before the president and the members of Congress as well as to others. The burden of his message was the near coming of Christ.

William Miller

The advent message was preached by about seven hundred leading ministers in England. It was also preached in South America, in France, Switzerland, Russia, Germany, and the countries of Scandinavia, and in some of the islands of the sea. It is said that William Miller had the names and addresses of three thousand ministers in various parts of the globe who between 1840 and 1844 were proclaiming, "Fear God, and give glory to Him; for the hour of His Judgment is come." The message was carried to every mission station and to every seaport in the world.

4. Children Preaching the Message. It was in Sweden, and to some extent in Norway and Germany, where the message was proclaimed by little children, some of them not more than six or eight years of age. The children, led by the Spirit of God, used the very language of this message, "Fear God, and give glory to

In Sweden the first angel's message was proclaimed by little children.

Him; for the hour of His Judgment is come." In one place in Sweden Satan tried to stop this work by causing the arrest of two boys, one eighteen and the other fifteen years of age, who were giving the message. These boys were whipped until their bare backs were bruised and bleeding. Then they were cast into prison. When the wounds healed, their persecutors took them out of prison, demanding, "Will you cease preaching this doctrine?" These brave boys answered quietly, but firmly, "We will preach whatever the Lord bids us." Then they were beaten a second time.

At last, the king of Sweden told the authorities to release those boys from prison, and let them alone.

We are told that in the closing work of this message "children who are receiving a Christian education will be witnesses for Christ. . . . In these last days, children's voices will be raised to give the last message of warning. . . . When . . . men are no longer permitted to present the truth, the Spirit of God will come upon the children, and they will do a work in the proclamation of the truth which the older workers cannot do, because their way will be hedged up."

5. The Message Was with "a Loud Voice." Great crowds of people attended the meetings where this message was preached, and the power of God was present. People realized that they were facing God's great Judgment day, and that they must prepare for His coming. Satan often stirred up opposition, but this only brought more people to listen to the words of truth. This message, which was preached by Dr. Wolff as early as 1821, continued to be preached until the close of the 2300 days in 1844. Especially during the last few years it was preached "with a loud voice." As a part of the great threefold message, it is still sounding throughout the world, and will continue to be preached "to every nation, and kindred, and tongue, and people" until "the hour of His Judgment" closes.

How to Study: Keep a map of the world before you as you study this lesson, and point out the different countries where the first angel's message was preached by Dr. Wolff and others. Review the diagram of the 2300 days, because this was the prophecy which was the basis of the first angel's message. Read Daniel 8:14 and 9:24-27. Who was president of the United States in 1837, when Dr. Wolff preached the message to the United States Congress?

On pages 137 and 138 of "Great Second Advent Movement," there is an interesting description of a meeting held at this time. Perhaps you would like to read it.

Use of Concordance: Find the verse starred in paragraph 1. Key word: generation. In what part of the Bible will you look for it?

Memory Work: Memorize Revelation 14:6, 7. This is part of the fourth memory certificate section.

2. "BABYLON IS FALLEN"

The Second Angel's Message — Rev. 14:8

"And there followed another angel, saying, Babylon is fallen, is fallen." Rev. 14:8.

1. The First Disappointment. Those who preached the first angel's message expected the Saviour to come sometime during the year 1843, because 1843 years A. D. plus 457 years B. C. (the time when the 2300 days began) make 2300 years. They did not know just when in the year; but it could not be later than the spring of

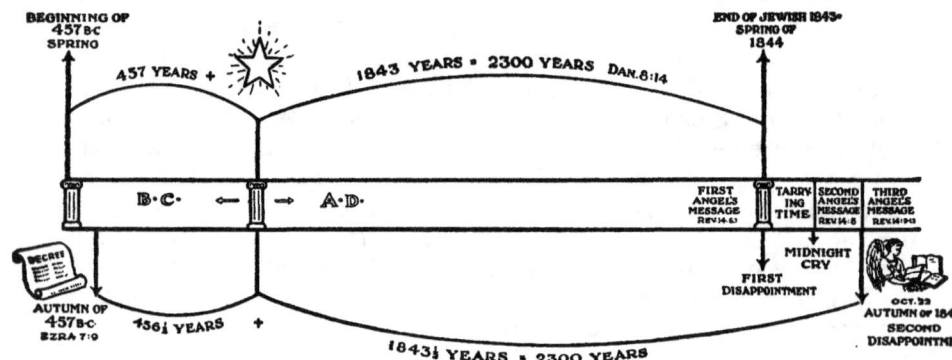

DIAGRAM NO. 12. The two disappointments

1844, because the Jewish year 1843 ended then. When the last day of that year passed and Jesus had not come, they were greatly perplexed. Had they been misled? Those who had accepted the message from fear now turned against it. They were the "evil servant" that Christ described, who said in his heart, "My lord delayeth his coming," and who therefore stopped looking for him.

2. Light from the Bible. But the true servants of God knew that He had been leading them, and they could not give up their faith. As they studied the Bible, they found encouragement in the parable of the ten virgins, who went out to meet their lord; for this parable said that the *"bridegroom [meaning Jesus] *tarried.*" They also found hope in these words of the Lord to Habbakuk: *"Write the vision, and make it plain upon tables, that he may

---

References Used: S. A. M., pp. 177, 184; Matt. 24: 48, 49; 25: 1-13.

run that readeth it. For the vision is yet for an appointed time, but at the end [of the 2300-day vision] it shall speak, and not lie: though it *tarry* [beyond the time you expected], *wait for it;* because it will surely come, it will not tarry."

They believed that the Lord had permitted the disappointment in order to test their sincerity. Those who did not really want to see Jesus were glad that He had not come, and they began "to eat and drink with the drunken." Those who did want to see the Saviour were disappointed but not discouraged. They made the prophecy "plain upon tables" by drawing charts and diagrams that would make it plain to themselves and others. This helped them to see their mistake. They had figured that the 2300 days began with the *first day* of 457, which, according to the Jewish time, was in the spring. But Ezra's record of the commandment to restore and to build Jerusalem showed that this decree did not take effect until the autumn of that year. So, of course, the 2300 days could not end until the autumn of 1844. They thought that the cleansing of the sanctuary, the event that was to come at the end of the 2300 days, was the cleansing of this world from sin, or its destruction by fire. By studying the services of the earthly sanctuary they learned that the cleansing of the earthly sanctuary always occurred on the tenth day of the seventh month, which in 1844 would be October 22. Therefore, they reasoned, "The end of the world will come October 22, 1844."

3. The Midnight Cry. At first, people were slow to accept this new idea, for fear that they might be mistaken again. But the more they studied it, the plainer it seemed. In July, the middle of the summer, a large number of them met to study the Bible together. As they prayed and studied, they felt convinced that October 22 must be the correct time. Then another great movement began, a preparation to meet the Lord on October 22 of that year. The proclamation of this message was called "the midnight cry," because it was a fulfillment of that part of the parable of the ten virgins which says, "At midnight there was a cry made, Behold, the bridegroom cometh." Besides, this movement really did begin at the midnight of a Jewish prophetic day, which would be midsummer of the literal year.

4. Effect of the Midnight Cry. People who lived at that time and who wrote about this wonderful experience said that this cry swept over the land with remarkable rapidity. Everywhere people were moved to repentance. They saw that even their mistake was a part of the prophecy. Thousands of people sincerely believed that in a few short weeks they would see Jesus coming in the clouds of heaven, and that the world would then be destroyed. These people felt that the giving of this message to their friends and neighbors and to others whom they could reach was the only thing worth while. Men who had sown and planted their fields in the spring were not interested in the harvest, so they left their crops standing in the fields, thus showing their faith by their works. Others sold their homes and used the money to print and distribute papers and tracts, and to support those who could leave home to preach the message. Some held on to their money until it was too late to invest it. These afterward laid thousands of dollars before those who were printing the truth, but were told that it was too late, as they already had all they could use before the end would come.

5. Opposition of Professed Christians. It seems impossible and yet it is true that many professed Christian churches bitterly opposed the preaching of the second coming of Christ. At last, they even refused to retain as members of their churches any who would speak of their hope in His coming. Ministers headed mobs determined to tar and feather those who preached the message. Meetings were often broken up by mob violence. With such a spirit in the hearts of professed Christians, it is not surprising that evil crept into the churches. It was at this time that church suppers, lotteries, and pleasure making of various kinds, were introduced in order to keep the people interested in *religion!* Surely this farce must have pleased Satan.

6. The Second Angel's Message. When William Miller and others began to preach the message of the coming of Jesus, they had no thought of organizing a separate church, or separating the people from their own churches. Their whole burden was to help them prepare to meet the Lord. But when these honest believers were not allowed to express their faith, and in many instances were excluded from the church to which they had belonged, the second angel's message was sounded, "Babylon is fallen, is fallen." "Come out of her, My people." Like the first angel's message, this call continues to be given, for in Babylon there are still many of God's precious jewels.

7. **October 22, 1844.** At last, the tenth day of the seventh month came, the day when thousands upon thousands expected, face to face, to meet the Judge of all the earth. They had made no provision for anything beyond that date. They had thought they would need nothing more for this life. They had done all they could to warn their neighbors and friends. In sorrow they had said good-by to those who had not given their hearts to God, for they never expected to see them again. And now in sober, solemn anxiety they assembled at their places of worship, expecting any moment to hear "the voice of the Archangel and the trump of God," and to see the heavens ablaze with the glory of their coming King.

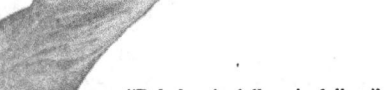
"Babylon is fallen, is fallen."

8. **The Second and Great Disappointment.** The hours passed slowly by, and when at last the sun sank below the western horizon, the tenth day of the seventh month was ended, and Jesus had not come. The shades of night spread their gloomy pall over the world; and with that darkness came a pang of sadness to the hearts of the advent believers, such as can find a parallel only in the sorrow of the disciples of our Lord, as they solemnly wended their way to their homes on the night following the crucifixion and burial of Him whom but a little while before they had triumphantly escorted into Jerusalem as their King.

How to Study: Be able to explain why the mistake in *time* was made. Why was October 22 set as the day for Christ to come? Be able to explain that the midnight of a prophetic day would come in midsummer. Why was the second angel's message necessary?

Use of Concordance: Find the two texts starred in paragraph 2. Key word: Use "tarry" for both verses. Before you begin to hunt, decide in what books of the Bible to look.

For Your Workbook: Draw a diagram of the three angels' messages, showing the two disappointments. Show also when the first angel's message was given, the tarrying time, the midnight cry, and the second angel's message. The blank for this diagram is a page in "Bible Workbook" for the eighth grade.

Memory Work: Memorize Revelation 14: 8.

---

3. SATAN'S PLOT UNMASKED
The Third Angel's Message — Rev. 14: 9-20

"Here is the patience of the saints: here are they that keep the commandments of God, and the faith of Jesus." Rev. 14:12.

1. Struggles After the Disappointment. As the disappointed ones took up life's duties once more, for years they had to meet the scorn and sneers of a scoffing world. Even the children in school were insulted by other children. But if our own hearts are right before God, sneers can hurt only those who give them. It took a long time and a great deal of patient labor before those who had sold their homes and given the money to advance the message, once more had even the common comforts of life. But God's truth was worth more to them than houses and lands.

In New Hampshire a man whose name was Mr. Hastings had a large field of fine potatoes which he had left undug. "Let us dig them for you and put them into your cellar," said some of his neighbors, "for you may need them." "No!" answered Mr. Hastings. "I am going to let that field of potatoes preach my faith in the Lord's soon coming." And so the potatoes stayed in the ground. That autumn the potato crop in all that section of the country was almost a total loss on account of the "potato rot." But when Mr. Hastings finally dug his, he had a fine crop, entirely free from the rot. Consequently he had an abundant supply for himself, and in the spring his neighbors were obliged to buy seed potatoes of him, and they were glad to pay a good price for them. Who shall say that God's hand was not over this potato field which had silently preached the message?

2. More Light from the Bible. These sincere Christians had learned where to find comfort and help, and to the Bible again they went with many prayers for light and understanding. In Revelation 10:11 they read, "Thou must prophesy *again* before many

---

References Used: S. A. M., pp. 166, 167; Mal. 4:1.

peoples, and nations, and tongues, and kings." But what should they prophesy? Then they began to study the third angel's message and the sanctuary. In this study, they found no mistake with the *time* they had set, but they learned that the cleansing of the sanctuary, the *event* that closed the 2300 days, was the Judgment in the heavenly sanctuary, and not the cleansing of this earth by fire. A little later they learned that the Sabbath of God's law is the seventh day of the week, and not the first day. The Lord also mercifully gave these people the spirit of prophecy, to lead them over the rough path that lay before them, and to help them understand the special truth He desired to give to the world. In Revelation 12:17 these people are called "the remnant," because they are the last part of God's church on earth, the few who will remain true and loyal. They are the ones "which keep the commandments of God, and have the testimony of Jesus Christ," which is "the spirit of prophecy." They are the ones who will give God's last message to the world before His second coming.

"The third angel followed them."

3. Why the Dragon Is Wroth with the Remnant. The dragon is wroth with this church because the third angel's message, which they proclaim, is a warning against the beast and his image and Satan's whole system of iniquity. Long enough has Satan blinded men's eyes. Long enough has he turned them away from God's law. "Every nation, and kindred, and tongue, and people" shall hear the truth of the everlasting gospel. Satan's plan to overthrow the government of God and set up a government of his own shall be exposed. Everyone must know his deceptive schemes. Then each one must decide for himself whether he will receive "the seal of God" and march under God's banner, or receive "the mark of the beast" and march under Satan's banner.

4. The Loud Cry (18:1, 2). As the dangers thicken and the end draws still nearer, God's great anxiety for the children of earth deepens. A short time before probation closes, the heavenly Parent sends a special angel "having great power" to cry "mightily with a strong voice," emphasizing the words of the angels of Revelation 14; and the whole earth is "lightened with his glory," so that all who do not willfully close their eyes to the truth shall clearly see the wicked plans and schemes of Satan, and the righteous requirements of a just and loving Father. The open doors into all coun-

"I saw another angel come down from heaven, and the earth was lightened with his glory."

tries, and the rapidity and power with which the message of Revelation 14 is now going to the whole world, indicate that even now we can hear some strains of the loud cry of this mighty angel.

5. Result of Rejecting God (14:9, 10). "If any man worship the beast and his image, and receive his mark in his forehead, or in his hand, the same shall drink of the wine of the wrath of God, which is poured out without mixture [not mixed with mercy] into the cup of His indignation; and he shall be tormented with fire and brimstone in the presence of the holy angels, and in the presence of the Lamb." This destruction takes place at the end of the thousand years, when Jesus and His redeemed people descend to this earth. This is the day described by Malachi: "For, behold, the day cometh, that shall burn as an oven; and all the proud, yea, and all that do wickedly, shall be stubble: and the day that cometh shall burn them up, saith the Lord of hosts, that it shall leave them neither root nor branch." No one shall be able to quench that awful fire; it is unquenchable, burning till the last vestige of sin is entirely consumed.

6. Commandment Keepers (14:12). While those who have chosen to worship the beast and his image and walk under the banner that Satan has set up are destroyed in the lake of fire, the angel shows John another company who have chosen to obey God and walk under *His banner.* Of these the angel says, "Here is the

"Upon the cloud One sat like unto the Son of man."

patience of the saints: here are they that keep the commandments of God, and the faith of Jesus."

7. Coming of the Son of Man (14:14-16). Again the prophet looked, and he saw "a white cloud, and upon the cloud One sat like unto the Son of man, having on His head a golden crown, and in His hand a sharp sickle." This shows Jesus as He is preparing to leave heaven to come to this earth for His people. The angel of mercy has left the earth and returned to heaven. Angels in heaven are hastening to and fro. One "angel came out of the temple, crying with a loud voice to Him that sat on the cloud, Thrust in Thy sickle, and reap: for the time is come for Thee to reap; for the harvest of the earth is ripe. . . . Another angel came out of the temple which is in heaven, he also having a sharp sickle. And another angel came out from the altar." This is the destroying angel having "power over fire." This angel "cried with a loud cry to him [the angel] that had the sharp sickle, saying, Thrust in thy sharp sickle, and gather the clusters of the vine of the earth [the wicked]; for her grapes are fully ripe." So while Jesus gathers the righteous, the destroying angel thrusts in his sickle into the earth, and gathers the vine of the earth, and casts it into the great wine press of the wrath of God.

How to Study: Study to recite from the paragraph topics. Remember that the first disappointment showed a mistake in *time;* the second, a mistake in *event.* What scripture showed their mistakes? The study of what subject gave them further light? Why are these people called the remnant? Explain why Satan is wroth with them.

Memory Work: Finish memorizing the three angels' messages, including Revelation 12:17 with 19:10, last part. When this work is completed, you are entitled to the fourth star on your memory certificate.

For Your Workbook: On your diagram of the messages, indicate the place for the third angel's message. Both of the first two messages continue to be given with the third message.

REVIEW OF REVELATION 14

Test Questions:
1. What time does the giving of the third angel's message cover? Show how many years of "this generation" are now past.
2. What is God's purpose in sending this message to men?
3. Why does Satan so bitterly oppose it?
4. In what four prophecies is the first angel's message found?
5. How extensively was it preached? Show on the map.
6. Explain the two disappointments — cause, time, and how understood.
7. Why were the churches called Babylon?
8. What was the midnight cry?
9. What is "the faith of Jesus" or "the testimony of Jesus"?
10. Explain that the cleansing of the heavenly sanctuary is the Investigative Judgment.
11. What are the two characteristics of the remnant church? Why does Satan hate these two things?
12. What event follows the giving of this message?

Dates to Remember:
  First angel's message,—1831 to the end
  Second angel's message,— summer of 1844 to the end
  Third angel's message,— autumn of 1844 to the end

Chapter Drill: What prophecy is found in Revelation 14? Give in order the general subject of each chapter in Revelation from 1 to 14.

Verse-Finding Drill: See how quickly you can find the verse containing each of the following. (Others may be added from previous reviews.)
  1. I saw another angel . . . having the everlasting gospel to preach.
  2. The hour of His Judgment is come.
  3. Babylon is fallen, is fallen.
  4. Here are they that keep the commandments of God, and the faith of Jesus.
  5. Blessed are the dead which die in the Lord from henceforth.
  6. I looked, and behold a white cloud, and upon the cloud One sat like unto the Son of man.
  7. The testimony of Jesus is the spirit of prophecy.
  8. The dragon . . . went to make war with the remnant.

Memory Drill: Rev. 14: 6-12.

OUTLINE OF CHAPTER XII

Symbols — The Seven Last Plagues
Time   — "One Day,"— the Last Year of the Reign of Sin
Result — Destruction of the Whole Earth
          Satan Cast into the Lake of Fire

Topics —

                                                        Revelation

Preparation for the Seven Last Plagues 15
First Five Plagues Poured Out ....⎤
The Sixth Plague .... ⎬ 16
The Seventh Plague ....⎦
Review

CHAPTER XII

The Climax of Satan's Destructive Reign

1. PREPARATION FOR THE SEVEN LAST PLAGUES
Revelation 15

"I saw another sign in heaven, great and marvelous, seven angels having the seven last plagues." Rev. 15:1.

1. The Sixth Division of Revelation. The sixth division of the prophecies given in the Revelation is recorded in chapters 15, 16, 17, and 18. Chapter 15 introduces the prophecy, giving a description of the seven angels having the seven last plagues, and a description of the temple in heaven during the time the plagues are poured out. Chapter 16 tells about the pouring out of the plagues. Chapter 17 describes the woman who represents "the synagogue of Satan" and who is called "Mystery, Babylon the Great." Chapter 18 tells of the fall and final destruction of this Babylon during the plagues.

2. Events Leading to the Plagues. When Jesus rose from the dead and ascended to heaven, the work in the first apartment of the heavenly sanctuary began. This continued until 1844. Then His work in the second apartment began,—the investigation of the records of those whose names have at some time been entered in the book of life. The cases of the righteous dead of all past ages are first investigated. When these are finished, the cases of the righteous living will be examined. This work will close when the third angel's message, which God sends to tell everyone about the Judgment, has gone to all the world, God's people are all sealed, and the full number of Christ's family which He planned in "times eternal" is made up. Then the angel of mercy will leave the earth, and the decree will go forth, "He that is unjust, let him be unjust still: and he which is filthy, let him be filthy still: and he that is righteous, let him be righteous still: and he that is holy, let him

References Used: G. C., pp. 613, 614, 618, 619; Matt. 24:14; Rev. 22:11; 8:5; Dan. 12:1; Isa. 59:16; 1 Cor. 4:9; Job 1:8-12; 2:6.

be holy still." The work of Christ as our High Priest will then be finished. He will cast His censer into the earth, and leave the sanctuary. At that time the plagues will be poured out.

3. Angels with the Plagues (15: 6-8). "The seven angels came out of the temple, . . . clothed in pure and white linen, and . . . girded with golden girdles. And one of the four living creatures gave unto the seven angels seven golden vials full of the wrath of God." John saw that as soon as these angels left the temple, it was immediately filled with the glory and power of God, so that no one was able to enter it until the seven angels had finished their work. During all this time, there will be * "no intercessor" in the heavenly sanctuary. Then will begin the "time of trouble, such as never was since there was a nation." The wrath of God will be poured out upon those who "worship the beast and his image." It will be poured out "without mixture"—without mercy—because sinners have entirely rejected God's mercy.

4. Why God Tries His People. During the time of trouble, the righteous and the wicked will be on this earth together. Have you ever wondered why God will leave His children to go through these terrible times *after* probation closes? Why did God leave Job in Satan's power? Why did He turn away His face from Jesus as He hung upon the cross? God's people * "are made a spectacle [or theater] unto the world, and to angels, and to men." Satan has accused God of being partial and unjust, of favoring His own children while not giving *him* a fair chance. Whenever he is defeated, he claims that God has taken unfair advantage of him.

So it was in the case of Job. "Hast thou considered My servant Job, that there is none like him in the earth, a perfect and an upright man, one that feareth God, and escheweth evil?" said God to Satan. Satan angrily answered: * "Doth Job fear God for naught? Hast not Thou made an hedge about him, and about his house, and about all that he hath? . . . But put forth Thine hand now, and touch all that he hath, and he will curse Thee to Thy face." Then the Lord said to Satan, "Behold, he is in thine hand; but save his life."

Satan feels the same toward God's people to-day. "He declares that the Lord cannot in justice forgive their sins, and yet destroy him and his angels. He claims them as *his* prey, and demands that they be given into his hands to destroy." It is as if he should say to God: "Remove the hedge You have placed about them, and they will curse You to Your face. They will quickly come over onto my side." Will any one of us do this?

Jesus will not leave one stone unturned to settle the question, even with fallen angels, that God is just. So He steps out of the sanctuary and leaves His own children in the land of the enemy, without an intercessor. God's only restriction during this time is that Satan may not take their lives. This is Satan's supreme opportunity. "As Satan accuses the people of God on account of their sins, the Lord permits him to try them to the uttermost. Their confidence in God, their faith and firmness, will be severely tested. . . . He [Satan] hopes . . . that they will yield to his temptations, and turn from their allegiance to God."

Our next lesson will tell us what sort of world this would be if it were under Satan's sole rule. It will show us, too, whether God is unjust or whether Satan himself is the cruel and unjust one.

How to Study: The chief points to get out of this lesson are, when the plagues are to be poured out, on whom, and why. Turn to the chapters in the Bible that deal with the plagues, and notice the general contents of each.

Use of Concordance: Find the three texts starred under topics 3 and 4. Key words: intercessor, spectacle, hedge.

Chapter to Remember: Revelation 15 — preparing to pour out the seven last plagues.

---

2. FIRST FIVE PLAGUES POURED OUT
Rev. 16:1-11

"I heard a great voice . . . saying to the seven angels, Go your ways, and pour out the vials of the wrath of God upon the earth." Rev. 16:1.

1. The Plagues: Duration, Extent, Character (18:8). The Bible says that the "plagues come in one day." This is generally understood to be a prophetic day, which of course would mean one year. "These plagues are not universal, or the inhabitants of the earth would be wholly cut off. Yet they will be the most awful

---
References Used: G. C., pp. 618-620, 628, 629; Hab. 3:17; Hag. 1:10; Ps. 91:3, 4; 121:5, 6; Isa. 33:16; Joel 1:11, 12, 18, 20; Amos 8:3; Gen. 32:26.

scourges that have ever been known to mortals." They will be similar to those which fell upon Egypt just before Israel was delivered from Egyptian bondage.

2. The First Plague (16: 2). The first plague will be poured out upon the earth. As a result, "the fig tree shall not blossom, neither shall fruit be in the vines; the labor of the olive shall fail, and the fields shall yield no meat; the flock shall be cut off from the fold, and there shall be no herd in the stalls." "The heaven over you is stayed from dew, and the earth is stayed from her fruit." Because of this drought and famine, "there fell a noisome and grievous sore upon the men which had the mark of the beast, and upon them which worshiped his image." But God's people have obeyed the laws of life, they have practiced right health habits, and in this time, though they will suffer from hunger, they have the promise, * "He shall deliver thee . . . from the noisome pestilence. . . . His truth shall be thy shield and buckler." Shall we at that time be able to claim this promise if now, during our time of probation, we fail to practice right habits of health?

3. The Second and Third Plagues (16: 3-7). Under these plagues, the water of the sea and of the rivers becomes as the blood of a dead man, and all that are in the sea die. So terrible are the plagues that it would seem that they cannot last long, or everyone would perish. Deadly though they are, they are just, for the wicked "have shed the blood of saints and prophets." Though the righteous suffer from thirst, yet they do not perish, for God's promise is fulfilled: * "Bread shall be given him; his waters shall be sure."

4. The Fourth Plague (16: 8, 9). John saw the fourth plague poured upon the sun, "and men were scorched with great heat." Because of this extreme heat, "the harvest of the field is perished," and "all the trees of the field are withered." "The beasts groan, the herds of cattle are perplexed, because they have no pasture. . . . The rivers of waters are dried up." "There shall be many dead bodies in every place," so many that it will be impossible to have funeral services, and "they shall cast them forth with silence." During this terrible time the wicked blaspheme the name of God because of the plague; but the righteous, although not free from suffering, have learned to trust God, and to be patient under trial.

They thank God for the promise: * "The Lord is thy keeper: the Lord is thy shade upon thy right hand. The sun shall not smite thee."

5. The Fifth Plague (16:10, 11). The fifth plague is poured out "upon the seat of the beast; and his kingdom was full of darkness; and they gnawed their tongues for pain, and blasphemed the God of heaven because of their pains and their sores."

When mercy and love fail to draw sinners to repentance, affliction is often needed. But when neither avails, the case is hopeless. These people have deliberately chosen to be on Satan's side, they have refused every opportunity to

The waters became blood, "and every living soul died in the sea."

turn to Jesus. Now their last breath is spent in blaspheming the God whose resources of infinite love to save them from their sins have been persistently rejected.

God's people see serious trouble ahead. "Satan . . . does not know that their cases have been decided in the sanctuary above." Nor do they know it. They are not afraid to meet death, but "they fear that every sin has not been repented of." Still they cannot remember one that is unconfessed. "Though suffering the keenest anxiety, terror, and distress, they do not cease their intercessions. They lay hold of the strength of God as Jacob laid hold of the Angel; and the language of their souls is, 'I will not let Thee go, except Thou bless me.'"

How to Study: Be able to tell the nature of each of the first five plagues, and how God's people are protected under each. What particular promise is their help in each case?

Use of Concordance: Find the three starred verses under topics 2, 3, 4. Key words: shield, bread, shade.

Dictionary: Noisome.

3. THE SIXTH PLAGUE
Rev. 16: 12-16

"And he gathered them together into a place called in the Hebrew tongue Armageddon." Rev. 16:16.

1. Chief Event of the Sixth Plague (16:16). The great event of the sixth plague is the last great battle that will be fought before Jesus comes. It is called the battle of Armageddon, named from the place where it will be fought.

2. The Power Back of Armageddon (16:13, 14). When God showed John this great battle, He also showed him the power that would urge forward this final warfare. Said John: "I saw three unclean spirits like frogs come out of the mouth of the dragon, and out of the mouth of the beast, and out of the mouth of the false prophet. For they are the spirits of devils, working miracles, which go forth unto the kings of the earth and of the whole world, to gather them to the battle of that great day of God Almighty." This shows that Satan is really the general of Armageddon, and

References Used: G. C., pp. 588, 590, 592, 612, 615, 624-626, 630-633.

that he will work through "the dragon," which represents paganism (those who reject God or Christ), "the beast," which represents the papacy, and "the false prophet," which represents false or apostate Protestantism. In these three classes are included all who dwell upon the earth, except God's true children, those who steadfastly remain loyal to His commandments. These three pow-

"And he gathered them into a place called Armageddon."

ers will go forth to the kings, or rulers, of the earth, and by working miracles, they will lead these rulers to engage in this great world war.

Armageddon, the decisive battle of the war, is still future; but Satan is even now preparing his "unclean spirits" for that time. His great purpose in this war will be just what it always has been; namely, to destroy the influence of God's law on this earth, and to establish his own authority. How does he go about this work? He makes the Sabbath, which is the seal of *God's* authority, the great issue. He is determined to compel the whole world to recognize Sunday, which he has set up as the mark of *his* authority. In this way he thinks to make himself recognized as the supreme ruler of this earth.

3. **Apostate Protestantism.** You will remember that when Protestants first came into existence they *protested* against the claims of the papacy. They said that the church had no right to use the power of the state to force people to obey its demands. They said that everyone should be allowed to worship God just as he thought was right, and that the state had control only of his civil deportment. But Protestants as a body have become false to their original profession. They are called "the false prophet," for they are now trying to secure the power of civil rulers to compel everyone in religious matters, and they have centered their efforts on compulsory Sunday observance. For many years they have thus been busy forming "an image to the beast,"— an image to the papacy.

4. **War Against the Remnant (12:17; 19:10).** In the time of trouble which is soon to come upon the world, we shall see fulfilled the words of the prophet: "The dragon [Satan] was wroth with the woman, and went to make war with the remnant of her seed, which keep the commandments of God, and have the testimony of Jesus Christ," which is "the spirit of prophecy." The efforts that Protestants have for years been putting forth to secure Sunday laws have been largely defeated by the counterworking of those who "keep the commandments of God." This makes Satan very angry. He is now urging Protestants to unite with the papacy and with those who make no profession, in order to accomplish their purpose. Under this threefold union, miracles will be wrought through spiritualism, which in many ways is already a common belief among all these classes of people.

5. **Commandment Keepers Falsely Accused.** As troubles develop, the plagues continue. Worse and worse grows the situation. The "unclean spirits" are desperate. They persuade rulers that those who "keep the commandments of God" are the cause of all these evils. They declare that the calamities which are upon the world "will not cease until Sunday observance is strictly enforced." And to prove that they are right they will perform miracles, healing the sick, and doing other "lying wonders." As the apostles were accused of treason, so commandment keepers will also be accused of rebellion against the government because they refuse to obey man-made laws that require them to disobey God.

"Like the melody of angel songs, the words fall upon the ear, 'Stand fast to your allegiance. Help is coming.' "

6. Satan's Last Great Deception. At last Satan will appear in person as an angel of light, even as Christ Himself. Through spiritualism he will work miracles and will perform many undeniable wonders. He will profess to believe the Bible, and to have respect for the church. Everywhere people are deceived. They think Christ has come. They "prostrate themselves in adoration before him, while he lifts up his hands, and pronounces a blessing upon them. . . . Then . . . he claims to have changed the Sabbath to Sunday, and commands all to hallow the day which he has blessed." But those who have studied the Bible know that he is an impostor, for the Bible says that Christ will come in the clouds of heaven, and as the lightning flashes from one end of heaven to the other. They know, too, that his claims are false, because they are not in harmony with God's word.

7. The Death Decree. When Satan fails to deceive God's true children, his rage knows no bounds. He then causes a decree to be issued "against those who hallow the Sabbath of the fourth commandment, denouncing them as deserving of the severest punishment, and giving the people liberty, after a certain time, to put them to death." This is the time when they will not be able to buy or sell, and their property will be confiscated. Then "the people of God will flee from the cities and villages, and associate together in companies, dwelling in the most desolate and solitary places. Many . . . will be cast into the most unjust and cruel bondage."

8. Help Assured. "Some are assailed in their flight from the cities and villages; but the swords raised against them break and fall as powerless as a straw." Angels see their distress, and hear their prayers, and protect them. "They are waiting the word of their Commander to snatch them from their peril." But as it was with Jesus in the garden of Gethsemane, so God's people must drink of the cup and be baptized with the baptism. As they continue to pray, "the veil separating them from the unseen seems almost withdrawn. The heavens glow with the dawning of eternal day, and, like the melody of angel songs, the words fall upon the ear, 'Stand fast to your allegiance. Help is coming.'"

How to Study: Point out Armageddon on the map. Be sure you know what is represented by the "unclean spirits" of devils, and what part these act in preparing for the battle of Armageddon. Why does Satan make Sunday laws the great issue in this war? Why is the war finally directed against the "remnant"?

Where is the Bible text quoted under topic 4 found? Where is the text which says that the time will come when God's people will not be allowed to buy or sell?

---

4. THE SEVENTH PLAGUE
Rev. 16: 17-21

"And there came a great voice . . . from the throne, saying, It is done." Rev. 16:17.

1. Deliverance from the Death Decree. As the time draws near when the death decree is to go into effect, it will be as it was in the days of Esther. In different lands "it will be determined to strike in one night a decisive blow" to destroy the hated sect. "Throngs of evil men are about to rush upon their prey, when lo, a dense blackness, deeper than the darkness of the night, falls upon the earth. Then a rainbow, shining with the glory from the throne of God, spans the heavens, and seems to encircle each praying company. The angry multitudes are suddenly arrested. Their mocking cries die away. . . .

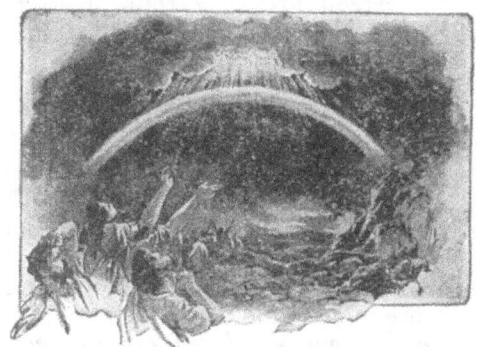

"A rainbow, shining with the glory from the throne of God, seems to encircle each praying company."

With fearful forebodings they gaze upon the symbol of God's covenant."

2. Events at Midnight (16:17, 18). As when God delivered His people from Egyptian oppression, as when the Angel met Jacob to deliver him, so at this time "it is at midnight that God manifests His power for the deliverance of His people. The sun appears, shining in its strength. Signs and wonders follow in quick succession. . . . Everything in nature seems turned out of its course. The streams cease to flow. Dark, heavy clouds come up, and clash against each other. In the midst of the angry heavens

---

References Used: G. C., pp. 635-641, 644, 645; Isa. 35:5, 6; 1 Cor. 15:52; Matt. 24:31.

is one clear space of indescribable glory," whence comes "a great voice out of the temple of heaven, from the throne, saying, It is done. And there were voices, and thunders, and lightnings; and there was a great earthquake, such as was not since men were upon the earth, so mighty an earthquake, and so great." This earthquake opens many graves, and there is a special resurrection of "all who have died in the faith of the third angel's message." * "They also which pierced Him" are raised to behold His glory.

It is then that "there appears against the sky a hand holding two tables of stone folded together. . . . The hand opens the tables, and there are seen the precepts of the Decalogue, traced as with a pen of fire." Then God's blessing is pronounced upon those who have honored Him by keeping His Sabbath holy. * "Blessed are they that do His commandments, that they may have right to the tree of life, and may enter in through the gates into the city."

3. Destruction of Babylon (16:19-21; 18:9, 11, 17, 20). After the special resurrection, the terrible destruction of the seventh plague is poured out upon the wicked world, which is called Babylon. "And the great city was divided into three parts, and the cities of the nations fell: and great Babylon came in remembrance before God, to give unto her the cup of the wine of the fierceness of His wrath. And every island fled away, and the mountains were not found. And there fell upon men a great hail out of heaven, every stone about the weight of a talent [about fifty-seven pounds]: and men blasphemed God because of the plague of the hail; for the plague thereof was exceeding great."

Babylon and its destruction are more fully described in Revelation 17 and 18. The kings of the earth, the merchants of the earth, and every shipmaster, and as many as trade by sea, mourned over Babylon, saying, "Alas, alas that great city Babylon, that mighty city! for in one hour is thy judgment come." It is thought by many that this "one hour" is prophetic time, and that therefore this terrible plague will last fifteen days. Whether this be true or not, let us hope that it will be but a short time.

4. The Sign of the Son of Man. At this time "the voice of God is heard from heaven, declaring the day and hour of Jesus' coming. . . . Like peals of loudest thunder, His words roll through the earth." "Soon there appears in the east a small black cloud, about half the size of a man's hand. It is the cloud which surrounds the Saviour, and which seems in the distance to be shrouded in darkness. The people of God know this to be the sign of the Son of man. In solemn silence they gaze upon it as it draws nearer the earth, becoming lighter and more glorious, until it is a great white cloud, its base a glory like consuming fire, and above it the rainbow of the covenant."

Then the heavens depart as a scroll when it is rolled together, and as the people of God look upon the scene, the sky seems filled with shining angels, and they hear the music of the heavenly anthem. At first they cannot see Jesus, but "as the living cloud comes still nearer, every eye beholds the Prince of life. . . . Before His presence, 'all faces are turned into paleness.'" The wicked feel the terror of eternal despair, and call for the rocks and mountains to fall upon them and destroy them. Even "the righteous cry with trembling, 'Who shall be able to stand?' The angels' song is hushed, and there is a period of awful silence. Then the voice of Jesus is heard, saying, 'My grace is sufficient for you.' The faces of the righteous are lighted up, and joy fills every heart. And the

Graves are opened, and angels gather together the elect, and they are caught up to meet the Lord in the air.

angels strike a note higher, and sing again, as they draw still nearer to the earth."

5. The Resurrection of the Righteous. "Amid the reeling of the earth, the flash of lightning, and the roar of thunder, the voice of the Son of God calls forth the sleeping saints. . . . 'Awake, awake, awake, ye that sleep in the dust, and arise!' Throughout the length and breadth of the earth, the dead shall hear that voice; and they that hear shall live. . . . All come forth from their graves the same in stature as when they entered the tomb. Adam . . . presents a marked contrast to the people of later generations. . . . But all arise with the freshness and vigor of eternal youth. . . . Christ . . . will change our vile bodies, and fashion

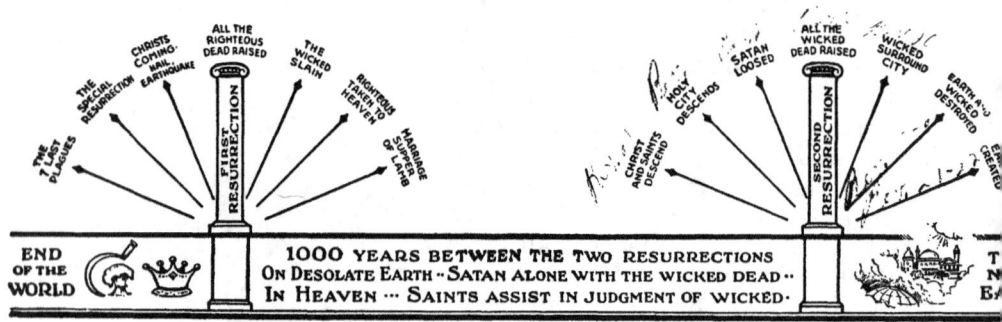

This shows the events that cluster around the beginning and end of the millennium.

them like unto His glorious body. The mortal, corruptible form, devoid of comeliness, once polluted with sin, becomes perfect, beautiful, and immortal. All blemishes and deformities are left in the grave." *"Then the eyes of the blind shall be opened, and the ears of the deaf shall be unstopped. Then shall the lame man leap as an hart, and the tongue of the dumb sing."

6. The Righteous Changed and Translated. The living righteous are changed *"in a moment, in the twinkling of an eye." "They are made immortal, and with the risen saints are caught up to meet their Lord in the air. Angels 'gather together the elect from the four winds, from one end of heaven to the other.' Little children are borne by holy angels to their mothers' arms. Friends long separated by death are united, nevermore to part, and with songs of gladness ascend together to the city of God."

REVIEW OF THE SEVEN LAST PLAGUES

Test Questions:
1. In what chapters are the plagues described?
2. Are they poured out before or after probation closes? What verse in Revelation 15 shows this?
3. Why are they poured out "without mixture"?
4. Tell in order upon what each plague will be poured out, and the effect. What special promises encourage the righteous at this time?
5. How long will the plagues continue? Give verse.
6. Under what plague is the battle of Armageddon?
7. What three powers does Satan use in this battle?
8. Why is Satan especially angry with "the remnant"?
9. Through what power will Satan work miracles?
10. When Satan appears as Christ, how may we know that he is a deceiver?
11. What decree is passed under the sixth plague that will be like the one passed in Esther's day?
12. In what way will the deliverance of God's people at this time be like their deliverance from Egypt anciently?
13. Name the events of the seventh plague.
14. What is the sign of the Son of man?
15. When does God say, "It is done"?
16. When does the special resurrection take place? What two classes are raised at this time? What verses tell this?
17. When are the rest of the righteous raised?

Chapter Drill: To previous chapter drills on Revelation, add the following:
Revelation 15. Angels appointed to pour out the plagues
Revelation 16. The plagues poured out
Revelation 17. Wicked Babylon described
Revelation 18. Destruction of Babylon

Verse-Finding Drill: How many of these can you find in five minutes?

1. No man was able to enter into the temple.
2. I saw . . . seven angels having the seven last plagues.
3. The first . . . poured out his vial upon the earth.
4. The second angel poured out his vial upon the sea
5. The third angel poured out his vial upon the rivers.
6. The fourth angel poured out his vial upon the sun.
7. The fifth angel poured out his vial upon the seat of the beast.
8. The sixth angel poured out his vial upon the . . . Euphrates.
9. The seventh angel poured out his vial into the air.
10. I saw three unclean spirits . . . the spirits of devils.
11. He gathered them . . . into a place called . . . Armageddon.
12. There came a . . . voice . . . from the throne, saying, "It is done."
13. There was a great earthquake.
14. The plague of the hail . . . was exceeding great.
15. Her plagues come in one day.

For Your Workbook: Begin the diagram of the one thousand years, entering the events you have had that take place at the beginning of this time. The blank for this diagram is a page in "Bible Workbook" for the eighth grade.

OUTLINE OF CHAPTER XIII

Subject — God's Great Family "Home Coming"
A New Heaven and a New Earth

Time — One Thousand Years; Then Eternity

Result — No More Sin
"No more death, neither sorrow, nor crying," for "The Lord God omnipotent reigneth"

Topics —

	Revelation
The Hallelujah Chorus at the Marriage of the Lamb	19
Satan's Time for Undisturbed Reflection	20
A New Heaven and a New Earth	} 21
The Holy City	
God's Plan Finished — "It Is Done"	22

Review

CHAPTER XIII

The Triumph of God's Plan

1. THE HALLELUJAH CHORUS AT THE MARRIAGE OF THE LAMB
Rev. 19:1-10

"I heard a great voice of much people in heaven, saying, Alleluia; . . . for the Lord God omnipotent reigneth." Rev. 19:1, 6.

1. The Homeward Journey (15:3). The last four chapters of Revelation tell the triumph of God's plan, and the great family home-coming. When all the righteous dead are released from Satan's prison house, and they with the righteous living have been * "caught up together . . . in the clouds, to meet the Lord in the air," then begins that wonderful seven-day journey to heaven. "On each side of the cloudy chariot are wings, and beneath it are living wheels; and as the chariot rolls upward, the wheels cry, 'Holy,' and the wings, as they move, cry, 'Holy,' and the retinue of angels cry, 'Holy, holy, holy, Lord God Almighty.' And the redeemed shout 'Alleluia!' as the chariot moves onward toward the New Jerusalem."

In speaking of this grand journey, Uriah Smith says: "From our little world we pass out to our sun, ninety-three million miles away; on to its nearest neighboring sun, nineteen thousand million miles away; on to the great double polestar, from which it takes light, in its electric flight of one hundred ninety-two thousand miles a second, forty years to reach our world; on past systems, groups, constellations, till we reach the great star Alcyone, in the Pleiades, shining with the power of twelve thousand suns like ours!" Is it any wonder that after such a journey the great company of the redeemed break forth in that song of victory, saying, "Great and marvelous are Thy works, Lord God Almighty"?

2. Words of the Hallelujah Chorus (19:1-3). After the redeemed reach heaven, John heard that great company singing the

---
References Used: G. C., p. 645; E. W., p. 19; D. R. on lesson text; 1 Thess. 4:17; Eph. 3:15; 5:27; Isa. 64:6.

(483)

Alleluia chorus. He does not attempt to tell how many voices there were in this chorus, but merely says, "I heard a great voice of much people." The words he heard them singing were, "Alleluia; salvation, and glory, and honor, and power, unto the Lord our God." Their first thought is not the benefit they themselves

As the living chariot of God moves upward, the wheels cry, "Holy, holy, holy."

receive; it is not the beautiful crowns and harps that have been given them, nor the splendid mansions that are to be their eternal home. No! their first thought is to honor their King by expressions of gratitude and love.

"True and righteous are His judgments: for He . . . hath avenged the blood of His servants." The heavenly beings and the saints rejoice in the righteous judgments of God, not because they have enmity toward the unfortunate subjects of those judgments, but because God's wisdom, His justice, His goodness, stand fully vindicated. The wicked were invited and urged to come, but they despised the invitation and killed those who brought it to them.

"And again they said, Alleluia."

3. Special Parts in the Chorus (19:4-7). Then special singers render their parts, for "the four and twenty elders and the four living creatures fell down and worshiped God that sat on the throne, saying, Amen; Alleluia."

Then a solo follows, for "a voice came out of the throne, saying, Praise our God, all ye His servants, and ye that fear Him, both small and great."

Then the full chorus, "a great multitude," joined the triumphant song. Some of the voices are as the sound "of many waters," clear and sweet; others are the bass voices, "as the voice of mighty thunderings," saying, "Alleluia: for the Lord God omnipotent reigneth. Let us be glad and rejoice, and give honor to Him: for the marriage of the Lamb is come, and His wife hath made herself ready."

4. The Oratorio "Messiah." If you have ever listened to the great oratorio "Messiah," composed by that master musician, Handel, you have heard one of the grandest pieces of music ever written by man. This masterpiece is sung each year at Easter time in London by a chorus of three thousand trained voices. It is most thrilling. Every breath of air vibrates with its inspiring harmony, until the soul seems almost to be transported to heaven and to be listening to the angel choir as they sing the praises of Messiah their King. The climax of this oratorio is called "the Hallelujah Chorus." This chorus is based on the scripture which is the text of to-day's lesson.

5. The Marriage Supper (19:8, 9). The occasion of this chorus is the marriage supper of the Lamb. After the great reception before the throne of God is over, Jesus says, "Come, My people, you have come out of great tribulation, and done My will; suffered for Me; come in to supper, for I will gird Myself, and serve you." There before their eyes is a table of pure silver, many miles in length. On the table is the fruit of the tree of life, the manna, almonds, figs, pomegranates, grapes, and many other kinds of fruit. What a sight that will be, and what a blessed privilege it will be to sit down to that table at the time of the great reunion of God's * "whole family in heaven and earth"!

May not one of the boys and girls who study these lessons be missing on that great occasion. May we all have on the wedding garment, "the fine linen, clean and white," the garment of righteousness which is without "spot, or wrinkle, or any such thing." Now is the time to let Jesus take away the filthy rags of our sins and clothe us with a change of raiment. Christ must not only be on us as a robe, but in us as a life.

How to Study: How long was there "silence in heaven"? This shows how long it will take to make the journey to heaven. When will the alleluia chorus be sung? Where? By whom? In whose honor? On what occasion? What are the terms of admission? Describe the parts of this chorus.

Write in figures the numbers given under topic 1. In connection with each topic read the Bible verses referred to.

Use of Concordance: Find the two texts starred under topics 1 and 5. Key words: caught, family.

For Your Workbook: Continue the diagram of the one thousand years, entering the events of this lesson.

For the Ambitious Student: On the first clear night find the Pleiades.

How many miles long would a table have to be to seat 144,000 people, giving to each person 3 feet of space, and seating the people along both sides of the table? Suppose each of the 144,000 is the head of a family of ten, how long a table will be needed to seat all the families?

2. SATAN'S TIME FOR UNDISTURBED REFLECTION
Revelation 20

"I saw an angel . . . having . . . a great chain in his hand. And he laid hold on . . . Satan, and bound him a thousand years." Rev. 20: 1, 2.

1. Satan in the Bottomless Pit (20: 1-3). When the righteous are taken to heaven, Satan is left alone with his evil angels on this desolate earth. The bodies of the wicked, slain by the brightness of the coming of Jesus, are strewn from one end of the earth to the other, with no one to mourn over or bury them,— terrible feast for the fowls of the air. The very foundations of the earth have been shaken by the voice of God; the great earthquake has leveled the mightiest works of man; everywhere the seven last plagues have left their desolating effect. Here, in this limitless waste, this "bottomless pit," Satan is confined for a thousand years. He cannot leave the planet, and he has no one to deceive or annoy. Here he is left to behold and reflect upon the ruin he has wrought. This is the third time that he has been "cast out."

References Used: G. C., pp. 658-666, 668, 669, 673; E. W., pp. 17, 18, 41, 291; Jer. 25: 33; Matt. 19: 28; 1 Cor. 6: 3; Zech. 14: 4; Acts 1: 11; Isa. 34: 9; 2 Peter 3: 10.

2. Judgment of the Wicked (20:4-6, 12, 15). While Satan is wandering about on this earth, John sees the righteous sitting on thrones; "and judgment was given unto them; . . . and they lived and reigned with Christ a thousand years." Jesus foretold this time when He said to His disciples, * "Ye which have followed Me, in the regeneration when the Son of man shall sit in the throne of His glory, ye also shall sit upon twelve thrones, judging the twelve tribes of Israel." This is the judgment of the wicked, "whosoever was not found written in the book of life." "And the books were opened, . . . and the dead were judged out of those things which were written in the books, according to their works." "The portion which the wicked must suffer is meted out, . . . and it is recorded against their names in the book of death." Satan and the evil angels also are judged at this time; as Paul says, * "Know ye not that we shall judge angels?"

3. The Coming of Jesus. At the close of the thousand years Christ, with all the redeemed and a host of angels, descends to this earth. As He descends, * "His feet shall stand . . . upon the Mount of Olives, which is before Jerusalem on the east, and the Mount of Olives shall cleave in the midst thereof, . . . and there shall be a very great

Here, on this desolate earth, Satan is confined for a thousand years.

The New Jerusalem coming down from God out of heaven

valley." This was the very spot from which, after His resurrection, He ascended. It was here that the angels said to the disciples as they stood gazing after Him, "This same Jesus, which is taken up from you into heaven, shall so come in like manner as ye have seen Him go into heaven." The touch of Jesus purifies the "very great valley" made by His coming.

4. Descent of the Holy City (20:5; 21:2, 10). Then the heavens are parted and rolled back, and looking through the open space in Orion, the saints see the New Jerusalem in all its glory and beauty "coming down from God out of heaven, prepared as a bride adorned for her husband." A mighty angel stands at each gate. The city "rests upon the place purified and made ready to receive it, and Christ, with His people and the angels, enters the holy city." The promise that Jerusalem should stand forever is at last fulfilled. Then Jesus calls forth the wicked dead, "the rest of the dead," who "lived not again until the thousand years were finished."

5. Preparing to Capture the City (20:7-9). When the wicked dead are raised to life, "Satan shall be loosed out of his prison," and he at once goes out "to deceive the nations, . . . to gather them together to battle." It is an immense multitude, "as the sand of the sea." First he tells them that by *his* power *he* has brought them from their graves. He says that Christ is a tyrant who plans to rule over the earth, which by right belongs to him and to them. He points to their great numbers,— many more than are in the city,— and assures them that they can easily capture the city and take possession. Then he makes the weak strong and performs other wonders. Among this host "are kings and generals who conquered nations, valiant men who never lost a battle, proud, ambitious warriors." They are ready to follow Satan's directions. They prepare for battle. They construct implements of war. They organize their millions into companies and divisions.

"At last the order to advance is given, and the countless host moves on,— an army such as was never summoned by earthly conquerors, such as the combined forces of all ages since war began on earth could never equal. Satan . . . leads the van, and his angels unite their forces for this final struggle." They "compassed the camp of the saints about, and the beloved city."

6. Final Coronation of Jesus (20:11). As the armies surround the city, the gates are closed. Then far above the city they see Jesus sitting upon "a great white throne" which rests upon a foundation of burnished gold. Around Him are the redeemed. "The brightness of His presence fills the city of God, . . . flooding the

They "compassed the camp of the saints about, and the beloved city."

whole earth with its radiance. . . . In the presence of the assembled inhabitants of earth and heaven the final coronation of the Son of God takes place."

Satan sees "the crown placed upon the head of Christ by an angel of lofty stature and majestic presence, and he knows that the exalted position of this angel might have been his." But in his pride of heart he spurned it. He knows that he alone is to blame. He sees that his willful rebellion has unfitted him for heaven, and even if he could be admitted now, it would be supreme torture to obey Jesus.

7. The Death Sentence (19:21; 15:3, 4). Then the book of death is opened. Satan's name heads the list, and to his account have been transferred all the sins that he has tempted the righteous to commit. As Jesus looks upon the wicked, they remember every sin they have ever committed. Above the throne they see a great cross, and in this seems to be pictured like a living panorama God's great plan to save them. They see all that Jesus has done and suffered that man might be saved. They see that they are without excuse. By their lives they have declared, "We will not have this Jesus to reign over us." The death sentence — the sword which proceeded out of the mouth of Jesus — is pronounced upon Satan and all his followers, and they all with one accord confess that the sentence is just and merciful. All the nations of earth, both loyal and rebellious, declare, "Just and true are Thy ways, Thou King of saints, . . . for Thy judgments are made manifest."

8. The Wicked Destroyed (20:9, 10, 14; 19:20). Then "fire came down from God out of heaven, and devoured them." "And the beast was taken, and with him the false prophet that wrought miracles before him, with which he deceived them that had received the mark of the beast, and them that worshiped his image. These both were cast alive into a lake of fire burning with brimstone." "And the devil that deceived them was cast into the lake of fire and brimstone, where the beast and the false prophet are." Even death itself and the grave "were cast into the lake of fire."

9. The Earth Purified (21:11). Fire not only comes down from heaven, but it bursts forth from every chasm of earth, for the earth is stored with fire. "The streams thereof shall be turned into pitch, and the dust thereof into brimstone, and the land thereof shall become burning pitch." The rocks and all the elements of earth * "melt with fervent heat." The very "heavens being on fire shall be dissolved." In this cleansing fiery lake the wicked are destroyed, root and branch,— Satan the root, his followers the branches. Upon this sea of fire the holy city rides safely, as the ark of Noah rode on the waters of the flood.

How to Study: Get a clear idea of what is going on during the thousand years,— where Satan is and what he is doing, where the wicked are, where the righteous are and their work; also the events at the close of the thousand years,— the descent of Christ and the righteous, the descent of the city, the resurrection of the wicked, preparation for the battle of "Gog and Magog" (Rev. 20: 8), the coronation of Jesus, the book of death, the death sentence, the lake of fire in which Satan and his followers are utterly destroyed.

Use of Concordance: Find the four texts starred under topics 2, 3, 9. Key words: regeneration, angel, feet, fervent.

For Your Workbook: Enter the events of this lesson on your diagram of the thousand years.

For Class Discussion: Locate the constellation Orion; "the open space" in Orion. The middle of the three stars in Orion's sword consists of a number of stars. The telescope reveals four principal stars forming a four-sided figure. Within this figure is located what astronomers call "the open space."

---

3. A NEW HEAVEN AND A NEW EARTH
Rev. 21:1-7
"Behold, I make all things new." Rev. 21:5.

1. "The Earth and the Heaven Fled Away" (20:11). From the face of Jesus "the earth and the heaven fled away; and there was found no place for them." "It is well known," says a prominent writer, "that with a sufficient degree of heat, any substance on this earth can be reduced to the condition of gas, and thus become invisible. So will it be then with this whole earth. The heat being raised to a sufficient degree of intensity, would not the whole earth be converted into gas, and become invisible, and thus appear most literally to flee away, so that no place is found for it? But the elements are not destroyed. They are only, by that process, purged from the last and minutest taint of sin, and every token of the curse."

2. A New Creation (21:5). Then from the great white throne issues that mighty proclamation, "Behold, I make all things new." "Behold!" Yes, the redeemed, gazing with wonder and admiration from the holy city, shall see the work of creation — the re-creation of a new heaven and a new earth. At the announcement, "I make all things new," the elements combine again to form a new world. At the first creation, "the morning stars sang together, and all the sons of God shouted for joy." At this new creation, that song and shout will be increased by the glad voices of the redeemed.

3. The Sea (21:1). The new earth will differ in many ways from the earth as we now see it. When John saw it, he said,

---

References Used: D. R. on lesson text; E. W., pp. 17-19; G. C., p. 675; Job 38:7; Ps. 121:6; Isa. 11:6, 7, 9; 30:26; 32:18; 33:24; 35:1, 2, 5, 6, 8-10; 40:31; 49:10; 55:12, 13; 60:18; 65:17, 21, 22; 66:23.

"There was no more sea." The great oceans which now occupy so large a part of the earth's surface will be no more. God made the earth to be inhabited; and that this purpose may be fulfilled, the ocean space will be a beautiful landscape, dotted with small seas and lakes, and diversified by charming streams.

4. The Earth. "The wilderness and the solitary place shall be glad for them; and the desert shall rejoice, and blossom as the

Not only "all the sons of God" but all the redeemed shout for joy when this earth is re-created.

rose. It shall blossom abundantly." And the blossoms will never droop and die, for there will be no death there. We are told that the grass will be a living green, with a reflection of silver and gold, as it waves proudly to the glory of King Jesus. The woods will not be dark and gloomy, but light and glorious. "Instead of the thorn shall come up the fir tree, and instead of the brier shall come up the myrtle tree." The mountains will not be rough, bleak, and dangerous, covered with eternal snow. On the beautiful hills and the lofty summits of the mountains will grow a wealth of roses and lilies and other vegetation. "The mountains and the hills shall break forth before you into singing, and all the trees of the field shall clap their hands."

5. The Highway to Zion. "And an highway shall be there, . . . and it shall be called the Way of Holiness; the unclean shall not pass over it. . . . No . . . ravenous beast shall go up thereon; . . . but the redeemed shall walk there, and . . . shall return, and come to Zion with songs and everlasting joy upon their heads: they shall obtain joy and gladness, and sorrow and sighing shall flee away." "From one new moon to another, and from one Sabbath to another, shall all flesh come to worship before Me, saith the Lord."

The eternal home of the redeemed

6. The Animals. "The wolf also shall dwell with the lamb, and the leopard shall lie down with the kid; and the calf and the young lion and the fatling together; and a little child shall lead them. And the cow and the bear shall feed; their young ones shall lie down together: and the lion shall eat straw like the ox. . . . They shall not hurt nor destroy in all My holy mountain."

7. The Light. "Moreover the light of the moon shall be as the light of the sun, and the light of the sun shall be sevenfold." Yet "the sun shall not smite thee by day, nor the moon by night." "For He that hath mercy on them shall lead them, even by the springs of water shall He guide them."

8. The People (21: 4, 7). "He that overcometh shall inherit all things." "Then the eyes of the blind shall be opened, and the ears of the deaf shall be unstopped. Then shall the lame man leap as an hart, and the tongue of the dumb sing." "And the inhabitant shall not say, I am sick." "But they that wait upon the Lord shall renew their strength; they shall mount up with wings as eagles;

"A little child shall lead them."

they shall run, and not be weary; and they shall walk, and not faint." "And God shall wipe away all tears from their eyes; and there shall be no more death, neither sorrow, nor crying, neither shall there be any more pain: for the former things are passed away,"— they "shall not be remembered, nor come into mind." The greatest trials that we have ever had here will be so small compared with the glory that surrounds us that they will seem like nothing, and we shall feel that, secured at any cost of suffering and self-denial, heaven is cheap enough.

9. The Occupation of the People. "My people shall dwell in a peaceable habitation, and in sure dwellings, and in quiet resting places." "Violence shall no more be heard in thy land, wasting nor destruction within thy borders; but thou shalt call thy walls Salvation, and thy gates Praise." "They shall build houses, and inhabit them; and they shall plant vineyards, and eat the fruit of them. They shall not build, and another inhabit; they shall not plant, and another eat. . . . Mine elect shall long enjoy the work of their hands."

How to Study: Prepare to recite from the lesson topics.

Use of Concordance: Find one text used in each of paragraphs 4-9 — six texts in all. Most of the texts used, outside of the lesson text, are found in Isaiah, the great "new earth book."

Memory Work: Memorize Revelation 21:1-7 for the fifth star on your memory certificate.

For Your Workbook: Finish your diagram of the thousand years.

4. THE HOLY CITY
Rev. 21:11-27; 22:1-5

"Blessed are they that do His commandments, that they may have right to the tree of life, and may enter in through the gates into the city." Rev. 22:14.

1. Capital of the New Earth (21:3, 22; 22:3). The holy city, the New Jerusalem, is to be the capital of the new earth. It shall be "a crown of glory in the hand of the Lord, and a royal diadem in the hand of thy God." And "the throne of God and of the Lamb shall be in it." John heard a great voice out of heaven saying, "Behold, the tabernacle of God is with men, and He will dwell with them, and they shall be His people, and God Himself shall be with them, and be their God. . . . And I saw no temple therein: for the Lord God Almighty and the Lamb are the temple of it." The capital of a state or nation is the center of its government. The presence of the throne of God shows that the New Jerusalem will be the capital of the new earth, the center of its government.

2. Size and Shape of the City (21:16). "The city lieth foursquare, and the length is as large as the breadth: and he measured

---
References Used: D. R. on lesson text; E. W., p. 17; Isa. 62:3, 4; 1 Cor. 2:9; Zech. 8:5; Gen. 2:10.

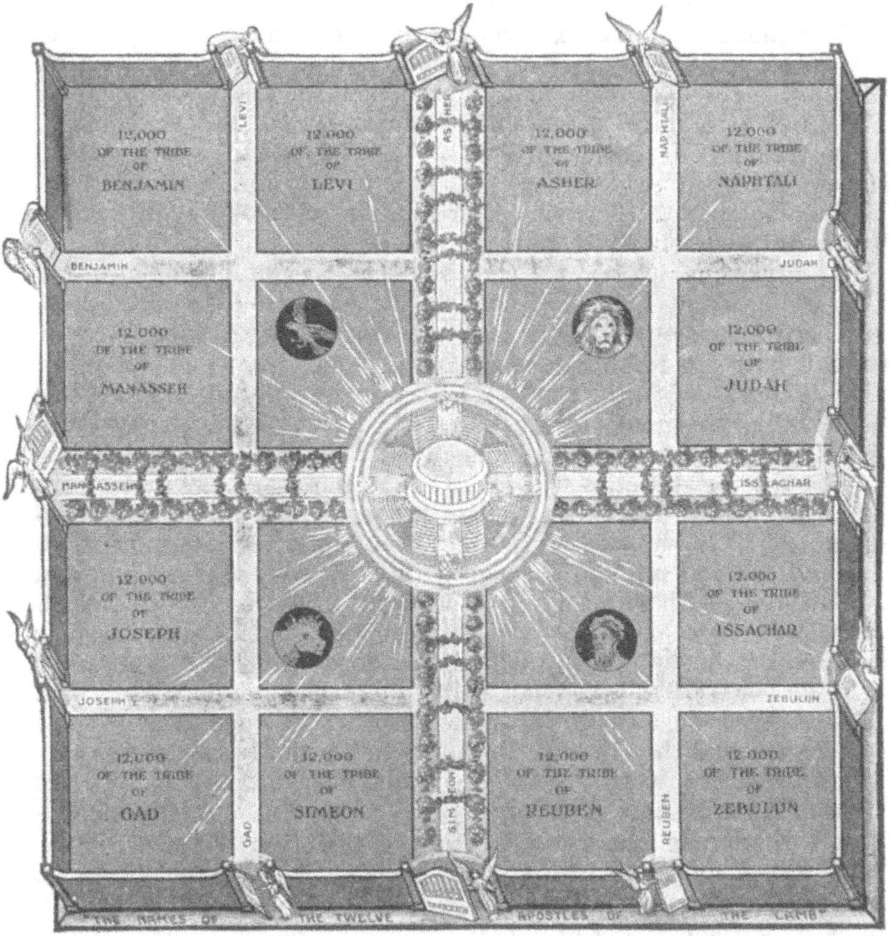

DIAGRAM No. 14. This diagram of the holy city is based on Isaiah 6:1; Revelation 4:3, 6, 7; 7:4-8; 21:12-25; 22:1, 2; Ezekiel 47:12; and Genesis 2:9, 10.

the city with the reed, twelve thousand furlongs. The length and the breadth and the height of it are equal." The ancient method of measuring a city was to measure the entire distance around it. According to this rule, the New Jerusalem will be 1,500 miles around, or 375 miles on each side, since it is a perfect square.

33—B. L., Eighth Grade

It would be impossible, except by comparison, to gain any true idea of so large a city. In the United States of America in 1910 there were 786 cities that contained a population of 8,000 or more. The total area of all these cities was about 9,000 square miles, while the New Jerusalem will cover 140,625 square miles, nearly sixteen times as much surface. That is to say, all the cities of the United States in 1910 having a population of 8,000 or more could be put into one sixteenth part, or one of the large squares, of the New Jerusalem. When we consider that the total population of all these cities was about 35,000,000 we get some idea of the vast number of people who could meet for worship within the walls of the holy city from Sabbath to Sabbath. This one city will have an area almost equal to the combined area of the states of Maine, New Hampshire, Vermont, Massachusetts, Rhode Island, Connecticut, New Jersey, Delaware, Maryland, West Virginia, and Indiana.

From later statistics we learn that in the year 1920 there were 62 large cities in the United States having a population of 100,000 or more. This included, of course, New York with its more than five and one half million, Chicago with its nearly three million, and Philadelphia with its nearly two million. The area of all these 62 cities was equal to about one third of one of the sixteen large squares of the holy city. Their combined population was more than 26,000,000. Do you not think there will be abundant room in the New Jerusalem for mansions for all the redeemed?

We are told that the length and breadth and height of the city are equal. The word "equal" does not always mean having the same dimensions; it often means *in proportion*. And doubtless that is the thought here,— the height of the city will be in proportion to its length and width. The ancient city of Babylon, which was Satan's counterfeit of the New Jerusalem, had wonderful hanging gardens that rose terrace above terrace until they equaled in height the walls of the city. The height of the New Jerusalem would indicate more imposing elevations and towers than it would be possible for human mind to conceive. "Eye hath not seen, nor ear heard, neither have entered into the heart of man, the things which God hath prepared for them that love Him."

3. **The City Wall (21: 12, 17, 18).** The city has "a wall great and high," which, when the angel measured it, was found to be "an hundred and forty and four cubits," or about 264 feet. "And the

building of the wall of it was of jasper." Jasper is a precious stone said to be wavy with the various colors of the rainbow. And this jasper will be "clear as crystal," revealing all the glories within the city.

4. **The Gates (21:12, 13, 21, 25).** The wall has twelve gates, three on each side. Each gate is of one solid pearl. On each gate is written the name of one of the twelve tribes of the children of Israel. "And the gates . . . shall not be shut at all by day: for there shall be no night there." In and out through these gates pass those who are sealed of the twelve tribes, according to the name on the gate. It is very fitting that the gates of the city are made of pearl, for the redeemed who pass through them have come out of great tribulation. The pearl is the result of pain and suffering caused by some foreign substance, perhaps only a tiny grain of sand, getting within the shell of the oyster. The oyster cannot expel the substance; if it should try to do so, its tender body would become torn and lacerated in the vain effort. So it quietly submits and covers the cruel substance with a secretion from its own body. This secretion gradually develops into the beautiful, polished, costly gem. If we meet the little annoyances of each day, believing that God sends them to develop in our characters a sweet, Christlike meekness and patience, we shall be fitted to enter these pearly gates.

5. **The Foundation (21:14, 19, 20).** The wall of the city has twelve foundations of precious stones. The first is jasper, like the walls; the second, a sapphire, which is described to be beautiful sky-blue color almost as glittering as a diamond; the third, a chalcedony, a kind of agate similar to the onyx; the fourth, an emerald of living green; the fifth, a sardonyx, which is like a pink carnelian; the sixth, sardius, a stone like a red carnelian; the seventh, a chrysolite, which is the color of gold; the eighth, a sea-green beryl; the ninth, a topaz, a pale yellowish green stone; the tenth, a chrysoprasus, similar to the topaz; the eleventh, a jacinth (or hyacinth) of a deep red or violet color; the twelfth, a brilliant violet-colored amethyst. These precious stones are not always the same color, and they are often streaked or wavy or spotted with various colors, so that with the glory of God shining through them, all the possible changes of every color in the most magnificent combinations would be revealed.

On each foundation is written the name of one of the twelve apostles. These precious stones are mentioned in two other places in the Bible; once in the description of the breastplate of the high priest, and again of the covering of Lucifer —the rainbow about the throne of God.

6. The Light of the City (21:11, 23). "The city had no need of the sun, neither of the moon, to shine in it: for the glory of God did lighten it, and the Lamb is the light thereof." We have learned that outside the city, the moon will be as bright as the sun is now, and the sun will be seven times as bright as now; but the glory of the throne of God illuminating the holy city is so much greater that there the sun is not noticed. No wonder we are thrice told, "There shall be no night there"!

7. The Golden Streets (21:21). "And the street of the city was pure gold, as it were transparent glass." The thought evidently is that the gold is like a mirror, so highly polished as to reflect the gorgeous palaces, the beautiful gardens, and the dome of heaven. "The mansions on either side of the street, having equal powers of reflection, would marvelously multiply both palaces and people, and conspire to render the whole scene novel, pleasing, beautiful, and grand beyond description." We are not told the width of the streets; but with so spacious a city, there would be abundance of room for generous avenues. *"And the streets of the city shall be full of boys and girls playing in the streets thereof."

8. The River of Life (22:1, R. V.). "And he showed me a river of water of life, bright as crystal, proceeding out of the throne of God and of the Lamb, in the midst of the street thereof." Beneath the throne of God is an inexhaustible fountain of the water of life, the source of all the waters of the earth. This river is in the garden of Eden, which was transplanted to heaven just before the flood. Of the first creation of the earth we are told that "a river went out of Eden to water the garden; and from thence it was parted, and became into four heads." Doubtless in the same way the river of life will go out from the city in every direction to water and beautify the earth.

9. The Tree of Life (22:2). "On either side of the river, was there the tree of life, which bare twelve manner of fruits, and yielded her fruit every month: and the leaves of the tree were for the healing of the nations." This is John's description. Another who in vision has been permitted to see the heavenly land, says of the tree of life: "At first I thought I saw two trees. I looked again, and saw that they were united at the top in one tree. So it was the tree of life on either side of the river of life. Its branches bowed to the place where we stood, and the fruit was glorious; it looked like gold mixed with silver."

The banyan tree grows in a similar way. From its branches roots grow, that finally reach the earth, and become trunks, and give out other branches. In just this way the tree of life is supposed by some to extend all along both sides of the four branches of the river of life, thus forming four magnificent avenues from the center of the city or the throne of God, to the wall in four directions. The length of each of these four avenues would be about one hundred eighty miles.

Every month, as the tree of life puts forth a new fruit, "shall all flesh come to worship" before the throne. Every month all will partake anew of the life-giving fruit, and enjoy a special feast of good things.

How to Study: Try to picture in your mind each part of the description of the city as you read. Why is the city called the capital of the new earth? Be able to figure the size of the city from the statement in Revelation 21: 16 — its length, breadth, and area in miles. How many such states as the one you live in could it contain? How far between the gates? If each mansion were given ten acres how many mansions would the city contain?

How does the highest building in your town compare in height with the city wall?

Allowing 15 miles for the width of the three streets and the river on each side of the city, what would be the length of each of the sixteen squares? How many square miles would each contain? How many acres?

If each of the 12,000 of a tribe is the head of a family, how many acres would each family average?

Dictionary Work: Be sure you can correctly pronounce the names of the jewels in the foundation.

Use of Concordance: Find the verse starred under topic 7. Key word: play.

Memory Work: Memorize Revelation 22: 1-5, 11-14, 17, for the sixth and last star on your memory certificate. When this is earned the teacher will sign your certificate.

For Your Workbook: On blank diagram No. 14 given in the workbook, draw a plan of the holy city, showing the location of wall, gates, main streets, river of life, tree of life, throne of God. Place also the names of the tribes, in their proper places, and "a rainbow round about the throne." Color the golden streets, the tree of life, the river of life, and the wall. Draw a square on the map of your country, showing the proportionate size of the city.

5. GOD'S PLAN FINISHED—"IT IS DONE"
Rev. 22:4, 10, 17

He shall see of the travail of His soul, and shall be satisfied." Isa. 53:11.

1. The Father Is Satisfied. At last God's great plan is finished. The long, long struggle is ended. The everlasting victory is won. Freedom from Satan's prison house has been dearly purchased. But it is forever secure. The "first dominion," the earth, originally given to Adam as his kingdom, betrayed by him into the hands of Satan, and so long held by the mighty foe, has been fully restored. Yes, it is even more beautiful than if it had never needed redemption, for it is glorified by the cleansing of divine blood. The righteous family which God planned in times eternal are all at home, care-free and happy. Never again shall affliction mar "My Father's house." As He looks upon the multitude of the redeemed, who without a fault stand before His presence with exceeding joy, as He sees His entire family gathered about Him, the Father is satisfied.

2. Jesus Is Satisfied. It was "for the joy that was set before Him," that He might bring "many sons unto glory," that Jesus "endured the cross, despising the shame." The sorrow and the shame were great, but the joy and the glory are greater. In the redeemed the Son of God sees His "brethren," children of His Father. As their elder Brother, He looks upon them bearing once more the divine image, reflecting again the likeness of their King. He beholds in them the result of the travail of His soul, and as He sees their unbounded joy and His Father's pleasure, Jesus is satisfied.

3. Angels and Unfallen Worlds Are Satisfied. The controversy that has been fought out on this earth has been "a spectacle [or theater] unto the world, and to angels, and to men." As, with intense interest, the angels and the unfallen worlds have watched this vast theater, as they have seen Satan deceive and destroy, as they have followed the working out of his wicked devices and cruel plans, as they have realized his determination to wreck and ruin, as they have witnessed his unjust persecution of those who desired to serve God, and especially as they saw him exult over the Son of God when He hung in agony on the cross, they are abundantly

---
References Used: G. C., p. 677; Isa. 61:3; Jer. 31:14; Ps. 17:15; 36:8.

satisfied that Satan was "a murderer from the beginning," "a liar, and the father of it." In their eyes God's mercy and love, His righteousness and justice, are fully vindicated. Angels and unfallen worlds are abundantly satisfied.

4. Are the Redeemed Satisfied (22:4)? And what about the redeemed? Are *they* satisfied? They have "beauty for ashes, the

Proclaim joy and gladness throughout God's universe, for "there shall be no more curse."

oil of joy for mourning, the garment of praise for the spirit of heaviness." No longer are they feeble and sick. No longer are they poor and in distress. They have the freshness and vigor of eternal youth, and are clad in richer robes than the most honored of earth ever wore. Their crowns are more glorious than were ever placed upon the brow of earthly kings. All the riches of heaven are theirs. Do you think they are satisfied — perfectly satisfied?

Have you ever desired to be a great musician, or a great artist, or a great traveler, or to attain great heights in knowledge? There every longing of your heart will be satisfied. There "every faculty will be developed, every capacity increased. The acquirement of knowledge will not weary the mind or exhaust the energies. There the grandest enterprises may be carried forward, the loftiest aspirations reached, the highest ambitions realized; and still there will arise new heights to surmount, new wonders to admire, new truths to comprehend, fresh objects to call forth the powers of mind and soul and body." "My people shall be satisfied with My goodness, saith the Lord." "They shall be abundantly satisfied with the fatness of Thy house; and Thou shalt make them drink of the river of Thy pleasures."

The joy of the Lord is to see souls saved in His kingdom. And the redeemed enter into His joy. Above riches and all the good things that are provided for personal comfort and pleasure, those who walk the golden streets of the city will gain joy in associating with others whom they have encouraged and have helped to gain a home in heaven. The joy of earth lies not in things that money can buy, but in the love and society of our friends. There we shall have the companionship not only of the redeemed but of angels. More than that, we "shall see *His* face." Satisfied? Oh, yes! "I shall be satisfied, when I awake, with Thy likeness."

5. The Song of Universal Satisfaction (5:13). When God's Great Plan is finished, one harmonious note of supreme, unbounded satisfaction will sound throughout His entire universe, for "every creature which is in heaven, and on the earth, and under the earth, and such as are in the sea, and all that are in them, heard I saying, Blessing, and honor, and glory, and power, be unto Him that sitteth upon the throne, and unto the Lamb forever and ever."

6. "Come! Come! For the Time Is at Hand" (22:17). This wonderful book of Revelation closes with the Spirit's appeal to our hearts: "The Spirit and the bride say, Come. And let him that heareth say, Come. And let him that is athirst come. And whosoever will, let him take the water of life freely." Do not our hearts respond to this invitation? The new earth, the holy city, with all their beauty, their advantages and opportunities, speak to our hearts with that still small voice, saying, "Come! Come! For the time is at hand."

> "I want to be there, I mean to be there,
>   I expect to be there, I do;
> I want to be there, I mean to be there,
>   I expect to be there, don't you?"

REVIEW OF REVELATION 19, 20, 21, 22

Test Questions:
1. Who will sing the "hallelujah chorus"? When? Where?
2. How long will it take the redeemed to go from earth to heaven? Give reference.
3. What song do the redeemed sing on that trip?
4. What is meant by the marriage of the Lamb? Who serves at the marriage supper? What is the wedding garment?
5. Where and how is Satan chained during the one thousand years?
6. What is going on in heaven during the one thousand years?
7. Name the events that take place at the beginning of the one thousand years; at the end.
8. When does the final coronation of Jesus take place?
9. Describe the battle of "Gog and Magog."
10. Describe the cleansing of the earth by fire. Give two texts.
11. Describe the new earth—sea, earth, animals, light, highway to Zion, people, occupation of people. In what two books of the Bible is this largely told?
12. Describe the holy city—capital, size, shape, wall, gates, foundation, light, streets, river of life, tree of life. What chapters tell?

Memory Drill: Rev. 21:1-7; 22:1-5, 11-14, 17.

Verse-Finding Drill: See how many of these you can find in ten minutes, without concordance:
1. And again they said, Alleluia.
2. The Lord God omnipotent reigneth.
3. The fine linen is the righteousness of saints.
4. Blessed are they which are called unto the marriage supper.
5. The testimony of Jesus is the spirit of prophecy.
6. The beast . . . and . . . the false prophet . . . were cast alive into a lake of fire.
7. The rest of the dead lived not again until the thousand years were finished.
8. Blessed and holy is he that hath part in the first resurrection.
9. They . . . compassed the camp of the saints about.
10. I saw a new heaven and a new earth.
11. The earth and the heaven fled away.
12. He . . . showed me . . . the holy Jerusalem, descending out of heaven.
13. He that overcometh shall inherit all things.
14. He said unto me, It is done.
15. There shall be no night there.
16. I will be his God, and he shall be My son.
17. And they shall see His face.
18. Blessed are they that do His commandments.
19. Behold, I come quickly.
20. Whosoever will, let him take the water of life freely.

Concordance Time Drill: See how many of these verses you can find in ten minutes, using concordance. The key word is starred.
1. Eye hath not seen, nor *ear heard, . . . the things which God hath prepared.

2. The streets of the city shall be full of boys and *girls playing.
3. My people shall be *satisfied with My goodness.
4. I shall be satisfied, when I *awake, with Thy likeness.
5. Then we . . . shall be *caught up together . . . in the clouds, to meet the Lord.
6. Know ye not that we shall judge *angels?
7. His *feet shall stand . . . upon the Mount of Olives, . . . and the Mount of Olives shall cleave in the midst thereof.
8. The elements shall melt with *fervent heat.
9. Instead of the *thorn shall come up the fir tree.
10. The desert shall rejoice, and *blossom as the rose.
11. The hills shall break forth before you into singing, and all the trees of the field shall *clap their hands.
12. An highway shall be there, and . . . the redeemed shall *walk there.
13. The cow and the *bear shall feed; their young ones shall lie down together.
14. The *inhabitant shall not say, I am sick.
15. They shall build houses, and *inhabit them.

General Chapter Drill:
Give in order the main subject of each chapter in Revelation.
Find the chapters that tell about the following:
1. Little book open
2. Book sealed with seven seals
3. New earth*
4. Appearance of Christ
5. Hallelujah chorus
6. United States in prophecy
7. God's two witnesses
8. The 1260-day period
9. Sealing the 144,000
10. Destruction of the wicked
11. River of life
12. War in heaven
13. Second coming of Christ
14. Silence in heaven
15. Marriage supper of the Lamb
16. Image of the beast
17. Throne of God
18. Four beasts and twenty-four elders
19. Decree at close of probation
20. Redeemed in heaven

SUMMARY OF IMPORTANT DATES
Starred dates should be memorized

B. C.
*4004 Creation; the fall of man
2348 The flood
1921 The promise to Abraham
1921-1491 — The 430 years of sojourn in Canaan and in Egypt
1491 Birthday of the missionary nation Israel
   The law given at Sinai
1491-1451 — The 40 years of wandering in the wilderness
1451 The nation established in Canaan
 975 End of the united kingdom
 606 End of the divided kingdom
 606-536 Babylonish captivity of 70 years
* 538 Fall of Babylon; rise of Medo-Persia
 457 (Autumn) Decree of Cyrus, Darius, and Artaxerxes to restore Jerusalem
* 457-1844 A. D.— The 2300-day period
 397 Last of Old Testament prophets
* 331 End of the Medo-Persian world kingdom
   Beginning of the Grecian world kingdom

```
*  168 End of the Grecian world kingdom
       Beginning of the Roman world kingdom
   A. D.
     27 (Autumn) Baptism of Christ
     31 (Spring) Crucifixion of Christ
        Birthday of the Christian church
        Christ's work begun in the holy place of the heavenly sanctuary
     34 Jewish nation rejected
     96 John given the Revelation on Patmos
*   313 Constantine proclaimed religious liberty to the world
*   321 Edict of Constantine, making Sunday a holiday,—the first Sunday law
*   476 Downfall of pagan Rome. End of ancient history
*   538 Papal Rome established. Beginning of the Dark Ages
*   538-1798 — The 1260 years of papal persecution
    622 Rise of Mohammedanism
*  1380 Wycliffe translated Bible into English
   1453 Constantinople captured by Turks
*  1456 First Bible printed from movable type — printed in Latin
*  1492 Discovery of America. Beginning of modern history
*  1517 Beginning of Reformation. Work of Luther
*  1529 The first Protestants
*  1535 First complete Bible printed in English
*  1620 Landing of Pilgrims in New World
*  1755 (Nov. 1) Lisbon earthquake
*  1780 (May 19) Sun darkened
   1789 United States government organized. French Revolution began
*  1798 End of 1260 years of papal persecution
   1804 British and Foreign Bible Society organized — the first of its kind
*  1833 (Nov. 13) Falling of the stars
*  1844 (Oct. 22) Investigative Judgment began,—Christ's work in the most holy
        place
```

Babylonian Kings During the Time of Daniel

```
B. C
606–561 Nebuchadnezzar (this includes two years' reign with his father
            Nabopolassar)
561–559 Evil Merodach
559–556 Neriglissor
556     Labarosoarchod
555–538 Nabonidus, his son Belshazzar ruling with him a part of the time
```

Dates of Events Recorded in Daniel

```
         Daniel
606       1. Daniel in the king's school
603       2. Nebuchadnezzar's dream of the image
580       3. The golden image set up
569–563   4. Insanity of Nebuchadnezzar
540       7. Vision of the four beasts in the first year of Belshazzar
538       8. Vision of the ram and the he-goat in the third year of Belshazzar
538       5. Capture of Babylon by Darius the Mede
538       6. Daniel in the lions' den
538       9. Daniel's prayer and explanation of the 2300 days in the first year
             of Darius
534      10. Daniel's three-week prayer season
         12. His last vision
```

CHRONOLOGICAL TABLE FROM ADAM TO JOSHUA

PATRIARCHS	AGE	References
1. ADAM	930	
2. SETH	912	
3. ENOS	905	
4. CAINAN	910	
5. MAHALALEEL	895	GEN. 5
6. JARED	962	
7. ENOCH	365	
8. METHUSELAH	969	
9. LAMECH	777	
10. NOAH	950	GEN. 5:29,32; 7:6; 9:28
11. SHEM	600	
12. ARPHAXAD	438	
13. SALAH	433	
14. EBER	464	
15. PELEG	239	GEN. 11:10-26
16. REU	239	
17. SERUG	230	
18. NAHOR	148	
19. TERAH	205	GEN. 11:32
20. ABRAHAM	175	GEN. 11:32; 12:4; 25:7 ACTS 7:4
21. ISAAC	180	GEN. 21:5; 35:28
22. JACOB	147	GEN. 25:26; 48:21
23. LEVI	137	GEN. 29:34 EX. 6:16
24. KOHATH	133	EX. 6:18
25. AMRAM	137	EX. 6:20
26. MOSES	120	DEUT. 34:7
27. JOSHUA	110	JOSH. 24:29

The figures at the ends of each line show the dates of the birth and death of the corresponding person. This table shows the length of each life, what persons were living at the same time; the rapid decrease of life after the Flood. By the heavy dotted lines, representing irregular steps, it is easy to see through how few persons the story of Eden and the Flood came down to Moses by whom they were written in the Book. Adam lived with Noah's father for 56 years, Lamech lived with Shem 93 years, and Shem himself, who lived nearly a century before the Flood, talked with Abraham and Isaac only a little while before the children of Israel took possession of Canaan.

We invite you to view the complete
selection of titles we publish at:

www.TEACHServices.com

Scan with your mobile
device to go directly
to our website

Please write or email us your praises, reactions, or
thoughts about this or any other book we publish at:

TEACH Services, Inc.
PUBLISHING
www.TEACHServices.com • (800) 367-1844

P.O. Box 954
Ringgold, GA 30736

info@TEACHServices.com

TEACH Services, Inc., titles may be purchased in bulk for
educational, business, fund-raising, or sales promotional use.
For information, please e-mail:

BulkSales@TEACHServices.com

Finally, if you are interested in seeing
your own book in print, please contact us at

publishing@TEACHServices.com

We would be happy to review your manuscript for free.

www.ingramcontent.com/pod-product-compliance
Lightning Source LLC
Chambersburg PA
CBHW071824230426
43672CB00013B/2752